CARNAGE AND CARE ON THE EASTERN FRONT

Carnage and Care on the Eastern Front

The War Diaries of Bernhard Bardach, 1914–1918

Translated and edited by
Peter C. Appelbaum

berghahn
NEW YORK · OXFORD
www.berghahnbooks.com

First published by
Berghahn Books
www.berghahnbooks.com

English-language edition
© 2018, 2025 Peter C. Appelbaum
First paperback edition published in 2025

All rights reserved. Except for the quotation of short passages for the purposes of criticism and review, no part of this book may be reproduced in any form or by any means, electronic or mechanical, including photocopying, recording, or any information storage and retrieval system now known or to be invented, without written permission of the publisher.

Translated from German

Library of Congress Cataloging-in-Publication Data
A C.I.P. cataloging record is available from the Library of Congress

British Library Cataloguing in Publication Data
A catalogue record for this book is available from the British Library

ISBN 978-1-78533-978-3 hardback
ISBN 978-1-80539-746-5 paperback
ISBN 978-1-80539-922-3 epub
ISBN 978-1-78533-979-0 web pdf

https://doi.org/10.3167/9781785339783

This translation is dedicated to my wife's father, Murray (a Pole from Rzeszów); her grandfather Louis (a Galicianer from Rozwadów); and my own Grandpa Louis—the opposition—a Litvak from Neishtot Sugint (Žemaičių Naumiestis), in memory of all the Jews in Eastern Europe who could not emigrate and were murdered by the Nazis.

Contents

List of Illustrations	viii
Foreword. All Quiet on the Eastern Front: The War Diaries of Bernhard Bardach *Jay Winter*	x
Acknowledgments	xiv
Note on Town Names	xv
Translator's Introduction	xvi
Introduction. Bernhard Bardach: A Biographical Sketch *Helmut Konrad*	1
Chapter 1. 1914: Poland, Russia, Carpathians	17
Chapter 2. 1915: Carpathians, Gorlice-Tarnów, Southern and Western Ukraine	52
Chapter 3. 1916: The Brusilov Offensive and Its Aftermath	107
Chapter 4. 1917: Winter in Ukraine—Inspections—Blockade—Worsening Shortages	175
Chapter 5. 1918: Treaty of Brest Litovsk—Crippling Shortages—Piave—War's End	240
Appendixes	289
Bibliography	292
Index	293

Illustrations

Maps

0.1. The Brusilov Offensive, June to September 1917. Ellipse marks Bernhard Bardach's theater of activity. 16

Figures

All images courtesy of the Leo Baeck Institute.

0.1. Bardach with easel and paintbrush during a rest period. xi

0.2. Dr. Bernhard Bardach. Oil painting (1905) by Roman Gozdawa-Kawecki, 1868–1938. xvii

1.1. "Toilette" out in the open. 21

1.2. Morning prayer in the field of Jewish refugees expelled from their homes. The caption states "Lublin," but this was seen everywhere expulsions occurred. 28

1.3. "Types." Poor Jewish inhabitants in an Eastern European town. 38

1.4. The caption reads "teachers: relaxation hour." Prostitutes, possibly being examined for venereal diseases. 41

1.5. A lone Russian body on the battlefield. By the end of the war, nearly two million Russian soldiers would be killed. 44

1.6. Church with dome hit by artillery shells. 45

2.1. A Russian prisoner of war combing a fellow prisoner's hair for lice (*russisches Kulturbild*). 53

2.2. Gravestone of Dr. M. Reitzes, who died of typhoid fever in Krasnoyarsk, Siberia. 72

2.3. Jewish beggar in Grubieszow.	84
2.4. Painting by Bardach of a card game in which he kibitzes.	94
3.1. Soldiers wearing gas masks in a trench on the Eastern Front.	113
3.2. Men lining up for cholera inoculation.	119
3.3. An open fracture of the lower leg before plaster of paris application.	121
3.4. Bardach and colleagues look proudly at an aseptically treated lower leg wound that has not become infected.	122
3.5. A man with bandaged eyes being led out of regimental command.	125
3.6. A picture of despair. Amputations and eye damage.	126
3.7. Surgeon examining his patient postoperatively.	151
3.8. Eastern European synagogue: one tiny part of a world destroyed by the Holocaust.	158
4.1. Medical care in a first aid station.	176
4.2. Burial in the field.	177
4.3. Bardach's sketch of bathhouse facilities.	187
4.4. Dress-up pantomime with amateur players.	197
4.5. Bernhard Bardach at his desk with accumulated paperwork and reading material.	202
4.6. Memorial service in the field.	204
4.7. A visit to the dentist in the Austro-Hungarian Army.	214
4.8. Kaiser Karl praying with the troops.	223
5.1. A theater group: not all the soldiers appear to be appreciative.	248
5.2. Bathing facilities carefully marked for rank-and-file soldiers only.	253
5.3. Delousing facility.	254

Foreword
All Quiet on the Eastern Front
The War Diaries of Bernhard Bardach

JAY WINTER

It has been a long time coming, but the effort to move the center of gravity of the historiography of the Great War to the east, from Paris to Warsaw, or from London to Lemberg (Lviv) finally is bearing fruit. The publication of this diary is evidence of this geographical shift of attention, enabling us to develop an archivally rich account of the Eastern Front in World War I.

Furthermore, during the centennial of the Great War, there has been an avalanche of publications, exhibitions, and historical studies on the local and national level, broadening our vision of the multiple theaters of military operations. This book is part of this wave of historical writing. Its subject is daily life on the southern sector of the Eastern Front, covering the vast space from east of Brest-Litovsk in the north to Lemberg, Ternopil, and Czernowitz in the south. Today, all are in Ukraine. It was there that in 1916, the Austro-Hungarian Army faced the Russian army's last great offensive, the Brusilov Offensive.

In late 1915 and in concert with her Allies, Russia agreed to launch an offensive in the late spring and summer of 1916. The objectives were the cities of Lemberg and Lutsk. The Russians massed four armies of forty infantry divisions and fifteen cavalry divisions on this sector, giving them a real but limited numerical advantage against the thirty-nine Austrian infantry divisions and ten cavalry divisions facing them.

Assisting these Austrian troops were numerous medical and sanitary facilities staffed by physicians like Bernhard Bardach. Their function was not only to deal with casualties but also to prevent the spread of endemic and epidemic diseases, rife on the Eastern Front. Bardach's diary is a close-up look at the medical support system and daily life of Austrian troops before, during, and after the Brusilov Offensive. From his comments, we can appreciate not only the gravity of this attack on Austrian forces but also the back-and-forth movements on the front that ultimately blunted the offensive. In this document, we have a first-person account of a campaign that exhausted both the attacking and the defending forces.

In one sense, the Brusilov Offensive was a success, showing that Russian forces had the capacity to organize and sustain an assault on enemy lines on a front two hundred kilometers long. In June, the Russian broke through Austrian lines, taking two hundred thousand Austrian prisoners, and almost captured the Austrian commander, Archduke Joseph Ferdinand. Further gains were made in the southern sector, all the way to the Carpathians. But in a matter of days, Russian supply lines became overextended, forcing them to consolidate their gains rather than continuing their advance.

To stabilize this front, the German commander Erich von Falkenhayn ordered German troops supporting Verdun to move to the east. He knew that after Brusilov, the Austro-Hungarian Army was a spent force. What he did not know was that so was the Russian army. Whatever territory the Russians seized, the strategic balance in this sector did not change. In this respect, the Brusilov Offensive paralleled the stalemate produced at Verdun and the Somme at the very same time. What Bardach's diary shows is the wearing down of both sides in this sector, thereby anticipating an end to the offensive capacity of not one but two mass armies.

The consequences of this erosion of the military capacity of both sides were evident sooner in Russia than in Austria. The February revolution of 1917 was the first of a series of popular movements against a war that had produced no strategic advantage for either side at the cost of tens of thousands of lives. The Brusilov Offensive precipitated this turn away from war in Russia in 1917 and, indirectly, in Austria-Hungary a year later.

Bernhard Bardach was not aware of this sea change in the military fortunes of both sides.

Figure 0.1. Bardach with easel and paintbrush during a rest period. Photograph courtesy of the Leo Baeck Institute.

He was an educated physician who saw himself as an artist. In his diary entries, we find a somewhat limited man with conventional views, an Austrian officer proud of that fact, sensitive not only to the weather but to medals and honors and to the efflorescence of rank and titles in the Austro-Hungarian Army. Like most soldiers, he saw a narrow sector of the front and had no strategic overview. He knew that the Brusilov Offensive was a grave moment for his side, but he did not see that in blunting that offensive, the Austrians had effectively reached the limits of their military effectiveness as a fighting force.

Bardach knew very well about the shortages afflicting the home front. He bought and sent home substantial stores of food to his family in Vienna, meticulously listing every single item in his diaries. And yet, like most soldiers in the field, he did not see that starving the home front endangered the war effort as a whole. In this sense, he was a nineteenth-century man engaged in a twentieth-century war. His myopia was not unusual at the time, and it helps account for his sense of shock and bitterness when he realized that the war was lost. Bardach, like most physicians, was not a political analyst. He saw what was in front of him, not what was undermining the ground under his feet and that of his family and his nation at war.

Bardach was transferred to the Italian front in 1918 and learned there of the unraveling of the war effort of the Central Powers and of the Austro-Hungarian Monarchy itself. His response is striking. He was one of the few Jewish officers who adhered to the *Dolchstosslegende*, the belief that his army had not been defeated but had been stabbed in the back by civilians, and by the treachery of US President Woodrow Wilson, who had promised a peace without victory, and then proceeded, as punishment, to carve up his beloved empire. The one nation still standing, Germany, was where he thought he could still serve at the end of the war, but that was not to be. He was demobilized, returned to Vienna where he tried to bring his family life back to something approaching normality.

As Helmut Konrad's introduction to this diary shows, by the late 1930s, that too was impossible. *Anschluss* forced him to migrate to the United States, where he lived in relative poverty and absolute bitterness about the failure of the new Austrian state to honor his pension rights. His fault, in the eyes of a series of post-1945 Austrian bureaucrats, was that in 1939 he had not followed procedures the Nazi authorities used to deal with those emigrating from Austria. This mix of hardly veiled, lingering anti-Semitism and administrative cruelty marked his last years.

Bardach's diaries are important for a number of reasons. They shed considerable light on daily life on the Eastern Front, on the medical services supporting the fighting, and on the attitude of a highly cultivated Viennese doctor to the uprooted and miserable Jewish population of Galicia and Volhynia caught in the crossfire. His writings offer us a singular view of what it felt like to be at war on the Eastern Front.

Bardach resembled Stendhal's Fabrizio in *The Charterhouse of Parma*, a man who passed through the battlefield of Waterloo seeing everything and nothing at the same time. He saw the landscape but wondered if a battle had occurred, and if so, who won, and why? Bardach saw everything but had no idea why the position of his army became increasingly untenable during and after the Brusilov Offensive. His myopia (and Fabrizio's) are hardly surprising. What determined victory in the Great War was by and large a structural matter: the way in which the Central Powers waged war led to real suffering among civilians, without creating an arsenal capable of a strategic breakthrough on either the Western or the Eastern fronts. There was to be no breakthrough, either there or anywhere else. That is what distinguished nineteenth-century war and those who fought in it from twentieth-century warfare. In this sense, Bardach was a nineteenth-century man, cultivated and loyal, serving in an army that could not win the war. The same was true of many men who served in the German army, who were similarly seduced into believing that they had not lost the war in the field.

Like many other diaries, this one is informative in ways its author never knew. But to understand its importance, we must recognize that it is only a part of the archive Bardach's family left to the Leo Baeck Institute in New York. There we also find a collection of 997 photographs he took during his military service, most of which remain unexplored. The subjects he chose to photograph are widely varied: many are of civilians trapped in this sector of the war, but others are of military life and the damage hostilities did to the Volhynian landscape.

As an assimilated Jew, Bardach took a particular interest in the vivid face of Jewish life in this region. Refugees are everywhere, uprooted by war and wandering in search of safety. His photographs of this world are respectful and sensitive, almost anthropological in nature. His gaze is that of a civilized observer facing people still observing the calendar and rituals of traditional Jewish life. Bardach himself attended High Holiday services for Jewish soldiers serving on this sector of the front, but his camera captured another world entirely, that of the shtetl at a moment of crisis. As such, this collection provides us with a rich assembly of images of the antechamber of the Holocaust, that time during the Great War when the Pale of Settlement was torn apart, a little more than two decades before it vanished forever. Taken together, the diary and photographs of Bernhard Bardach are unique documents, which show vividly not only the fabric of daily life on the Eastern Front but also how the 1914–1918 conflict opened a new era of violence, extending from one world war to another.

Jay Winter is the Charles J. Stille Professor of History emeritus at Yale University. He holds honorary doctorates from the University of Graz, KU Leuven, and the University of Paris.

Acknowledgments

I thank Jay Winter for his valued encouragement, wise counsel, reading and critiquing the entire manuscript, and helping with the choice of photographs, and I thank both Jay Winter and Helmut Konrad for gracing it with informative introductions. Frank Mecklenberg, Michael Simonson, and Tracey Feder at the Leo Baeck Institute in New York City are thanked for archival and photographic assistance; Manfried Rauchensteiner, Erwin Schmidl, Martin Senekowitsch, Thorsten Eisengerich, and Jürgen Ortner for help with the complex medical and nonmedical ranks in the Austro-Hungarian Army; Stanislava Caravoulias for help with Hungarian and Slovak names of Carpathian towns large and small; Marion Berghahn, Chris Chappell, Amanda Horn, and Lizzie Martinez at Berghahn Books for their meticulous editorial work; and Larry Sweazy for index compilation. Dagmar Stadtherr-Brenecke provided the meticulous transcription of 557 diary pages handwritten in Sütterlin into readable German, as well as help with abbreviations, recalcitrant words, Austrian dialect, and names of towns that have since changed names and hands (some more than once).* My dear wife, Addie (*eishet chayil mi yimtza*), read through the entire manuscript, providing her usual insights and a loving home background that allowed me to mumble uninterrupted in two languages, and my daughter, Madeleine, was ready at all times with a daughter's love.

Any errors in text or translation are entirely mine.

Peter C. Appelbaum
Land O' Lakes, Florida
July 2017

---

* It should be noted that two transcriptions of this diary exist: the other was done by Petra Ernst (University of Graz), who is since deceased. Petra was going to send me the entire transcription when illness intervened.

Note on Town Names

I have tried my best to find modern-day names of towns, using maps, Google, and a recognized gazette.* For simplicity, unless town names are completely different (e.g., Hungary and Slovak Republic), diacritical marks are in endnotes only. I am responsible for all errors.

---

* Gary Mokotoff and Sallyann Amdur Sack, *Where Once We Walked: A Guide to the Jewish Communities Destroyed in the Holocaust* (Teaneck, NJ: Avotaynu, 1991).

Translator's Introduction

Bernhard Bardach was born in Lemberg on 3 August 1866 as the son of a wholesale merchant. After attending gymnasium, he entered medical school, first in Vienna and later in Graz, where he graduated in 1893. He immediately entered the military, where he had already been promoted senior surgeon by the time war broke out.

Bernhard Bardach's diary[1] is important on many levels. He provides a blow-by-blow commentary of the entire war, either from personal experience or war news. He was present during the Austro-Hungarian retreat into the Carpathians from 1914 to 1915 and the 1916 Gorlice-Tarnów Offensive, and (importantly) he had a front row seat for the Brusilov Offensive, which is reported in great detail, from hour to hour and day to day. During the first weeks of the offensive and until German command and reinforcements were brought up, a note of panic creeps into his diary: the seemingly leaderless army in chaos, streaming to the rear, and blocking roads. Throughout his diary, Bardach comments scathingly on the ineptitude of Austro-Hungarian leadership; disorder, mixed signals, supplies and provisions arriving either late or not at all, officers more interested in throwing their weight around, going on leave, or spending a few weeks at the front just to obtain a medal. Germans are presented in a much better light. Russians are presented as brave fighters but with inept leadership (except for Brusilov).

Religion was of secondary importance to Bardach. Apart from High Holidays, no other Jewish festival (or Sabbath eve) service is mentioned, and his synagogue attendance on Rosh Hashanah and even Yom Kippur is perfunctory, even given exigencies of war. When he fasted on Yom Kippur, it was at his convenience, not for the prescribed twenty-five hour period. He did not adhere to the dietary laws and did not mention relationships with other Jewish comrades. Only two brief comments on anti-Semitism occur in the entire diary: Jews experienced less discrimination, and more opportunities for advancement, in the Austro-Hungarian than the other two armies fighting on the Eastern Front. Bardach showed respect and reverence to Kaiser Franz Joseph and to

Peter C. Appelbaum ❧ xvii

Figure 0.2. Dr. Bernhard Bardach. Oil painting (1905) by Roman Gozdawa-Kawecki, 1868–1938. Photo courtesy of the Leo Baeck Institute.

the newly crowned Kaiser Karl; his allegiance to the monarchy was absolute. In this, Jews in Austro-Hungary were similar to those in Germany, with the exception that Germany was one nation, not a supranational empire made up of many nationalities.

Bardach's medical duties, surprisingly, do not comprise the major part of his diary. He worked in field hospitals, inspected surrounding medical facilities, and saw to it that bathhouses were properly built and maintained and that men were adequately inoculated against cholera and typhoid, and provided with a continuous supply of safe, clean water. Apart from emergency procedures such as trepanation of the skull, he did not perform surgical procedures (on his own, at any rate), which were performed by specialists from command. He worked in collaboration with a bacteriologist, on hand to culture specimens and water and look for transmissible pathogens. The standard of microbiology and understanding of epidemiology of infectious diseases in Austro-Hungary before the war was high. Bardach was alert to the danger (and prevention) of malaria in Italy, and coped well with outbreaks of cholera and bacterial dysentery (with a bacteriologist, where available) but not so well with malaria. His inspections and other travels took place in every kind of weather: heat and humidity, rain and mud, ice and snow. His diary is replete with descriptions of endless mud, which sometimes make roads impassable so that he could not leave his quarters, and bitterly cold winds whipping up deep snowdrifts. Cars were not the rule, and he often had to march short distances, or use horse and cart. Although Bardach's duties took place in the rear of the fighting, this does not mean that he was not in the firing line. Indeed, he was lucky to survive the entire war unscathed.. However, the long war took a toll on his health, with constant colds, sciatica, and swollen feet, apart from psychological problems and constant worry about his family.

Bardach respected Russian soldiers, but regarded Italians (referred to consistently as "wops") and Romanians with contempt because both joined the Anglo-Russian Entente more than a year after the war started, to pounce on potential spoils. Italy was a special object of his ire, because it had been, when war began, at least nominally, part of the Central Powers. Bardach places great emphasis on the comfort of his quarters, the quality of the food and drink, and companionship. As befits a physician in Kaiser Franz Joseph's army, he is a bit of a snob. All senior officers are referred to by full name and titles, and he is fixated on acquisition of decorations. He sets great store on seating arrangements in the mess and how near he is seated to senior officers and aristocracy. His batman built his winter quarters and saw to his needs; quarters were cleaned and heated for him. Bardach's weather descriptions are accurate and precise, hour by hour. He even describes eclipses of the sun and moon. His descriptions of the Russian Revolution are insightful and accurate, given that he did not witness it at firsthand. Battles of the Isonzo and the Romanian campaign are also reported in detail.

Bardach's descriptions (and photographs) of Eastern European Jews caught in between two great armies are arresting. Devastated towns and impoverished, hungry, desperate civilians greeted him at every turn. As soon as the Russian army moved into Galicia and Bukowina in August 1914, mass deportations began, with a total of about six hundred thousand Jews displaced from their homes and about two hundred thousand killed as a result of the war.[2] When war ended, Jews in Galicia and Bukowina (newly severed from the Empire) had to contend with pogroms for several years. Then, a scant two decades after the political situation had calmed down, the Holocaust completely destroyed their entire world. Bardach describes an Austro-Hungarian medical corps that reflected weaknesses similar to those of the leadership itself. It is not the standard of medicine that is inferior, but rather the organization of the corps and its choice of leaders. When necessary, Bardach worked well with his German counterparts. He holds Czech, Ruthenian, and Bosnian soldiers in low esteem.

From 1917 onward and with increasing desperation, his emphasis turns to food. Bardach's wife and four daughters in Vienna come under increasing pressure due to the blockade and worsening food shortages. Bardach tries to procure as much food for them as possible, irrespective of whether it contains pork, and entries are replete with lists of food and other commodities, which he sends home from the front, to help feed his family. Toward the end of the war, he has to obtain thread, shoes, canvas material, even toilet paper; practically nothing is available at home (unless at exorbitant prices on the black market). He is so concerned about the condition of his family (especially his wife Olga, who bears the brunt of keeping the family fed), that he brings them out to live on what was—before 1918—the Eastern Front, to obtain better provisions. The children fall prey to whooping cough, and they come down with the 1918 "Spanish flu," which luckily, in their case, is not severe.[3]

Bernhard Bardach is briefly noted by Marsha Rozenblit as having served as a military physician throughout the war, mainly on the Eastern but also briefly on the Italian Front. His joy over victories on the Eastern Front contrasts with less enthusiasm for successes on the Italian Front,[4] leavened by scathing criticism of Austro-Hungarian leadership on the Eastern Front, and constant denigration of Italians as "wops" and traitors. By the time he and his division were transferred to the Piave in 1918, hunger, shortages, and exhaustion had changed the tenor of his narrative. Bardach has a very low opinion of US President Woodrow Wilson, whom he describes as a huckster who only sees dollar signs, and an unfaithful partner for peace.

Jay Winter, in his books on memory, devotes several pages to some of Bardach's large collection of war photographs,[5] illustrating the complex nature of the Austro-Hungarian Army of Occupation on the Eastern Front, the plight of Jewish civilians and refugees (including medical issues), villages on fire, murder of civilians, graves of Jewish physicians and deceased Austrian officers who died on active duty, and many others. This volume expands on Winter's book, by utilizing Bardach's own photographs, to illustrate points made in his own complete diary, which is presented here in English for the first time.

One of Bardach's last entries, just before the armistice, is powerfully ironic, in view of subsequent events. After the Empire breaks up, he rejects the opportunity to join the Polish Army but remains with the Germans, because, "despite their known anti-Semitism, he feels more comfortable with them."

To conclude, it is hoped that this volume will help open up the Eastern Front of World War I, a theater of action that up until now has received insufficient attention but was just as important as the Western Front in prosecution of the war.

Notes

1. Bernhard Bardach, *War Diaries, 1914–1918: Bernhard Bardach Collection* (New York: Archives of the Leo Baeck Institute, ME 1164 [1919]. Transcribed into printed German, with editorial assistance, by Dagmar Stadtherr-Brenecke.
2. Frank M. Schuster, *Zwischen allen Fronten.Osteuropäische Juden während des ersten Weltkrieges (1914–1919)* (Cologne: Böhlau Verlag, 2004), 125; Petra Ernst, "Der erste Weltkrieg in deutschsprachig-jüdischer Literatur und Publizistik in Österreich," in *Krieg: Erinnerung, Geschichtswissenschaft*, ed. Siegfried Mattl, Gerhard Botz, Stefan Karner, and Helmut Konrad, (Vienna: Böhlau Verlag, 2009), 68–72.
3. The 1918 flu pandemic (January 1918 to December 1920) was an unusually deadly influenza pandemic involving H1N1 influenza virus. It infected five hundred million people across the world, and resulted in the deaths of fifty to one hundred million (3 to 5 percent of the world's population).
4. Marsha L. Rozenblit, *Reconstructing a National Identity: The Jews of Habsburg Austria during World War 1* (New York: Oxford University Press, 2004), 88–9.
5. Jay Winter, *Remembering War: The Great War between Memory and History in the Twentieth History* (New Haven, CT: Yale University Press, 2006), 91–102; Jay Winter, *War beyond Words: Language of Remembrance from the Great War to the Present* (Cambridge: Cambridge University Press, 2017), 49–53.

INTRODUCTION

Bernard Bardach
A Biographical Sketch

HELMUT KONRAD

The Bernhard Bardach collection comprises a unique treasure in the archival holdings of the Leo Baeck Institute in New York—a personal archive that bears witness to the horrors of the twentieth century. On the one hand, the Bardach war diaries—published here in the English language for the first time—preserve the impressions and experiences of a senior military physician during the whole of World War I—6 August 1914 through 1 January 1919—described in minute detail.[1] On the other hand, and just as relevant, are his photo albums, which tell not only of the Eastern Front but also of the civilian population caught up between the opposing sides in the vortex of fighting. These albums comprise an inexhaustible repository for visual history of World War I's Eastern front.[2] The six volumes of diaries and the albums permit a unique, in-depth look at everyday events on the Eastern Front, which, in contrast to other fronts in this war, remained at least partially mobile. Availability of all this material in easily accessed digitized form greatly facilitates research.

The diaries and albums tell us a great deal about Bardach's life during the four years of the war; however, much less is known about his life before and after the conflict. His daughter Miki Denhof prepared a short biography of her father for the Leo Baeck Institute, with as complete an overview of his life as she could manage. Tanja Grössing has included the latter report in the short biographical sketches of her noteworthy master's thesis (in collaboration with Petra Ernst) at the University of Graz.[3] I have complemented and clarified parts of Bardach's biography using additional documents from the Austrian State Archives[4] and the University of Graz[5] to provide as accurate a glimpse as I can into the life of Dr. Bernhard Bardach before, during, and after the war.

Bardach's Life before 1914

Bardach was born in Lemberg, in Austrian Galicia, one of the centers of Jewish life, both assimilated and orthodox. The great jurists Raphael Lemkin and Hersch Lauterpacht were born there. Martin Buber was raised there, and the novelist Joseph Roth was born at Brody (Ukraine), nearby.[6] An extract of the Lemberg (Lviv, Ukraine) birth register confirms that "Berisch Bardach, son of Israel... Bardach and his wife Rive was born on 3 August 1866."[7] Names of the midwife and witnesses are also recorded. His father was a merchant.

After several years in a Jewish elementary school, Bernhard moved to the Lemberg gymnasium (German academic high school), followed by the second upper school (gymnasium), where he graduated. At the age of twenty, he entered the University of Vienna, to study medicine. Every fifth semester, he studied in both Vienna and Graz. On the enrollment page, his mother tongue is given as German, and his religion as Jewish (*mosaisch*). From the winter semester of 1887/88 to the end of winter semester 1892/93, he was enrolled, first as ordinary, then (in the 1893 summer semester) as senior student, before passing the final oral examination. He passed the first oral examination on 24 March 1890, the second on 1 December 1892, and, only five days after the third examination on 22 June 1893, he graduated as doctor of general medicine.[8] His academic career was satisfactory, though not particularly distinguished. In 1892, he obtained two excellent evaluations in internal medicine; other than that, all examinations are marked "satisfactory," all on the first attempt.[9] It may be assumed, but not definitely proven with existing documentation, that anti-Semitism played a role in his "satisfactory" examination results at the University of Graz.

On 23 April 1888, Bardach registered as a one-year volunteer in the Habsburg army: this guaranteed him a study stipend, but entailed six years of active service thereafter. In 1893, a few weeks after his graduation, he was appointed secondary physician and then senior physician on active service. In 1908, he successfully passed the test for surgeon major.[10] His list of service assignments before the war is long. He had to interrupt his studies from 1 April to 30 September 1890, to perform his obligatory six-month service in the thirtieth Lemberg infantry regiment.

Bardach served his first year as military physician at the twenty-third garrison hospital in Agram (Zagreb, Croatia), as secondary physician in the surgical department. He spent most of the following four years in Fiume (now part of Italy) among other duties as representative of the chief regimental physician. From 1 September 1898, he taught at the infantry cadet school in Kamenitz (Kamenice nad Lipou, Czech Republic), where he functioned as "teacher and chief school physician." The following year, he served as interim commandant of the fifth Ulan Regiment troop hospital in Warasdin (Varaždin, Croatia), until he was again transferred on 1 May 1900, to Czortkow (Chortkiv, Ukraine), as chief regimental physician, chief garrison physician, and commandant of the troop hospital of the first Ulan Regiment.

Five years later, Bardach was transferred back to the thirtieth infantry regiment in Lemberg, where he spent the next four years as chief physician in command and at times as chief regimental physician. In August 1909, he was transferred again, as chief physician to the fourth Bosnian-Herzegovinian infantry regiment in Trieste, which would be his main place of residence for several years. Although his war archive documents classify him as a "dental specialist," his job was to prove himself proficient in all fields of medical treatment.

In 1885, his personal file states that he "cannot ride." By 1897, his "riding has improved," and finally in 1902 he is "capable of riding for official duties"—a skill that he would need urgently, during the coming war. His service evaluations do not deviate from the norm, and he was promoted "according to rank and period of duty." His military career reflects the possibility that Jews could make a career—especially a medical one—in the Austro-Hungarian Army, without often being confronted by open anti-Semitism. Mobility, however, was an absolute prerequisite, and Bardach's many transfers before the war were not at all unusual.

Bardach's 1911 service evaluation provides detailed information about his military career and private relationships. His 1912 evaluation states tersely "as in 1911" without any additions. In 1911, the following are noted:

> Rank: Surgeon major, Regimental chief physician
>
> Knowledge of languages: Excellent written and spoken German, very eloquent style, excellent communication skills. Polish, Croatian: military usage sufficient for service needs.
>
> Private relationships: Married with secure annual income of 1,600 crowns, assets inherited from his deceased first wife. Two daughters: Bettina born in 1900, Ega born in 1904. Married again in 1909, against a security indemnity of 40,000 crowns. Finances in good order.
>
> Health: Fit for war service. Very shortsighted, uses glasses. Medium height, strong build.
>
> Character: Upright character, performs duties conscientiously.[11]

This document tells us a great deal. Pointedly, perhaps, no mention is made of religion; by contrast, detailed information on his knowledge and abilities inside the military, leadership qualities, and especially private relationships, are noted.

Bardach married soon after the end of his studies and entry into military service. His first wife, Henia, was the daughter of a Jewish landowner. The marriage yielded two daughters, Bettina and Ega. Henia died soon after the birth of their second child, and, five years later, he remarried. His second wife, Olga, daughter of a textile manufacturer named Krieger, was born 21 February 1886 in Bielitz, Silesia (Bielsko-Biała, Poland), and was twenty years younger than her husband. The second marriage yielded two more daughters, Miki and Mary, the latter of whom was born during the war. Bardach refers repeatedly to Olga and his four daughters in his war diary. This family—Olga with two of her own children and two from his previous marriage—were his emotional fulcrum, throughout the turmoil of a war, which drove him through different regions of Central and Eastern Europe, the Balkans, and Italy. We will meet them again in the description of his life during the decades after the Great War. After the outbreak of the war, Olga moved from Trieste to Vienna with the four children.

Military documents show that Bardach was awarded two decorations during peacetime: The Jubilee Memorial Medal of the Armed Forces, and the Military Jubilee Cross. Both awards reflect his long period of service. Bernard Bardach was already forty-eight when the long period of peace, during which he grew up, ended. He was born during the last great battle of the Habsburg Empire and had experienced no warlike confrontations in his twenty years of service. He went to the front as a mature man of senior military-medical rank, and decided to record his experiences there in word and photograph.

The War Years

Bernhard Bardach's war diary—presented here in its first complete English translation—describes the fifty-three months of war that followed accurately and in great detail. Bardach's writing style is sober, with a great deal of medical terminology. The text is peppered with foreign words and many abbreviations, indicating that the diary was meant only for his personal reading, not for others, let alone a wider reading public.[12] Tanja Grössing has comparatively analyzed the Bardach diaries and those of Egon Ernst Kisch, which were meant for publication. She shows that the first few volumes underwent only light revision, not of content but rather of grammar and syntax. The writing style, however, remains the same. Bardach's written expressiveness is, as noted in his previous service evaluations, excellent. Once one has become used to his Gothic cursive handwriting, texts are easily deciphered. However, in order to obtain a complete picture of his emotional experiences, the photo albums, which are much more than supplementation of the written material, are essential. The photographs show what Bardach considered worthy of preservation: they include everyday occurrences as well as an astonished, almost colonial, view of the indigenous population, especially the Jews of Central and Eastern Europe. The photos also cast a pitiless eye on the victims of this terrible war.

The albums are worthy of a separate analytical book; Jay Winter has made extensive use of these in lectures and publications.

Bardach's diaries permit an exact reconstruction of his frontline service. His written notes begin with an almost semiofficial introduction, from the viewpoint of a loyal member of the Habsburg Empire. He summarizes the period between the murder of the heir to the throne until the declaration of war, in a scant six diary pages. His personal war diary follows. The diary eschews all sentimentality. Among the darkness and tears at the Trieste railway station, he remarks tersely: "I am happy that I spared my family the pain of accompanying me to the station." The journey to the front leaves him with ambivalent feelings. "Beautiful maidens crowd around our carriages, throw flowers at us, like going to a dance" alternates with "even if we are victorious, if it goes on like this, there will be mass murder and the destruction of untold numbers of lives." The author is too worldly-wise to resemble a young war enthusiast, but is fully prepared to do his duty conscientiously and with absolute dedication.

Bardach arrives at the front in Glogowiec near Katowice (Poland) and is immediately confronted with the horrors of war. Three hundred men have fallen into a Russian ambush and been killed. On the other hand, the diary proudly documents the functioning of Austrian administration in an occupied Russian village. This introduction does not have sufficient space to reproduce accurately Bardach's route during the course of the war. In brief, it can be said that he was very rapidly confronted with war's realities, in the form of hundreds of badly wounded men, as stated in an entry on 24 August 1914, a sort of "baptism by fire." This strenuous effort exacted a cost. On 29 August 1914, Bardach writes: "I am completely exhausted, and also have severe stomach cramps." The war rapidly reveals what is to be expected on the other the side of simple war propaganda. Necessity for support by German troops, to maintain the front line against the Russians, is also made clear early on.

During the first few weeks of the war, the acculturated Jewish physician who has lived in large cities like Vienna, Graz, and Trieste, gets his first glimpse of the lives of the Jewish population of Eastern Europe during the war. The view of a physician like Bardach, fully integrated into big city life, is characterized by compassion but also by emotional distance:

> The sight of the Jewish exodus from Rudniki is very moving. Very few are able to obtain some sort of conveyance, and there is no space for so many people. They lie in heaps one on top of the other. Most are old people, women, and children, who make the journey back—loaded with bundles—on foot. A picture of the greatest misery!

However, he sees "the Jews from Rudniki" with objective compassion and has long separated himself from this part of the East/Middle European Jewish community. He speaks of the "poor Jews" on the San, "who are terrified, pack all their belongings, wring their hands at each thunder of the cannons, and run through the streets like madmen, bundles on their backs, not knowing where to go." Two things are apparent, perusing the photographs: first, an almost ethnological and dispassionate curiosity of the "exotic creatures" whom he sees; second, an extremely distanced and prosaic empathy, which is sometimes not detectable at all. Reciprocal cross-references between diary and photographs are unfortunately not present, and one often finds two separate emotional worlds between the photographer and the chronicler. Luckily, Bardach labeled all his photos, allowing added (though retrospective) insight into his war service.

The army allows Bardach to practice his faith and puts no obstacles in his way. The detailed entry of 7 October 1916 makes this abundantly clear:

> Yom Kippur. By invitation from Chaplain Dr. Levi, I travel to Vladimir Volynsky [Ukraine] with the general's own car, taking Senior Physician Dr. Deutsch from the second division medical unit with me.
>
> The journey takes one and a quarter hours; the weather is very unpleasant: overcast, rain at times. I spend the entire day in the synagogue in a place of honor next to Chaplain Dr. Levi with the exception of the afternoon pause from 2:00 to 4:00 p.m., during which time I visit the local medical supply branch, to purchase supplies. I return to the synagogue and remain there until 5:30 p.m., at which time I return, arriving at command at 7:00 p.m. (The car remains at my disposal all day.) I fast easily and am not plagued by hunger. The sermon is much better than the one for New Year. The service was solemn and very good—an outstanding cantor—but the number of men was a lot smaller, only common soldiers and poor Russian Jews.

This excerpt explains a great deal: first, the self-evidence of religious practice, and acceptance of Jews in the Habsburg Army, which goes so far as to allow him to use the general's own car to travel to synagogue. One also sees Bardach's responsibility as a physician, in that he uses the afternoon break and the car to order medical supplies, for onward transportation to the front. He observes *some* religious commandments as a matter of course, by fasting. But at the same time, he clearly differentiates himself from "common soldiers," with whom the high-ranking surgeon major has no emotional connection. The Russian Jew remains to him an exotic and marginal figure.

Anti-Semitism did not pose any particular challenge to Bardach. Apparently he could humorously circumvent it. He writes about a dinner on 1 October 1915: "We are invited to dine there. The menu is simple but very good—I sit to the right of Dr. Raday, who is very friendly, but whose anti-Semitism does not seem to have changed much." The diary does not show any real outrage about small talk with an anti-Semite during dinner.

Bardach's war service decoration record is clearly set down in the archives. In December 1914, he was put up for the Knights Cross Award: the application is based on his "cold-blooded personal commitment to performance of his medical duties under the most dangerous conditions."[13] In November 1915, Bardach was promoted to Oberstabsarzt II Klasse (with the rank of lieutenant colonel), and a few months later, he was again put up for a decoration: this time for his:

> steadfast sense of duty and tireless activity including (but not limited to) organization of the medical corps. He has in many cases given valuable service as a devoted general physician. The fact that the troops—even when they entered the cholera-infested region of Kowel [Kovel, Ukraine]—were practically unaffected by infection, is entirely due to his constant care and supervision of all preventive hygienic measures.[14]

A final award proposal in September 1917 cites his "brave and steadfast behavior against the enemy."[15] He succeeded in containing the infectious diseases prevalent amongst the soldiers during the static warfare in Volhynia (region consisting of contiguous areas of Poland, Ukraine, and Belarus). Bardach's nine military awards are preserved at the Leo Baeck Institute in New York and are digitally available for those interested. The main register page of his personal file in the war archives also lists these awards, together with his raised salary qualifications between 1915 and 1917.

Decoration proposals show that Bardach worked not only as a hospital organizer but also in the field of preventative medicine. Moreover, he provided medical care to the civilian population. As the diary entry of 30 July 1915 indicates, he has to pay a visit to a farmer's wife to try and help with her difficult birth:

> An arm has prolapsed and the head is stuck deep in the pelvis. Rotation impossible despite hours of trying, and no other surgical procedures are possible because of lack of instruments. Spontaneous birth around 11:00 p.m., but the infant is born dead.

On 16 August 1915:

> There is quite a lot of cholera here; corpses pass along the road near me all the time. The civilians are mainly poor Jews. In addition to inoculation of the command baggage train, I also inoculate Assistant Physician Schwarz and, as far as my vaccine supplies last, the civilian population. The people crowd around me and must be held at arm's length, by force if necessary. Women, men old and young, children as well—in total about four hundred are inoculated.

As far as can be gathered from his diary, Bardach was a dutiful and loyal subject of the Habsburg Monarchy. He served with great personal commitment but without any illusions about the nature of the war. At the outset, during his initial journey from Trieste to the front, he noted, (as has been mentioned):

"even if we are victorious, if it goes on like this, there will be mass murder and the destruction of untold numbers of lives."

The diary contains an unusually complete account of the unfolding of the Brusilov Offensive in 1916, which exhausted both the Russian and the Austro-Hungarian armies. We can see from the diary that the Brusilov Offensive revealed the hopelessness of their situation: "terrible news from the front: unbelievable losses—whole battalions, especially of fortieth and eighty-second infantry regiments, have been trapped during the breakthrough, and trenches are filled with piles of corpses. My heart dies in my throat." Bardach relates that the fourth army has lost forty thousand men during this offensive, and ten thousand from his original unit of eleven thousand. The turbulent pages of his diary during this period reveal his most difficult days at the front during the entire war.

The diary is generally sober and prosaic and, apart from the early period of the Brusilov Offensive, rarely reveals tumultuous emotions. However, the entry of 16 December 1914—early in the war—states:

> The ride through the battlefields of the past four weeks reveals a picture of destruction horrible to behold. Whole heaps of Russian and Austrian bodies lie around everywhere. Endless amounts of war material. Churches and houses destroyed either by bombardment or burned down—a picture of misery and wretchedness!

By the time of the Brusilov Offensive in 1916, the true horror of war and hopelessness of the Austrian position has become all too obvious. Bardach is no longer convinced that the war can be won, but his loyal sense of duty and commitment—honed for decades in the army—does not budge.

The diary is seldom private. Bardach reports on his often-venturesome attempts to collect provisions for his family before he goes on leave, to alleviate their hunger in starving Vienna by bringing food along with him or sending it on ahead. His family plays a central role in the diary only once when, after the end of the Brusilov Offensive, he is finally granted leave and spends three weeks with his family between 14 October and 12 November 1916:

> I find my family well, just thinner, especially my Olga. I can see her joy and happiness that I have arrived: she is very animated and will not leave my side—my dear, good wifey, affectionate as a little child. My eldest daughter, Bettina, has become a splendid, lively woman. Her thinner appearance looks very good on her, and she is both modest and lively. She fills me with joy. Ega is a pretty, dear young girl, still doesn't learn much but certainly knows more than she did last year and has made excellent progress in piano playing. She has real talent. Miki is a magnificent young girl, deft and agile, but always modest—she cozies up shamelessly against her Dad and is a real enfant terrible. My youngest daughter, Mary, is dear and sweet: actually, this is the first time I really see her. This sweet

little thing is very good, hardly cries at all, so that one does not even know that an eight-month-old baby is there.

These are the words of a classical patriarch: loving, but in charge of the five women in his Vienna family. His wife is described affectionately, but as a childlike, feminine being. He is not only the rooster in the henhouse but also the one who without doubt has the primary say in domestic affairs, despite his family having had to manage without him for such a long time. That his wife was twenty years his junior may have played a part in the unfolding of their conventional marriage.

Eight months pass before Bardach manages to get home leave, in summer 1917. In April 1918, he laboriously collects a package of family provisions to be delivered by his batman (including ten kilograms of bacon and four and a half kilograms of ham), without any guarantee that the goods would be delivered. In April 1918, Bardach is finally transferred from the former Eastern Front to the front lines in upper Italy, first to Montfalcone and finally to Portogruaro. During this time, a note of increased resignation appears in his diary. He cannot even pray on Yom Kippur, because of the daily realities of war.

On 20 September, Bardach, heavily laden with provisions (including no less than forty kilograms of flour) is able to visit his family in Vienna again. By that time, the Spanish flu has already gripped the city: luckily, his daughters become infected with just a light, passing fever. Soaring inflation complicates everyday activities on all levels.

Bardach experiences the last weeks of the war back at the Italian Front, where—as a senior officer—he is most struck by the weakness of the home front. He sees the army in the field as yet unconquered and is appalled at the Monarchy's inner decay. This is particularly striking, in that it shows the similarities between the thinking of a loyal Jewish Austrian and that of radical right-wing soldiers convinced that the war effort had been betrayed at home, by socialists and Jews. Bardach's mild version of the *Dolchstosslegende* (stab in the back myth) is a reflection of his innate patriotism, his conservative outlook, and his downcast attitude at the end of the war.

On 3 November, Bardach rejects entry into the Polish Army, despite his birth city of Lemberg, because he considers the Poles a corrupt and incompetent nation: "The Germans are not kindly disposed to the Jews but at least they are cultivated and assiduous and more honest, so I will join them." He decides clearly in favor of German national identity to what—after the fall of the Monarchy—is now called German-Austria (Deutsch-Österreich).

War's end finds him on the Italian Front, described prosaically in his diary: "So the war has ended for me, and I close my diary!!" He travels back to Vienna by train and reports immediately to the German-Austrian army. He has to travel to his appropriate military command in Graz to complete the necessary admission formalities. On 20 November, he reports for duty at garrison hospital no. 1, but two days later is sent to a spa for treatment of his rheumatism, a result of his many years of strenuous service at the front. After his spa cure, he enters the private Clinic Finger for training as a specialist in skin and venereal diseases. So ends his nearly thirty years of military service.

Civilian Life

Adaptation to civilian life could not have been easy, but not because of his financial situation, which was comfortable. When Bardach finally retired from the army in 1920 as Oberstabsarzt I Klasse (colonel), after thirty-three years, two months, and twenty-nine days of active service, he was entitled, starting in 1921, to draw an old-age pension. Additionally, he obtained a salary from the Clinic Finger, and after the end of his training, he opened a private practice in Vienna (about which we unfortunately have no documentation).

But first his citizenship had to be clarified. As prescribed at the end of the Habsburg Monarchy, he had the right to claim Lemberg, his birthplace, as home. However, on 1 November 1918, the West Ukrainian People's Republic was established. Civil war followed. After three weeks, Polish troops entered Lemberg and a bloody pogrom against the Jewish population followed. Self-evidently, he neither could nor wanted to return there.

Vienna became the center of their lives. Bardach worked in the demobilization center for returning soldiers of the German-Austrian army until 1 August 1920.[16] On 1 January 1920, he was promoted to the next pay level. On 21 December 1918, he had already handed in his declaration of citizenship to the district magistrate in the seventh district of Vienna, stating that he wished to belong to, and be, a loyal citizen of the Republic of German-Austria.[17]

Many Viennese were filled with mistrust of Jews from Eastern Europe who now wished to remain. Other biographies indicate that bribery was often necessary for them to obtain Austrian citizenship. In Bardach's case, there is no indication that this was the case. However, perhaps this is why it took until 7 June 1920, when he and his family obtained permission from the provincial government of Lower Austria for right of residence and Austrian citizenship. On 30 June 1930, his provisional pension payments were changed to regular retirement benefits by the Ministry of Defense.

Meanwhile, the children grew up and flew the coop into the wider world. The eldest immigrated to the United States in 1922 and, when Miki did the same in 1939, she was the third Bardach daughter who had chosen to live in America. Miki had studied at the Reimann School of Art and Design in Berlin, and a notable career as editor and designer lay before her.[18] It's thanks to her that the Bardach Collection was gifted to the Leo Baeck Institute in New

York. When Miki Denhof died in 2000 at the age of eighty-eight, the *New York Times* issue of 8 June 2000 dedicated an extensive obituary to her, with recognition of her artistic achievements. It also highlighted the donation of her father's collection to the Leo Baeck Institute.

One of the daughters went to Italy, married in Florence, and survived World War II hiding in the Abruzzi. Olga and Bernard Bardach experienced the end of the Austrian Republic alone; by that time, Bernhard was already sixty-two. They attempted to live in Vienna through early 1939, so as not to give up all they owned. But by then then situation had become intolerable, and emigration was the only option—in their case, tantamount to expulsion from their homeland.

Humiliation

Bardach's lifelong medical service, including his service in uniform and in the field on the side of the Central Powers during the war, counted for absolutely nothing after the Anschluss. Incorporation of Austria into the German Reich meant that they, together with the other two hundred thousand Jews of Vienna, were excluded from the Volk. The lengths to which this ostracism would go were not yet clear, but living in Austria had become practically impossible.

Olga and Bernhard, who at the time were living in 62 Kaiserstrasse, seventh district, submitted a departure application to allow them to join their daughters in the United States, and so the chicanery began. Both were required to hand in a list of the private articles that they wanted to take with them to the Vienna foreign currency office in Teinfaltstrasse. Obviously, no articles of value could be included: even Bardach's military service medals had to be stamped "not made of precious metals" by the authorities. Bardach listed 151 objects, among these about thirty-six handkerchiefs and fourteen pairs of underpants. Olga had only thirty objects, including three packages of letters from her children. With very few exceptions—such as these letters—the list comprises only articles of clothing, and nothing of value. They signed a letter confirming that they had neither property nor debts in Austria, and no property out of the country. The lists were handed in on 26 April 1939, with a "provisional" departure date for the United States of 2 May.[19]

On 2 May, Bardach informed the pension office in Vienna, that he had requested his bank—Creditanstalt Bankverein—to open a special account to facilitate further pension deposits. The settlement was still outstanding, because the bank required disclosure of the exact deposit amount from the pension office:

> I hereby inform the pension office that I am still awaiting approval from the bank, and that I will be leaving Germany in the next few days, with an interme-

diary stop in Florence with, once visa formalities have been completed, further travel to the USA.[20]

From Italy, Bardach tried unsuccessfully to control his financial affairs. The authority wrote tersely:

> The Jew has left Reich territory. The Vienna foreign currency office has approved payment into a special account until 31 March 1940. The authorized payee has not yet submitted official notification of the authorized opening of this account at Österreichischer Creditanstalt Wiener Bankverein. Therefore, no reason for the establishment of a special account exists, and pension payment will cease from 1 June.

This is followed, thickly underlined, by "until he reports in person."[21] Bardach would have had to return to Vienna to deal further with this issue. On 8 July, the Vienna pension office demanded that the pension payment be returned by the bank, writing: "The Vienna pension office has erroneously paid out a pension benefit in the amount of RM 582.66 into the special account of the Jew Dr. Bernhard Bardach. Bardach is out of the country without the permission of the Ministry of External Affairs, and the money must therefore be returned."[22]

Bardach sent two separate letters—one typed, one handwritten—from Viareggio to the Senior Finance Presidium in Vienna on 6 September 1939, again requesting payment of the previously approved sums.[23] The Gestapo had already informed the pension office on 22 September that they had "no objections to the Jew Dr. Bernhard Bardach changing his place of residence."[24] However, all forms of payment—no matter how small—were consistently refused, and Bernhard and Olga fled from Italy via Portugal to New York, finally arriving in 1941, without a penny in their pockets.

Compensation?

There was obviously no hope of financial compensation for the Bardach family from National Socialist Germany. But after their comprehensive defeat, the breakup of the Habsburg Empire, and the establishment of the Austrian Republic, one could hope that new life would be breathed into their old pension claims. However, this was to take time.

Eleven months after war's end, Bardach addressed a clearly handwritten letter to the "War Ministry":

> With respect to the renewal of my pension payments, I report that my last payment in the amount of RM 296.33 occurred on 1 May 1939. Since then, despite repeated valid requests, I have received nothing.

I therefore request retroactive renewal of my pension payments. These are needed all the more because as an eighty-year-old man I am unable to practice my profession anymore, and am totally dependent on charitable support from my family.[25]

A letter from the Ministry of Finance dated 14 October (only received on 10 December) informed Bardach that his pension had been canceled in 1939, "because you left the country."[26] This elicited a clearer and even more emotional response: Bardach wrote that he had been forced to emigrate "with only RM 10 in my pocket." All promises to pay his pension into a blocked account had been broken, "despite my urgent requests, repeated so many times that they have worn me out." He continued:

> I, who served my Fatherland faithfully for a total of thirty-two years in war and peace, have had to live for the past seven years on the charity of my two unmarried, unprovided-for daughters, who must work very hard indeed to provide our daily bread. From the days of my youth, I have avoided being a burden on anyone; but now, as a retired Austrian officer, I do not possess a single cent to call my own.[27]

On 31 March 1946, Bernhard Bardach became a naturalized American citizen. But he didn't have much longer to live, and died in 1947 of a myocardial infarct. Existing documents put the date of his death at 6 June 1947.

It took until 1955 before attorney Dr. Odelga in Vienna successfully took up the financial interests of the Bardach family in Vienna. From 1 October 1955, Olga received a monthly widow's benefit of 1,355.70 schillings; her widow's pension claim from 1950 to 1955 was also paid into an Austrian blocked account. However, Bernhard received no retroactive reparation: "Because, at the time he acquired American citizenship, he did not possess pension authorization during his residence overseas, his pension benefits have lapsed."[28] The cynicism of Austrian officials about Jewish expulsion, even a decade after war's end, is obvious. Overseas residence forfeited pension claims. What "overseas residence" really meant for the Bardach family, played no role in the argument whatsoever. Neither did the fact that had he remained in Vienna, he would have been subject to deportation and extermination. "Overseas residence" meant staying alive, and that was the bureaucratic sticking point in providing him with the pension he so evidently deserved. The bureaucratic shadow of the Holocaust continued to darken Jewish lives long after the end of the war.

Olga Bardach died on 25 August 1968. The Central Pensions Office wrote laconically that the daughter, Miki Denhof, was entitled to a pension balance of 1,044.30 schillings, less court costs.[29] A disgraceful chapter in the history of postwar Austria thus came to an end.

Both international and Austrian research are today able to enjoy the wonderful components of the Bardach collection at the Leo Baeck Institute in New York, and through them obtain ever newer and deeper insights on the history of World War I, especially the war on the Eastern Front. However, the history behind these documents must not be forgotten. The life of Bernhard Bardach and his family, described here in broad terms, demonstrates the fate of people on whom deep wounds were inflicted by the politics of Austria (including Austria both under National Socialism and after its downfall). Bernard Bardach's loyalty to the state, demonstrated by decades of military service, in the end came to nothing.

Helmut Konrad is Emeritus Professor of Contemporary History at the University of Graz. He has held visiting fellowships at Cornell University, University of Waterloo, European University Institute Firenze and Yale University.

Notes

1. The diaries comprise six volumes of clearly written German Gothic cursive. They are available in digital form on the Leo Baeck Institute New York homepage, archive no. AR 6632.
2. See Jay Winter, *War beyond Words: Language of Remembrance from the Great War to the Present* (Cambridge: Cambridge University Press, 2017), 49–53.
3. Tanja Grössing, *Der Bleistift zitterte und das Herz zitterte, als dieses Manuskript entstand: Untersuchungen der Kriegstagebücher von Egon Erwin Kisch und Bernhard Bardach*, MA thesis, University of Graz, 2015.
4. Personal file of Bernhard Bardach, Österreichisches Staatsarchiv, Kriegsarchiv, Vienna. I thank Frau Archivdirektorin Renate Dommanich for competent assistance during my examination of the extensive material.
5. I thank Professor Doctor Alois Kernbauer, Director of the Graz University Archives, most sincerely for placing Bardach's examination details at my disposal.
6. On Lemberg and Lvov, see Philippe Sands, *East-West Street: On the Origins of "Genocide" and "Crimes against Humanity"* (New York: Knopf, 2016).
7. Birth certificate in Bardach personal file, *Kriegsarchiv*.
8. Examination file, Graz University Archives.
9. Ibid.
10. Personal file, *Kriegsarchiv*.
11. Service assessment of Surgeon-Major Dr. Bernhard Bardach, 1911, *Kriegsarchiv*.
12. Grössing, *Der Bleistift zitterte*, 29.
13. Decoration proposal of 30 December 1914 in personal file, *Kriegsarchiv*.
14. Decoration proposal of 20 December 1915 in personal file, *Kriegsarchiv*.
15. Decoration proposal of 25 September 1915 in personal file, *Kriegsarchiv*.
16. Confirmation in provisional Austrian personnel files of medical corps company 1, Vienna of 6 November 1920. Personal file, *Kriegsarchiv*.

17. Citizenship declaration of Dr. Bernhard Bardach, 21 December 1918. Personal file, *Kriegsarchiv*.
18. "Miki G. Denhof Nèe Bardach, Editor and Designer," in *Biographia, Lexicon österreichischer Frauen*, vol. 1 A-H, Vienna, 2016, 574.
19. Application to the Vienna foreign currency office of 26 April 1939 submitted by Bernhard and Olga Bardach. Personal file, *Kriegsarchiv*.
20. Letter from Bardach to the pension office, Vienna, 2 May 1939. Personal file, *Staatsarchiv*.
21. Handwritten decision on the request by Bernhard Bardach on 16 May 1939. Personal file, *Kriegsarchiv*.
22. Letter from sixteenth pension bureau in Vienna to Austrian Creditanstalt, Wiener Bankverein, Filiale Westbahnstraße, 8 July 1939. Personal file, *Kriegsarchiv*.
23. Two identically worded letters, one typed the other handwritten, from Bardach to the Vienna *Oberfinanzpräsidium*, section 7b, 6 September 1939 from Viareggio, Italy. Personal file, *Kriegsarchiv*.
24. Letter from Gestapo, Staatspolizeileitstelle Vienna, to pension office of 22 August 1939. Personal file, *Kriegsarchiv*.
25. Handwritten letter from "*Oberstabsarzt* Dr. Bernhard Bardach, New York, 740 West 187th Street" to the Austrian War Ministry, 9 April 1946. Personal file, *Kriegsarchiv*.
26. Letter from the Ministry of Finance Zl 109.585/46—pension section B, to Dr. Bernhard Bardach, New York, 14 October 1946. Personal file *Kriegsarchiv*.
27. Letter from Dr. Bernhard Bardach, New York to the Ministry of Finance in Vienna 12 December 1946. Personal file *Kriegsarchiv*.
28. Letter from Ministry of Finance to the central pensions Office, June,1954. Personal file *Kriegsarchiv*.
29. Correspondence from Central Pay Office to the Regional Court of Central Vienna, 8 November 1918. Decision and attachments to Mrs. M Denhof. Personal file, *Kriegsarchiv*.

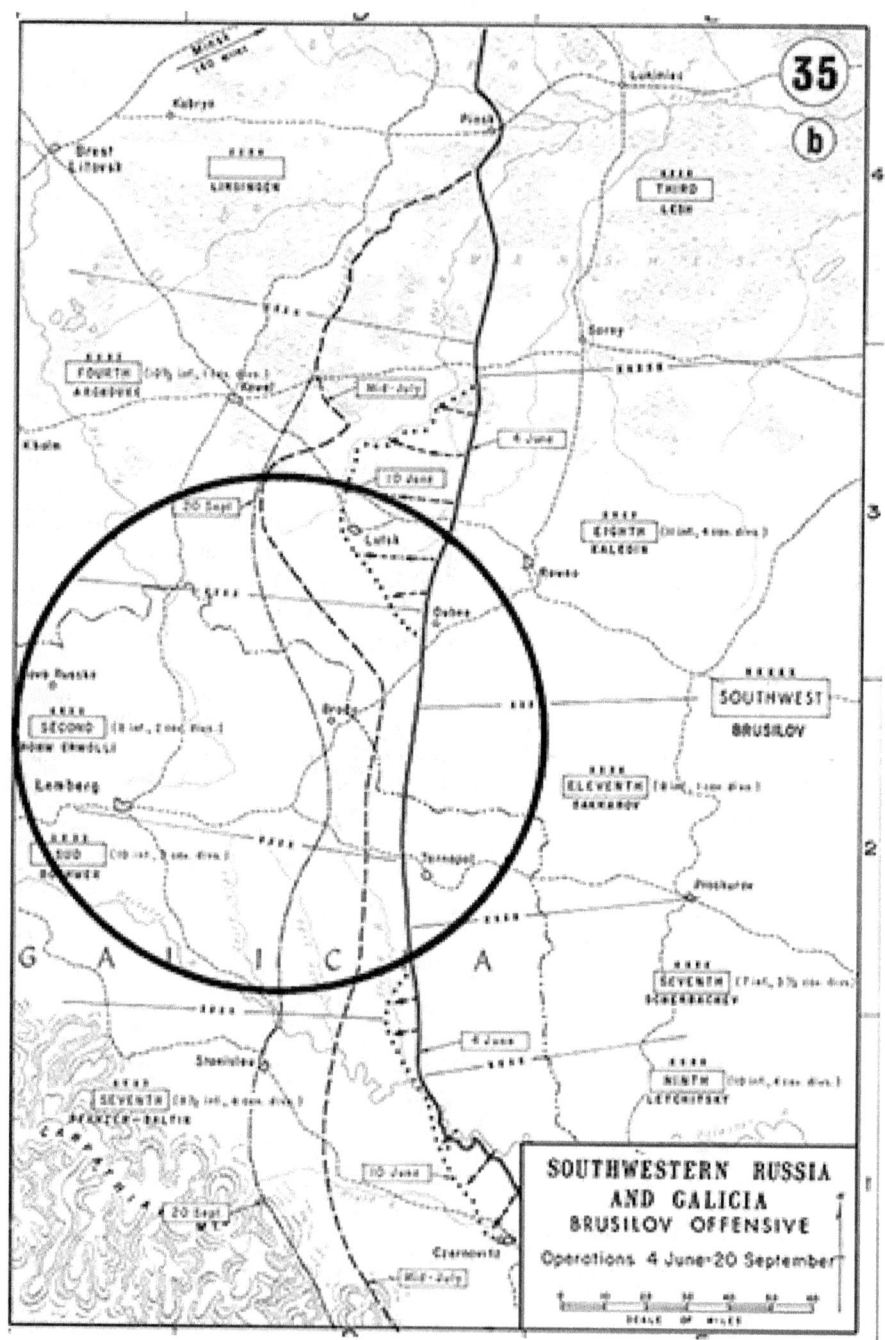

Map 0.1. The Brusilov Offensive, June to September 1917. Ellipse marks Bernhard Bardach's theater of activity. Wikimedia Commons, public domain.

CHAPTER 1

1914
Poland, Russia, Carpathians

On the fateful date 28 June 1914, the heir to the throne Franz Ferdinand d'Este and his wife Duchess Sophie Hohenburg were murdered in Sarajevo. This earthshaking event instantly clarified the political situation in which our Monarchy and its ally Germany found themselves. By this deed, Serbia faithfully fulfilled its deadly mission by organizing the assassination, together with its preceding scandalous propaganda. Russia immediately delivered its preplanned declaration, that it wants nothing untoward to happen to Serbia, and ordered official mobilization that, in fact, had been in process for quite a long time. France, believing that the moment for *la revanche* had arrived, followed the call of its Entente partners as well as perfidious Albion, and opened hostilities by indiscriminate bombing—forbidden by international law—of open German cities.

England, who carefully instigated Russia and France and dragged Belgium into the war, now openly joined the Entente against the Central Powers—something that in fact they had already done in secret—and entered the war, to destroy German commerce, and oust this dangerous rival from the world scene. On 25 July 1914, after the Serbian rejection of our ultimatum, declaration of war followed, by proclamation of general mobilization on 31 July 1914.

4 AUGUST. Day 1 of general mobilization. Preparation of my regimental battalion in Trieste is already far along, with our men already fully clothed and equipped, so that they can begin the journey to Karlstadt[1] on 6 August at 1:36 a.m. (for supplemental equipment to put the battalion on full war footing).

Despite the very late hour, the whole of Trieste is awake and humming: columns echo with continuous cheering of *eviva!* and *alla guerra!* The platform is crowded with people, and there is no end of leave taking by waving scarves and handkerchiefs, until finally the train leaves the station. There are many tears, especially from women and children, and I am happy that I spared my family the pain of accompanying me to the station.

8 AUGUST. Arrival in Karlstadt at 2:00 a.m. after a boring and uncomfortable journey. Four of us share a first-class coupé (Lieutenant Colonel Tuschner, Captain Alexandrovitsch, First Lieutenant Quartermaster Steiner, and myself). Weather cool and partly overcast, with rain. My quarters in Karlstadt are simple, but clean and private. Very hot, with plenty of work to do. My primary mission the first day is acquiring a horse, because the two horses given to me by the regiment here are absolutely impossible to ride. They have not yet been broken in, and resemble Galician farmers' horses (*koniki*). After a great deal of searching in the horse market, with assistance from Lieutenant Colonel Tuschner, Captain von Martini, and the regimental horn player, I buy an iron-gray horse for 850 crowns. The horse looks good, young (four and a half years old), large enough, without blemish, and, as the seller assured me, very good natured and well behaved, despite having thrown its previous rider twice while galloping. The rider was to blame for this, for riding without saddle and stirrup, and thus not being able to stop the horse. He may be correct. We will see!

The main occurrence today is the sudden order from command that all Serbian soldiers are unreliable and must be removed from service as soon as possible. This measure proves to be totally uncalled for. As a group, they would certainly have done their duty, and there were many courageous, intelligent men among them.

In this way, an entire battalion is eliminated, including Major Lesic; Captains Kobelnic, Diappa, Deischl, and Kukla; First Lieutenants Buchta, David, Kartner, Maiuran, and Siemetsberger. What a blot on the regiment's escutcheon! The companies are now, because of removal of the Serbs, fully occupied with reorganization. I am naturally less involved, having already almost completed the outfitting of my stretcher-bearers and dressing carriers.

Weather favorable, with some afternoon rain, only lasting about two hours and clearing later. Music at the square: I meet the widow of my former chief physician, Mrs. Aschkenasy. The poor woman has gone very old: she was always small, but has become very fat and bloated in the face—she is now as hideous as she was once pretty! Regimental Physician Aschkenasy fell in love with her casually during a long-ago summer concert, but his love disappeared as quickly as it appeared, almost immediately after the honeymoon. The poor man committed suicide a few years ago—he never was completely normal. Their daughter, to whom the woman introduced me, is a seventeen-year-old, sweet, small, pale, badly developed young lady—face and nature just like her father. Overeffusive, daydreams only over music and theater—otherwise very modest. Whether—with her looks—she will be able to succeed in her passion is another question.

9 AUGUST. Sunday morning. I am occupied determining irregularities in bread production, and, in the afternoon, with further issuance of emergency medical services material. Weather very nice!

10–11 AUGUST. Nothing special.

12 AUGUST. The regiment is sworn in and photographed. I am extremely upset to find that my horse has never been ridden and is therefore absolutely useless as a cavalry horse. I am saved from last-minute embarrassment by the willingness of Lieutenant Colonel Tuschner and Captain Diappa to exchange my horse for one of theirs.

13 AUGUST. At 8:40 a.m. the regiment departs into the unknown, general direction Russia. The first day is very hot, but it gets progressively cooler. Provisions are good, but the mood is miserable. No wonder! The situation is getting worse and worse: even if we are victorious, if it goes on like this, there will be mass murder and destruction of untold numbers of lives.

We travel through Agram,[2] Budapest (not the main railway station), Kaschau, Chynow, Jaroslau,[3] and Przeworsk: there we decamp and reach Glogowiecz[4]—fourteen kilometers from the Russian border—on foot, the following afternoon.

17 AUGUST. Great enthusiasm for us at all larger rest stops by civilian population, consisting mainly of women, girls, half-grown lads, and cripples (on state pension). Beautiful maidens crowd around our coupés, throw flowers at us, give the soldiers cigarettes, sing, and rejoice, like going to at a dance. This mood becomes more serious, the nearer we reach the enemy. News brought to us in Przeworsk by Captain von Martini—who had been sent on ahead as billeting officer—is shattering: the Russians have lured the colonel of the *Deutschmeister* Division, with three hundred men, into an ambush, and killed them. The colonel's body has been completely plundered, and left lying in his undershirt. The body is sent back to Vienna.

19 AUGUST. Inspection by Commander of the Infantry Lipošćak

20 AUGUST. 5:00 a.m. departure from Glogowiecz. Lieutenant Colonel Schenk is ordered back to Agram, where he takes over command of the Serbian front. Beautiful summer weather, which doesn't help our mood at all. The order for "travel march" is given, but, in reality, without disturbance by the enemy, we move forward rapidly. In several places, huge numbers of troops jam the roads. A picture of badly organized maneuvers.

At 10:30 a.m. we cross the border and enter the notoriously sandy Tanew[5] region. A peculiar feeling creeps into each of us; joy, clouded by thought of the fighting that lies ahead: it's clear to everyone that coming battles will be very fierce.

Almost at the border, we see the first signs of war destruction; the Austrian and Russian customs buildings have been completely burned down.

We cross the border with cries of "hurrah," and "to our victory," waving our caps in the air, decorating them with Russian oak leaves. We travel for an hour through a thick forest of firs, whose only road is almost impassable because of huge amounts of sand. Our valiant pioneers and sappers have long since been at work, building a wide log path for the baggage train on one side of the road. Russian women and farmers work hard to help us.

After marching for hours, we quarter temporarily on Russian soil in Wola Rozaniecka[6] south of Tarnogrod,[7] at 3:00 p.m.

During the late afternoon, we can already see signs of introduction of Austrian administration on Russian soil. A special political administrator calls the village farmers together: they immediately choose a community representative (*wójt*),[8] after having declared the previous one deposed. They take the oath on our constitution, sealing the procedure by removal of the Russian emblem from the town hall, and replacement with an Austrian one. The regiment takes the Russian emblem as a war souvenir.

21 AUGUST. Advance! We fall in at 5:00 a.m. and travel north without stopping. A beautiful region—many forests. We hear the thunder of cannons for the first time around 12:30 p.m.—still about fifteen to twenty kilometers from here. Nevertheless, it has an effect on every one of us: we become very serious very quickly. It is difficult to guess, let alone describe, the feelings of others. Each man thinks and experiences things in a different way. My feelings are peculiar: neither anxiety nor fear. Maybe something in between. We hear the thunder of artillery of varying intensity, for a few hours.

Around 2:00 p.m., we are able to see the scheduled eclipse of the sun very clearly. We were in the forest when the sun—which had shone down fiercely all day—gradually began to darken: the entire forest glowed with a peculiar color—a magnificent picture. But all the while it remained bright enough for many not to notice what was happening, unless they were paying attention. We had a short rest and, when this spectacle ended half an hour later, continued our march, arriving in Stary Bidaczow[9] at 4:00 p.m.

22 AUGUST. Our preliminary encampment is changed to Wola.[10]

23 AUGUST. Advance: the enemy have announced themselves, and fighting has been going on for two days. We reckon on an encounter probably today, certainly tomorrow.

Last night I finally slept well, after three nearly sleepless nights. The plague of fleas that first night on the Russian lakes was so bad that I asked to sleep in the mayor's bed. After this experience, I have decided never to sleep in a bed of such doubtful quality again, and have tried to sleep in a barn the past two nights. The trouble with this is that one cannot undress in a barn because of the cold nights.

My sleeping equipment is very poor; I miss a sleeping bag greatly, and a rubber washbasin seems superfluous, and useless into the bargain.

We march away at 5:00 a.m., despite the fact that it is Sunday. One doesn't know what day it is at all, unless reminded of it daily.

After a forced march of thirty-eight kilometers, we arrive at 6:30 p.m. in our place of encampment in Krzemien.[11]

24 august. First day of fighting: our regiment receives its baptism of fire. Today was supposed to be a day of rest: the troops are so exhausted that at first no further marching is ordered. We install ourselves comfortably, with much washing, shaving, etc. Our batman is busy washing our clothes, when at 11:00 a.m. we suddenly hear loud cannon thunder—immediate alarm, and we march off. Hardly have we reached the edge of the village, when shrapnel and shells whizz past our heads, falling to our left and right. It seems impossible for my medical staff and myself to leave the town. Lieutenant Colonel Bisenius, who whizzes by me on his horse, warns me about the fighting. (I did not think that I had seen this splendid man for the last time.) We stay behind for a while until the sound of fighting disappears, and continue our march in the direction of the regiment.

Figure 1.1. "Toilette" out in the open. Photograph courtesy of the Leo Baeck Institute.

At 3:00 p.m., an infantry battle begins: soon wounded soldiers and officers begin arriving for treatment. Because I lack anything resembling a building like a farmhouse, I install my first aid station in a hollow. The first wounded officer is First Lieutenant Suk, who tells me the sad news that Lieutenant Colonel Bisenius has already been killed, together with Captains Katušic and Ditz, Machine Gun Commander First Lieutenant Schatzmann, and many others. I wait here until dark, and then march with my walking wounded to the estate Godziszow,[12] where the first aid station of another regiment is already fully active, with already over five hundred wounded (two-thirds of them Russians). We work all night. Transfer of the division medical unit is in full swing, and evacuation to the nearest first aid unit is complete by next morning at 9:00 a.m.

25 august. I search for my own regiment and find it in Branewka[13] around 1:00 p.m. The regiment lies there completely exhausted; the neighboring unit is just as tired out, so it's a very good thing that they had no other duties that day. Yesterday's fighting led to six officers killed, six wounded; thirty-four men killed, sixty-six wounded; a total of forty killed, seventy-two wounded. Apart from those listed above, also Lieutenants Steurer and Koreis, killed; wounded: First Lieutenant Suk, Lieutenants Zgaga and Henschel, Cadet Trtnik, Lieutenant Kraus, Cadet Jenaw.

26 august. We break camp at 6:00 a.m. and march, without encountering the enemy, until 3:00 p.m, resting in the forest near Turobin.[14] As it turns out, we must spend the night here as well. I sleep under a tree—not so bad. No provisions at all today.

27 AUGUST. We pass through the forest. Today there is fighting in for crossing of the Por River: the twenty-fourth infantry division is fighting there.

28 AUGUST. Battle of Turobin: a great victory for our side. Crossing of the Por is greatly impeded by Russian resistance: if they would have succeeded in throwing us back, it would have made all our successes thus far illusory—for that reason the many dead and wounded on our side. The night of 27 to 28 August is very restless. Because we believe that the Russians have set fire to Turobin, or bombarded our baggage train early, our troops remain dug in. I am located in a roadside ditch with the regimental staff. No question of sleep, of course: very cold and wet. Life begins anew at 2:00 a.m., and at 4:00 a.m. we march off in a northeasterly direction. The Russians retreat during the night. We march until noon without encountering them, and finally make a rest stop in Zolkiew.[15] The regimental staff are directed to a Jewish house. Only old people, half-grown young boys, and girls can be seen. They make a very good impression, are intelligent, and are interested in the fighting, because they read only of Russian victories in their newspapers. They give us tea and white bread; we would have surely received provisions here, had we not been alarmed at 6:00 p.m., and marched off at once. We march for three full hours without seeing a soul; by the time we return to our quarters, it's already 10:00 p.m.

29 AUGUST. Today should also have been a rest day, earmarked for thorough washing and cleaning. But we are again disappointed: it is already 11:00 a.m., and rations are about to be distributed, but we receive the alarm again and march off immediately. We march without stopping until 8:00 p.m., without finding the enemy, and halt in Sobieska Wola.[16] We are quartered in a barn, together with the entire regimental staff. I am completely exhausted, with severe stomach cramps for the first time in this campaign. Lunch and dinner are revolting: I cannot eat the food, despite being very hungry, and satisfy my hunger with dry bread and cheese: I go to sleep at 8:00 p.m. and sleep beautifully until 4:00 a.m.: the first good sleep in three days.

30 AUGUST. We break camp at 5:00 a.m., and march in circles, without advancing a single kilometer. It's already 10:00 a.m. by the time the regiment adopts a defensive position at Radomirka,[17] and the men start to dig in. I encamp, together with the entire medical staff of 150 behind the regimental reserves in a deep hollow. We install ourselves comfortably and enjoy an opulent second breakfast[18] with sardines, wine, etc. We have just started to brew tea when, at 1:00 p.m., enemy artillery starts to shoot into our hollow. We all scatter quickly, leaving everything behind. The stableman from D Camp is slightly wounded in the head by a piece of shrapnel. After a while, the fire stops: we hurry into the hollow again and try to dig ourselves in, because we have to hold out here until dark.

In the evening, we go to regimental command, where we obtain hot food and really hot tea, always the best provision of all. We lie under a tree and rest. The night is horrible: the wind blows, rustling the leaves ceaselessly. Because I have no covering, my entire body is frozen. Apart from that, my neighbors on both sides snore atrociously, so I do not close an eye until morning.

31 AUGUST. Early, at 4:00 a.m., we search our hollow out again and remain there, dug in, until 3:00 p.m. Then, advance! We march uninterruptedly until 11:00 p.m. and are surprised by rain on the way for the first time since our departure from Karlstadt. We eventually arrive in Izdebno,[19] where the entire staff spend the night in a barn: I sleep very well.

1 SEPTEMBER. We should, according to orders, have marched off at 9:00 a.m. but are surprised, and almost overrun, by the Russians at 6:00 a.m. Apparently we have been betrayed by the civilian population. Heavy enemy artillery fire: a small panic ensues but does not last for long. Our valiant artillery take up position and open up a murderous fire on the Russians, who appear to retreat, because their artillery fire ceases, and our infantry pursues them. Soon heavy defensive fire is heard.

On the same morning, we receive the news that the Germans have captured seventy thousand men from the Russian 2nd army.[20] The news is received with a loud "hurrah." At 9:30 a.m. I establish my first aid station in an estate (Xanerówka):[21] very soon, masses of our wounded start to stream in. The division commandant rides by: he requests from the chief medical officer of the fifth division, through me, that as many wounded as possible be evacuated. By evening I have evacuated 150 of the mostly seriously wounded to the divisional medical unit, among them Captain Redel. Because the regiment takes up position in front of us around evening, we remain where we are overnight.

2 SEPTEMBER. Departure 5:00 a.m. After marching a short distance, we encounter enemy artillery: heavy fighting on both sides—it's obvious that we are heavily outnumbered and outgunned. We come under cross fire and must retreat, under uninterrupted enemy artillery fire. We retreat, and arrive in Siedliska Wielkic (Suchodoly),[22] where I take charge of a first aid station already established by the eighty-ninth infantry regiment: 110 wounded are already gathered there. When everyone finally streams back, I have to leave the wounded who cannot be evacuated—together with ensigns Krešic and Kušec, one-year medical volunteers Sošic and Mazukrek, and half my medical patrol—behind; I march back to Izdebno with the regiment. In Izdebno, the regiment adopts a defensive position, while I establish a first aid station at the southern end of the town. The medical personnel whom I left behind are all taken prisoner by the Russians; after this, I will not leave medical personnel with the wounded again if something similar recurs.

Today is a terrible one for the regiment. We lose Captains Nemenz, Naic, and Rosam, the first killed the other two wounded and taken prisoner. Captain Schwarz is evacuated with bladder catarrh,[23] a not unwelcome occurrence for him. We doctors only come through unharmed by lucky chance; our danger there was very great. The mood in the regiment is very dejected.

3 SEPTEMBER. We are hot on the enemy's heels: firing opens up on both sides at 6:00 a.m. Our regiment is ordered to hold this position at all costs. Our troops have already been decimated; battalions have been formed out of regiments, and companies out of battalions: this depresses us even more. Nevertheless, we hold our position for the day.

4 SEPTEMBER. Situation very unfavorable. The enemy arrives from Lublin by train, which we can hear whistling and bringing ever more enemy forces to the front. By contrast, we have been fighting uninterruptedly for a whole day, without reinforcements. The enemy is advancing on both flanks; this could be very dangerous, because our troops are combined together in one place.

Torrential rain since early morning. At noon, our position gets even worse: heavy artillery fire into the town of Izdebno begins—we cannot remain at the first aid station, and retreat. Soon, we are followed by the ninetieth infantry regiment, on our left flank. It seems as if only our regiment has not received the order to retreat. Finally, we retreat through pouring rain via Orchowiec;[24] we see other troops retreating in the same direction, so as not to lose sight of the division. Exhausted and soaked to the skin, we arrive in Czysta Debina[25] at 6:30 p.m., where we are quartered in one room. We are joined by Captain Peuker (a very special hero!), Captain Alexandrovitz, the imam, and First Lieutenant Quartermaster Steiner.

I am awakened at 2:00 a.m., with the news that our regimental commandant, Colonel Klein, is lying wounded in the neighboring barn. The mud is already knee-deep; I can barely manage one hundred paces with a horse, but we finally bring the colonel into a room with a bed in it. His teeth chatter from cold. When I dress his wound properly, I see what amazing luck he has had. The bullet has gone clean through his left groin between the bone and great vessels, without damaging anything. I find out from him that our regiment, lacking orders to retreat, have remained where they are: The entire regiment is surely lost!

5 SEPTEMBER. Rain continues—but weather clears, with only intermittent, transient rain showers. After I have treated Colonel Klein, we march south in the early morning. We are informed that the enemy are pressing strongly toward us and will soon have our position under bombardment. On the way, we meet up with large baggage trains and many different troop sections, all marching in the same direction. On their heels, I find the small remnants of a battalion with Lieutenant Colonel Tuschner. We find out from him for the first time, how terrible the night of 4 September really was. Around 2:00 a.m., the Russians stormed our front line and could not be halted. Everyone ran away, leaving armaments and even rifles behind. Many were killed, and many taken prisoner—the unholiest confusion!

Hardly sixty men remain from the entire regiment; we all continue our retreat, together with an incalculable number of baggage trains, when suddenly the Russians let loose a hail of shrapnel. Everyone scatters, to escape the rain of fire, and no one can be stopped until we finally reach Turobin and rest. Hardly have two hours passed, before the situation again becomes insecure. The baggage train of the entire corps passes through, in order to arrive at the Por River Bridge on time. We want this obstacle behind us as well, and continue our march. Among others, Assistant Physician Dr. Rubeš and many other men disappear from sight—they have apparently taken another direction. We continue our march south: it's already dark when we arrive in Huta Turobinska[26] and come upon three hundred Bosnians. We take them under our command and quarter there for the night. After having received no provisions the last three days, it's not difficult to fall asleep without food here as well.

6 SEPTEMBER. I sleep more soundly than I can remember, until 6:00 a.m.: the best remedy for my exhaustion. Soon our traveling kitchen appears again: after an absence of several days, we greet it with rejoicing. Finally, something hot to drink (tea, black coffee). Revitalized, we march back to Tokary,[27] where the regiment has assembled. Around 2:00 p.m., we take up position at Huta Turobinska, to prevent the enemy from crossing the Por. The regiment, comprising just eight hundred men, appears to be completely demoralized, and I have the feeling that very little can be achieved with these remnants, at least in the near term. All three of our machine guns have fallen into enemy hands.

To my consternation, I find out that Army Brudermann has been completely routed and that Lemberg[28] is now besieged! How terrible!

7 SEPTEMBER. An awful night, which I spend with Dr. Luger in a badly built tent: the cold inside leaves me in a pitiable state, and I leave the tent at 2:30 p.m. to warm myself at the campfire.

The regiment forms up together into two battalions of about eight hundred men, with remnants of the seventh light infantry battalion number four (one officer, 130 men) and brigades on both sides, under command of Lieutenant Colonel Tuschner. A small shift in our holding positions follows. At night we camp where we can again—I look for the nearest barn, where I sleep fitfully, dreaming of retreat and destruction.

It is rumored that a German corps is on the march east of us—the fourth army (under Archduke Joseph Ferdinand) is coming to meet us from Serbia. If only this were true, because they could really help us out of our precarious position!

8 SEPTEMBER. Cannon thunder very early *on the Por!* A German corps has attacked there. We stay in our positions near Dalekoviec[29] all day, ready to march off, when an aerial report around 8:00 p.m. informs us that the Russians are marching to our rear from the south: we march off immediately. Despite it being moon bright, we advance with difficulty, standing and lying about a great deal. At 6:00 a.m. we are still six kilometers from Dalekoviec. A Prussian division suffered a small setback yesterday, and we must come to their aid and support. I am terribly tired after last night—my entire body is frozen, and I am so exhausted that I can hardly stay on my horse.

9 SEPTEMBER. "The Prussians have come, the Prussians are here!" goes from mouth to mouth. Everyone breathes more easily, because arrival of the Prussians means victory. They are splendid fellows, clean, trim, and neat in their pork pie helmets—so sure of victory and enthusiastic in their conduct that one unconsciously feels safe in their presence. Unfortunately, their numbers here are small for the moment—only two divisions—until they finish the French off; then several corps will follow these. The Russians can only be conquered by large masses of men who are fresh and properly rested.

It's already 2:00 p.m. and we still lie in reserve positions. We have slept well and been strengthened by our traveling kitchen, when we get the news that the Prussians have beaten the Russians back. We advance to Tokary, where we make open camp.

Suddenly . . . at 9:00 a.m. alarm and order to march back: we follow the orders and halt at 2:30 a.m. in front of Branewka,[30] where I fall fast asleep in a food supply wagon, until 6:00 a.m.

10 SEPTEMBER. We march off and arrive in Frampol,[31] Celinka estate at noon. Open camp. We are not appraised of the general situation, and know nothing for sure: not even whether we are retreating on purpose or because we are being forced to do so. We hear that a great battle near Lemberg is in preparation.

At 4:00 p.m. Alarm! We march on to Bilgoraj.[32] The enemy is approaching in great strength—we march until 9:00 p.m. without seeing the enemy, and take up camp—I am again in a food supply wagon: but this time I sleep miserably. Alarm at 2:30 a.m. proves, thank God, to be false, and from then on I sleep well until 6:00 a.m.

11 SEPTEMBER. A terrible day! Our corps retreats, and our regiment consists only of the small second battalion, some *Landsturm*[33] men and the third cavalry division with its artillery: all under the command of Major General Packeny. We must serve as rearguard to cover the retreat. A thankless and dangerous task, considering the few tired, beaten troops. I notice that our Lieutenant Colonel Tuschner is really upset, but resigned to this. We find out that the Russians are advancing on Bilgoraj from three sides. For this reason, we leave Bilgoraj as soon as it is dark, and spend the night in Sol.[34] The regimental staff are quartered in the local estate with the troop commandant Major General Packeny and his staff. We are welcomed by the owner with great hospitality and dine splendidly. We are not used to the wonderful dinner, served so beautifully. But we still sleep on straw, because of lack of sufficient bedding for everyone. My mood remains miserable. I have found out how bad the situation in Lemberg is—the city has already fallen and been devastated by the Russians.[35] There is great confusion in the city, and I have no news of my loved ones!! Additionally, the situation here is awful! The Russians on our heels, our physical and moral strength so low!

12 SEPTEMBER. We march off early at 3:00 a.m., direction Tarnogrod. The Russians have dug themselves in at Bilgoraj for the night and must have wondered in the early morning hours, when they could find no trace of us. We presume that there will also be enemy forces in Tarnogrod. Because our hole is becoming ever smaller, and escape seems impossible, we are understandably very dejected. We already see ourselves as literally wiped out, or at the very least in enemy hands.

We have hardly been marching for an hour when we get the news that Tarnogrod has been occupied by the enemy in force and that, by royal decree, we are ordered to march in a westerly direction through Harasiuki,[36] a few kilometers from the border. We breathe a lot easier and march off cheerfully, arriving at 3:00 p.m. We take up camp in the village, protected from attack. The staff sleeps comfortably in a barn. We are reinvigorated by a good night's sleep.

13 SEPTEMBER. We decamp at 6:00 a.m. for Rudniki[37] behind the San River, where we finally meet up again with our second infantry division. The march is not forced, and disturbed only by rain that started yesterday and continues in torrents all day today. At 11:00 a.m. we cross the San near Rzeszow,[38] on a splendid bridge constructed by our pioneers, and set foot again on Austrian soil. An indescribably joyful feeling. All six staff members take up quarters in a small barn, where, packed together like herrings, we still sleep well, and our mood is good.

14 SEPTEMBER. We get up at early at 6:00 a.m.! Great opportunity for thorough washing and cleaning after such a long, long time: it's absolutely necessary by now; we feel fresh again, and revitalized for new undertakings.

Fighting on the San continues, and the thunder of cannons is heard. The civil population, mostly poor Jews and farmers, are terrified, pack their belongings, wring their hands at each thunder of the cannons, and run through the streets like madmen, bundles on their backs, not knowing where to go. Many flee the town on scheduled trains, others on wagons. All stores are shut—there is nothing left to sell. The soldiers are besieged with a tremendous number of enquiries and can hardly fend the people off. No wonder! Everything is confused, and troops are continually marching through.

We are the division's reserve and have a preliminary rest day. At 1:30 p.m.: we are having lunch—test alarm. Nothing significant; we are back in our quarters less than an hour later. But a downpour starts, and in a very short time we are soaked through.

15 SEPTEMBER. Our entire army (first army, Captain Dankl) starts the retreat and leaves the San open to the enemy. There have to be good reasons for this decision, which cannot be criticized by laymen. The splendid bridge over which we have crossed so many times is blown up; likewise the railway station and the provisions store near it, with its huge stockpile, are burned to the ground.

Retreat begins at 9:00 a.m., and we arrive at 3:00 p.m. in Lowisko,[39] where the entire division digs in, with a Prussian division on our flank. So I am condemned to spend yet another night under canvas.

The sight of the Jewish exodus from Rudniki is very moving. Very few are able to obtain some sort of conveyance, and there is no space for so many people. They lie in heaps one on top of the other. Most are old people, women, and children, who make the journey back—loaded with bundles—on foot. A picture of greatest misery!

16 SEPTEMBER. The retreat continues, from 7:00 a.m. to 3:00 p.m., overnight in the village of Staniszewskie.[40] Staff overnights in a barn: it is a good thing to not have to sleep outside, because nights are already quite cold.

17 SEPTEMBER. Occupation of farms north of Staniszewskie and Zielonka:[41] according to reports, the enemy is moving in that direction. The regiment digs in; my personnel and I return to the first house in Zielonka, where I establish the first aid station. No sign of the enemy—it rains pitilessly during the night: the regiment must have suffered a great deal out in the open.

18 SEPTEMBER. All troops continue their retreat. Our battalion leaves at 7:30 a.m.; I ride past, and join the ranks of my own battalion. Pouring rain

Figure 1.2. Morning prayer in the field of Jewish refugees expelled from their homes. The caption states "Lublin," but this was seen everywhere expulsions occurred. Photograph courtesy of the Leo Baeck Institute.

and strong winds, which continue until noon, followed by clearing. Arrive in Kupno[42] at 3:30 p.m.: open camp, officers in barns.

19 SEPTEMBER. Retreat continues starting at 6:00 a.m. The enemy dogs our heels, but always stays about three kilometers behind us, without attacking. They don't appear to be strong. We reach Zdziary[43] at 2:00 p.m. Weather good: clouding over toward evening, followed by rain.

20 SEPTEMBER. A very tiring day, continuous rain! We march off at 4:00 a.m., while it is still completely dark. We travel through Debica to Podgrodzie,[44] where we only arrive at 4:30 p.m., even though the distance is not even twenty-four kilometers. Bottomless roads are horribly softened by the rain, and baggage trains in front of us often get stuck in the mud: these stoppages, which often last for hours, happen frequently. We arrive soaked to the skin and, with great difficulty, obtain room for Lieutenant Colonels Tuschner and Krinninger, and myself, adjoining the farm family. As a sign of thanks for their shelter and protection, we give the farmers an unnecessary sum of twenty crowns.

21 SEPTEMBER. A day of rest, partially spent in refitting, which has become very urgent. So again, after a long pause, thorough washing of our bodies. The weather is favorable: the troops are happy. I travel to Debica in the afternoon to make some purchases. All stores are closed, both because it is Rosh Hashanah and because they have nothing more to sell. The town makes a sad impression.

22 SEPTEMBER. Rest day! Major Šešić arrives and joins our regiment with the remnants of his battalion's seven hundred men and a few reserve officers. Thick fog early, rain by afternoon, which carries on uninterruptedly until evening, making roads completely impassable: just terrible!

23 SEPTEMBER. At 9:00 a.m. the regiment takes up a position of readiness north of Podgrodzie. A sharp, cold wind continues to blow. It is 1:00 p.m., and hardly has it died down when it starts to rain again, but rain is moderate and does not last long. Toward evening, one of the battalions establishes forward posts; the remainder encamps in Podgrodzie.

24 SEPTEMBER. Break camp at 3:00 a.m. in the pitch dark: March over the bridge to Pilzno.[45] Occupation of the Pilzno heights, while the staff quarters in the town. I have a very nice room and sleep well for the first time in three nights. I don't have to suffer my neighbors' snores, and the plague of fleas is also less. Weather quite good. The bridge is blown and set on fire toward afternoon. It is still burning brightly by evening: a terrible but beautiful sight. Pilzno is a nicer town than Debica.

25 SEPTEMBER. The retreat continues, from Pilzno to Poskle.[46] March begins at 7:45 a.m, arrival at 12:30 p.m. Pickets are placed again, and the entire staff is quartered in *one* room. The nights are too cold to use the barns anymore.

In the afternoon, we meet up with the reinstated Serbian battalion, Major Kötschet, Captains Kobelnigg, Diappa, and Roschitz. I am very happy to see them here, especially Captain Kobelnigg, who brings me greetings from my wife. Weather very nice in the morning, very cool toward evening.

26 SEPTEMBER. Departure 7:00 a.m. for Tarnow.[47] We take up positions immediately in front of the town, in Rzedzin,[48] as division reserves. The regiment remains inactive all day. Out of sheer boredom, I go into the town to make purchases. Unfortunately, things are mostly sold out, but I manage to buy a small sleeveless fur coat. The town is large, very nice in parts, and expanded in modern fashion, with several good coffeehouses. Huge movement, pushing and shoving in the streets: the population appears to be very restless, depressed, and worried about the loss of the whole of Galicia.[49] The afternoon goes by very quickly—I return to the regiment around 6:00 p.m.; it has already taken up quarters in Rzedzin. I am given a nice room that I share with Captain Penker, with only one bed, but no furniture. I sleep well, but only until 2:00 a.m. Weather overcast, quite cold, but no rain.

27 SEPTEMBER. Rest day. Lieutenant Colonel Tuschner joins me instead of Captain Penker: we get the best room in the village. I spend the whole day in Tarnow again. My yearning for people is so great that I cannot bear to be in a village, when a "large city" is so near—weather nice, afternoon overcast.

28 SEPTEMBER. Rest day. Obligatory visit to Tarnow in the morning. In the afternoon, medals for bravery are handed out for the regiment. Fancy ceremony. Otherwise very boring—rain.

29 SEPTEMBER. Like yesterday. Strong wind in the morning, rain in the afternoon, which does not prevent my trip into town.

30 SEPTEMBER. Intermittent rain and hail almost the entire day. I go into the town at 11:00 a.m. and remain in the temple (Yom Kippur) until 1:30 p.m. After that some errands to run, and at I return to camp at 4:00 p.m. Walking to and from the town, and walking through it, have made me very tired.

1 OCTOBER. We are still in Rzedzin near Tarnow. Weather overcast, windy, periods of sunshine. I visit the town morning and afternoon: the change does me good.

2 OCTOBER. Weather miserable: impossible to go into town—no reading material, so I am very bored. Cholera[50] makes its appearance. The forty-third *Landwehr* infantry division, which has just joined our own corps, has had to be isolated because of several cases of cholera.

3 OCTOBER. The offensive is taken up again! Departure 7:00 a.m., advance to Czarna,[51] where we arrive at 3:00 p.m. Camp and forward posts, staff in a farmhouse; sleeping quarters on straw. Dinner at 6:00 p.m. Weather unstable: cold, wind, periods of rain and hail. Toward evening, arrival of our newly appointed Regimental Commandant Colonel Basrig. We are not bothered much by the enemy today; there are a few Cossack artillery positions in front of Czarna, but they do us no harm.

4 OCTOBER. Continued advance from Czarna to Poreby Kedzielski near Ruda.[52] Departure 8:00 a.m., arrival 6:00 p.m. Marching with the column's baggage trains is terribly boring, because no progress can be made on the bad roads. Only a very small distance is covered during an entire day. Unpleasant weather: strong, cold winds, periods of rain. Miserable.

In the station we meet up with Colonel Klein, who has recovered and rejoined his regiment, not knowing that his position is already occupied. He awaits a decision from command.

5 OCTOBER. Today we cross the Vistula River. The second battalion (Major Kötschet) has been tasked to cross it at 5:00 a.m. and clean up any opposition on the other side: they succeed in doing so with very little resistance and no losses. We are ready to march at 5:00 a.m. but only depart at 10:00 a.m., through Wylow to Zaborze[53]—hardly two kilometers; we stop again, have dinner around 5:00 p.m., and cross over pontoon bridges near Goleszow,[54] constructed in less than two hours: a technical masterpiece massive, beautiful, and imposing. Great difficulty in getting the wagons with war material across the bottomless road leads to long delays. Apart from that, the enemy must first be driven away from Rzochow.[55] The regiment makes camp in the open. My room is very cold, so I sleep badly.

6 OCTOBER. March continues through ¤ 236,[56] Przylek to Trzesowka.[57] An exhausting day: starting at noon, it rains uninterruptedly almost all day. The roads are horribly softened and impassable. Baggage trains remain stuck—we march all day and arrive in in Cmolas,[58] in pouring rain and soaked to the skin, at 8:30 p.m. We are quartered in a priest's house. The Russians departed just before our arrival, taking the priest with them. Captain von Glossner, who has been ordered to search the town for Russians before we arrive, is standing in the entrance to the village on our arrival: he tells us that he has not been able to go out because of night fog, so the staff themselves do the inspection. The priest's house is roomy but devastated by the Russians: divans have been ripped open, horsehair and covers removed. But we can still use them to sleep on. No provisions today: but at least we can heat the room and dry out as best we can.

7 OCTOBER. Naturally a rest day! Our baggage trains and especially artillery are stuck in the mud on the way here. Our traveling kitchen arrives during the night, and we get yesterday's lunch at 8:00 a.m. today: schnitzel with potato salad! Not a very suitable menu for this early hour! Weather favorable, only a short-lived rain shower in the afternoon. But our room is comfortably heated, and we all feel very good. The missing Adjutant Dr. Rubeš arrives back to the regiment, after investigation!

8 OCTOBER. The march continues at 5:30 a.m., arrival in Koziolek[59] at noon. Weather fine at first, then a cold wind blows with a brief snowfall. The march wouldn't have been so bad had I not torn a muscle in my right thigh while sitting up. So I can neither march nor ride, and the pain is bad. Quarters are miserable: a small farm room for ten men! Because the cold can already be clearly felt, the overheated farm room is doubly comfortable.

9 OCTOBER. The most important occurrence of the day is that, unfortunately, Colonel Klein retains regimental command. Otherwise, the march is continued in a northerly direction. Departure 6:00 a.m., arrival in Maziarnia[60] at 2:00 p.m. Five of us are quartered in one farm room. Weather very unpleasant, biting wind, cold, and wet: I have already put my fur waistcoat on. My muscle pains have diminished somewhat, but nevertheless I walk most of the way, to spare my horse who has an open saddle wound again. I was properly taken in with this miserable nag by Lieutenant Colonel Tuschner—he exchanged it with me for my iron-gray horse and promised to pay me the 350 crowns difference. I have not received the money, and the horse is an old, worn out sidekick that can absolutely not wake up properly, even with the greatest care and regular fodder. Heavy fighting in our vicinity; we will be involved shortly.

10 OCTOBER. We remain in our positions for the time being. Weather very unpleasant: overcast with a damp cold. Quarters miserable and dirty—at night we are plagued by fleas, bugs, and mice—no sleep.

11 OCTOBER. Unfortunately, another rest day in this miserable hole. To make things even more unpleasant, it starts raining very early—clearing for a while during the afternoon—then uninterrupted rain the rest of the day. For dinner, fish prepared by a Jew.

12 OCTOBER. We are still here. The pioneers march in front of us to improve the roads, which have become impassable because of the recent rain—which lasts all day today as well. Boredom is terrible—no sleep at night, and my appetite has greatly diminished.

13 OCTOBER. Why we are still here passes understanding. Rain continues all morning—clearing later, but the mud is very deep. I change my quarters and can sleep better. I have also succeeded in cadging an old newspaper from someone, so the time passes.

14 OCTOBER. We are still here in the morning—horrible! Luckily no more rain—the sun—which we haven't see for almost three weeks—even breaks through in the afternoon, which becomes beautiful, lifting all our spirits. Everyone is up and about, working outside without fear of the heavy cannon fire in the north, which has continued for the past three days.

15 OCTOBER. The division remains here today as well. Today has, quite unexpectedly, become very significant for me, and changed my position at one stroke—I become the division chief medical officer in place of the sick and evacuated Dr. Stach. I depart to take up my position this very afternoon. My heart beats with joy, but I cannot say anything out loud because of the many envious people! The officers—especially the colonel himself—are very sorry that I have to leave them: it seems the colonel really means it. After one hour of travel by wagon, I arrive at command in Stany.⁶¹ Commandant Lipošćak is waiting and is the first to greet me. He and the entire command greet me. Dr. Stach has already left, so I must make myself acquainted with the new and different duties on my own.

The first dinner here tastes wonderful—a peacetime meal in the truest sense of the word, so different from the traveling kitchen food, which I can't stomach anymore (everything tastes the *same*, always mixed with sand). Unfortunately, the castle has been completely burned down, so we must make do with mass quarters. I use the proximity of the post office to tell my so anxious wife the latest news.

16 OCTOBER. Relief of the thirty-seventh *Landwehr* infantry division from their position on the San. Departure with the staff at 8:00 a.m., then to tenth corps command, where I report personally to Corps Chief Medical Officer Oberstabsarzt 1 Klasse Zapatowicz. After completion of the service agenda and consumption of a splendid second breakfast, we ride to Grebow,⁶² where during two hours of rest, orders are handed out: then we ride further to Zaleszany,⁶³ where we arrive when it is dark, at 5:30 p.m. The ride is very tiring: on a bad road with a lot of trotting, which doesn't suit my poor nag at all—it lags behind the whole way. Our baggage train for the traveling kitchen remains stuck in the mud and only arrives at 2:00 a.m., with my personnel. So we remain without hot food all day, and I spend the night on my old, tattered divan in the local school, half-sitting, half-lying and fully dressed. The first day at command is very shabby. Luckily, the weather is beautiful: lovely springlike weather.

17 OCTOBER. We are very near the enemy, who are on the other side of the San. Firing continues day and night—mainly artillery—very unpleasant—apparently both sides intend to keep themselves busy here, to postpone transfer to the front—for the moment, the San is not forced by either side. During dinner, news comes of the decoration of our commandant, General of the Infantry Lipošćak, with the Crown Order Second Class: we immediately break out the champagne and remain together until 11:00 p.m.

18 OCTOBER. Situation unchanged. Sunday atmosphere, interrupted at times by artillery fire on the San, to which no one reacts anymore. Weather nice and warm, splendid lunch; immediately before that I am surprised by the visit of my old friend Surgeon Major Dr. Berger, who as chief medical officer of 110th *Landsturm* brigade (commandant Major General Matašić, also an old regimental comrade from the seventy-ninth infantry regiment), is now under my command. We are very happy to see each other and chat for a few hours each day.

19 OCTOBER. Weather nice and warm, a real summer's day. The front is quiet, cannon firing here and there. At 11:45 p.m. sudden heavy rifle fire on the San—alarm! My batman—a cowardly Bosnian—is hysterical with terror: he thinks that the Russians have already arrived and that we have all been taken captive. The sound of fighting can be heard in our immediate vicinity. Quiet returns after two hours, but doesn't last long—at 3:00 a.m., heavy rifle fire starts up—alarm again—quiet only returns around 4:15 a.m. Apparently this is a Russian demonstration designed to hold us fast at the San. But such night alarms are always very painful—we lack an overview of the general situation and believe that, at every step, Russians will appear.

20 OCTOBER. We remain in our positions, and the day passes quietly. Planes can be seen almost daily. Weather generally good, somewhat overcast, but no rain. The night also passes quietly, but it rains heavily.

21 OCTOBER. Mud after the overnight rain is quite bad. Weather overcast but warm. My two room companions, Lieutenant Colonel Berger and his adjutant First Lieutenant Steinbock from my pioneer battalion, are departing today, leaving me alone in my room. I sleep very well on one divan. Splendid meals with the staff. Afternoon rain, mud makes the roads impassable.

22 OCTOBER. Endless mud—otherwise nothing new. At Nisko,[64] an entire Russian division has succeeded in crossing the San—hard-fought battle with the twenty-fourth infantry division, lasting two whole days. It seems that the ninth cavalry division are to blame for this, because they failed to prevent it. The sentries on the San were apparently asleep and killed by Russians, allowing the enemy to cross the river.

23 OCTOBER. The battle at Nisko continues, without any progress. So we are still stuck here. The weather is good, but mud does not dry properly. I pass the time reading. My friend Berger has given me a Polish book (*Zlisdrenie* by Schnitzler, in German *Berta Garlan*)—a very good book, in Schnitzler's style—only the Vienna dialect doesn't do well in Polish.

At dinnertime a magician appears. We laugh a great deal, while, at the same time, cannon thunder on the San becomes worse. It is raining and the mud is horrible. Steam rises at Nisko, and no progress is made. We are relieved by the sixth cavalry division and arrive in Gorzyce. The commandant's staff arrive just in time for lunch. The Russians see this movement and instantly greet us with heavy shrapnel fire. Shrapnel falls on both sides of our mess, and we are lucky that nothing falls inside.

Departure at 2:30 p.m., and after an hour's ride we arrive in Gorlice.[65] We are quartered with a farmer, three of us at a time. A noticeably clean room; the farmers of this village are especially clean compared to others—I even sleep in a real bed, very clean, no vermin. Cholera vaccine arrives immediately before we march off: I must take it with me.

25 OCTOBER. Advance through Sandomierz to Sobotka.[66] At Sandomierz we cross the Weichsel,[67] reaching Russian territory at 9:30 a.m. Traffic is mediated by an ad hoc constructed bridge and a second military bridge for the constant traffic. The town itself is very interesting: it is located on a height, and visible from miles around. We arrive at the estate in Sobotka at 4:00 p.m. The rooms are nice and clean, but we sleep on straw. Weather very good—the ground is starting to dry.

26 OCTOBER. Advance via Ozarow to Tarlow.[68] Departure 7:30 a.m., arrival 1:30 p.m. We have to trot a great deal, and my horse absolutely refuses to do so—it lags behind, and I have great difficulty coaxing it forward. Lieutenant Colonel Tuschner has taken me in completely and hasn't even paid me the three hundred crowns difference. From tomorrow, I will ride my predecessor Dr. Stach's horse.

The situation today has deteriorated greatly. The enemy is attempting to cross the Weichsel at Jozefow.[69] Part of our division is already fighting—tomorrow the entire division will attack. But this does not prevent us from enjoying an excellent lunch and even more so the new wine, which is meant only for sipping. However, some men notice its good taste quite late after their first sip and conduct themselves comically. I have never seen Private First Class Grinchowski so jolly before. The weather is good, and the ground is drying out more and more. Command is quartered in the rectory; I am quartered in the Landsturm brigade medical unit, which has already been established here, and sleep very well on a real bed.

27 OCTOBER. We stay in our position during the morning. The news about the enemy gets worse and worse; eventually we depart at 3:00 p.m. and arrive at 4:30 p.m. via Zemborzyn to Sluszczyn.[70] While on the march, we meet up with a wounded transport of about three hundred men. In Sluszczyn I find a Landwehr brigade medical unit in fullest activity. Commandant Surgeon Major Dr. Beigel, Second Physician Dr. Meisels, who was command physician in Lemberg. The third man is a dentist, and an idiot. The situation is so bad, and the work remaining to be done so great, that I do not hesitate, roll up my sleeves, and get to work myself. By 10:00 p.m. we have evacuated one hundred more wounded, among them many Bosnians who, as my prior patients, do me no honor, because many have left hand wounds probably caused by self-mutilation. The medical unit soon goes back, and I overnight in the surgeon major's quarters on straw, fully clothed. I find all three of our ordinance officers here. They are resigned to being here, because command has neither food nor quarters. The Russians have attacked our division again, and we must retreat because of their superior forces.

28 OCTOBER. We start our retreat early at 4:00 a.m., in the pitch dark. We travel on foot through Alexandrow, to Sienna-Olechow,[71] where we arrive at 2:00 p.m., the enemy at our heels. The weather has cleared up and is pleasant. We eat at 4:00 p.m., no quarters—we all, including our commandant, sleep on straw in a barn, fully dressed. It's awfully cold, and I have nothing with which to cover myself except a light plaid blanket. We break camp at 1:00 a.m. and depart at 2:00 a.m., again in a southerly direction, because the Russians are pressing in on us. The route takes us through Cmielow to Przeuszyn,[72] where we arrive at 2:00 p.m., in other words after a twelve-hour march. A miserable dump, but there is a beautiful castle nearby, where we quarter in a beautiful, warm room with impeccable, old-fashioned, tasteful furniture. This does us a world of good after three such exhausting days, during which we could not undress or wash.

30 OCTOBER. After an excellent night's sleep, we must, unfortunately, leave this beautiful place, and the retreat begins at 7:00 a.m. We go through Tudorow to Grocholice,[73] where we quarter as best we can in an estate, I in an adjacent building with Captain Krämer. The caretaker is a miserable fellow, Russia-friendly, interested only about his own household, complaining every time soldiers approach. Our situation is quite critical. Fifth corps has been attacked in Ostrowiec and forced back to Opatow.[74] All our bridges over the Weichsel have been demolished, and the enemy is very near, with strong enemy columns on the march southwest from us. We are ordered to hold our positions at all costs.

About six kilometers from Opatow, we come upon a splendid sugar factory, built with German capital. This entire region looks rich and very fertile, so different from the wilderness in the Tanew region. Since yesterday, the weather has suddenly become very cold, with a strong cold wind—fall has arrived.

31 OCTOBER. We remain here. Weather like yesterday. The sky is miserably gray—real snow weather. At 10:30 a.m., alarm to be ready to march. The enemy has attacked our left flank in division strength, in an effort to push it back. Unfortunately, we have lost communication with fifth corps, but this is soon repaired. It's 3:00 p.m., and the fighting on the front continues. We remain ready to march at precisely the time the traveling kitchen arrives. It's completely dark at 5:30 p.m., and fighting stops. We get our first meal at 7:30 p.m.

Today the Bosnians flee at the first sign of shrapnel fire, and can be stopped only with difficulty. We are very disappointed, and Commander Lipošćak feels constrained to condemn six of the men to death: they are shot the next day at the front. Toward evening, he himself finds a Bosnian, who has fled here from the front, hiding in one of the houses. He commands that the man be shot on the spot. Hopefully, this dreadful example will help, because this business will remain as a permanent blot on our regimental escutcheon. After a miserable night, with hardly two hours of sleep, alarm at 6:00 a.m.! Fighting has started again, and the Bosnians are again retreating to Grocholice, despite the fact that our secure position does not give them any reason to do so. Our commandant is very upset about this: new forces are brought in, and during the course of the day the situation improves, although we had sufficient men without them during the critical time. The beautiful sugar factory has been bombarded and set ablaze by the Russians, and burns brightly. Weather is still cold and overcast, hardly 1°C. There is enough to do at the division medical unit, but it cannot be compared to the onerous duty of the doctor one the front line, who must remain in this awful cold day and night, out in the open.

At 3:30 p.m., shrapnel and shells start falling about three hundred paces from our estate: a truly awful day. Men are completely exhausted—the night watch is not reliable anymore, so an attack on us is quite possible. For security, we ride in the evening to Przepiorow,[75] where we overnight in an estate. Rooms are very cold and cannot be warmed up, so I sleep miserably, fully clothed, on a threadbare decoration divan.

2 NOVEMBER. It's lucky that we left because, at 3:00 a.m., the Russians attack the fortieth, who have to retreat to Grocholice under heavy fire. The division medical unit in Swojkow[76] is also heavily bombarded and has to evacuate in haste, leaving a great deal of material behind. They are ordered to set up again in Kujawi.[77] At 8:00 a.m., the fortieth are back in their positions, and the sugar factory and the castle (Wdostow) are again in our hands by evening. But for how long? Fighting ebbs and flows all day, and a shortage of artillery shells leads to an order for us to retreat. Divisional staff go back to Szczeglice.[78] The general mood is depressed: Russians are threatening us and appear to want to drive us into the Weichsel. Temperature 1°C.

3 NOVEMBER. Retreat is definitely decided—today we must travel to Staszow.[79] The staff leave at 5:00 a.m. Yesterday was one of the most terrible days in the entire war so far. We have lost two batteries and a number of officers, and the men are decimated, leaving only small fractions of regiments available. In sharp contrast to our mood, the sun is just beautiful: 10°C, a real summerlike day. We remain in Sielec[80] south of Staszow. The Russians do not press us—a sign of how heavily they have suffered as well—just now, 1,500 Russian prisoners have passed by us.

My sneezing is in full bloom. Colonel Klein takes dinner with us this evening—he is very timid, and therefore I led the discussion (we know why!).

4 NOVEMBER. Retreat continues. We depart at 7:00 a.m., after I have an excellent night's sleep. I go with the staff to Stopnica,[81] where we arrive at 11:00 a.m. An unsympathetic place: the Jewish quarter is in the courthouse area, dilapidated and unpleasant looking. The weather is good, but not as nice as yesterday. I have a terrible cold. Cannon thunder toward afternoon, originating from first or fifth corps.

5 NOVEMBER. We continue in a southwesterly direction. Departure at 7:00 a.m. Line of march: Zborow, Zukow, Piasek, Strozyska, Szczytniki, military bridge at Ostrow to Sokolina.[82] Arrival at 4:00 p.m. The march is very strenuous, about thirty-four kilometers, but weather is not bad. We are quartered in groups of six at the schoolteacher's house. I sleep on a divan. Dinner at 9:00 p.m.

6 NOVEMBER. We are ordered to fortify our positions and stand fast in Sokolina. The Germans have been pressed in on their left flank, and there is a

Figure 1.3. "Types." Poor Jewish inhabitants in an Eastern European town. Photograph courtesy of the Leo Baeck Institute.

danger that our entire division could be encircled. For that reason, new orders come in at the last moment to continue our retreat.

Departure for Kamienczyce[83] at 9:00 a.m. Overcast and rainy: typical November weather. My cold is somewhat better, but I have chest catarrh. Our general situation is really unfavorable. Our troops have been complemented by the first battalion. The young lads are still rosy cheeked, well dressed, and full of hope—reserve officers no less than men. They do not yet guess the breadth of the sorrow and misery of this war.

Arrival at 4:00 p.m. Good quarters in the estate of an Austrian army supplier. Food to be served soon, by women—Lieutenant Count Goluchowski is evacuated home because of illness, and I give him greetings to my Olga.

7 NOVEMBER. The retreat continues. Departure 7:00 a.m., arrival in Slomniki[84] at 3:00 p.m. The enemy can better be seen from here—a great deal of cannon fire from the north—obviously rearguard actions with other corps. I am quartered with Captain Krämer. Despite this being the house of an ordinary village Jew, the room and bed (nickel and wire mattress) are immaculately clean—but I do not sleep particularly well.

8 NOVEMBER. We leave at 6:00 a.m. for Saspow near Skala,[85] where we arrive at 4:30 p.m. A hard day—the roads are bad with many gullies, hills, and rocks (similar to the Hinterbrühl).[86] Roads are jammed up with baggage trains, and the weather is lousy: damp cold, with intermittent rain. The village is a wretched little place—quarters in a stinking farmer's room, with a clay floor on straw. I share quarters with Senior Logistics Officer Rosenberg, a very unsympathetic roommate. Our baggage train only arrives at 3.00 a.m., so no hot food today.

9 NOVEMBER. Depart at 8:00 a.m., arrive in Gorenice,[87] one and a half kilometers from the border, at 11:00 a.m. Weather unpleasant, like yesterday—but finally we are well quartered in an estate, with a bed, food at 5:00 p.m., and I sleep very well.

10 NOVEMBER. The division remains where it is. The troops fortify their positions, and we have a chance to relax—correspondence, laundry, washing ourselves, etc. A day like this does us all good.

11 NOVEMBER. We remain in our current position. No sign of the enemy—I use the free time to inoculate the staff against cholera. I inoculate Assistant Physician Dr. Scheuer of the division medical unit (a very lively person) and our housekeeper, who is a teacher. Unfortunately, weather is overcast and foggy; otherwise, our stay here is very pleasant. The rooms are cozy and warm. Mass quarters.

12 NOVEMBER. Situation the same. The enemy has moved in a northeasterly direction, causing great relief to our troops. A day of rest—relaxation is noticeable in command as well. A very heavy storm with wind and rain begins during the night, which breaks one of our windowpanes and causes consternation among my roommates until it is repaired. The inoculation reaction, which was quite severe last evening among almost all the men, has gone down significantly.[88] As a worthy conclusion to today, a lively card game (*frische Vier*) is organized: I participate only as kibitzer.

13 NOVEMBER. Rest day! A great deal of mail after a long, long time without it—I too am richly endowed with mail: six cards and one letter from my valiant Olga; I have had to wait long enough for them. I start my reply immediately and start numbering my letters. The first one becomes a letter six pages long. Today is the first snowfall, but only moderate, because the cold is not yet severe, and the snow melts almost immediately.

14 NOVEMBER. We remain here—I am not too unhappy about this, because our stay is very pleasant. In the morning a visit from our corps commander Feldzeugmeister Meixner—he refuses a preprepared excellent breakfast—all the more for us!

One case of cholera each is reported from our battalion and the eighty-ninth infantry regiment—that is less pleasant; hopefully these cases will remain isolated.

15 NOVEMBER. Cholera cases accumulate—also, many men from command have colds, so there is much to do and I am busy all day, but still have time to write a long letter to my Olga Suddenly, at 11:00 p.m., we receive an order to depart tomorrow, to the north.

16 NOVEMBER. Depart at 9:00 a.m. for Przeginia.[89] Frost overnight, continuing into the next day—water frozen everywhere. The ride is short—a bit more than an hour—but unpleasant because of cold weather which has now really arrived. The chief of our general staff Major Ginsel suddenly becomes ill with a very high fever and is evacuated—and so, men one after the other crumble away. Next in line is our commandant, who has a severe attack of nerves—during today's march he suddenly develops a severe case of sciatica. Quarters in the priest's house, which has very few rooms, so mass quarters on straw—I am quartered in the general staff office.

We receive the joyful news that the Germans have taken twenty-four thousand Russians captive, together with fifty machine guns. Perhaps this will hasten the end of the war, which is otherwise nowhere in sight.

17 NOVEMBER. I have a bad night. No rest in the general staff office—the telephone rings all night—between 1:00 and 2.00 a.m., orders are drafted and distributed. Apart from that, we are eleven in one room. Undressing and washing in the morning are unthinkable (the latter mainly because of unreliability of the water due to cholera in the vicinity). Cannon thunder begins early and continues all day—an intense battle develops. There are more than three hundred wounded, and I am moved when toward 7:00 p.m. Captain Schwartz is brought to me with a stomach wound. Because of lack of space at the division medical unit, I take his case over and place him in my room in the priest's house. His general condition is good; hopefully the intestines are not damaged, or at least not badly affected.[90] After I bandage him, he remains on his stretcher, with instructions for strict rest and no intake of food or drink.

Despite intense fighting, little ground is gained—the Russians resist tenaciously. The weather is very bad: damp cold, some snow, complete winter.

18 NOVEMBER. This next night is no less busy, and the office lamp burns all night—the main reason why I get no sleep. The battle continues just as intensely all day without any ground gained.

Captain Schwarz is doing well, no fever. Weather lousy, like yesterday—a covering of snow can be seen everywhere.

19 NOVEMBER. A calm night, so I get a good night's rest. But at 5:00 a.m., while still dark, fighting starts all over again. Snow falls almost all day, but the cold is not severe. Only toward evening do our troops succeed in partially penetrating the Russian position—great German victories over the Russian third corps are reported, as well as victories of our troops near Cracow, lifting our spirits greatly. Today we still remain here but will probably advance tomorrow.

20 NOVEMBER. Another terrible night! Fighting continues uninterruptedly—repeated attacks by both sides—much activity in the office. Despite this obstinate three-day battle, we have not advanced a single kilometer. Additionally, this freezing weather: the men must remain outside without regular hot food—it's simply awful! Captain Schwarz is doing well, no signs of intestinal damage.

21 NOVEMBER. A decent night. Reasonably quiet until 4:00 a.m., but then it becomes noisy again. Beautiful weather—sunshine and blue skies. We have entered a decisive stage. Captain Schwarz continues to do well, so he can be evacuated gently this afternoon. I take over the corner of the room in which he has been cared for, and now share the room with the priest. The decisive battle does not materialize, but a Russian attack is expected very soon.

22 NOVEMBER. The first night with the priest—not good: better quarters but a bad camp bed. Things are very unsettled because of increased activity in the adjacent telephone room relative to the expected attack, which begins at 3:00 a.m. and takes a murderous course. Lieutenant Colonel Kötschet is killed, Lieutenant Colonel Tuschner is shot in the head, and Captains Wratschil and Deischel are wounded. The battalion has lost almost all of its active officers. The fighting during the day is indecisive, and we still occupy our original position.

23 NOVEMBER. Temperature −8°C, wind and sun. A truly beautiful winter's day. The only thing is that the men are suffering terribly from the cold at

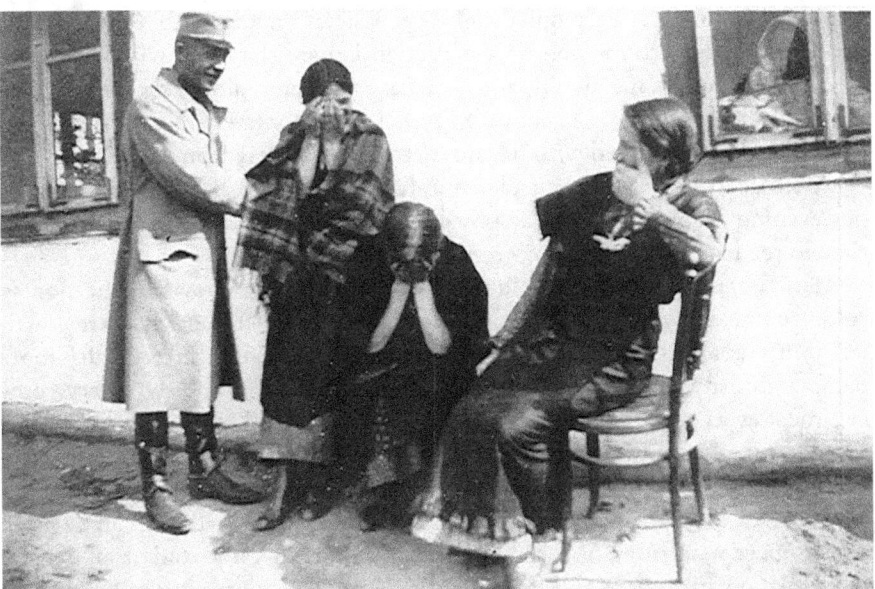

Figure 1.4. The caption reads "teachers: relaxation hour." Prostitutes, possibly being examined for venereal diseases. Photograph courtesy of the Leo Baeck Institute.

night—significant frostbite during the day as well. Today's fighting takes place on our front—men dig in.

I am content at the priest's house—I have the room to myself all day, and even manage to have a primitive, and very urgent, bath. The first "blondes"[91] make their appearance today and surprise me most unpleasantly... considerable confusion.

Frost increases toward evening and the wind howls: a real storm. Sudden alarm at 9:00 p.m.—Russians are said to have broken through the ninth infantry division. This proves to be untrue, and calm returns.

24 NOVEMBER. Temperature −10°C. Great excitement very early. A violent cannonade at 5:30 a.m.: the fourth infantry brigade has taken the important crossing point over which we have fought for days: more than one thousand Russians are taken prisoner. But during the course of further fighting, we lose all the ground we have gained to the enemy again and so remain where we were before. There are enough wounded—since 17 November, 2,580 wounded received in my own unit alone. Among the Bosnians, Colonel Barwig is wounded.

25 NOVEMBER. A quiet night. Both sides are exhausted. The frost has broken; temperature early this morning was only −1°C. Despite the pause in the fighting, we still have plenty of wounded coming in daily. Both lines of fire lie in wait in their shelters near one other. If a lookout even sticks his head out, he is shot at immediately.

26 NOVEMBER. A very quiet night, yet I sleep only until 2:30 a.m. I have been very lucky with my quarters. Although I share the room with the priest, he does not bother me all day, and I can use the room alone; by contrast, the others are eight to ten to a room, and have to lie on straw. Most of them seem to be plentifully supplied with "blondes," but I keep away from them.

27 NOVEMBER. Weather is pleasant, fresh but with a clammy wind. Glorious evening moonlight. The day passes easily with normal activity. I have free time to read and work on my correspondence.

28 NOVEMBER. Night absolutely silent—moderate snowfall but not so cold. An unearthly quiet at the front during the day. Hectic activity in my medical unit has also stopped. For two days I have had only thirty to fifty more patients, mostly sick: isolated cases of suspected cholera and dysentery come in almost every day.

29 NOVEMBER. Like yesterday. Weather good, artillery fire at times. According to prisoner information, the Russians intend to attack our positions tonight. But the anticipated attack does not occur, so no credence can be given to prisoners' assertions. Weather beautiful—sunshine, not cold at all—a few fliers take off from here and land again smoothly: two first lieutenants under leadership of Captain Kaiserfeld, all involved in reconnaissance of enemy artillery positions.

1 DECEMBER. Another beautiful winter's day with sunshine and not so cold. Fliers appear before 9:00 a.m.—I permit myself the luxury of a bath again today.

2 DECEMBER. Situation unchanged—moonlit night, used by Russians for an attack, to try a breakthrough in one sector or another—but they are bloodily repulsed. Violent rifle clatter always sounds unearthly at night, but there are very few wounded, since both sides seem to be shooting in the air. Our men have finally learned to keep proper watch at night, and dig themselves in well. One bad experience is enough: they have learned their lesson.

3 DECEMBER. A lovely day, no less beautiful than a similar day in Trieste. Otherwise nothing new. We are gradually establishing winter quarters: earthen huts that can be heated are built, also blockhouses for officers. The wigwam built by Lieutenant Szwejkowski and the telephone section installation are worth seeing.

4 DECEMBER. Unchanged: warm, but not as nice as yesterday.

5 DECEMBER. Glorious weather, like on 3 December. Otherwise no changes—a very nice Nikolo[92] celebration with many jokes and fun. General amusement at a fake alarm telegraph drafted by General Staff Captain Schejwl (enclosed). A goodly number of fun gifts. For example: for Senior Logistics Officer Rosenberg a motor burning firewood and a fake transfer to staff headquarters, a truss for Captain Pistelka, a condom for the chaste First Lieutenant Spetzler—all accompanied by comical verses—a miniature general's hat for captain Schejwl, etc.

6 DECEMBER. Rain and snow today for a change, unpleasant after so many fine days.

7 DECEMBER. Sunshine and snow melt.

8 DECEMBER. Snow has completely melted. Major Ginzel, who, after his illness on 16 December, has joined us again, is definitely evacuated because of lung catarrh. Commandant Lipoščak goes to Teschen[93] for a few days, for consultation.

9 DECEMBER. Weather glorious. Winter quarters for officers and men of our command almost complete. I am still staying with the priest and am very satisfied there. At least I am spared the plague of vermin, under which most of the men suffer.

10 DECEMBER. No changes on our front—complete calm—beautiful mild weather.

11 DECEMBER. Nothing of importance. Lively shooting at night from the neighboring division, but of no significance. Weather good.

12 DECEMBER. Today is a very good day. I receive photographs of my children, which make me very happy. Photos are beautiful, and they all look very well. I also receive the fur coat sent by my family, which I don't really need at the moment. Weather very nice.

13 december. Weather somewhat overcast, intermittent rain—otherwise nothing new.

14 december. False alarm at 3:00 a.m., based on the false report that one of our battalions has been thrown back from their position. But until clarification is obtained, an entire hour passes. Arrival of our commander around 5:00 p.m.: he is in a very good mood, with a lot to say. We remain together until midnight.

15 december. Very early in the morning, we hear that the Russians have departed. A great surprise, with differing reactions. Those with beautiful winter quarters are very glum—otherwise, there is general rejoicing: So we advance again. First, reconnaissance detachments are sent out—during the afternoon, the men are sent out after them. But command remains here for the moment.

16 december. Departure from Przeginia at 7:00 a.m., weather beautiful. First, though, a moving parting from the priest and his aunt. He kisses me so heartily on both cheeks that I am much moved.

Our horses are so overexcited from so much standing around that they can hardly be held back. And so it goes, without enemy interference, until noon, when we take up quarters in Wysocice.[94] Out of custom, I take quarters with the local priest again: at least there, cleanliness is assured. He directs me to his office: a nice, clean room and a well-upholstered bench that will serve as my bed.

The ride through the battlefields of the past four weeks (Suloszowa and Gotkowice)[95] reveals a picture of destruction horrible to behold. Whole heaps

Figure 1.5. A lone Russian body on the battlefield. By the end of the war, nearly two million Russian soldiers would be killed. Photograph courtesy of the Leo Baeck Institute.

of Russian and Austrian bodies lie around everywhere. Endless amounts of war material. Churches and houses destroyed or damaged either by bombardment or burned down—a picture of misery and wretchedness!

17 DECEMBER. A pleasant night with the priest in Wysocice,—the clean room and good sleeping quarters help. By contrast, orders from the general staff office give me no rest. Hardly have I gone to bed at midnight when three hours later the command comes to give up further pursuit of the Russians and march in the direction of Cracow, where further preparations will follow—where to? And so ends any possibility of sleep. Early at 9:00 a.m. we depart, arriving at the estate of Szerodrokowice,[96] where we find a terrible scene of devastation and destruction by the Russians. Most articles of furniture have been carried away; those that remain have been demolished. After three hours' rest, we continue the march and arrive in Wilczkowice[97] at 4:00 p.m., when it is getting dark. It rains all day; the roads are all softened by mud, and impassable in places—baggage trains and traveling kitchens cannot advance, so all I eat that day are four pieces of bread and butter and two sardines. We sit around—around twenty men in one room around the table in the estate—most of us go to bed around midnight. I share a divan with Colonel Wscislak—other divans are taken by the commandant and Colonel Rosenzweig. Captain Krämer sleeps in an armchair. We spend the night fully clothed.

18 DECEMBER. Departure at 9:00 a.m. and arrival in Cracow at noon. The ride is unpleasant—awful mud because of rain during the morning. The

Figure 1.6. Church with dome hit by artillery shells. Photograph courtesy of the Leo Baeck Institute.

weather today becomes favorable and warm, 2.5°C, with sunshine at times. We quarter in the Hotel Poller—a very good first-class hotel. I don't need to describe how pleasant a stay in a comfortable room is, after such a long time of deprivation. Tour of the city, shopping for small items—I send money and postcards to my Olga and the children. Good food and drink in the hotel. I am overjoyed over a good bed and a good sleep after the miserable night in Wilczkowice.

19 DECEMBER. Cracow! After a glorious night of uninterrupted sleep, I spend the morning—which passes all too quickly—with visits to coffeehouse and steam bath, and shopping for small items. Departure at 3.00 p.m. in the direction of Oderberg[98] (dinner) and Kaschau.

20 DECEMBER. Beautiful day—complete winter landscape. Midday station at Iglo:[99] we know now that we are in the Carpathians.

21 DECEMBER. We travel through Garbócbogdány, Töketerebes, and Nagymihály[100] (breakfast). We have great difficulty leaving, because of the jam of columns in decampment station.

22 DECEMBER. At 9:30 a.m. we arrive in Mezö-Laborcz,[101] where we decamp. Rain and endless mud. The railway station is completely destroyed, the place itself mostly burned down. After orders have been handed out, we march on to Vidrany.[102] I travel there, on invitation, in the car with our commander. This town has also been badly damaged, plundered, burned, the priest's house empty: but still we remain there overnight, I on a divan in our commander's room (on his invitation). However, I sleep badly because of the plague of fleas and miserable bed: also because, in the middle of the night, orders come down to advance to Rymanow.[103] The most awful mud, rain during the night. The commandant, Colonel Rosenzweig, and I refresh ourselves as best we can at the station-catering center. Our commander causes me great embarrassment by unexpectedly asking me directly: do I want a decoration, or an out-of-turn promotion? I must tell him straight! I am totally embarrassed, and look to Colonel Rosenzweig for a hint of advice, which he does not give me. I do not want to keep him waiting, so I declare for the decoration. I do the right thing, because an application for out-of-turn promotion might not go through, and I could come out empty-handed. Even if the promotion were approved, it would be no particular advantage to me, because even without it I have a high rank and have only been in line for a year—Colonel Rosenzweig, when questioned afterward, confirms that I have done the right thing. After the end of this strange interlude, we return to Vydrany.

23 DECEMBER. Departure at 7:30 a.m., in pouring rain and awful mud to Habura (Laborcz-fö).[104] Command takes up mass quarters on straw in the school: I have quarters in an abandoned priest's house, where a lieutenant from the ammunition pool resided before—he leaves me an excellent bed: I sleep from 8:30 p.m. to 4:30 a.m. I have not slept at all for the last two nights.

24 december. It rains all night, with a strong southeast wind. The mud and filth get ever deeper. We ride off at 7:00 a.m. and arrive—spattered with mud from head to toe—in Jasliska,[105] where we have quarters in the local convent. The nuns withdraw into their separate cells, leaving the large rooms for us, and the chapel, for our mess. The rooms are bare as barrack rooms, with just beds in them, like our camp beds. General staff takes one of the rooms as headquarters, and I am given a bed that doesn't look very inviting and gives little confidence in its cleanliness, with jumping and crawling company. We have an evening Christmas tree in our mess: modest, but full of atmosphere. The nuns have worked diligently to help decorate the tree. Dinner without fasting dishes: fish is replaced by roast lung, which, perhaps because it is what it is, does not taste as good. Our mood is very depressed: an attack is coming tomorrow, whose planning does not give us much room for hope. We remain together until midnight, less from enjoyment than to await the corps dispatch, which arrives at 4:00 a.m. Orders are immediately put into effect, and given to the men at 5:00 a.m., and attack ordered for tomorrow, general direction Rymanow.

25 december. With all the goings on, another sleepless night, as is always the case when I have the high honor of obtaining quarters in the general staff's office—despite the fact that the bed is unexpectedly comfortable and clean. But constant light—the telephone, gas cooker—these are all worthy institutions, but incompatible with sleep.

The attack is scheduled to begin at 9:00 a.m.: we stay here for the moment. Thick fog early, temperature 7°C. Advance appears very slow, without any special progress. But our position, relative to the neighboring troops, proves to be so miserable that any victory seems hopeless. In fact, the order comes at night to retreat and regroup (oh, how awful), so we remain here tonight as well—wonderful prospects for a good night's rest! We are under command of seventh corps under Archduke Joseph Ferdinand for a few days.

26 december. No sleep, of course. At 7:30 a.m., we say farewell to the nuns and retreat to Czeremcha,[106] where we arrive in the afternoon. A miserable dump, mostly burned down by the Russians. Many of us are quartered in a wretched, stinking farmhouse in the first reasonably large room, next to the farmer's family. A revolting little hole. Colonel Rosenzweig and I camp on straw on a floor without wooden planks. Men are not too unhappy with their lot, because the young farmer's daughter is pretty and lively—she has two rows of blindingly white, beautiful teeth.

27 december. Exhausted after two sleepless nights, I sleep well from 11:00 p.m. to 5:00 a.m. It rains uninterruptedly, and mud is terrible, so we cannot make a stop anywhere, and stay here for the moment. Snow falls toward evening—only long letters that I receive today from my dear Olga are a sign of life in the midst of all this unpleasantness.

28 DECEMBER. It must have snowed continuously all night, because by early morning snow reaches up to above our ankles. Trees are completely snow-covered—a complete winter landscape—but not terribly cold, so again a mess. Fighting along the entire line, at least on our front. Third and seventh corps, on the left, have to retreat. Heavy shelling toward afternoon, also in our village, so that, at 2:00 p.m., our division is ordered to retreat. We leave Czeremcha at 3:00 p.m., under bombs and shells. Naturally, I am left with wet laundry. Having laundry done seems to conspire against me. Orders are handed out in Habura, and then we ride back to Mező-Laborcz, where we arrive around 10:00 p.m. I am quartered in the civilian pharmacy with the Honvéd hussars. Our commandant is First Lieutenant Count Tisza, an exceptionally quiet and charming man. We camp on a wire mattress on the floor where, despite the many mice, I sleep well until 5:00 a.m.

29 DECEMBER. Weather still miserable and overcast, unbelievable mud, rain during the day. Yesterday's snow has already disappeared, at least in some areas.

30 DECEMBER. I sleep very well and am happy with the hussars, who are very attentive. First Lieutenant Baczi from the Satzberg area takes good care of me. My quarters are significantly improved. Fighting advances very slowly—the division medical unit is, unfortunately, in Boro.[107] It is always a disadvantage not to have a second physician. But, during the course of the day, the twenty-fourth division medical unit does indeed arrive (Commandant Surgeon Major Kolbe) and gives me at least a measure of support. The same horrible weather—what a mess!

31 DECEMBER. A quiet night. The weather has improved a bit—no sign of frost. Today our attack is scheduled to restart, and we are ready to march. Unfortunately, we are losing our Commandant Lipošćak. Because of a difference in opinions between him and the new army commandant, he has had, of course, to draw the shorter straw. I have already written an excellent recommendation for him. Yesterday, he signed off on my decoration application with the Order of Franz Joseph. At:3.00 p.m., we ride together, under snow squalls, to Habura (Laborcz-fö), where I lodge in my previous quarters, this time with the three ordinance officers First Lieutenants Count Trautmannsdorf and Schlesinger, and Baron Jesenski.

A very shabby, miserable New Year's Eve, despite a tombola and other funny events. Because of the tactlessness of our quartermaster, I do not take New Year's Eve dinner with the other officers. Captain Schejwl gives me a small bag of money, as my winnings.

Notes

1. Karlovac (Croatia).
2. Zagreb (Croatia).
3. Košice (Slovak Republic); Chynów, Jarosław (Poland).
4. Przeworsk and Glogowiecz are both in Poland.
5. River in southeast Poland, a tributary of the San.
6. Wola Różaniecka (Poland).
7. Tarnogród (Poland).
8. Mayor (Polish).
9. Stary Bidaczów (Poland).
10. Wola (Poland).
11. Krzemień (Poland).
12. Godziszów (Poland).
13. Branewka (Poland).
14. Turobin (Poland).
15. Zhovkva (Ukraine).
16. Sobieska Wola Pierwsza (Poland).
17. Radomirka (Poland).
18. Austrian *Gabelfrühstück*.
19. Izdebno (Poland).
20. Bardach is referring to the Battle of Tannenberg (26–30 August 1914), which resulted in the almost complete destruction of the Russian 2nd Army and the suicide of its commanding general, Alexander Samsonov.
21. Not found.
22. Siedliska-Wielkic (Suchodoły), Poland.
23. Possibly gonococcal cystitis.
24. Orchowiec (Poland)
25. Czysta Dębina (Poland).
26. Huta Turobińska (Poland).
27. Tokary (Poland).
28. Former capital of Austrian Galicia. Now Lviv (Ukraine)
29. Dalekowice (Poland).
30. Branewka (Poland).
31. Frampol (Poland).
32. Biłgoraj (Poland).
33. Reserve force that consisted of men aged thirty-four to fifty-five years.
34. Sól (Poland).
35. Lemberg fell to the Russians on 3 September.
36. Harasiuki (Poland).
37. Rudniki (Poland).
38. Rzeszów (Poland).
39. Łowisko (Poland).
40. Staniszewskie (Poland).
41. Zielonka (Poland).
42. Kupno (Poland).
43. Ždziary (Poland).

44. Dębica and Podgrodzie (Poland).
45. Pilzno (Poland).
46. Pośkle (Poland).
47. Tarnów (Poland).
48. Rzedzin (Poland).
49. In the early stages of the war, the Austro-Hungarian Army was severely defeated and forced out of Galicia, while the Russians captured Lemberg and, for approximately nine months, ruled Eastern Galicia.
50. Signs of an unsafe water supply/sewage disposal system.
51. Czarna (Poland).
52. Poreby Kędzierski and Ruda (Poland).
53. Wylów, Zaborze (Poland).
54. Goleszów (Poland).
55. Rzochów (Poland).
56. Throughout the text (and succeeding chapters), this symbol means map/grid location or height.
57. Przyłęk, Trzesowka (Poland).
58. Cmolas (Poland).
59. Koziolek (Poland).
60. Maziarnia (Poland).
61. Stany (Poland).
62. Grębów (Poland).
63. Zaleszany (Poland).
64. Nisko (Poland).
65. Gorzyce and Gorlice are both in Poland.
66. Sandomierz, Sobótka (Poland).
67. Vistula River.
68. Ożarów, Tarłów (Poland).
69. Józefów (Poland).
70. Zemborzyn, Słuszczyn (Poland).
71. Alexandrow, Sienna-Olechów (Poland).
72. Ćmielów, Przeuszyn (Poland).
73. Tudorów, Grocholice (Poland).
74. Ostrowiecz, Opatów (Poland).
75. Przepiórów (Poland).
76. Swojków (Poland).
77. Kujawy (Poland).
78. Szcze(y)glice (Poland).
79. Staszów (Poland).
80. Sielec (Poland).
81. Stopnica (Poland).
82. Zborów, Zuków, Piasek, Strozyska, Szczytniki, military bridge at Ostrów to Sokolina (all in Poland).
83. Kamieńczyce (Poland).
84. Słomniki (Poland).
85. Sąspów, Skala (Poland).
86. A town in the district of Mödling in Lower Austria, home to the Seegrotte, a system of caves including Europe's largest underground lake.

87. Gorenice (Poland).
88. The original cholera vaccine, made from killed bacteria, routinely elicited severe local and systemic reactions, and boosters had to be given on a regular basis.
89. Przeginia (Poland).
90. Intestinal damage with leakage would have led to fatal peritonitis in the pre-antibiotic era.
91. Prostitutes. Euphemized in Figure 1.4 as "teachers."
92. Saint Nicholas Day.
93. Cieszyn (Poland) and Český Těšín (Czech Republic). The town lies right on the border and has been the subject of numerous disputes.
94. Wysocice (Poland).
95. Sułoszowa, Gotkowice (Poland).
96. Not found (Poland?).
97. Wilczkowice (Poland).
98. Bohumín (Czech Republic).
99. Spišská Nová Ves (Slovak Republic).
100. Bohdanovce, Trebišov, Michalovce (Slovak Republic).
101. Also known as Laborcz-Mező/Medzilaborce (Slovak Republic).
102. Vydrany (Slovak Republic).
103. Rymanów (Poland).
104. Habura (Slovak Republic).
105. Jaśliska (Poland).
106. Czeremcha (Poland).
107. Borov (Slovak Republic).

CHAPTER 2

1915
Carpathians, Gorlice-Tarnów, Southern and Western Ukraine

1 JANUARY. Glorious winter's day. Not so cold, about 1 to 2°C, with sunshine and dry ground. Weather becomes overcast toward afternoon, but remains cold and dry.

2 JANUARY. Weather as yesterday: no changes. Fighting remains where it is, except for small shifts.

3 JANUARY. Thawing weather again: by afternoon, mud is again as deep as it was a few days ago. Today's fighting in Jasiel[1] is successful, and the commandant is in a better mood.

4 JANUARY. Unchanged—weather miserable. Afternoon rain, which lasts all night.

5 JANUARY. Like yesterday. Snow alternating with rain. Clearing in the afternoon. The mud is terrible.

6 JANUARY. A powerful storm roars in from the south during the night, and it has been snowing heavily since early morning. During dinner, our commander is handed a sealed envelope from army command; its contents announce his replacement by Major General Langer. Great resentment on our side, in stark contrast to Commander Lipošćak himself, who comforts us and is talkative the entire evening. He feels justified, in that Corps Commandant Meixner—who shares his military opinion—has been relieved of command as well.

7 JANUARY. Sudden alarm at 5:00 a.m. Loud noise of fighting not too far away. Our commander arrives, Diogenes-like with his electric lamp, in our room to wake us up. But we are already up and about, dressing. Heavy fighting for ¤ 704, which we lost yesterday but are now commanded to retake. This occurs, and fortieth regiment takes about three hundred Russian prisoners and three machine guns. The enemy retreats along the entire line—Commander Lipošćak is very pleased with this conclusion of his command here, we no less than he. The weather is very favorable—sunshine—mud ever present, but the

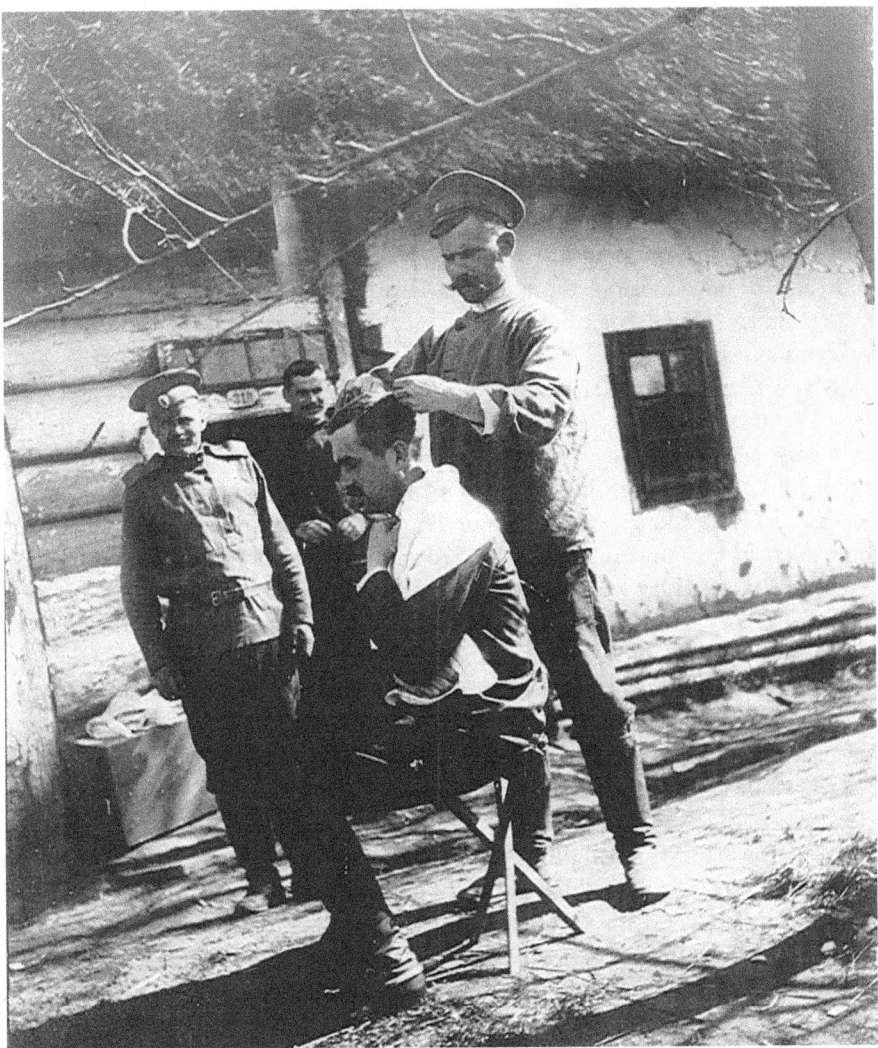

Figure 2.1. A Russian prisoner of war combing a fellow prisoner's hair for lice (*russisches Kulturbild*). Photograph courtesy of the Leo Baeck Institute.

afternoon is not too cold. To crown the day, Count Trautmannsdorf photographs us with our commander during the afternoon.

8 JANUARY. Unchanged—wet snow and mud.

9 JANUARY. The same.

10 JANUARY. Heavy snowfall, temperature a bit warmer, so we literally swim in a sea of muddy water—terrible! Weather improves a bit toward evening. Other than that, the situation is unchanged. Apparently another division

is marching toward us, and we will probably advance again in a few days' time. Meanwhile, great relocations inside the division, giving man and beast no rest.

11 JANUARY. Heavy snowfall early—snow begins to melt in the afternoon, with sunshine—mud gets ever worse. Black ice toward evening—otherwise no changes.

12 JANUARY. Winter landscape—thawing weather toward afternoon—light frost in the evening.

13 JANUARY. Temperature −3°C early, then thawing weather. Arrival at 7:00 a.m. of new division commander, Major General von Langer. Immediately before that, Colonel Klein takes official leave of Commander Lipošćak. Tears on both sides.

Major General von Langer makes a bad impression: he is nervous and restless. We must vacate our quarters for him. Commander Lipošćak leaves me his room, but he is remaining here for another two or three days. As a stopgap, we all move into a very large riding schoolroom, in which Lieutenant Colonel Rosenzweig and Dworzak, as well as Senior Logistics Officer Rosenberg, are already quartered. A fifth uncomfortable, cold room: I sleep really badly the first night.

14 JANUARY. Dry weather: moderately cold, sun in the afternoon, and evening frost.

15 JANUARY. Typical winter's day, with a lot of snow and quite cold. I suffer most in our new quarters, because this riding school cannot be heated throughout the entire day—certainly not at night, when the heating is turned off. My decoration proposal has apparently only left corps today.

16 JANUARY. Commander Lipošćak departs today at 9:00 a.m. Although he has treated Major General von Langer shamefully during the past few days—completely ignoring him during meals—General von Langer still prepares an imposing farewell for him: all men in command accompany the car in which Lipošćak and his ordinance officer Lieutenant Colonel Count Trautmannsdorf both travel, on horseback to the nearest village (Boro).[2] Small units of all army branches are deployed along the entire route: when the car passes by, they shout "hurrah." We ride in front of the car on arrival in Boro, and take up positions. When the car arrives, we shout out a loud "hurrah." Commander Lipošćak leaves the car, gives a moving farewell speech, shakes each one of our hands, and continues on. We turn back. Many photographs are taken. Upon our return, I take up quarters in the ordinary farmer's room, which he has left for me, and in which the farmer's family still live: accordingly, it isn't very clean, and we have some insect company. Morning clear and wintry, thawing in the afternoon with yet more mud.

17 JANUARY. Thawing weather continues.

18 JANUARY. Lovely winter's day—dry, sunny, −4°C. A beautiful, snowy landscape—otherwise, very boring: No mail for four days, and therefore I have no desire to write myself. Such a day crawls by very slowly indeed.

19 JANUARY. Heavy snow during the night. Strong north wind during the day, with corresponding cold, which is still bearable. Feast of the Epiphany in Russia.

20 JANUARY. Cold worsens rapidly. The new offensive is to begin tonight—great preparations, but with reserve provisions for only the next five days.

21 JANUARY. Severe frost, about −10°C. Sun in the afternoon, a small let-up in the cold. I put my fur coat on for the first time. Large troop movements through our area: apparently, the battle is about to begin.

22 JANUARY. A little less cold. During lunch, our new chief of the general staff, Major Heller, arrives. Our division is about to leave—command rides with the immediate staff straight after breakfast, to Chwostcjow:[3] this village consists of five houses, of which two are at least one hundred paces from the other group of three houses. All wretched, stinking farmers' hovels. I share such a hole in the wall with Captain Jelen, First Lieutenant Zorn, afterward with Captain Pockel and Officer Kalab. The stove has been destroyed by a shell, so a reserve stove has been placed there, on which all officers' food is cooked. This place serves as mess for lunch and dinner. We prepare our beds on the tables.

23 JANUARY. Start of general offensive across the entire Carpathian Front, including Bukowina,[4] where two German corps are fighting. Command arrives at the day's vantage point ⌑ 742. Beautiful, sunny winter weather, surroundings covered in snow, −5°C. Significant warming by afternoon. The attack proceeds smoothly, and we gain several heights. For a while, we are imperiled by enemy artillery fire, but this passes. We receive a full second breakfast, with tea, at 2:00 p.m. When darkness falls, we return to Chwostcjow and our beautiful quarters, for our main meal. Nothing much to see at this stage.

24 JANUARY. Lousy weather: strong wind and heavy fog. The attack continues; ⌑ 742 is attacked and taken again by the Russians; we fight for this height all day again and only retake it in the evening. Command remains in Chwostcjow—heavy snow toward evening.

25 JANUARY. Cold has let up. The fighting is now mainly on our line. Neighboring division can also not advance properly; therefore, we are quartered again, most inhumanly, in this lousy place. We could just as well have stayed in Laborcz-fö[5]—the anxious general!

26 JANUARY. A sad day! Cold, overcast, snowdrifts. Fighting is static; our troops are even retreating a bit. Losses quite heavy, more than 350 wounded in the last three days, a few hundred dead. Number missing and captured still unknown—according to reports, all together more than two thousand men. General mood miserable.

27 JANUARY. Heavy snowdrifts during the night—in places the snow is more than one meter high. Both sides attack repeatedly during the night, with many prisoners taken on both sides. The men cannot advance, and there is a threat that they may be completely snowed in.

28 JANUARY. Fighting is not going well. Toward evening, the situation becomes so critical that the order to retreat is given. Around 7:00 p.m. we begin to march back to Laborcz-fö. Riding is impossible because the horses sink deep into the snow, so we trudge down the mountains and arrive in Laborcz-fö after an exhausting, hour-long march. I am quartered with Surgeon Major Dr. Müller. The number of wounded and those suffering from frostbite is high: about 1,700 men in the few days since 23 January.

29 JANUARY. Quite cold, with snow. The day passes miserably—toward evening we receive news that Russians are moving into our positions—we are ready to march by 10:00 p.m. but remain here for now.

30 JANUARY. A great deal of snow—the front is quiet—I write letters diligently.

31 JANUARY. Snowfall continues—heavy fighting on our left flank with seventh corps—unfortunately, they do not succeed, and the order to retreat comes toward evening: our command must retreat to Boro. We depart at 11:00 p.m. and march in the freezing weather (−12°C) over crunching snow through a road jam-packed with baggage trains. We arrive at our quarters at 12:30 a.m., in the school, where I share a room with Colonel von Rosenzweig and Senior Logistics Officer Rosenberg. We bed down on straw on the ground. General staff are quartered in the priest's house.

1 FEBRUARY. The day is calm: fighting only starts toward evening. At 1:00 a.m., while we are soundly asleep, the order comes to be "ready to march" we depart at 3:00 a.m., arriving in Mező-Laborcz[6] at 4:30 a.m. We are quartered in the same room that served previously as our mess: but in the meantime horses have been stabled here, so it first has to be thoroughly cleaned. So we lie in the horse stench on the wet ground until 7:00 a.m.

2 FEBRUARY. Lovely sunny winter's day—not too cold. The snow has frozen. On the lookout for better quarters, I meet up again with the Honvéd hussars: they make a nice, clean room, with a good divan, available to me, and I sleep excellently all night. Toward evening we receive as reinforcements three battle-ready battalions from the eighty-eighth infantry regiment: excellent German troops, and our mood and hope for victory are raised.

3 FEBRUARY. Beautiful winter weather continues, just colder: temperature −17°C. The sound of fighting gets louder and louder: we are ready to march. In the morning, eighty-first regiment arrives with four thousand men but is unfortunately assigned to seventh corps. During the afternoon, shelling of the church in which the general staff is located becomes so heavy that remaining there becomes impossible; we move to the southern part of the town and take positions in a part of the rooms of corps command. Corps command is still here for the moment, so everything becomes very crowded. We remain ready to march during the night, and lie fully dressed, squeezed onto the floor like herrings. Night passes relatively quietly—the trains are withdrawn to Izbugya-

Radvány,[7] and the abandoned station is a picture of terrible devastation—there is great danger of being cut off by the Russians. God help the poor troops who are sidelined, unable to fight.

4 FEBRUARY. Weather favorable, not too cold. Quiet in the morning on the front, but the sound of fighting is audible west of us in the twentieth infantry division. Heavier artillery fire during the course of the day from our side—shells and shrapnel fall everywhere. Toward evening the weather changes: snow falls and it becomes less cold. Both corps command and command of the twenty-fourth infantry division are located here—what courage! Sudden alarm around 8:30 p.m., ready to march, the Russians are attacking Mező-Laborcz. Corps command whizzes away in cars. The sound of fighting gets ever louder: infantry and machine gunfire from very nearby. There is fighting in the town entrance, and command departs at 11:30 p.m., to the convent of Monastir Saint Basiloarda,[8] where we are blocked by a flood of retreating baggage trains. We arrive in the convent at 1:00 a.m.: it's occupied by rear echelon staff. However, as soon as they hear that the Cossacks are coming, they immediately make themselves scarce. At 2:00 a.m., news comes that Mező-Laborcz is in Russian hands. Our division has been beaten completely and is streaming back. If we would have remained there thirty minutes longer, we would hardly have been able to escape. Great consternation: another order is given to prepare to leave. At 4:00 a.m. we depart. Unbelievable baggage train congestion with retreating troops together on the road—a total mix-up. Additionally, strong snow squalls. We remain on the road and, with all our strength, restore some semblance of order, and then quarter in a huntsman's house on the side of the street. All sorts of reports and orders are handed out—at daybreak, 6:00 a.m., we continue our march along the baggage train columns and, by rapid march, arrive at 7:30 a.m. the next day.

5 FEBRUARY. Alsöczebeny.[9] Here for the first time we receive the sad news that barely 450 fighting-ready men remain of our entire division—so, in effect, our division has been completely wiped out. Because of lack of proper provisions, sleepless nights and excessive exertion during the past few days, most of us are so exhausted that, at 11:00 a.m., after a frugal breakfast, almost all fall sound asleep in a heap on the ground. I myself, despite being no less tired, cannot sleep in such a place and am therefore writing down these lines.

We continue our retreat today and intend, by forced marches, to pry ourselves loose from the enemy as rapidly as possible, come what may. Our offensive has completely collapsed: between 23 January and 4 February, we have lost about ten thousand men: what a debacle! We depart at 2:30 p.m. and arrive in Laborczradvány[10] at 4:00 p.m.: an insignificant farmer's village. At 6:30 p.m. we get our first hot food of the day.

6 FEBRUARY. A quiet night: less quiet for me, because my roommate First Lieutenant Baron Jesenski has to leave at 1:00 a.m. and—out of worry that we might suddenly have to depart without my hearing of it because my quarters are secluded—I cannot fall asleep again. But it has been completely quiet, and we remain here for the moment. The weather is lovely, although quite brisk in the morning −15°C. Sun in the afternoon: a glorious winter landscape.

7 FEBRUARY. Situation unchanged; thawing weather begins. We have significantly less accommodation space, because it must be shared with the farmers. Even our mess has farmers in it, and we must sometimes dine to the music of a squealing infant. Most of us are bothered less by this for a change, because the mother is so young and pretty: a real Madonna face with a Junoesque appearance. The men feast their eyes on the mother calming the child.

8 FEBRUARY. Sudden alarm at 5:00 a.m. Ready to march. Apparently, Russians have attacked our battery, and the entire communications section goes into motion. But it proves to be a false alarm, and the state of readiness is canceled at 9:00 a.m. Beautiful spring weather, with snowmelt. My batman, whom I have recently changed in Laborcz-fö, has unfortunately taken ill and been evacuated: my replacement, from the staff company, is a village teacher.

9 FEBRUARY. A glorious springlike day, with a great deal of snow melting—the roads will soon become impassable. We leave our quarters, and our beautiful Madonna, at 3:00 p.m. and move to the neighboring village, Izbugya-Radvány,[11] which is bigger and nicer, with better quarters. We must set up here and prepare for a fairly long stay. I am quartered in a huntsman's house, where I share a large, clean room with Captain Jelen, First Lieutenant Schlesinger, and Baron Jesenski. My bed consists of a wire mattress on a cupboard upended on the floor—a good resonant floor! My stomach has had it.

10 FEBRUARY. I remain in bed all day, taking in no solid food, I have had two cholera-like stools and am feeling terrible, so dehydrated that I have passed no urine for almost an entire day.

11 FEBRUARY. I feel a lot better, get out of bed, and sit comfortably in a large club armchair. My diet continues.

12 FEBRUARY. I feel almost completely recovered, and my appetite has returned—I eat normal food. The order to be ready to march has been in effect since 8:00 a.m., because the offensive has restarted along the line. But still, we do not depart. The weather is tepid and a great deal of snow is melting: ugh!

13 FEBRUARY. Snowmelt continues: the mountains are almost all a dirty gray color now, and the Laborcza River[12] rises as we watch, overflowing its banks in places. Otherwise nothing new: we remain here for the time being. Two 30.5-centimeter mortars have arrived and are positioned south of Okreske.[13] Their assembly takes one entire afternoon: very complicated and interesting.

14 FEBRUARY. The mortars are in action today already—all the windowpanes in their vicinity are broken. Weather overcast, roads bottomless.

15 FEBRUARY. Weather overcast, very unpleasant, rain. Corps Commandant Krautwald inspects the division. In the afternoon, our neighboring sev-

enth corps begins the attack; we are held in reserve. The mortars are kept very busy.

16 FEBRUARY. Beautiful early spring weather—a lot of sun—but the most dreadful mud. Our troops have actually advanced, but command remains here for the moment. The immediate staff are at the day's vantage point near the mortars.

17 FEBRUARY. Weather like yesterday, quite warm—light frost toward evening. Fighting on the front advances slowly. In the evening, we receive the joyful news that Hindenburg has taken fifty thousand Russians captive in East Prussia.[14]

18 FEBRUARY. Situation unchanged—weather like yesterday. The mountains are already almost completely snow-free. Splendid advances in East Galicia—Czernowitz[15] is again in our hands.

19 FEBRUARY. Weather less favorable—damp cold. Some improvement in the afternoon, the sun tries to break through—wind.

20 FEBRUARY. A warmer wind, rain in the afternoon that lasts all night. Mud is immeasurable, and roads completely impassable.

21 FEBRUARY. Fighting continues—slow advance. And so we are still here. I would be very happy if only I didn't have to share the room with Captain Jelen. His office activities occupy him far into the night, often until midnight and even later, and he cannot be made to get out of bed early: certainly not before 9:00 to 9:30 a.m. I cannot sleep when the light is on. It's all terribly unpleasant. Suddenly alarm: order to be ready to march at 10:30 p.m. The Russians are said to have broken through our position at the Convent of Saint Basiloarda. We sit on chairs in the mess, half asleep, half awake, until 1:30 a.m., when news comes that the Russians have been repulsed again.

22 FEBRUARY. Weather better—no more rain but endless mud. Immediate staff go to the daily vantage point. Mortars are withdrawn, apparently because of yesterday's incident when they were in great danger, and are transported to the Koskocz[16] railway station. With yesterday's attack, the Russians have got rid of an unpleasant companion: it must have been terribly uncomfortable for them.

23 FEBRUARY. The immediate staff are moving to Okreske, while we are remaining here. Not such a bad thing, just a pity that Captain Jelen is not going with them. Weather is less pleasant.

24 FEBRUARY. Situation unchanged. The Russians are trying to break through with all their strength, but so far they have been repulsed. Hindenburg has apparently captured 110,000 Russians, three hundred artillery pieces, and many hundreds of machine guns at the Masurian Lakes. So the Russians must be feeling quite under the weather and want to at least force a victory here: especially because they are not doing very well in Bukowina and East Galicia. We will see!

25 FEBRUARY. Weather favorable: light evening frost, but by day the mud remains. In the morning, I make a visit to command in Okreske by car. This is a pleasant outing for me. I am back at 2:00 p.m., after taking lunch there. Captain Jelen and his ordinance officer have been ordered away permanently—hurray! So I remain alone in my uncomfortable room with the comfortable club armchair: it can't get any better. I spend the morning at the *Landwehr* division medical unit whose commandant, Surgeon Major Beykowski, is a very pleasant fellow. I spend a lot of time in the Red Cross refreshment train that has been located here at the station the past few days. The train leader is delegate banker Huiber, a very pleasant man—good reading material is available inside.

26 FEBRUARY. Weather good. No real changes at the front. Some command officers are shepherded back to Okreske on a daily basis—today was Senior Logistics Officer Rosenberg's turn—no loss either. Hopefully I will not be among them, because quarters there are miserable. Captain Jelen's batman made short work of my new pair of galoshes yesterday: there was nobody else in the room.

27 FEBRUARY. Weather favorable today as well. The general surprises us with his visit after we have dined: he visits the refreshment train, and we remain together until his departure. Baron Hauerstein, the new ordinance officer, arrives.

28 FEBRUARY. Weather glorious: roads already almost completely dry. Lively activity at the railway station continues. This is the end station, from where the evacuation train with the sick and wounded leaves. Evacuation Leader surgeon Major Dr. Schipek, is a lively fellow. A mobile reserve hospital with three doctors as evacuation station, a hospital train, and permanent train for the sick (and wounded) are at the station on a daily basis. So there is sufficient variety and relief.

1 MARCH. March roars in like a lion. Real March weather overnight. Wet snow covers the ground again: it melts, and then falls again. More mud—horrible. Otherwise nothing special. Chief Medical Officer Zapatowicz inspects the station.

2 MARCH. Weather similar to yesterday—periods of sunshine—unbelievable amounts of mud.

3 MARCH. Situation and weather unchanged.

4 MARCH. A hospital train from the Vienna Volunteer Rescue Association[17] has arrived, commanded by old Count Hilerek—Colonel Dr. Charas and two additional physicians have also come along. They bring gifts from home and take wounded in. The train is well equipped, and a wounded man can count himself lucky to be in such a train. The sleeping and dining coaches for the association's senior staff are splendid. Dr. Charas is a less than sympathetic character: educated, but puffed up. Today an offensive involving our neighboring troops occurs, with little success: more wounded and killed.

5 MARCH. Situation the same. Afternoon visit at command in Okreske.

6 MARCH. I spend the morning at the Red Cross refreshment station. The people are very pleasant and forthcoming. Heavy snowfall toward evening.

7 MARCH. Winter reappears, with heavy snow, wind, and biting cold.

8 MARCH. Morning and night frosts. Midday sunshine—very pretty, except for the mud: the roads have been softened up again.

9 MARCH. Weather like yesterday. Afternoon visit by the generals to inspect the refreshment station.

10 MARCH. The ground has frozen solid, with a really cold wind. Morning overcast. Journey with the refreshment station delegate Herr Huber to the corps chief medical officer for introduction, and extension of his activity to the first aid station.

11 MARCH. Very cold with a strong north wind: an exceptionally chilly winter day. Lieutenant Schlesinger, who has lain sick in my room for several days, may well have typhus/typhoid.[18] Today is my official evaluation of Dr. Stach's horse, which I exchange for my old nag. Finally, I have a really good horse!

12 MARCH. Cold has eased up a bit. Morning transportation of Lieutenant Schlesinger to the evacuation station, and disinfection of our room with potassium permanganate and formalin, which I obtain in the refreshment station. Because of this, I spend overnight in the refreshment station's coach, together with Herr Huber.

13 MARCH. Heavy snowfall, followed by snow melt—horrible! Second cholera inoculation at command. Most men, including myself, have a really strong reaction—shivering spells toward evening, so I refuse food. In the evening, news comes of the decoration of our Senior Logistics Officer Rosenberg with the Order of Franz Joseph. He will be thrilled about this—it has taken long enough.

14 MARCH. Inoculation reactions are more or less gone after a day. A great deal of snow everywhere: what a mess! But it will not last: it melts under our feet already.

15 MARCH. Thawing weather—periods of rain—the most revolting mud.

16 MARCH. Weather really awful—rain mixed with snow—terrible mud, yet I must go out to command in Okreske—behind me, Corps Commandant Krautwald has also appeared.

17 MARCH. Snowmelt—situation unchanged. In the evening, fourth mobile battalion under the leadership of Captain Kobelnigg arrives by train: we are very happy to see each other. He also brings me a package (a field bed and a shoulder cape), which could hardly have arrived at a better time. However, on the way from the station they are lost/stolen—I am furious and spend a sleepless night over this.

18 MARCH. Weather unchanged: mild, with mud. The rescue association train arrives again.

19 March. Weather unchanged. In the morning, I visit with the chief medical officer to write a letter of recognition for the Red Cross delegate. News of a favorable conclusion of negotiations with Italy do the rounds. Good news: we hope for a rapid peace agreement.[19]

20 March. Mud gets ever deeper. Strong wind toward afternoon. The Russians have attempted an energetic breakthrough today, which is, just as energetically, promptly repulsed. Many prisoners pass by us all day, but the fourth battalion also has heavy losses.

21 March. First day of spring, not only on the calendar but in reality. A more beautiful and warmer day can hardly be imagined—only clouded by the news that I must immediately return to command in Okreske. I part from my comrades and splendid quarters with a heavy heart. On the way there, I meet Captain Kobelnigg, who has been wounded and is being evacuated—he is radiant with happiness, because his has a million-dollar wound: a bullet wound in the soft tissue in the right upper thigh. I am, by contrast, decidedly unhappy: my package is lost forever.

Great excitement at command about an imminent attack. We ride off to Balin Pusta[20]—the horses are restless because they have been inactive for a long while, and now this glorious spring air makes them very frolicsome. We leave our horses and travel on foot over the mountains, in part deep in snow, and arrive in the as yet unfinished hunting lodge in Škoda[21]—it is already 3:00 p.m., and apart from my breakfast coffee I have not eaten anything and am ravenously hungry. Luckily, our "nutrition father" Chromy arrives soon: the good fellow unpacks something for me from his horse: the piece of sausage with bread taste wonderful. We travel further across the mountains to ¤ 600, our vantage position for the day. We see no sign of fighting, however, and telephone communication from here is difficult. Agreed—but it is ordered that command must stand at the daily vantage point! We return to the hunting lodge at the onset of darkness, where hot food is prepared for us. It is already 9:00 p.m by the time we get to sleep: a straw bed is on the floor.

22 March. At 9:30 a.m. we are at our daily vantage position but return to the hunting lodge at 1:00 p.m., because our losses have been so enormous that another attack on our side is unthinkable. Weather glorious, like yesterday, only some wind. Still feels cold at night.

23 March. Lovely weather continues—much sun, blue sky. We consolidate our holding positions, and command arrives in Izbugya-Belá.[22] Captain Krämer returns from distributing provisions and is the first to hand me the news of my decoration with the Order of Franz Joseph. This makes me very happy, because now I have caught up with my comrades, many of whom received this decoration some time ago. This joy does not pass unclouded: in the evening, we receive the news of the fall of Przemysl![23]

24 MARCH. I am so upset about the fall of Przemysl that I don't even feel like writing to Olga—to say nothing of Commander Liposćak to thank him for the decoration. Izbugya-Belá is a pleasant place—perhaps that is the reason for its name—and quarters are quite passable, although in a farmer's house shared with the farmers. The room is clean, and the female farmer is the sister of the Madonna from Izbugya-Radvány, no less beautiful and vivacious than her sister. First Lieutenant Baron Jesenski is my roommate.

25 MARCH. Situation unchanged. Weather remains very good.

26 MARCH. The weather changes. Rain mixed with snow in the afternoon—a loud sound of fighting can be heard: Russians attack the Kobila and Javirska heights, but are repulsed.

27 MARCH. Weather improved. Significant mud after yesterday's rain. Joint afternoon inspection of the division medical unit baggage train with Senior Logistics Officer Rosenberg.

28 MARCH. Overcast with rain, which lasts all afternoon. Endless mud. The mood is not cheerful anymore, mainly because of the attitude of our faithful ally Italy, who is making ever greater and more unreasonable demands for territorial annexation. It's totally unreasonable! Troop transports to the east must be held up in Marburg[24] and directed straight to the Italian border.

At 6:00 p.m. heavy Russian attack along our entire line: a violent cannonade is heard—we remain on watch and assembled until 1:00 a.m., when there is a lull in the fighting. However, fighting soon begins again and lasts all night without any real success, except for the fact that ⌑ 600 is now in the neutral zone. About 150 wounded on our side.

29 MARCH. A quiet day. In the morning, I travel to the division medical unit in Laborczradvány, from there to the Red Cross refreshment station, returning around 1:00 p.m. Morning weather favorable, only horrible mud everywhere. Weather deteriorates during the afternoon, with light snowfall. Toward evening, the Russians start the same game as yesterday, but are repelled quickly and the night is quite calm.

30 MARCH. Complete winter landscape with a lot of snow on all visible slopes—even without the snow the weather is bad. Cannon thunder early. Evening attacks today as well, as during the past few days, but with the same results—the Russians are repulsed.

31 MARCH. Miserable weather: rain, wet snow, bottomless mud. Yesterday we had to vacate our quarters to make room for two new Hungarian battalions, and we occupy one room in which, apart from the farmers, five children—from three months to fifteen years—also live.

The wailing of this little group, mixed with the cannon thunder, yields such pleasant music that it would be a pity to sleep. Russian attacks are again repulsed.

1 April. Revolting weather—significant snow, which is already melting, during the night, so the mud is awful. The two Hungarian battalions have departed, so I return to my previous quarters, where there are only two children, to whose bad habits I have already become accustomed. Afternoon sun brings with it a cessation in the snow, but increases mud all the more.

We hear that Commander Lipošćak is returning: his friend Commandant Meixner has, during the past few days, been honorably reinstated. We are all happy about this, because his replacement in corps command, Commander Krautwald may make an excellent sergeant—but as general? Never!

2 April. Good Friday. A beautiful fine day as far as weather is concerned, otherwise a terrible day of fighting! The Russians start heavy artillery fire in the early morning hours, which gets more violent and lasts for several hours. After that, their infantry goes over to the attack along the entire front, including troops that had been occupied with the siege of Przemysl. Rifle fire comes ever nearer, and Izbugya-Belá is fired upon as well. It happens very quickly and violently, and soon our infantry comes streaming back. Around 2:00 p.m., the order comes to retreat, and command is ordered to return to Laborczradvány. Fighting only recedes toward evening, when finally our divisional cavalry is put into action as our last reserves. Count Tisza is seriously wounded in this fighting, Count Bellegarde is wounded and taken prisoner, First Lieutenant Kaposi killed, etc.

German troops arrive toward evening, and the two Hungarian battalions are ordered back. They immediately start to march against the enemy. There are no quarters—we lie on the ground in groups of five.

3 April. Early on a beautiful morning, command arrives at ¤ 454, from which we have an excellent view of the entire battlefield. Fighting is in full swing, and the Germans have penetrated significantly. Our position is not spared from Russian shells and shrapnel, so we have to change positions a few times. Around 4:00 p.m. our troops are ordered to dig into their holding positions, and command returns to their quarters at 6:00 p.m.

4 April. Fighting for the Kobila and Javirska heights continues. A further German division joins in the attack: we fight together with them, advancing slowly—at 7:30 p.m. we return from daily vantage point ¤ 454. The heights are not yet taken today. During the day, Duke Otto Windischgratz takes command. Weather beautiful today as well.

5 April. We ride together to our position at 7:00 a.m.: today represents a great victory. All calibers of our artillery begin a powerful preparatory bombardment that lasts until 4:00 p.m., after which our infantry go over to the attack; Kobila and Javirska are very soon in our hands. Russians give up in entire large groups: 2,500 prisoners, two artillery pieces, twelve machine guns and huge amounts of rifles, ammunition, etc.: our joyful mood is indescribable—we return, drunk with victory, to our quarters in Laborczradvány at 6:00 p.m.

6 APRIL. Beautiful warm spring weather continues—we arrive at our daily vantage point at 9:30 a.m.; our division stands fast today; the neighboring divisions do the fighting, to take the neighboring heights—we return to quarters at 6:00 p.m.

7 APRIL. Our division returns to Mező-Laborcz for refitting and is replaced by German troops. We do not go out to our vantage point today and are occupied solely bringing in the booty. There are mountains of rifles, ammunition, and other war material—both artillery pieces have also been brought in.

8 APRIL. We ride off to Mező-Laborcz at 10:00 a.m., arriving there at 11:00 a.m. A nice, quiet, extended village, with a row of houses lining the street. The house themselves have tin roofs. Unfortunately, the entire town has been occupied by the Germans; it's already evening before a plan can be made for the Germans to vacate the place. I share a room with Senior Logistics Officer Rosenberg. Toward evening, we get the news that Commander Lipošćak is on the way—he is at Homonna[25] at the moment.

9 APRIL. Commander Lipošćak arrives at 9:00 a.m.: we await him ready to cooperate as much as we can, and greet him cordially. Great joy on all faces except that of our General Langer, on which consternation is seen: he has to take a brigade command again. This does not suit him at all: he reports sick and promptly disappears during the night without even saying goodbye.

Rain toward afternoon, which continues uninterruptedly in the evening. After only an hour, the mud is so deep that the roads will soon be impassable. The division medical unit is here.

10 APRIL. At night, the unexpected order comes to march back to Homonna. We start the journey at 8:30 a.m., arriving at our destination at 11:00 a.m. A nice town, not very big—the Russians have partially burned down the town center. I quarter with First Lieutenant Count von Trautmannsdorf at the home of a Jewish family—not bad. Catering like in a restaurant, expensive and bad. Weather good.

11 APRIL. We depart again at 8:30 a.m. I ride with Surgeon Major Phlebs; we ride too rapidly, with a great deal of trotting and galloping, so that we travel the twenty-four kilometers in two and a half hours, arriving in Mező-Körtvelyes,[26] a nice, clean village with a beautiful castle belonging to Captain of the Reserve Moscovits, in which command is quartered. The rooms are splendid, beautifully and elegantly appointed. There is a magnificent dining hall with terrace and free staircase. I am quartered alone in the adjacent building—something that I prefer—in a splendid field bed. There is a beautiful park, but the weather is not good: otherwise, we feel exceptionally comfortable here.

12 APRIL. We will refit here. Additional men and equipment are on the way. The weather is, unfortunately, not good yet. However, buds are already abundant, and new green growth can be seen everywhere. Life reawakens, and we have a desire to live again: if only this awful war would end!

13 APRIL. A memorable day! Army Commandant Archduke Friederich inspects our division—the heir to the throne, who is also expected, has canceled at the last minute. Kaiser Weather—the troops are deployed about one and a half kilometers from our quarters. The Archduke arrives at 9:00 a.m. in a large suite of cars and inspects the troops: he honors several men by addressing them—including me, whom our commander introduces with the words: "An excellent chief medical officer." The Archduke enquires about the medical conditions in the division. The solemn ceremony ends at 9:30 a.m., and we fall out.

14 APRIL. Service for the fallen at 9:00 a.m. Because of the pouring rain all day, the field mass is replaced by church readings. Horrible mud, which significantly influences our refitting.

15 APRIL. Rain all morning. Clearing only by afternoon. But roads remain impassable because of the huge amounts of mud.

16 APRIL. Beautiful sunshine, which dries out the ground rapidly. Just before lunch, I am solemnly decorated with the order of Franz Joseph before the assembled corps of division command. Commander Liposćak gives a very flattering speech, to which I respond to with thanks and recognition. He then pins the order on my chest. My upbeat mood today is understandable.

17 APRIL. Good weather, a splendid stay here—unfortunately much too short, because the order comes this afternoon to prepare for departure tomorrow.

18 APRIL. Glorious, warm weather. Noise of departure preparation can be heard everywhere. I take the opportunity to take a splendid bath at 8:00 a.m. early. We depart at 5:00 p.m. for the encampment station of Örmező,[27] where we arrive after a rapid ride of 1.75 hours. Large, nice village with a beautiful castle, already occupied by the Germans: so we are quartered in farmers' houses. The Germans have established a convalescent home here: nice and clean, just like in peacetime.

19 APRIL. Nice, warm weather persists. Encampment at 3:00 p.m. and departure via Kaschau,[28] where we arrive at midnight.

20 APRIL. We depart from Kaschau at 10:00 a.m. and spend 6:00 to 10:00 a.m. at the station and in the town—we meet Captain Krämer with his wife: he traveled ahead three days ago, for a rendezvous with his wife. From here we travel to Eperies;[29] lunch noon to 1:00 p.m. in Abos.[30] Arrival in Eperies at 3:45 p.m. Lovely weather, really warm. Arrival in Muszyna[31] at 10:00 p.m., where we decamp. We must look for quarters ourselves. I find quarters in a farmhouse with Captain Prachowny and climb into bed without any bedding—brr!

21 APRIL. We ride off at 8:30 a.m.: weather splendid. Arrive in Krynica[32] at 10:00 a.m. A beautiful spa town with lovely parks and gardens, splendid villas, electric lights, and baths. Command is accommodated in one of the largest establishments, each man in a separate room with an excellent bed, etc., if only we could remain in this wonderful place!

22 APRIL. Today as well, we wallow in happiness. The town's notables are invited to dine with us. Weather very good. We are dressed for summer and have sent our winter clothes off already. My weight today is 76.2 kilograms.

23 APRIL. Opening of mineral baths especially for us today. We all take a bath and are delighted with it. In the afternoon, departure for Muszyna to visit the corps chief medical officer and local Red Cross refreshment station. Requisition of a new camp bed and a *Rekordspritze*[33] to replace what was stolen/mislaid. The division medical unit, which has been traveling on foot, will only arrive tomorrow. Conditions here are wonderful, but unfortunately we have to leave this evening.

24 APRIL. We depart from Krynica via Polany to Brunary.[34] We depart at 10:00 a.m. and arrive at 2:00 p.m. Glorious summer weather, really hot at times. The town is a wretched dump, no quarters at all; I share a farmer's hut with the senior logistics officer and Captain Krämer.

25 APRIL. Travel from Brunary via Leszczyny to Nowica.[35] Depart 8:00 a.m., arrival 1:00 p.m. Just as miserable a dump as yesterday—I share a room with the senior logistics officer, in which the farmer's family also lives. Our horses stand in the entrance behind the door.

26 APRIL. We remain here—our division is relieving ninth corps. Weather good, our stay here is quiet but boring. In the afternoon, Commander Lipoščak shares a confidential communication with Colonels Klein and Rosenzweig and me concerning a memorandum which he wants present to His Majesty. He wants our prior opinions about it: I am greatly honored to have been asked my opinion.

27 APRIL. Quiet at the front, with cannon fire here and there. Weather more overcast, periods of rain in the afternoon.

28 APRIL. Weather nice, just quite cold because of the wind. Our guests for lunch are Corps Commandant Martini and four gentlemen from his staff, as well as the brigadier of the forty-fifth infantry division Major General Nemeczek, whom I already know from Gastein.

29 APRIL. Beautiful weather: sunny and warm. Corps Commander Martini rides out daily to the front with several men and returns at noon.

30 APRIL. Weather remains good. Finally, my furniture sent from Trieste has arrived in Vienna in good condition. Both my wife and I are very pleased about this—we are relieved of this worry.

1 MAY. During the night, I am taken to Colonel Klein, who has fractured a rib from falling off his horse. He is evacuated today. A great offensive[36] is being prepared: the division medical unit is transferred here; corps command and its immediate staff are coming here as well. Weather very favorable.

2 MAY. Start of a great offensive across our entire front. We ride to the battle areas, ⌧ 814, where we remain until 8:00 p.m. and then return to our station. An initial preparation by the artillery: thundering and roaring such has not been seen or heard before. Then the infantry advances; Russians give up in droves; those that do not, flee precipitately. Wonderful to see! Our troops reach their assigned destination. We see from afar the petroleum refinery in Gorlice go up in flames. A powerful fire, which will surely burn on for several days. One can get an idea of the artillery fire when one thinks that our corps alone shot 9,620 salvoes. During the day, we receive a visit from the army commandant. The day passes very rapidly with exceptional excitement over the splendid results of our recent battle.

3 MAY. We ride out today at 7:00 a.m. to ¤ 814. The weather is not as good—windy and cold, with fog that limits visibility. Today the division has a small task, to take ¤ 757—slow going, but the goal is achieved. The Germans move forward smoothly: corps command leaves the vantage point at noon; the weather improves at 5:00 p.m.

4 MAY. Good weather early, then overcast and quite cold. We ride off today at 9:00 a.m., because our division is stationary—first the Magura heights must be taken by the twenty-first *Landwehr* infantry division, and that is a difficult task. Our time on ¤ 814 today is uncomfortable and boring, because of the cold and lack of visibility, yet we have to hold out until 7:30 p.m. Magura is taken and the Germans progress well.

5 MAY. A day of rejoicing of the first order! Russians are retreating along the entire front in forced marches, leaving endless amounts of material behind. We depart from Nowica at 7:00 a.m., on the road to Petna,[37] where First Lieutenant Buchta, who was killed two days ago, has been buried. I have the time to find his grave, which looks very dignified. We ride off to Banica[38] a few hours later. Not a Russian in sight—only prisoners and war booty. We arrive in Wolowiec[39] at 7:00 p.m., toward evening, and take up quarters. We find an entire supply depot filled with Russian infantry ammunition: more than forty thousand cartridges. The division medical unit arrives in Petna.

6 MAY. Alarm early at 2:30 p.m.: preparation to depart, to catch the fleeing Russians. Departure at 4:45 a.m. through Nieznajowa—Krepna—Olchowiec, with a long rest in Polany. We arrive in Tylawa[40] when it is already dark, at 7:00 p.m. A very stressful march of more than thirty-five kilometers. The baggage train arrives even later, so we get our first hot food around 11:00 p.m.: an unappetizing stew. The village is, like all others, completely burned down, only two farmhouses standing: we take mass quarters in a wretched, stinking farmer's room. We find no more Russians, but our neighboring division, the forty-fifth infantry and fourth cavalry divisions, have had colossal success, taking prisoner one general, one colonel, fourteen officers, 1,300 men, twenty light and five heavy artillery pieces of modern construction, baggage trains, and a lot more war booty. Our soldiers' jubilation is indescribable. The Russians have fled precipitately, and we are nipping at their heels.

7 MAY. After hardly four hours of sleep, our entire division is on the move again. The Russians cannot be allowed to get away this time. Departure 5:00 a.m., direction Jasliska,[41] the same station that is a sacred memory from last Christmas Eve. There is still fighting on the mountain slopes, apparently with Russian rearguards. Arrival in Jasliska at 7:00 p.m. In the evening, we receive, as compensation for yesterday, an excellent and generous dinner. From today, we are assigned to seventeenth corps.

8 MAY. Pursuit of the enemy continues in a northeasterly direction. We march through Tarnaewka,[42] where the enemy rearguard is still in position, attempting to cut us off on the Wislok.[43] Shells and shrapnel whistle uncomfortably over our heads, and we make quite a long stop to distribute new dispositions. Russian fire stops after about an hour. First Lieutenant Spetzler, dispatched with an order to brigade command, is hit in the lower back by a stone ricocheting from a shell—no visible wound, apparently severe bone contusion. He is evacuated.

The Russians do not yield, and a violent artillery duel ensues, which lasts until dark, when the Russians finally retreat, leaving about eight hundred prisoners. We quarter in Tarnawka:[44] wretched farmhouses without chimneys, so that the upper part of the room is filled to the ceiling with smoke. Standing upright is impossible. Therefore, I quarter in a barn. Start of summer vacation season. Not cold, little rest. Toward midnight, a house catches fire, causing great excitement. Afternoon weather overcast, rain toward evening.

9 MAY. Rain continues, although lighter, into the day. We march off at 6:30 a.m. through Rudawka Rymanowska,[45] where we soon come under such heavy artillery fire that we can hardly find a small place to shelter. Once we find somewhere safe, we remain there until darkness falls and then return to Rudawka Rymanowska for the night. The Russians have become much tougher adversaries—they have apparently obtained reinforcements, and today we advance very slowly. I suddenly experience severe pains in the small of my back that extend into my left hip and make any movement difficult.

10 MAY. Rain again during the night, clearing by 9:00 a.m. with a fresh wind. We remain here for the moment. During the night, the Russians repulse our attack, with heavy losses on our side. Fighting goes on without a break: a very heavy artillery duel. Finally, toward evening, the matter is decided and Russians flee, leaving behind many prisoners: on our entire front about twenty thousand prisoners, many machine guns, endless amounts of ammunition. We spend the night here; I share a very small but clean room with First Lieutenant Count Trautmannsdorf and First Lieutenant Auditor Pfaff.

11 MAY. We carry on without a stop. The weather is glorious. We march in an easterly direction, parallel to the railway, to Sanok, through Odrzechowa and Wygnanka.[46] The heights north of the railway station are occupied early, but empty out during the course of the morning, so we can finally march without fighting. Depart 7:00 a.m., arrival in Struze Wielkie[47] at 8:00 p.m. The baggage train only arrives at 9:00 p.m. The march is very strenuous.

12 MAY. Only a short march today, hardly forty-five minutes, to Posada Olchowska[48] near Sanok. We arrive at 9:00 a.m., and enjoy an all-too-short rest day. Weather beautiful, already quite hot. I do not go into Sanok, which is devastated and empty, all stores shuttered, railway station and the adjacent storehouses—which were filled with Russian supplies—demolished and burned down. The car factory right next to the storehouses is completely demolished, all machines rendered unusable. The large supplies of wood have mostly been taken back to Russia. Factory rooms have been used as stables. Our accommodation is very good; I am quartered in a nice, well-furnished room on the first floor.

13 MAY. Today our troops must cross the San. Because the bridges have been blown, only two pontoon bridges are available. Our division arrives there in the afternoon, and command at 3:00 p.m., just as it really starts to rain. It is also quite humid. At 6:00 p.m., we arrive in Siemuszowa[49]—a wretched village with wretched accommodation. But, because I now have my own camp bed, I don't mind so much anymore. We go back to tenth corps, and join the German mountain corps.

14 MAY. Regular march for our division: depart 5:30 a.m., arrival in Bircza[50] at 10:30 a.m. A typical, small, Galician Jewish village—the center has been burned down, only a few houses are left standing, including the house of Count Czernecka, a very elegant place where our staff office is quartered. However, the castle next door has been completely burned down, except for adjacent buildings, which we ourselves burn down because the Russians have used them to accommodate cholera patients. I am quartered on the first floor of a very nice house. Toward evening Colonel Klein returns, his fractured rib healed.

15 MAY. We march against Przemysl again, leaving at 5:30 a.m. during bad, rainy weather. But after an hour, the weather clears and the *kalte Sophie*[51] blows the rain away. We are the corps reserve, and remain in Cisowa,[52] where we arrive at 9:30 a.m. and quarter in small farm rooms: I in a smaller room, the larger one for the ordinance officers, on whom I depend for my meals. The weather remains overcast. At 4:00 p.m. we suddenly get the order to depart for Olszany[53]—a few hours march away. The village has been completely burned down; not a single house is left standing. The troops make open camp, while command returns to Cisowa.

16 MAY. We ride off at 6:30 a.m. to the same vantage point as yesterday. The division is inactive today as well. At 7:00 p.m. we return to Cisowa. There is fighting in front of us, because the Russians are rapidly digging in and resisting strongly. But, in general, they are retreating along the entire front. Jaroslau, Sambor,[54] etc., are already in our hands. Weather nice in the morning: overcast afternoon with a lot of dust.

17 may. We ride to our daily vantage point at the bridge. Fighting in front of us continues without progress, and we come more and more to the conclusion that, without heavy artillery, we cannot take these positions. Corps command intervenes—we soon march away from our daily vantage point, not to Cisowa, but somewhat nearer the front, to Krzeczkowa,[55] where corps command is also going. The village has been completely burned down; the few houses left standing are occupied by corps command. We find a few houses being rebuilt, and a few officers and I choose a half-finished building for accommodation. Weather is warm, and our quarters—although letting air in—are clean and idyllically located; nothing around but lovely meadows on which the horses graze happily. Pure, clean air, glorious weather. A summerhouse is being built for the officers' mess.

18 may. Complete peace and quiet. We are suddenly awakened around 3:00 a.m. by a violent storm that causes excitement and disquiet. The wind blows through all the cracks and crevices, windows, and doors, and drops of water fall onto our heads. But the storm is soon over, and we go back to sleep. A lovely day, hot summer weather.

19 may. The hot weather continues, and I take the opportunity to take an early open-air bath. Sadly, my dolce far niente is disturbed by an order to report immediately to our position in Olszany. I dress quickly, swing onto my horse, and ride there in shortest possible time. We must receive Army Commandant Boroević. He arrives at 10:00 a.m., we introduce ourselves to him, and he enquires about the state of my medical unit and gives a speech orienting us on the general situation, which he describes as very favorable. Then he travels to the troops at the front; we await his return, which takes place at 11:30 a.m., and we ride back to Krzeczkowa. On the way, we inspect a demolished howitzer with tube damage. In the afternoon, most of the men bathe in the stream flowing by—I decide on a cold footbath but go so far as to take my leather waistcoat off. Another storm threatens toward evening, but doesn't occur; however, it cools the air down a bit. From today, we are in reserve. Our stay here cannot be for long; nevertheless, I start inoculating the men against typhoid fever.[56] The ski division is disbanded, and I exchange my batman, who excels only in his special stupidity, for a German lad named Schweiger. I believe that I have made a good deal because I have had nothing but bad luck with my batmen so far: this is my fifth one, already.

20 may. We are not masters of our own time! We have enjoyed it here so much; our summer huts are almost finished. Everything is wonderfully green, a narrow little stream flows through the meadows like a silver thread. And in addition this glorious warm summer weather—we thought we could establish ourselves in this lovely place, and live comfortably for a while. But no! Suddenly the order to depart arrives at 10:00 a.m. At 1:00 p.m., in torrid humidity, we mount our horses with full stomachs, trotting intermittently; we travel up and down the mountains until, at 6:30 p.m., we arrive, tired, faint, and exhausted, in Truszkowice.[57] The baggage train arrives only at 8:30 a.m., so dinner is also late and it is 12:30 a.m. before we can go to sleep. The farmers' houses are nice and clean; I share a room with Captain Prachowny.

21 MAY. Weather has deteriorated: rain hangs in the air but does not fall all day. We remain here—still in reserve. The eleventh infantry division is quartered in one half of the village. The chief medical officer is Oberstabsarzt I Klasse Dr. Jun.

22 MAY. Order to march off at 3:00 a.m.; we ride off at 4:00 a.m., traveling through Biblo,[58] home of the seventeenth royal commandos. We take our directives and ride off to Radochonce,[59] where we join up with the mountain corps, with orders to travel north to Medica-Mosciska.[60] In the evening, I receive the terribly sad news from Loreia[61] that Mila has died in Krasnoyarsk. I do not need to describe how deeply this shakes me. I cannot escape from this thought for a minute—it's just terrible.

23 MAY. Whit Sunday! A great battle looms but does not develop; apparently we are not completely prepared for it yet. Italy concerns us greatly, because war will surely come with our dear friend and ally.

24 MAY. The attack scheduled for yesterday begins today at 3:30 a.m.: tremendous cannon fire. Our front would have advanced had the right flank not been blocked because of heavy Russian artillery fire from the flank. The Russian attack weakens after two hours of battle; the front is quiet for the rest of the day.

Figure 2.2. Gravestone of Dr. M. Reitzes, who died of typhoid fever in Krasnoyarsk, Siberia. Photograph courtesy of the Leo Baeck Institute.

During the afternoon, news comes that Italy has declared war on us.[62] We have already become accustomed to the idea that this would happen, so the occurrence itself does not make such a big impression on us. But still, it is our only topic of conversation all day. A night attack is planned, to occupy the railway section of Moscicska.[63] We are with German troops—even our quarters are mixed one with the other. A German dragoon Lieutenant Baron Schichtling is our regular dinner guest. German singers entertain us beautifully. I am put directly in charge of no. 3/9 mobile reserve hospital.

25 MAY. Heavy night fighting continuing into very early today, without significant success. Except for the plague of sand, which becomes greater with time, the weather is very good. Evenings are very pleasant: German singers sing patriotic songs, and we join in enthusiastically. This lasts until about 11:00 p.m. Our Army Commandant Boroević obtains a similar command on the Italian Front and is replaced by Commandant Prihalto.

26 MAY. The battle for Przemysl is extremely violent: each individual hilltop must be captured, one after the other. In the north, Mackensen is making great progress: in two days he has taken more than twenty-five thousand Russians captive, as well as sixty-four artillery pieces, many machine guns, and a great deal of other material. We too, together with the Germans, take 1,600 prisoners today—but little ground is won. Therefore, we still remain here. Weather beautiful—no mail.

27 MAY. The front is completely quiet: is this not the calm before the storm? We are still here. It's very hot and dusty: the ground has dried up, and we need rain badly. Our mess is an open barn on the side of the road, so our food contains a great deal of dust. During the evenings, the German Lieutenant Colonel von Schlichting keeps us company.

28 MAY. Command changes position from south to *north*. Living conditions here are better; we are closer together and not so dispersed, in the midst of the Germans—who like to take the best for themselves and leave nothing for others—but we are nearer the front, and shooting does not let up. As soon as we arrive, it starts to rain. For the first time this month, rain sees to it that we arrive in our new quarters soaked. It rains repeatedly during the course of the day, which is certainly good for the seeds. The air has cooled down significantly. In the evening, we invite the German Brigadier General von Jarocky with his chief of general staff and Lieutenant Colonel von Schlichting, over to us. A very animated and jolly evening; the German choir sings German war songs. We part at 10:30 p.m.—fairly quiet at the front.

29 MAY. Overcast weather all day—some rain toward evening. Heavy Russian fire during the afternoon, without significant success. The chief medical officer of seventeenth corps Dr. Jun appears this evening. He looks dreadful, dried up like a mummy, and every bit as rotten as he was fifteen years ago in Czostkow.[64] He still cannot look anyone directly in the eye—bad conscience!—

and acts as if he doesn't know me at all. Members of our general staff are invited to the Germans in Radochonce this evening for dinner.

30 MAY. A nice, sunny day—very hot. During the morning, I ride to our division medical unit, returning in the afternoon. An early violent cannonade against the southwest front before Przemysl—I have no idea whether it is successful. The whole day is quiet, but in the evening, news comes that tenth corps has stormed and taken the fortress of Pralkowce west of Przemysl[65]—great rejoicing everywhere. News from the Italian Front isn't bad either. The Italians run away after the first shot—what brave wops they are!

31 MAY. No change. We are still here, dining daily off the very favorable press reports from Italy. We are pleased with the successful shelling of Rimini and Ancona. Weather remains good.

1 JUNE. During the morning, a visit with Quartermaster First Lieutenant Steiner from fourth battalion, where I also meet Captain Redl. We are very pleased with the news that Stryj[66] has been taken—the Russians have apparently lost fifty officers and nine thousand men are taken captive, as well as sixty artillery pieces and a lot of other war material.

2 JUNE. A heavy bombardment is ordered, begins at 2:30 a.m., and lasts more than an hour, without any real success. The infantry cannot advance because of heavy fire from the flanks. Weather very good: just a little sprinkle toward evening.

3 JUNE. Early news comes that the Germans have broken through the northern Front of Przemysl and entered the city. At 9:00 a.m. our tenth corps enters its former peacetime garrison headquarters: enormous rejoicing everywhere. During the evening, a telegraph comes from the Hofburg that Corps Commandant Martini has been awarded the Crown Order First Class. Indescribable joy. Weather very good.

4 JUNE. As expected, the Russians depart during the night, in a northeasterly direction. Early in the morning, we take up pursuit. Command leaves Radochonce at 8:30 a.m. and travels first to ¤ 291, where they remain until 3:00 p.m., then on to ¤ 282. A terribly hot and humid day, smelling of heavy storms, which develop around 4:00 p.m. We take refuge in a barn in Moczerady.[67] The attack does not advance at the start, so our commander decides to stay here for the night. The quarters are wretched and filthy, with a million flies—just horrible—the storm changes to a steady rain, which lasts all night: very good for seeds, less good for our poor men in the trenches.

5 JUNE. Skies still overcast, but gradually sun breaks through and it becomes warm; the ground dries quickly. We stay here today as well—I change my filthy quarters for ones that are not much better—but at least I am alone there. The division medical unit arrives today; no. 3/9 mobile reserve hospital, which is under our control, is on the way to Radochonce. The Russians are here in a prepreared, fortified position and must be flushed out by our artillery.

6 JUNE. Situation unchanged. We still remain here—I change my quarters yet again, after I find crawling company; my new quarters are thoroughly cleansed. In the afternoon, the general staff—myself included—are invited for a nice chat with Lieutenant Colonel von Schlichting. In the evening, we invite four German gentlemen, physicians included, for dinner.

7 JUNE. The attack continues today—we ride to our vantage point on ¤ 260 on the Chausee Mosciska—we lie in wait in the forest on the road to Lemberg.[68] The attack does not go smoothly—we reach Balice,[69] while the division medical unit stays behind. In the evening, suddenly the order comes to relieve our seventeenth corps and march off to another battlefield. No more details known—the line of march is given as Bykow-Siedliska,[70] so the hope to march into a reconquered Lemberg, which I had so long and so happily looked forward to, has been dashed. Quarters in Balice are no less wretched; the farmer's room is awful, mainly because of the unbearable plague of flies—no more sleep from 3:00 a.m. onward.

8 JUNE. Ordinary march from Balice to Siedliska. Depart 7:30 a.m., arrival 11:00 a.m. During lunch, the order comes to depart for Przemysl. On the way, we inspect the fort at Siedliska, which is really worth seeing. It was thoroughly destroyed by our army before the fall of Przemysl: the picture of destruction is devastating. The weather is very hot, so the afternoon march is unpleasant. But all goes smoothly under the leadership of our Chief of General Staff Stetter, and we reach our destination after only one hour. Very good quarters, which make a good impression and are very clean. Nothing to buy in the shops that are open.

9 JUNE. March further along the San to Dubiecko[71]—a forced march of more than thirty-two kilometers for command, forty-two kilometers for rank and file. Our own line of march is south of the San, so the detour is necessary. The march is burdensome: very hot indeed, traveling almost all the way on the trot. Arrival in Dubiecko at 2:30 p.m. Quarters with Pharmacist Goldschmidt, a former gymnasium colleague. The room is spacious but its cleanliness not very impressive. His wife is hideous, despite multiple layers of makeup—if only she knew how little she impresses me. Dinner at 10:00 p.m.

10 JUNE. March (regular pace) continues: we travel twenty-seven kilometers through Bacorz, Delegowka to Zabratowka.[72] Departure early at 6:45 a.m., arrival 12:30 p.m. with two hours of rest. March is very unpleasant and strenuous today as well because of the heat. Very good quarters with Captain Auditor Schneider and Captain Prachowny at a basket weaver's home.

11 JUNE. Today a short march of only sixteen kilometers to Lancut.[73] Leave 7:00 a.m. early, arrive at 9:30 a.m. Heat is already unbearable early: the giant plague of choking dust makes things even worse. The troops are outside the town. Today we leave the realm of seventeenth corps and return again to tenth corps, which belongs to the fourth army—under command of the German

Field Marshal von Mackensen. Quarter in priest's house—I share a nice, clean room with the sexton and allow myself the luxury of a bath. The town itself looks nice and hasn't suffered much from the Russians. Castle Potocki is completely intact.

12 JUNE. A twenty-four kilometer march in great heat and huge amounts of dust: we have arrived in the sand region. The fast ride lasts from 7:00 a.m. early to noon, with a two-hour rest. The entire division is accommodated in Brzoza-Krolewska:[74] myself in the town center near the church (with the organist). The house has a piano and an old barrel organ. It's heated because of the baking of bread, but full of children and flies. I therefore prefer to sleep in the open under a temporary canvas. A humid night, so sleeping out in the open is not unpleasant.

13 JUNE. Rest day, which does all of us a great deal of good and has become urgent, to catch up with the mail, which almost doesn't function—not at all to the hinterland, and only very slowly indeed to us. Weather becomes overcast toward evening, with rain forecast tomorrow. A very strong wind at night, which threatens to carry away the tent canvas over my head—so no more sleep this night. In any event, the command to march off comes at 4:00 a.m. Our division is going over to the attack.

14 JUNE. Departure at 7:30 a.m.: first to vantage point ¤ 189 south of the church near Giedlarowa,[75] where we remain all day, only entering the village at 8:00 p.m., when darkness falls; we take up quarters near the church. I have a nice, clean room all to myself, a bit farther away from the church. Ninth corps command also has this vantage point—so I have the opportunity to talk to my old comrade Chief Medical Officer Dr. Radczy. The day is not very interesting, with uncomfortable, windy weather, a result of yesterday's storm. Finally, mail in the evening—one from Tinka, only *one* from my adored wife, and one from father.

15 JUNE. Weather really cold with rain at times; quite unpleasant. Everyone is cloaked up again. We depart for yesterday's vantage point at 7:00 a.m.—our troops are already over the San, but advancing slowly—they hardly manage to win ¤ 183. We return to our comfortable quarters (which are much appreciated) at 7:00 p.m.

16 JUNE. Command remains in the division for today. Unfortunately, we do not find out about this soon enough, and spend the entire day ready to march. Weather much warmer. Afternoon burial of a cadet from fourth battalion—the poor lad was hardly nineteen and had come direct from cadet school. At the burial, I meet Surgeon Major Dr. Breuer. His duties are the same as mine, but he blows them up out of all proportion. I would have to lie if I said the same thing about myself.

17 JUNE. The Russians have departed during the night, with our soldiers in hot pursuit in the early morning. Command rides off at 7:00 a.m. through

Rzuchow,[76] where we cross the San on a pontoon bridge: a permanent one is in the process of being built. We proceed through Kurylowka,[77] and to the north we cross into Russian territory again at 4:00 p.m. We travel further through Kulno to Lipy Dolny,[78] where command remains until the troops have marched to the Tanew River.[79] It's already 8:00 p.m. when we arrive at the huntsman's lodge, and the baggage train only arrives to 10:00 p.m., so dinner is at midnight. The day has been very strenuous, but luckily the weather remains good, not too hot. But instead of the heat, there is this awful dust—this Tanew region looks like a desert, with its huge sand drifts.

18 JUNE. The division remains here—troops fortify their positions on the Tanew. Weather very good. I am quartered alone in a small room of a very clean little house not far from the huntsman's lodge.

19 JUNE. Command with the immediate general staff ride out to our positions: we stay behind, enjoying the peace and quiet.

20 JUNE. Troops are preparing for long drawn out Russian resistance. Weather good: cooled down somewhat.

21 JUNE. Situation unchanged. Weather bad: overcast, cool, rain at times, heavy rain in the evening, lasting all night. The general staff are invited to dinner at corps command to Zagrody Nakliekic:[80] I am taken along as well. Return at 11:00 p.m. after a lively evening. The chief corps medical officer is ill and does not come to dinner. I find out from him that our Corps Surgeon General is General Terenkoczy.

22 JUNE. Overcast all day, but no rain. The sand has its advantages: there is no mud.

I spend the free time reading—I am currently reading *Alraune*, an interesting book. In the evening, we receive the happy news that my hometown of Lemberg is again in our hands. I am happier about that than anyone else.

23 JUNE. Another sunny, warm day. In the afternoon, Corps Commandant von Martini with five of his staff members dine with us—a splendid menu, with musical accompaniment from the eighty-ninth infantry regiment, which has just arrived with a new battalion. Our division is again as strong as it was when we left—about fourteen thousand men.

24 JUNE. Weather good, not too hot, a little rain toward evening. Otherwise nothing. I hand in my vacation request.

25 JUNE. Very humid, even very early in the morning. Afternoon visit with fourth battalion. I find the officers corps at table celebrating the decoration of an officer of the third with the Golden Medal of Bravery. I remain there until afternoon. At 5:00 p.m. I return with Commander Colonel Rosenzweig and Major Heller; we stay there until 7:00 p.m. A short storm toward evening.

26 JUNE. Today as well, a short-lived storm toward afternoon, which helps clean the air and does not disturb our very pleasant stay. I am very satisfied

with my quarters—Captains Krämer and Prehal and Major Groër are my neighbors.

27 JUNE. Situation unchanged. At dinner, we again have Corps Commandant Martini with eight members of his staff as guests. Music from the fortieth infantry division. A beautiful summerhouse serves as our mess. A beautiful stay in the country! Hopefully, the war is not prolonged by our laziness!

28 JUNE. Anniversary of the death of Archduke Franz Ferdinand. Field mass with fourth battalion to which command rides out. Commander Martini comes but is too late for the mass. But he does take the miserable march past. Weather glorious; by 9:30 a.m., after a moderate gallop, we are in our station again.

29 JUNE. As usual, the Russians have departed during the night. Our vanguard troops are immediately ordered to advance. Command rides off at 1:00 a.m. in the direction of Krzemien.[81] Meanwhile, I receive telephonic approval of my fourteen-day vacation request, at the same time as Captain Krämer and Second Lieutenant Landig. And so we do not march with the rest, and start our return trip home at noon. A tiring and thorny trip. First by car/wagon to Lezajsk;[82] this goes smoothly, taking less than two hours. We are supposed to travel further by car, but there are great difficulties and a long delay. Once we get going, we arrive in Lancut in less than an hour. There are unfortunately no regular trains—all are fully occupied transporting German troops. So there is nothing left but to jump onto one of the overfilled trains.

30 JUNE. We arrive in Cracow at 6:30 a.m. The regular local train only departs from here at 3:00 p.m. Finally, at 4:00 a.m. the next morning, we arrive in Vienna.

31 JUNE. I am met at the station by my darling Olga who, because of a misunderstanding, has spent the entire night at the station.

It is not the purpose of this diary to describe my vacation, so I leave it out. It is unfortunately too short; I spend the whole fourteen days in the bosom of my family in Helenental bei Baden.

13 JULY. Depart from Helenental in the afternoon and travel in the direction of Tarnow that evening. I arrive at the assembly point at 6:00 p.m. the next day.

14 JULY. I meet up again with Captain Krämer and Lieutenant Landig, stay there all day.

15 JULY. At 7.28 p.m., we travel on together to Przeworsk.[83] A very boring journey that lasts all night.

16 JULY. We find out here that our instructions have been incorrect and that we have to travel back to Debica, and from there on to Rudnik.[84] A train goes there after a two-hour delay, and we must travel back that same long way: an awful trip. Hardly have we traveled fourteen kilometers when the train stops on open track and stays there a full twelve hours, so we only arrive in Rozwadow[85] at 2:00 p.m. After refreshing ourselves at the station kiosk, we travel by truck to Zaklykow,[86] where we are put up comfortably for the night with a Jewish family.

18 JULY. Early at 8:00 a.m., we travel by wagon, first to Krasnik (location of tenth corps command), and from there on to Pulankowice[87] to the location of our own command: arrival there around 1:00 p.m. Command is at battle station. Immediately in front of the village, we are solemnly welcomed back by two Russian shells: the second lands hardly two hundred paces from us.

The division medical unit is in Krasnik. Weather very hot and humid—rain toward evening, which lasts all night. During my vacation, a change in division command has occurred. Commandant Lipošćak has been given command of a Croatian group in Bukowina and is replaced as commandant by General von Sellner, an artillery officer, who looks very young but is very polite and friendly. Militarily, he hardly measures up to our Commander Lipošćak. In contrast to Lipošćak, the opinion of chief of the general staff, Major Heller has a decisive influence on von Sellner's orders; he is very diligent riding out to the daily vantage point, even in cases when one can see as little from there as from quarters.

19 JULY. It keeps on raining. The Russians have apparently withdrawn during the night: this is later confirmed, and pursuit begins. Command rides off at 10:00 a.m. and arrives at ¤ Kazmierow;[88] toward evening we take quarters in Kempa Grange.[89] Accommodation miserable. To the right of the mess—acting simultaneously as mass quarters—is the general staff office, at its left the telephone room—so no rest. Weather continues to be bad, overcast, cool; just as we march off, rain comes down.

20 JULY. Command leaves at 8:00 a.m. for yesterday's vantage point. Attack on the Russians is scheduled for noon, so morning is quite boring. Lunch is brought out to us. At 4:30 p.m. attack, postponed that morning, is ordered to begin. Very heavy artillery fire begins: we are victorious in less than an hour. The Russians give up in droves: by evening, three thousand prisoners are in our hands; additionally five machine guns, four infantry munitions wagons; an unending number of rifles, ammunition, etc., are apparently still left in their positions. After orders have been handed out, we ride back to our quarters; a heavy rain comes down, just like yesterday. Excellent spirits at dinner, spoiled a bit by my stomach indisposition. The divisional medical unit advances by 6:00 p.m. to the eastern part of Kempa.

21 JULY. A restless night—at 3:00 a.m. the Russians try unsuccessfully to break through again and regain their lost ground. But we are all given the alarm and are up and about at 4:00 a.m. The day itself passes boringly, without fighting. The division stays where it is, because our neighboring troops have returned. Our commander rides to the daily vantage point alone.

Weather unstable: at noon the sun breaks through, but only for a while. I am fasting today because of a stomach condition. However, as if on purpose, my favorite dish appears at table. I remain steadfast until evening, but then I can no longer resist the culinary delight.

22 JULY. Another restless night, of course, because of the proximity of the general staff, which one should avoid at all costs. Orders arrive at midnight, so no sleep at all between midnight and 2:00 a.m. An attack is ordered for today. At 4:00 a.m. we are awakened and are already at our daily vantage point at 5:00 a.m., where we remain until 7:00 p.m. Fighting goes on all day and is quite successful. We take about eight hundred prisoners and win ground, so an advance can be expected tomorrow.

23 JULY. Another restless night. Corps orders arrive very late again, and we depart by 5:00 a.m.—first to yesterday's heights, where we receive orders to advance. At noon we set off again and arrive in Wierzchowiska.[90] Our division medical unit is already there. Weather very hot and humid, my stomach is kaput—I take quarters in a barn.

24 JULY. We take up position here, and troops dig in. Our task is to tie down the enemy—a short rest for the troops to recover. My quarters are splendid, and I sleep better than I have for quite a long time. This feeling alone is pleasant; my stomach has also recovered and is functioning normally. Weather lovely, very hot, so that, almost completely undressed, I spend the day in my quarters. This freedom, after such long exertions, does me an extraordinary amount of good, and I spend the entire afternoon restoring my body: bathing, washing, etc. My appetite has returned.

25 JULY. Field mass early: naturally I must be there—Decoration of General Prusenowsky, Captain Prehal, and Cadet Pasternak. Sudden rain by afternoon, which lasts all day and deep into the night. Tonight my barn proves to be too ventilated, but that isn't so bad: barns are the best and cleanest accommodation in summer, are they not?

26 JULY. Complete clearing. The front is quiet.

27 JULY. Situation unchanged. Weather unstable and windy. My barn remains in excellent shape; nevertheless, I have a spacious tent built for myself from Russian tent canvas: my field bed is nice and big, but there is still considerable room around it. The roof slants steeply on both sides—the frames have brackets that are held together by pegs. I can even stand up straight in it. At lunch, Captain Pistelka asks me a funny question: do I think about receiving the Red Cross Medal of Honor? Of course I say yes, and am now curious . . . when will it materialize?

28 JULY. Situation the same: great boredom. Weather fine and hot; storms start around 4:00 p.m., but rain worsens the boredom. Tomorrow our offensive is scheduled to begin again—good luck!

29 JULY. Start of offensive along the entire line. We are up and about by 5:00 a.m.—a violent bombardment. Corps command, with several staff members, comes to stay with us all day. Unfortunately, the attack doesn't make any real progress, and command rides back at 6:00 p.m.; we remain in our quarters. Weather good.

30 JULY. During the night, the enemy departs—at dawn our troops pursue them. We dine early and ride off by 11:00 a.m.: through Belzyce and Palikije,[91] where we take a fairly long rest. We tour Count Potowski's castle,[92] which has remained completely intact and is particularly striking because of its tasteful furniture. A large library, splendid, spacious rooms. A formal bathroom, with all possible bathing equipment. I allow myself to give vent to my stomach ailments. After orders are handed out, we ride further to Milotzin,[93] where I find quarters that evening in the local estate. I try out my new tent, which works splendidly.

Immediately before this, I must pay a visit to my farmer's wife to try to help with her difficult birth. An arm has prolapsed and the head is stuck deep in the pelvis. Rotation impossible despite hours of trying, and no other surgical procedures are possible because of lack of instruments. Spontaneous birth around 11:00 p.m., but the infant is born dead. The division medical unit is in Palikije, and naturally corps command is still there, enjoying the castle's amenities.

31 JULY. We remain here for the moment. Attack on the Russian position in the afternoon that lasts almost all night, with only a few interruptions. Partial success. Thus, command remains at the estate. By comparison, Lublin has been occupied today. Weather unstable, no rain.

1 AUGUST. Situation unchanged, so we are still here. Weather uncomfortable: wind, cold, rain threatens but does not fall yet. I have just found out that I have been put up for the Red Cross Medal of Honor, Second Class. The application was handed into corps two days ago, by Chief Medical Officer Count Vetter von der Lilie.

In the afternoon, renewed attack on Russian positions, which lasts into the night and starts again at dawn the next day, without gaining much ground. The Russians fight a masterful rearguard action. They do not depart until the main body of their troops has retreated and all their baggage trains have gone. No amount of force makes their rearguard move. Only when ordered do they depart of their own accord during the night.

2 AUGUST. Weather nice and warm. The attack is renewed this afternoon and lasts into the night through today, with little success. In the evening comes the news that eight outposts of Fortress Ivangorod[94] have already been taken. Great celebration.

3 AUGUST. Orders come in early that our division is to be transferred west, to relieve German troops. Therefore, lunch at 11:00 a.m. About six hundred wounded during these two days of fighting. Yesterday the divisional medical unit was moved here, after having been relieved by a field hospital. This is the third time during the campaign that this has happened, although according to regulations it should follow the regiment. Theory and practice do not always go together! During the afternoon, orders are altered, and we become corps reserve, marching at 5:00 p.m. to Lugow,[95] where we are accommodated in the castle together with the twenty-fourth infantry battalion.

4 AUGUST. True to form, the Russians depart during this night as well, and we take up pursuit again. We join eighth corps—immediate staff travel by car, the rest of us travel to Kurow[96] Estate by horse, where we arrive at 10:00 a.m. and are quartered in the castle, which has many beautiful rooms; I am given a beautiful, spacious room. We relieve a German division here. The chief medical officer here is Oberstabsarzt I Klasse Dr. Pick: I speak with him preliminarily by telephone. The division medical unit arrives in Plonki.[97]

5 AUGUST. Our division goes over to the attack. Command rides to the daily vantage point, initially in Paljichow Dimba[98] forest, early at 6:00 a.m. The division medical unit arrives in Kloda,[99] advancing very slowly. Suddenly at 4:00 p.m., news comes that Warsaw has fallen! Huge enthusiasm. Troops in the firing line are told immediately, and a giant "hurrah" goes up, musicians play—everyone congratulates each other . . . meanwhile, the artillery thunders on. Command leaves for Barlogi[100] around 6:00 p.m.—a wretched village. I find quarters in a farmhouse in a room that does not look too bad from the outside. But, next morning, the dirty floor that I see doesn't please me, so I pack my things and leave. Weather unstable, sprinkles at times.

6 AUGUST. We receive early notification that our division and present location are to be used for other purposes. The attack continues, but still without success, so we remain here for the moment. I transfer to my tent, where I sleep the next night as well. Weather good, and the stay here quite pleasant. Everything happens here in the open—mess as well.

7 AUGUST. Despite the heavy night attack, not much ground taken. First Ivangorod has fallen, today Lubartow.[101] The Russians are retreating across the Bug River—that is the reason for their obstinate resistance, to gain maneuvering space. Third cholera inoculation at command.

8 AUGUST. A miserable night, with uninterrupted rain: my tent remains waterproof, but continuous rain rattling on my roof disturbs me greatly—I only fall asleep toward morning and get up at 7:30 a.m. Rain lasts all day—horrible—we receive the order to attack this afternoon. Command remains where it is.

9 AUGUST. A rest day. The division stays put. Weather somewhat better. Major Groër and Lieutenant Colonel von Rosenzweig go off on leave: I give the latter a letter for my Olga.

10 AUGUST. Our division departs. We take leave of the seventh army (Archduke Joseph Ferdinand) and join up with the eleventh army under Field Marshal von Mackensen. Departure for Lublin. On the way, we bid farewell to the army commandant, who takes the divisional march past. Arrival in Lublin at noon. The troops remain outside, and command is quartered in the city. I find quarters with Senior Logistics Officer Rosenberg in the Hotel Europejski, which is very good and comfortable. The city is pleasant, with a large-city appearance: elegantly clothed women young and older—their immaculate shoes are striking. We dine in the Hotel Victorya—very good, relatively cheap, but the drinks are outrageously expensive: a small bottle of red wine (genuine French, it is true) costs five crowns, while lunch costs a total of only three crowns.

11 AUGUST. Morning still in the city. At 8:00 a.m., the division is received by Army Commandant Field Marshal von Mackensen. He overtakes us personally, with his reduced staff, and marches in front of the division into the city center, where he deploys and lets the entire division march past: a glorious sight, which lasts one and a half hours: the entire city watches. Command remains in the city all morning: we only depart after lunch. I travel in Captain Jelen's car to Piaski,[102] where we arrive at 3:00 p.m. A backwater of destitute Jews that the Russians have completely burned down. I stay in a tent next to the cemetery wall. Weather very good.

12 AUGUST. Continuation of march, in glorious weather, to Siedliska Wielkie:[103] the same town where we fought a year ago, and I, while still with fourth battalion, had to leave the seriously wounded behind because we were retreating. I travel by car with Captain Krämer, in a hunting vehicle, which he recently acquired from command. We are quartered in a castle that is a picture of most piteous devastation. It still shows signs of former comfort and elegance: electric lights, running water, good furniture—but is demolished. Pictures cut out of their frames, mirrors smashed, etc, etc. I stay in my tent, because there is an awful plague of flies in the rooms.

13 AUGUST. Somewhat overcast morning. I travel on in the car with Captain Krämer and our commander arrives in Surchow, south of Krasnostaw.[104] On the way, we stop for troop disbursement and remain there until this is completed. I can now see how well the echelon is paid: the troops can't understand this, and feel that these large sums should be reduced. We continue on: it becomes very hot, and we only reach our destination, at 2:00 p.m. I quarter in my tent, the others in the priest's house. There is cholera among the civil population. Mail arrives, after a long delay, including a newspaper from 8 August.

14 AUGUST. The march continues, in the same way: I with Captain Krämer in the car, then distribution of pay, then on to Wojslawice,[105] where command is accommodated in the castle of Count Poletylo, which has also been badly damaged, first by fighting, then plundering—this time by the Germans. Glorious beautifully kept park, our mess is decorated with green garlands. I sleep all alone in a nice, spacious room on an excellent bed. A small German harvest team is also here: their Captain is invited to our table. We take small objects with us as souvenirs: I take a marble ashtray and a small heavy photo frame, both basically worthless. We also take away the brass hinges of the doors and

windows, the copper components of the brewery a bronze statue, a gong, etc. But hardly have we departed when the Germans declare this booty as theirs, and our men have to unload everything from the vehicle. In our presence, perhaps they wouldn't have had the nerve to do so.

Figure 2.3. Jewish beggar in Grubieszow. Photograph courtesy of the Leo Baeck Institute.

15 AUGUST. We march forward, direction southeast. Command is divided today as well: one travels by car, the other by horse. I travel in the car with other officers. Weather very nice, only transient rain toward afternoon. After completion of pay distribution, we arrive at Grubieszow:[106] a fairly large and typical Jewish town. I stay at the Ringplatz, in the house of a pharmacist and his seven daughters. Commandant von Sellner is in a room to my right; on my left is an artillery commander, a deputy of Colonel Rosenzweig. Colonel Wolf. Corps command is here as well, and I take the opportunity to introduce myself to Chief Medical Officer Dr. Vetter. Not much to say about the seven daughters: all are flirtatious. Commandant Sellner, who is staying right next to the family room, tells me that out of curiosity he peeped through the keyhole at the same time as one of the daughters—just as curious—was doing the same thing. What a surprise: the one eye to almost touch the other's in the keyhole!

16 AUGUST. Departure early at 7:00 a.m.—our division has already occupied their position. Command arrives in Ustilug (also called Uscilug).[107] Today all of us must ride, because the cars have become unusable; there is no petrol. Weather good, except for a passing shower. At first, we quarter in the priest's house with very nice, clean rooms—I share such a room with Captains Pfefferer and Jelen. There is quite a lot of cholera here; corpses pass along the road near me all the time. Civilians are mainly poor Jews. In addition to inoculation of the command baggage train, I also inoculate Assistant Physician Schwarz and, as far as my vaccine supplies last, the civilian population. People crowd around me and must be held at arm's length, by force if necessary. Women, men old and young, children as well—in total about four hundred are inoculated. The men insist on having their photos taken with a group of buxom young girls.

17 AUGUST. Our division relieves a German cavalry brigade in their positions on the other side of the Bug, and command takes up quarters in the castle, which belongs to a Russian Captain. A beautiful property, with two lovely villas—tastefully furnished. Most of the furniture has been removed, including the many bedframes and wire mattresses, which are all beautiful. The nickel bolts on the doors and windows are exceptionally solid and impressive. Lush park, right next to the Bug.

18 AUGUST. The Kaiser's birthday! Several already celebrate very loudly the evening before. Our commander is very annoyed, and scolds us early in the morning. Church service at 9:00 a.m. The Catholic Church is very small and the Russian Orthodox Church larger. A festive luncheon during which our commander toasts the Kaiser with a well-prepared speech. Plenty of champagne, with the expected consequences. Weather bad since yesterday: rain and a fair amount of mud.

19 AUGUST. Sudden order to depart at 7:30 a.m. The Russians continue their retreat—yesterday Kowno[108] fell. Sadly, we must leave our beautiful quar-

ters. It would have been too good to be true, to stay here, in such a lovely, comfortable room, the best I have had during the entire campaign so far.

Departure after breakfast in a northeasterly direction; command travels to Worczyn.[109] German division command occupies our castle quarters. The men rush here: we are at table when they arrive, and of course they eat with us. Quarters here are miserable: I stay in my tent. Weather bad: overcast, rain in the air.

20 AUGUST. A terrible night. It starts to rain heavily at 2:00 a.m. and lasts for three full hours. Rain leaks through the seams into the tent so that my roof becomes very wet—I cannot wait until 5:00 a.m., and escape into our mess. I feel miserable today: headache, upset stomach—I put myself on a diet. Weather clears up only in the afternoon, but this does not last. More rain by evening. I sleep in mass quarters with ten other men, but the room is large. Is it clean? We shall see.

21 AUGUST. Early order to depart to Kowel.[110] Yesterday the news came that the Germans have taken Nowo Georgyevsk fortress;[111] a total of eighty-seven thousand prisoners, including six generals, and seven thousand artillery pieces. The Germans are ferocious lads! We depart at 7:00 a.m. in the rain, which soon stops. We march without stop all day, arriving at 7:00 p.m. in Duliby,[112] a wretched village, completely abandoned and partially burned down. A picture of what we see repeatedly all over the area. Because of the threat of rain, I take a room with the logistics officer. I am feeling awful, so I fast. The German fifth cavalry division joins us.

22 AUGUST. March to Kowel continues. We part from tenth corps and form our own group with another division. We again belong to the first army, Commandant Prihalto. Heavy fog early, which lifts and it becomes fine, but weather remains unstable. We ride to our daily vantage point early at 7:00 a.m., near the church in Kustycze.[113] Fighting together with the fifth German cavalry division lasts all day, but no significant progress is made. The Russians lob shells that fall around us, without hitting anyone. Toward evening, the twenty-sixth division arrives to reinforce us in tomorrow's fighting.

23 AUGUST. As usual, Russians depart during the night, so we continue our march to Kowel. Command rides off at 10:00 a.m., first to ♮ 200; after staying there for a few hours, we arrive in castle Ruzyn.[114] Very nice rooms, but completely abandoned and in terrible disorder. As a souvenir, I take an album from Dresden and a few unframed pictures. The Germans are fighting directly in front of Kowel: we can hear the noise.

24 AUGUST. The Russians depart again during the night, so we march into Kowel; we enter the town ceremoniously at 10:00 a.m., then off to ♮ 192 and return at 1:00 p.m. Kowel is a Jewish town of about ten thousand inhabitants, most of whom have already fled. The town itself is very dirty and not built up, with one- or at most two-floor houses, and no coffeehouses or inns—no comparison with Lublin. An unimpressive town. We take quarters in the Hotel Bellevue and in a priest's house. The fifth German corps command are also here.

25 AUGUST. We remain here, for the moment. During the morning, arrival of the first *Landwehr* infantry division. I have the job of chief garrison medical officer. I take a lot of supplies and other necessities for our medical unit from the civilian pharmacy. But I still have some time to relax.

26 AUGUST. Weather remains good. The division medical unit transfers to the gymnasium, a beautiful building, comfortably furnished with baths, etc. Dr. Müller is thrilled with his new home; unfortunately, news comes in the afternoon that we must be prepared to march off tomorrow, so again no rest.

27 AUGUST. Departure 6:30 a.m. early, very nice weather. Yesterday the Germans took the fortress of Brest Litovsk,[115] or perhaps, the truth is that the Russians departed from it. They don't have many more fortresses under their control and appear to want to depart from Galicia as well. Apparently, they cannot withstand our sudden march forward. In regular march, command arrives in Geloby[116]—a large town situated on a railway with a splendid station that looks like a glasshouse. The station's water works have been blown up and most the windowpanes shattered, but otherwise the building is intact. A nice-looking courthouse and a school near the station, which we occupy. I even have two rooms at my disposal.

28 AUGUST. Forward march! Departure at 7:00 a.m., with glorious summer weather. We arrive at Czeben[117] at 7:30 p.m.: a very small village with hardly any houses, but those that are there are very nice and clean, occupied by Germans. I take up quarter there with Captains Krämer and Prehal.

29 AUGUST. March further! First to Budiaczewo;[118] after we cross the military bridge near Czeben, we stop for a fairly long rest from noon to 7:00 p.m. We enter into Sikiryczy,[119] where we take quarters in a hunting lodge. This long rest has been wonderfully "successful" for us: the Russians have had the entire day to escape from Luck![120]

30 AUGUST. Battle! The Russians are still offering strong resistance; we have been fighting since yesterday evening, but appear to have pressed too far ahead. The batteries are set up right in front of our house. The heavy fire is very unpleasant and will become much worse if the Russians can seek out (and pinpoint) our own guns. For the moment, small rifle fire is being shot over us. At 4:00 p.m., a civilian driver from our baggage train is wounded in this way. The night is unpleasant, because our passage is a thoroughfare for all who pass to and from the telephone room. Weather very nice and warm, but overcast in the afternoon with rain in the evening.

Our main attack begins at 1:00 p.m.: our heavy artillery preparation works so well that our troops go over to the attack after only an hour. Success is crowned by 1,400 prisoners among them two officers, one colonel, and two doctors. The area on both sides of the railway track and the railway station in Kiwerczy[121] is also taken, with five locomotives, about 180 goods carriages, a few passenger cars, a lot of other war material, two cows, five machine guns, one ammunition wagon, etc.: all in all, very decent booty.

31 AUGUST. Torrential rain all morning, then clearing. Troops continue their advance south. Command rides off at 7:00 a.m. and stays in a small building adjacent to the Kiwerczy railway station. Afternoon, on to Buruchewo,[122] where, at the castle, we "usher out" General Prusenowsky, Lieutenant Colonel Kutchinsky, and the fourth battalion commandant. This is necessary, because during the afternoon the Russians attempt to break through fourth battalion. The moment is so critical that we let our baggage trains travel away and even ride forward to command. But, around 6:00 p.m., their attack stalls, and we return to the manor. We take a few souvenirs with us from there: I take a book on popular medicine written for housewives, unfortunately written in Polish, but with German translation. We stay here, four to a large room, after the little room given to the senior logistics officer and me proves much too small.

1 SEPTEMBER. The Russians have retreated, and our division advances all along the line of march. Command rides off at 1:00 p.m., along the main highway. There are still supposedly Cossacks in Palera,[123] who hold our march up for a while. Toward evening, we take quarters in Palera, with the Czech colony. I stay with Captain Pfefferer in a very dirty farm room. The "fortress" of Luck has been in our hands for two days. Generous provisions have been found, but there is no fortress there.

2 SEPTEMBER. The Russians continue their retreat—the division travels along the highway in an easterly direction. Command rides off at 7:30 a.m. and stays for a while at the Olyka[124] railway station. Fighting on both sides of Putilewka,[125] but no progress. Toward evening we return to the small nearby manor on the roadside, and take up quarters in the post house about five hundred paces away, myself together with the senior logistics officer and Captain Jelen. Weather good.

3 SEPTEMBER. Fighting becomes very heavy. The Russians are resisting fiercely, threatening to go over to attack our neighboring division. Fighting ebbs and flows around ¤ 252 all day; in the evening, the Russians succeed in occupying it, and our troops must retreat over the stream. Very heavy losses. When darkness falls, command goes back and takes up quarters at the Olyka railway station. Our departure seems to be taking place too rapidly: replenishment of provisions and munitions is encountering difficulties. I am staying with the senior logistics officer, in a room full of bugs. Weather overcast.

4 SEPTEMBER. Rain since 7:30 a.m., lasting all day. A pause in the fighting. At 9:00 a.m., we bury Captain Wiener, who was struck yesterday, dying on the spot by from a chance piece of shrapnel on the way from his observation position to his battery in the woods. The cadet who rode next to him was unharmed—fortunes of war. His grave is at the edge of the woods near the railway station. Captain Berner, my old friend from fourth battalion, has arrived here with the ninety-ninth infantry battalion. If the weather were not so miserable, I would go and visit him.

5 SEPTEMBER. Continued quiet at the front. The plan for our further offensive is that tenth corps makes a detour north of Rowno,[126] and then our division should enter Polesia,[127] to cover the corps' retreat.

6 SEPTEMBER. Quiet continues. Rain, with short interruptions, lasts all day, making the roads almost impassable. Our medical unit has worked hard to establish an evacuation stop at the railway station. This is especially good for me, because I can participate in work almost all day.

7 SEPTEMBER. Weather still overcast in the morning, quite cool; clearing in the afternoon. Still quiet at the front; large-scale preparations on our side for the already-mentioned offensive. Ten divisions are gathered together: a tremendous amount of artillery, including heavy cannon. The recently occupied Russian railway station and Russian rolling stock do yeoman service.

8 SEPTEMBER. Artillery preparation begins at 8:00 a.m.—powerful bombardment. But the attack advances slowly and tediously—weather is also unfavorable: it rains most of the day. In the evening, a heavily contested estate is taken.

9 SEPTEMBER. The Russians were so kind as to depart during the night; our troops immediately set out in pursuit. Command only rides out to Olyka at 3:30 p.m., finding quarters in the school and the priest's house in the eastern part of the town. The fourteenth corps command and third division command are accommodated in the west of the town in the famous, magnificent Radziwill castle. News comes in the evening of the fall of fortress Dubno.[128] So Rowno and Grodno,[129] in the far north, are the only Russian-occupied fortresses left.

10 SEPTEMBER. Weather still overcast in the morning, but clearing completely in the afternoon. Command goes back to ¤ 241, but only immediate staff return: I remain behind, using the afternoon to tour the castle. It has 150 completely equipped rooms; inner appointments have been removed, but furniture remains. Our division is tasked to hold its position. The division medical unit is relieved by a field hospital. I share my comfortable, spacious room with the senior logistics officer and Captain Krämer.

11 SEPTEMBER. Only the immediate staff go out to the daily vantage point today; I remain behind. Staff remains outside today until noon, because, in the meantime, the order comes for our division to leave during the night so that we can act as corps reserve. Troops also arrive at Olyka. Weather good; fall is beginning. After a three-day pause, the mail finally arrives, so there is much to read and write.

12 SEPTEMBER. Division rest day. To pass the time, I have started to learn Russian. There are elementary grammar books in the school. Weather glorious.

13 SEPTEMBER. Our rest does not last long. The Russians have broken through at Dereviani,[130] and our division must enter the fighting. Thus, our alternative assignments have been canceled, for the moment. I have no problem with this, because my nice quarters and good weather make this stay quite comfortable.

14 SEPTEMBER. Early departure; it takes most of the afternoon until the troops from the front have assembled here. Command rides out at 1:00 p.m. and arrives in the Konstantinowka[131] estate at 4:00 p.m. We are taking a southeasterly direction, northeast of Brody,[132] where, after we part from fourteenth corps (Roth) and the fourth army (Archduke Joseph Ferdinand), we join with second army (Böhm-Ermolli). Weather lovely, mass quarters in the estate are not bad, five to a room. Captain Jelen's boisterous mood contributes greatly to our amusement.

15 SEPTEMBER. Departure at 8:00 a.m. Weather good, almost too good so early in the morning, and indeed, it changes: at 2:00 p.m., just before we enter the station, we are properly soaked by a downpour. Command travels through Mlynow to Bokujma,[133] a poor, pathetic dump, no quarters—out of pity, the field hospital gives us two rooms, and the school serves as our mess quarters. Weather improves, but remains overcast. The ride was quite rapid, with much galloping, and down the mountain, which caused my horse to suffer a saddle sore.

16 SEPTEMBER. Immediately before our departure in the direction ordered, we are suddenly stopped by army command, to await further instructions, which are not long in coming. To our great surprise, we are ordered back to where we started. Apparently, things are going badly there. The troops march off at 2:00 p.m., and command rides off with them at the same time, the commandant in the car, I with Captain Krämer in the wagon—in consideration of my poor horse—and we arrive back at 6:00 p.m., where our quarters are the same as those on 14 September. The baggage train only arrives at midnight, so we must make do with a cold snack.

17 SEPTEMBER. Early order to return to Palera, where we act as army reserve for the fourth army while a brigade (Klein) is directed to ninth corps. Arrival in Palera in bad, overcast weather that soon turns to rain. In Palera, we hear of the fourth army's terrible debacle. The Russians have broken through in Polesia, and six divisions have been scattered to the four winds. The men are streaming back to Luck, and our division is ordered there as well. All roads are blocked by baggage trains; getting through them is almost impossible. We finally get in the wagon with Captain Krämer and arrive in Luck at 6:00 p.m. The weather has cleared up, but a cold wind is blowing. Unbroken rows of baggage train columns pass through the town, which otherwise gives a very good impression. Electric lights, quite clean, good restaurants in which not much is available, and what's there is really expensive. Quarters in a clean but unfur-

nished private house. Our own baggage train only arrives at 2:00 a.m.: until then I sit in my chair dozing, and only get to bed at 3:00 a.m.

18 SEPTEMBER. Baggage trains continue through the town to the west side of the Styr River. Lack of a decent number of bridges severely complicates the return of baggage trains, yet it occurs without complaint. The fourth army and rear echelon command, who had been quartered here, have left Luck very early and gone to Vladimir Volynsky.[134] Luck is to serve as a bridgehead, under command of fourteenth corps, with whom we newly join up, but only after we have joined with fourth brigade (Prusenowsky). The position is still being established, because rear echelon command has not bothered to do so—culpable negligence! The division medical unit reaches a beautifully equipped Russian Red Cross hospital, which has just been left by field hospital no. 10/2. At 5:30 p.m., a report suddenly arrives that Cossacks have bypassed our flank and are marching toward Luck. Colossal commotion at command: everything is made ready for departure. This only lasts until 8:00 p.m., when we get the report that the Cossacks have been driven back. Gradually, quiet returns—with anxious feelings and fear of the Cossacks, we arrive at 1:00 p.m. in the Hotel Victorya, where we quarter. A mean type of hotel, in which prostitutes go in and out—one can hardly go up the steps without encountering them. Weather unstable, alternating sun and rain, quite cold at night. Today is Yom Kippur!

19 SEPTEMBER. A quiet night. Morning very overcast, windy, and cold—real cough and cold weather. The division medical unit must, unfortunately, leave its nice quarters and go back to the other side of the Styr bridge to Krieninice[135] so that, if retreat would be necessary, this obstacle would not hold us up. We stay here for the moment: two German divisions are marching there from the north, also seventeenth corps from Vladimir Volynsky. Will they be here before the Russians arrive? At 10:30 p.m., just as I am going to bed, alarm to be ready to march is given: the Russians have broken through. Great agitation that only calms down, when we hear that we have repulsed the attack. Calm is restored at 11:30 p.m.

20 SEPTEMBER. A quiet day, and I can finish my correspondence. Weather unpleasant.

21 SEPTEMBER. Weather still unstable and cold, so I travel in the morning to the command train column in Krieninice, to get some warm clothing from my box. Quiet on the front, but a new offensive is already being planned.

22 SEPTEMBER. A terrible day! Early in the day, the Russians unleash a violent artillery bombardment, with no real success. Shooting lasts all day, with short interruptions. It only becomes uncomfortable for us toward evening when, during dinner, heavy Russian shells hurtle over our house. Shells are aimed in all directions, especially at the unfinished large new bridge over the Styr. We all meet immediately in the command office, where we soon receive a report that the Russians have broken through our neighbors the twenty-fourth, between the ninth and seventy-seventh infantry divisions, and taken most of them captive. These are all Ruthenian[136] troops, who fraternize with the Russians during this entire campaign: cowardly pigs, whom the Russians already know very well and designate as *nash* (ours). A soon as they know that there are Ruthenians on the front, they don't always challenge them immediately. Our entire front has now been broken through and Russians extend their attack on our neighboring divisions, with resultant panic. Troops rush back to Luck, pursued by the Russians. Cannon and small arms fire draw closer and closer, and the night is pitch dark. We have the feeling that there is already fighting in the town. Command stays where they are, and only retreat at dawn next day, when commands for retreat are received and new positions on the other side of the Styr have been delineated.

23 SEPTEMBER. An order to arrive on foot into the town, which is still under Russian fire. A difficult journey! But we cross the bridge unharmed: high time that we left, because soon after that the bridge is set on fire by our troops. The Russians are hot on our heels and extinguish the fire so that a Russian armored car hurtles right up to the bridge and, with heavy machine gunfire, prevents our troops from fleeing across the deeper provisional bridge. So, out of five divisions that occupied the bridgehead in front of the town, only a fraction of the number return. From our own division, which originally had about 5,000 men with rifles, only 1,400 return. A terrible debacle.

The remnants of our forces occupying the west bank of the Styr are driven back by the Russians and take up a second position at the forest edge in front of Bogoluby.[137] Command remains in a local house for a while. But soon Russian shells whizz toward us, and we must retreat even further back and ride to Bogoszuwa,[138] where, together with our commandant, we take up mass quarters in a farmhouse with a straw floor in groups of eight, fully clothed.

Our baggage train arrives around midnight and gives us an unappetizing stew: a few spoons of soup and a few bites of hard, bad meat, which I chew and swallow with great difficulty and then throw myself on my "bed," where I more or less sleep, undisturbed by the enemy, until dawn.

Command urgently orders that we hold our present position, because German troops under command of Feld Marshal Linsingen are on the way from the north. Weather not good: fall and cool, but no rain.

24 SEPTEMBER. Quiet all along the front. Early glorious sunshine: we set out at 8:00 a.m. to yesterday's vantage point. Unfortunately, the Germans will only make their presence felt on 28 September: can we hold on to our present positions until then? We can only do so if the Russians don't attack—and indeed, the Russians appear to be moving north. All we have here is airplane activity, and we notice that strong reserves are on the march behind our front. In the evening we change our quarters to the same place as yesterday: a bit more comfortable for us.

25 SEPTEMBER. Fine weather, and quiet on the front, continues. The Russians are gradually moving away: apparently, they are already feeling pressure from the Germans in the north. Toward evening, the order comes to move the division south and join with the third brigade (Klein) again. We also join with ninth corps, chief medical officer Oberstabsarzt I Klasse Dr. Raday.

26 SEPTEMBER. The Russians have vacated Luck again after having hit us so violently. Our troops march south today—command rides out at 1:00 p.m., in lovely weather, first to Ratniewo.[139] On the way, we receive news that the Russians have definitely departed, so we can continue our march to Polonka[140]—a mean little Russian farming village. Quarters in farmers' houses, I with Captain Jelen. By the time we arrive, it's completely dark.

27 SEPTEMBER. Departure 9:00 a.m. early; march continues to Ostrozec,[141] where we arrive at 2:00 p.m. We remain in preparation at the town square until evening and then take up quarters in farmers' rooms, because corps command is accommodated in the local castle. Join up with Brigade Klein. Weather has become unstable.

28 SEPTEMBER. We are reserves for the fourth army and take up our daily vantage points, as well as prepared positions, at Malin,[142] near a Czech steam mill. Quarter at 5:00 p.m. in the school: I in my own nice, clean little room. Pouring rain toward evening and at night. Bulgaria declares war on Serbia.[143]

29 SEPTEMBER. A reasonably quiet day: of the entire division, only the fourth brigade is in action, the third is still in reserve. Command remains here in its quarters. During the afternoon, Chief of General Staff Heller is decorated with the Crown Order. Weather good—no rain.

30 SEPTEMBER. Quiet, good weather continues—all we have to do is to hold our position.

1 OCTOBER. A glorious morning! We rise early at 5:00 a.m. and ride off at 6:00 a.m. Command moves from Malin to Piane,[144] where we arrive at 7:00 a.m. We quarter in the estate, which is only vacated by ninth corps command in the afternoon, and are invited to dine there. The menu is simple but very good—I sit to the right of Dr. Raday, who is very friendly, but whose anti-Semitism does not seem to have changed much. I use the morning for a visit to fourth battalion—it becomes summer warm. Straight after the meal, corps command leaves the manor house, and I obtain a nice, cozy little room for myself: I always prefer it that way.

2 OCTOBER. Quiet at the front. Glorious, sunny, warm fall weather. I have excellent quarters, but unfortunately, corps command have taken all the furniture away. The house has a bath. The keys of the doors are quite original: I take a set with me. In consideration of the quiet current situation, chief of the general staff Major Heller allows himself fourteen days' leave—our ranks have been quite depleted, after Senior Logistics Officer Rosenberg and Captains Pistelka and Jelen have also taken vacation.

3 OCTOBER. Continued quiet at the front, likewise lovely fall weather, despite the fact that leaves are rapidly falling from the trees, which is very sad. Our third brigade entrenches on the northeast edge of the town. Large military tattoo in the evening, with music, in honor of tomorrow, which is the Kaiser's name day.

4 OCTOBER. Field mass at 8:00 a.m.: the fourth battalion, eighty-ninth infantry battalion, fourth light infantry, and staff soldiers also take part. Corps Commandant Kralicek is present with a part of his staff and takes the march past at the conclusion. Immediately after the mass, we are visited by a Russian flier: this time bombs instead of propaganda cards are thrown down at us. The pilot seems to know that our good Pater Niezgoda is very sensitive to such acts of politeness. This doesn't hinder our antiaircraft guns, which welcome the plane solemnly—in the best sense of the word—with shrapnel.

All troop commanders are invited for luncheon. We lead a jolly life here, with singing and music. The cavalry have left one or two pianos behind, and from 5:00 to 7:30 p.m., our dining rooms are turned into a coffeehouse. No table is without its card game. Sellner has his own tarok game, in which I kibitz, and so the time passes very pleasantly.

5 OCTOBER. Work on the fortification is very active; otherwise calm—weather overcast, some rain toward evening.

6 OCTOBER. Overcast all day, rain in the afternoon and at night. Russian artillery is more active than usual today, but not on our front. I spend free time reading and dealing with correspondence.

Figure 2.4. Painting by Bardach of a card game in which he kibitzes. Photograph courtesy of the Leo Baeck Institute.

7 OCTOBER. More rain last evening. Weather is very important, because it's our experience that Russians like to use bad weather for attacks. The same night: telephone at 3:00 a.m. with report that the Russians have broken into our neighboring division and are attacking with hand grenades. More and more corroborating information comes in, and finally at 5:00 a.m. the order comes for us to be ready to march. Command remains here for the moment, while troops are ordered to counterattack. Fighting lasts all day, and all our reserves are thrown in. Finally, our troops succeed in pushing the Russians back to their old positions. The fighting is heavy and costly. Russians possess artillery and ammunition again, and do not spare their use. At night, our third brigade is again placed in their earlier reserve position, and we remain here as army reserves. It has been a hard day!

8 OCTOBER. Quiet at the front: the old order is reestablished. Unfortunately, the weather is not good any more: overcast with periods of rain.

9 OCTOBER. Situation generally unchanged. Because Dr. Müller of the division medical unit is on leave, I travel to Luck today to supervise and inspect medical material, and transfer what we need back to our unit. I leave at 7:30 a.m., returning at 3:30 p.m. The trip goes smoothly; the weather is very bad—overcast, rain at times, strong wind. The process goes smoothly: this branch is well supplied. The collected material that we need can only be transferred tomorrow morning in two transports. I am accompanied by one-year volunteer Pharmacist Alexandru: a very nice fellow. After I have finished, I take the liberty of visiting Major General Dr. Terenkoczy, His reception is friendly, and I remain with him for almost an hour. Late at night news comes that Belgrade has been reoccupied by Central Power troops. Great rejoicing![145]

10 OCTOBER. Very overcast early, with a lot of mud. It must have rained all last night. Clearing during the afternoon, blue sky. Complete quiet at the front. I have been developing a cold for the past few days, which unfortunately stops me from bathing: a pity, because facilities here are so convenient.

11 OCTOBER. It rains again at night, and at times during the day. Mud has become very bad, and my cold is in full bloom. French troops have landed in Saloniki, despite Greek protests.[146]

12 OCTOBER. Weather very nice early, but becoming heavily overcast by afternoon—cold—clearing by evening. My cold is bothering me badly today, and I feel really ill. Quiet at the front continues.

13 OCTOBER. A nice fall day with a great deal of sun—fresh, but not cold. My cold is somewhat better. A Russian pilot has bombed corps command in Ostrozec, wounding eight men. Quiet at the front continues.

14 OCTOBER. Beautiful weather. Our stay here is pleasant, with all sorts of conveniences. My cold is significantly better.

15 OCTOBER. Weather as yesterday, only quite a strong wind. Pilots arrive daily between 7:00 and 8:00 a.m. and bomb us—two today, but no damage.

Since yesterday, a surgery group with Regimental Physician First Class Dr. Demmer has been established here.

16 OCTOBER. Weather overcast, cold wind. Rooms are already being heated, and winter clothing begins to appear. Russians become active at night, but without any success. The entire ninety-first brigade command and surgery group are invited to dine with us.

17 OCTOBER. During the morning, all physicians of ninth corps assemble at field hospital no. 6/9 in Ostrozec for a scientific meeting. Lectures are given by Dr. Werndorf, assistant to Professor Lorenz (orthopedic surgeon in Vienna) and Dr. Demmer about their surgical experiences during the war. Very interesting and informative. I ride back with Dr. Demmer. Weather like yesterday—less pleasant. Occasional Russian firing, heavy at times.

18 OCTOBER. The ninety-first brigade leaves Piane today, and, unfortunately, with them the surgery group. A large part of my daily conversation goes with them. My chats with Dr. Demmer were very lively and pleasant. My only distraction now is the evening tarok games, in which I only kibitz and act as temporary substitute for one of the players. Overcast, mild weather.

19 OCTOBER. I go for a morning walk in the forest with Captain Auditor Schneider. Catwalk into the forest. We are impressed by how the sixty-eighth infantry regiment park their heavy equipment. It's amazing how the men have learned how to install themselves rapidly, even luxuriously. Shelters and huts often look like villas, and inner facilities are often simply incredible. Senior Logistics Officer Rosenberg and Captain Pistelka arrive back from leave during the afternoon and relate a lot of useless news from the hinterland—each one had a great time in his own way.

20 OCTOBER. Finally, another glorious clear fall day! I want to travel to the division medical unit, but the car comes too late. In the afternoon, the order came to move command to Novosiolki.[147] We are all depressed about this—myself especially, because I am doing so well here. My splendid quarters—baths, the lovely surroundings. The baggage train is packed and ready to depart when the change in order comes to postpone moving by a day. Little is gained by this, except that I can spend one more night in my splendid quarters. The baggage train grouses because they have to turn round, unpack, and start the whole process again tomorrow. On the last day I change my quarters one last time, after Count von Trautmannsdorf departs, leaving his quarters to me. The room is, if possible, even more comfortable than my existing one, only one disadvantage: it's in an adjacent building.

21 OCTOBER. Depart early at 6:30 a.m., arrive in Novosiolki at 8:30 a.m. A wretched farming village—the manor house has been burned down, only the school is left standing, so the general staff and the mess are quartered there. I have quarters to myself, but in a miserable farm room that I have to make habitable by all sorts of improvements. Only half the floor is covered with planks. Weather good in the morning, just with a sharp, cold wind. Evening overcast.

22 OCTOBER. We remain here, and our troops work on organization of their positions. Weather unpleasant because of the cold wind; otherwise, the stay is not much worse than in Piane. Our piano has arrived with us, also our mess amenities, which are housed in a very nice, big pub.

23 OCTOBER. Situation unchanged, weather the same. Lieutenant Colonel von Spanochi, chamberlain of the Duke of Toscana, is allocated here for four days of "service training." This is surely the first sign of an imminent peace agreement—when gentlemen from the hinterland crowd to the front to diligently "earn" war decorations! Otherwise, he is a pleasant man.

24 OCTOBER. An enjoyable Sunday morning, with a new physicians' meeting in Ostrozec. Oberstabsarzt I Klasse Scheidl talks about bullet wounds to the skull, and Regimental Physician First Class Kaspazek about infectious diseases—less interesting. A discussion follows the talks, chaired by Surgeon General Dr. Terenkoczy. I arrive there by car, with Dr. Müller.

25 OCTOBER. Cold has suddenly lessened—mild weather, even with transient sunshine. I have made my room livable. The floor boarding has been completed, and the walls mostly covered with my tent canvas, to protect myself from cold penetrating through the cracks.

26 OCTOBER. Rain at night—otherwise, mild weather continues. Major Heller returns from vacation.

27 OCTOBER. Overcast weather, but not unpleasant. Captain of the General Staff Scheiwel returns from vacation.

28 OCTOBER. First, transitory snowfall. Delivery of an apparatus to prepare drinking water to Dr. Luger at fourth battalion. The front continues to be quiet.

29 OCTOBER. A memorable day. Our army commandant Archduke Joseph Ferdinand and his brother Heinrich take lunch with us. It's very cozy—I sit opposite the archduke. Weather overcast, but not too bad.

30 OCTOBER. Heavy hoarfrost early, as if it has snowed, with a strong wind. A Russian flyer is fired upon by an antiaircraft gun of the twenty-ninth light infantry regiment in Piane, and forced to land in the area of the seventh infantry division. Unfortunately, Captain Scheiwel is transferred to the corps of Field Marshal Heinrich Fath.

31 OCTOBER. Snowy landscape! Biting wind and really cold. Quiet at the front. It looks like we will spend the winter here.

1 NOVEMBER. Complete weather change. Mild, overcast, no trace of snow. Major General Klein is decorated with the Leopold Order, which, of course, pleases him greatly.

2 NOVEMBER. Now Captain Prehal, the last member in command, has gone on leave: During the morning, I take the liberty of enjoying a bath at the divisional medical unit, which is splendidly equipped. Weather unfavorable, rain since afternoon. The roads will soon become impassable. Quiet at the front. It will soon become very boring here; at least I can pass the time reading.

3 NOVEMBER. A glorious morning, deep blue sky, sunny and warm. Toward afternoon, weather changes, overcast with passing rain showers, then clearing, so that the Saint Hubertus Hunt[148] can take place at 2:00 p.m. Large participation by officers on horseback, artillery and cavalry, especially command staff. I myself do not take an active part: better so, because the old gentlemen who do come out of it so pooped that it takes a good long time before, with my aid, their hearts and lungs are made to function normally again.

4 NOVEMBER. Another splendid morning, just like yesterday, and with the same change in the weather, almost to the hour. The Russians have been busy all afternoon: heavy cannon fire of all calibers; one killed, only a few wounded. Apparently, they just want to keep us busy and prevent our troops from being withdrawn.

5 NOVEMBER. Violent storm during the night, which continues next morning with very strong winds and overcast weather. Less wind during the afternoon, but increasing again toward evening. Nisch has been taken by the Bulgarians.[149]

6 NOVEMBER. Weather like yesterday, very unpleasant. Situation unchanged.

7 NOVEMBER. Snow during the night, continuing today, but not too heavy; disappears without a trace during the course of the day.

8 NOVEMBER. Damp, cold, overcast weather continues today. Russians have intercepted an advance column of the eighty-ninth infantry regiment but have been driven from their position in front of our line by artillery fire.

9 NOVEMBER. The expected Russian night attack does not materialize. Weather like yesterday.

10 NOVEMBER. Beautiful sunny morning, which I use to visit Malin with Dr. Müller, to inspect bathing and delousing facilities established there by first aid station of the eighty-ninth infantry regiment. They are exemplary in every way. Return at 1:00 p.m.

11 NOVEMBER. Overcast, windy weather again; I remain in my quarters. Heavy rain by evening, lasting all night.

12 NOVEMBER. Morning weather still brisk, clearing up in the afternoon. Daily orders bring news of my appointment as lieutenant colonel. I am privately very happy about this.

13 NOVEMBER. Morning inspection by the first aid station of fourth battalion in Bakoryn,[150] together with Dr. Müller.

14 NOVEMBER. Reconnaissance ride to Worotniewo[151] for no. 9/9 field hospital with Dr. Müller. Good, warm weather, although overcast, with afternoon rain.

15 NOVEMBER. Overcast, damp, cold weather continues with mud. The day is quite boring, but luckily I have a few books to read and there is enough entertainment in our mess during the evening. The regular tarok game with our commander is immortalized by a wonderful caricature by First Lieutenant Geldern. Sadly, like many of his other caricatures, it's commandeered by the general staff for their own collection. And this picture was dedicated to me!

16 NOVEMBER. Visit by Dr. Raday. He is a real nuisance, nagging us with establishment of bathing facilities for troops but not giving us the means to do it.

17 NOVEMBER. Snow all day: by evening we sink in at above the ankles.

18 NOVEMBER. During the night, a stormy wind howls. By morning, the temperature has risen and snow has partially disappeared. Horrible mud, roads almost impassable. East wind continues to blow.

19 NOVEMBER. Predominantly snowy landscape and not so cold, but with large amounts of mud. Our command again loses a member, Senior Logistics Officer Rosenberg, who is being sent on a special mission to Constantinople. He is very happy about this, and I am pleased to have one less unpleasant character among us. He has understood how to inveigle himself into the good graces of command through his bellicose demeanor. But he is their slave, even to the younger lieutenant colonels. He is revoltingly coarse and is, at the end of the day, nothing less than a friend of the Jews.[152] His official farewell takes place this evening: it goes off well but with little excitement. By way of exception, there is no drunkenness, at least while the commander is still present. Only Captain Bergmayer from division cavalry cannot resist the booze and has his obligatory mountainous mug: he cannot tolerate any more than that. The musical entertainment is very pleasant, with singing. Lieutenant Rohrbach, a professional opera singer, sings excellently, as does Major Groër, although he seems less well trained. At 11:30 p.m., we "older gentlemen" (myself included) take our leave.

20 NOVEMBER. More of a winter landscape, as well as the wretched mud.

21 NOVEMBER. Very heavy frost during the night which lasts all day. Temperature −5°C. Pain in my right instep since yesterday, which is getting worse.

22 NOVEMBER. Light frost continues, overcast skies, gray, gray, nothing but gray.

23 NOVEMBER. A beautiful, snowy, frosty winter's day. I would like to ride out to the troops but am stopped from doing so by pain in my foot, localized over the extensor tendon of the great toe. No hope of doing anything today. Since yesterday, together with my other duties, I have also been assigned to no. 9/9 field hospital in Worotniewo.

24 NOVEMBER. Continuing cold wind, which brings with it clouds, snow, and continued cold. Very unpleasant weather. Additionally, the pain in my foot, and the news that my father has developed erysipelas.[153] It's therefore understandable that my mood has dropped below zero. During the past two nights, we have attacked the Russians: last night we brought in thirty-seven wounded and sixty prisoners. I think that that will be it, for a while.

25 NOVEMBER. Weather like yesterday. The ground has almost frozen solid, snow toward evening.

26 NOVEMBER. Snow with moderate cold that lasts all day, so that by evening snow is quite deep. Thank God my father is doing better—unfortunately, I am not: it looks like metacarpophalangeal arthritis.

27 NOVEMBER. Lovely sunny winter's day with a lot of snow everywhere. Calm wind.

28 NOVEMBER. Heavy frost: the window is covered with ice crystals. Cold increases toward evening.

29 NOVEMBER. Frost continues, −15°C. A beautiful, sunny winter's landscape.

30 NOVEMBER. Cold, frosty weather like yesterday.

1 DECEMBER. The cold, frosty weather continues. Today there is also a biting, cold wind that makes remaining outside literally impossible. Moderate thawing weather toward evening. Yesterday I hand in the proposal to award the Signum Laudis to Dr. Müller of our division medical unit.

2 DECEMBER. The cold weather breaks—rain by noon—black ice.

3 DECEMBER. Thawing weather continues, with intermittent rain. The mud gets worse and worse: I try to wear normal shoes today instead of snowshoes, but because of increased pain I have to take them off again by evening.

4 DECEMBER. Snowmelt significantly increased. The mud is indescribable. Today, inspection of the baths under construction in Bakoryn—they are going to be splendid.

5 DECEMBER. Snow is gradually disappearing, but mud is appalling and roads are impassable. Fourth cholera inoculation at command. My own reaction is quite strong, and I am literally ill later in the day. This evening we have a musical evening of recitative. Captain Nestrozzi of the third infantry division, an excellent duet singer, with Major Groër as baritone, and Captain Krämer, an accomplished pianist, give us an excellent evening of diversion. The commander of the third and captain of the general staff are our guests. A delightful evening; it's midnight before we all go to bed. As a result of strong overnight winds, roads have dried out to a degree. The sun shines lovingly again, and the landscape has become friendlier looking. Afternoon overcast and rain again toward evening. My foot will not get better: the swelling has partially lessened but won't disappear completely.

7 DECEMBER. Snow has disappeared, but the mud is atrocious.

8 DECEMBER. Morning sunshine, afternoon overcast.

9 DECEMBER. The mud is gradually drying.

10 december. The ground is somewhat frozen. I put in my application for fourteen days of leave. If only my foot would improve!

11 december. Bad weather with light snowfall. Terrible mud. The night is as black as pitch, and, on the way back to my quarters, I get stuck in the mud—horrible!

12 december. Overcast, mild wind—but complete clearing during the early morning hours with beautiful clear sky and strong sunshine—it becomes so warm that we can dine at an open window. Only the mud is horrible. My leave has already been approved.

13 december. Weather overcast again, but not unpleasant. Corps chief medical officer Dr. Raday has been transferred to fourteenth corps, South Tirol. He was good enough, but liked a great deal of paperwork.

14 december. Overcast and cool, light snow in the afternoon, then increasing cold. Frost during the night. The application to award me with the Signum Laudis has been submitted today. Now I must wait for three months for it to be processed.

15 december. Frosty weather, but still bearable. Morning inspection of field hospital in Worotniewo—very nice: the church has been adapted for medical purposes. Baths and disinfection facilities are exemplary—I can once more wear normal shoes. The swelling hasn't gone away completely, but at least the pain has diminished.

16 december. Light, frosty weather continues—toward evening the cold diminishes, with thawing weather. Commandant Sellner starts his vacation today; Major General Klein takes over for him while he is away.

17 december. Overcast, mild weather

18 december. Same as yesterday.

19 december. Morning sunshine, afternoon overcast again. Springlike weather. I am very excited indeed by my upcoming leave, which I begin in two days' time, although I want to depart tomorrow. Today we are surprised by electric lighting of our command. Soon the trenches will also have electric lighting as soon as the roads improve, and transport of heavy trucks will become possible again. It's amazing what our country achieves in this war.

The new corps chief medical officer Oberstabsarzt I Klasse Dr. Danneberg has arrived and invites me for a discussion tomorrow, just at the time when I want to depart on leave at 8:00 a.m. As it turns out, however, I do not need to appear in person, and he will be satisfied by a meeting with my substitute, Dr. Müller.

20 december. I depart on vacation at 8:00 a.m. with the division medical unit's car with Captain Krämer, arrival in Luck at 11:30 a.m. After a very good lunch, departure at 12:32 p.m. in a first-class coupé that is, however, unheated. We hold out until we reach Kowel at 5:30 p.m., but then we climb into the carriage nearest to the locomotive, which is, at least, heated. Unfortunately, it's a packed-full third-class coach, so we spend the entire night in a sitting position.

21 december. Arrival in Lublin at 5.45 a.m. after a two-hour delay, so we miss our connection—another train departs soon, but only with third class. Captain Krämer leaves me here, because he has a rendezvous with his own wife. Kowel-Lublin is free of snow, but after that, there is a great deal of snow.

Arrival at Rozwadow at 1:00 p.m. The locomotive is attached to the other end of the train, and heating does not reach our coach any more: we are in a pitiable state, freezing cold, and there is no hint of lighting either. Arrival in Cracow at 11:55 p.m., and we travel immediately on to Oderberg,[154] arriving there the next day.

22 december. A horrible night journey, third class packed with people, no heat or electric lights, wretchedly cold. Departure from Oderberg at 6:02 a.m., in a first-class heated coupé—we can literally breathe properly again and the rest of the trip to Vienna goes smoothly: arrival at 2:28 p.m., and I fly into my Olga's arms!

Notes

1. Jasiel (Poland).
2. Borov (Slovak Republic).
3. Not found.
4. A historical region in Central Europe, divided between Romania and Ukraine, located on the northern slopes of the central Eastern Carpathians and the adjoining plains. Before 1918, part of the Austro-Hungarian Empire.
5. Habura (Slovak Republic).
6. Also Laborcz-Mező: Medzilaborce (Slovak Republic).
7. Vyšná Radvaň (Slovak Republic).
8. Probably Saint Basilskard Monastery (Slovak Republic).
9. Lower Szebény (Hungary)? Too far away to be likely.
10. Radvaň nad Laborcom (Slovak Republic).
11. Vyšná Radvaň (Slovak Republic).
12. Latorica River (Slovak Republic).
13. Oreské (Slovak Republic).
14. Second Battle of the Masurian Lakes. By February 1915, 36 percent of the German field army was in the east.
15. Chernivtsi (Ukraine). Czernowitz was the capital of Austro-Hungarian Bukowina; the region was captured by the Russians very early in the war, along with most of Eastern Galicia.
16. Koškovce (Slovak Republic).
17. The Wiener freiwillige Rettungsgesellschaft was the first rescue organization in Vienna, founded on private initiative in 1881.
18. "Tp" in the original.

19. When war began, Italy was nominally part of the Central Powers.
20. Not found.
21. Not found.
22. Zbudská Belá (Slovak Republic).
23. The investment of the fortress of Przemyśl (Poland) began on 16 September 1914 and was briefly suspended on 11 October because of an Austro-Hungarian offensive. The siege resumed on 9 November, and the Austro-Hungarian garrison surrendered on 22 March 1915, after holding out for 133 days.
24. Maribor (Slovenia).
25. Humenné (Slovak Republic).
26. Hrušov, Rožňava District (Slovak Republic).
27. Strážske (Slovak Republic).
28. Košice (Slovak Republic).
29. Eperi(j)es: Prešov (Slovak Republic).
30. Obišovce (Slovak Republic).
31. Muszyna (Poland).
32. Krynica-Zdrój (Poland), the biggest spa town in Poland, as well as a popular tourist and winter sports destination situated in the heart of the Beskids mountain range.
33. Special glass syringe und ingrained metal piston from Berlin instrument maker Dewitt & Hertz; can be assembled and disassembled.
34. Both in Poland.
35. Both in Poland.
36. The Gorlice-Tarnów offensive was the Central Powers' main effort of 1915, causing the total collapse of the Russian lines and their retreat far into Russia. The continued series of actions lasted for most of the campaigning season for 1915, starting in early May and only ending because of bad weather in October.
37. Pętna (Poland).
38. Banica (Poland).
39. Wołowiec (Poland).
40. Nieznajowa, Krępna, Olchowiec, Polany, Tylawa (Poland).
41. Jaśliska (Poland).
42. Tarnaewka (Poland).
43. Wisłok River (a tributary of the San).
44. Tarawka (Poland).
45. Rudawka Rymanowska (Poland).
46. All in Poland.
47. Stróże Wielkie (Poland).
48. Posada Olchowska (Poland).
49. Siemuszowa (Poland).
50. Bircza (Poland).
51. 11 to 15 May is the season of the Eisheiligen (Ice Saints). According to folklore, mild weather only becomes stable after 15 May (*kalte Sophie*).
52. Cisowa (Poland).
53. Olszany (Poland).
54. Jarosław (Poland); Sambir (Ukraine).
55. Krzeczkowa (Poland).
56. A killed typhoid vaccine, first developed by Sir Almroth Wright (1861–1947), had been tested successfully during the Second Boer War. All British and Empire soldiers

were inoculated against typhoid, saving many lives, and other countries followed suit. The vaccine was, like the cholera vaccine, locally toxic.
57. Trushevychi (Ukraine).
58. Byblo (Ukraine).
59. Radokhyntsi (Ukraine).
60. Medika (Poland); Mostys'ka (Ukraine).
61. Bardach's sister.
62. When World War I broke out, Italy declared itself neutral, despite its membership in the Triple Alliance alongside Germany and Austria-Hungary since 1882. Over the course of the months that followed, Italy and its leaders considered how to gain the greatest leverage from participation in the war. Italy received assurances in the Treaty of London, signed in April 1915, that it would gain control over territory on its border with Austria-Hungary stretching from Trentino through the South Tirol to Trieste. The Allies also promised the Italians parts of Dalmatia and numerous islands along Austria-Hungary's Adriatic coast; the Albanian port city of Vlora (Italian: Valona) and a central protectorate in Albania; and territory from the Ottoman Empire. The Italians called this *sacro egoismo* (sacred egoism). Initially, Italy declared war only on Austro-Hungary; Germany would follow a year later.
63. Mostýs'ka (Ukraine).
64. Czostków (Poland).
65. Prałkowce is a village within Przemyśl County.
66. Stryi (Ukraine).
67. Mocherady (Ukraine).
68. Lviv (Ukraine).
69. Balychi (Ukraine).
70. Byków-Siedliska (Poland).
71. Dubiecko (Poland).
72. Bachórz; Dylągówka, Zabratówka (Poland).
73. Łańcut (Poland).
74. Brzóza Królewska (Poland).
75. Giedlarowa (Poland).
76. Rzuchów (Poland).
77. Kuryłówka (Poland).
78. Kulno, Lipiny Dolne (Poland).
79. River in southeast Poland, a tributary of the San.
80. Probably Naklik (Poland).
81. Krzemień (Poland).
82. Leżajsk (Poland).
83. Przeworsk (Poland).
84. Dębica, Rudnik nad Sanem (Poland).
85. Rozwadów (Poland).
86. Zaklików (Poland).
87. Kraśnik, Pułankowice (Poland).
88. Kaźmierów (Poland).
89. Kępa (Poland).
90. Wierzchowiska (Poland).
91. Bełżyce and Palikije (Poland).
92. Probably Poniatowski.

93. Milocin (Poland).
94. Ivangorod Fortress (on Russia-Estonian border, overlooking the Narva River).
95.Ługów (Poland).
96. Kurow (Poland).
97. Płonki (Poland).
98. Not found.
99. Kłoda (Poland).
100. Barłogi (Poland).
101. Lubartów (Poland).
102. Piaski (Poland).
103. Siedliska Wielkie (Poland).
104. Surhów, Krasnystaw (Poland).
105. Wojsławice (Poland).
106. Hrubieszów (Poland).
107. Ustyluh (Ukraine).
108. Kaunas (Lithuania).
109. Worchyn (Ukraine).
110. Kovel' (Ukraine).
111. Twierdza Modlin (Poland).
112. Duliby (Ukraine).
113. Kustychi (Ukraine).
114. Rishyn (Ukraine).
115. Brest (Belarus).
116. Holoby (Ukraine).
117. Czebenie (Poland).
118. Bodyachiv (Ukraine).
119. Sokyrychi (Ukraine).
120. Lutsk (Ukraine).
121. Kivertsi (Ukraine).
122. Borokhiv (Ukraine).
123. Not found.
124. Olyka (Ukraine).
125. Putilyvka River (Ukraine).
126. Rivne (Ukraine).
127. Polesia, Polesie or Polesye is a natural and historical region of Eastern Europe, stretching from parts of Eastern Poland, straddling the Belarus—Ukraine border and into Western Russia.
128. Dubno (Ukraine).
129. Grodno (Hrodna)(Belarus).
130. Derev'yane (Ukraine).
131. Konstantin(i)ovka (Ukraine).
132. Brody (Ukraine).
133. Mlyniv, Bokijma (Ukraine).
134. Volodymyr-Volynskyi (Ukraine).
135. Kremenets' (Ukraine).
136. A group of Slavic peoples (also known as "Rus") with their own language and culture, the majority of whom live in southwestern Ukraine, eastern Slovakia, southesast Poland, northeast Hungary, and northwest Romania.

137. Boholyuby, near Lutsk (Ukraine).
138. Bohushivka (Ukraine).
139. Ratniv (Ukraine).
140. Hirka Polonka (Ukraine).
141. Ostrozhets' (Ukraine).
142. Malyn (Ukraine).
143. Although the smallest member of the Central Powers in area and in population, Bulgaria made vital contributions to their common war effort. Its entry to the war heralded the defeat of Serbia, thwarted the foreign-policy goals of Romania, and ensured the continuation of the Ottoman war effort by providing a geographical conduit for material assistance from Germany to Istanbul. The actual date of war declaration against Serbia was 14 October.
144. P'yanovichi (Ukraine)? Too far to reach within a day's riding.
145. After Bulgaria had joined the Central Powers, Serbia was attacked from three sides. Belgrade was taken, Serbia occupied, and the Serbian Army retreated over the high mountains to the Albanian coast with very heavy losses. They were evacuated to the Island of Corfu until 1918.
146. British, French, and other Entente troops started to arrive in Salonika (Thessaloniki) on 15 October 1915 to oppose Bulgarian advances into Macedonia. King Constantine blocked Prime Minister Eleftherios Venizelos's desire that Greece join the Entente until 1917, when Constantine was deposed and Greece declared war on the Central Powers.
147. Novoselki (Ukraine).
148. Saint Hubert (about 656 to 727 CE) is honored among sport hunters as the originator of ethical hunting behavior.
149. Niš (Serbia).
150. Bakoryn (Ukraine).
151. Vorotniv (Ukraine).
152. This doesn't make sense, unless Bardach is being sarcastic.
153. Subcutaneous infection caused by group A streptococci.
154. Bohumin (Czech Republic).

CHAPTER 3

1916
The Brusilov Offensive and Its Aftermath

20 JANUARY. After the end of my fourteen days' vacation, I return to my division, arriving in Novosiolki,[1] where it is still located, at 2:00 p.m. Everything is as it was before, except that our Commandant Sellner has "become ill" during his vacation and has taken six more weeks' leave. He is substituted for by Major General Prusenowsky. On the way to command, I stop in Ostrozec[2] to report to the new corps chief medical officer Dr. Danneberg. His nose is out of joint, because I failed to report personally before my vacation. He did not have the courage to demand this directly at the time, leaving it up to me. I did not think it essential at the time, but he certainly puts a flea in my ear about it now.

The weather here is far from being as mild as it was in Vienna. Even without the bad weather, the mood is depressed. Perhaps I am mistaken and ascribe my own bad mood to that of the others. I take up my old quarters, of course.

21 JANUARY. By command of the chief medical officer, I must depart for Romanow[3] to the eighty-ninth infantry regiment, which has recently reported a few typhoid and two typhus cases. Weather unpleasant, cold and damp. It's afternoon before I return. In the meantime, the order has arrived for the division to depart tomorrow, so I arrive just in time. The division is to be used in reserve. Command moves to Gerazdza:[4] we may soon be transferred, perhaps away from this corps. This would not trouble me in the least because I do not work well with my superior: he grumbles if conditions are not exactly like those in peacetime.

27 JANUARY. Command departs for Gerazdza: I travel in the car, because the commandant and Major Heller are not using it. This new situation may only be temporary—it's bad enough as it is. I see German soldiers all around me, worn out by war. I am accommodated next to Major General Prusenowsky in a narrow, small, greasy room.

Morning weather clear, sunny, but cold, afternoon thawing weather. A great deal has happened since my absence on leave:

On 11 January, capture of Lowcen.

On 14 January, occupation of Cetinje.[5]

On 17 January, Montenegro asks for a peace settlement. Such occurrences should not be underestimated.

23 JANUARY. We remain here for the troops to rest and reequip. Our accommodation is scattered around all over the place: the staff office, telephone room, and mess. March weather, sunshine alternating with overcast skies, and a strong wind. Food is very tight: we have become somewhat spoiled by our quarters in Novosiolki.

24 JANUARY. Unchanged, the weather as well. Great amounts of mud.

25 JANUARY. Morning inspection of fourth battalion, located in the same village. I have a big row with the commandant Lieutenant Colonel Kuchinka, because he demands a written order for this inspection, which I naturally do not have. I take the liberty of sending a fulminating report to command, but do nothing else about it. Nothing much will happen under the command of General Prusenowsky: if he just has good food and drink and can sleep a great deal, he is satisfied. Everything else takes a back seat.

The division medical unit is not prepared and ready—it's resting, for the first time during this war. Evacuation goes directly to field hospital no. 9/9 in Worotniewo.[6]

26 JANUARY. Rain during the night—sunshine and very warm weather (for this time of year) by afternoon, but oh, the mud!! From today, my room has electric lighting.

27 JANUARY. No changes. Weather unfavorable, with rain and mud.

28 JANUARY. Beautiful, sunny winter's day. A light frost so that the ground is dry.

29 JANUARY. Weather even better than yesterday: it's a pleasure to be outside. A high visit during the afternoon; the representative of Kritek, the furloughed army commandant of Archduke Joseph Ferdinand, inspects the troops and dines with us with some of his staff.

30 JANUARY. A boring, gloomy, overcast, cold day—I am frozen through.

31 JANUARY. Morning still overcast, clearing in the afternoon. Sunshine and moderately cold.

1 FEBRUARY. Glorious winter's day with a lot of sun and moderately cold.

2 FEBRUARY. Beautiful weather, just a few degrees below zero. Very sunny, wintry warm during the afternoon. Kaiser Weather to honor our Heir to the Throne, Archduke Karl Franz Joseph, who inspects the fourth army of our division. Today only the fortieth infantry division and the fourth light infantry battalion are inspected: I am not present.

3 FEBRUARY. Inspection continues: the Archduke is very genial, shakes the hand of each officer and every infantryman who is decorated. The lovely weather continues.

4 FEBRUARY. A beautiful day, a worthy successor to yesterday. No more beautiful days can be thought of at this time of year, during this season, and at this location—no sign of the fabled terrible Russian winter.

5 FEBRUARY. I spoke too soon. Today is overcast and cloudy again—not too cold.

6 FEBRUARY. Weather like yesterday. I travel to Luck[7] at 2:00 p.m. with Dr. Müller, arrival 3:00 p.m. Starting at 5:00 p.m., large German and Austrian physicians' meeting in the cinema hall. Impressive doctors' participation, even a few general staff officers are present. Chairman Surgeon General Terenkoczy gives a short but good opening talk, followed by several interesting lectures and demonstrations by Professor Ballner,[8] Colonel Dr. Scheidl, and many others. These are followed by discussion, in which the German physicians take an active part. By 8:00 p.m., only the first half of the program is completed; the meeting is ended for the day, and the balance of talks postponed until tomorrow. We assemble for a communal Souper[9] in the mess, in which about two hundred physicians participate; we are the guests of the station commander, although proper accommodation for all outside doctors has been secured. I return to Luck at 10:00 p.m. A very satisfying evening in all respects: instructive and lively.

7 FEBRUARY. Overcast, unfriendly weather. Many who had a good time last night now have awful hangovers, including Dr. Müller, who remained behind. I feel doubly better to have avoided this temptation by strength of will.

8 FEBRUARY. Overcast with snow, which doesn't remain long and just contributes to the mud and mess.

9 FEBRUARY. Beginning of divisional medical inspection by the corps chief medical officer, in which I naturally participate. Today it is the turn of fourth battalion in Gerazdza, then field hospital no. 9/9 and the division medical section in Worotniewo in the afternoon. In between, the corps chief medical officer is my guest at lunch. The inspection takes all day until 5:00 p.m., after which he quarters with me overnight. Weather not very good, but still bearable.

10 FEBRUARY. Inspection continues. Departure at 7:00 a.m. to the eighty-ninth infantry battalion in Romanow, from there to the ninetieth infantry battalion in Botyn,[10] where we take lunch, and then on to Novosiolki, where we overnight. Weather very unpleasant, wet snow with a lot of mud. What a mess! Getting in and out of vehicles in the mud is very difficult. In Novosiolki, where brigade command Klein and the fortieth infantry regiment are situated, the regiment arranges a lively evening in our honor with music and singing. We stay together in a jolly mood until 12:15 a.m.

11 FEBRUARY. Continuation and conclusion of inspection. We begin at 8:00 a.m. at the fortieth infantry division, then on to Wierchowka[11] and the

fourth light infantry battalion, located in dugouts on the forest edge. Men have created a splendid underground village here. The officers' shelters are excellent, even luxurious—the nicest and cleanest we have visited during our entire inspection tour.

From here, our ways part—I return to Gerazdza, while the corps medical chief goes on to Ostrozec. I arrive back at 1:30 p.m. The weather today is much better, with the ground already partially dried. The sky is clear and blue.

12 FEBRUARY. Moderate snowfall, which starts at night and continues all day. Fog and not too cold.

13 FEBRUARY. Overcast, moderately cold continues. A lot of residual work is waiting for me to complete, so little time remains to rest from the exertions of the inspection tour.

14 FEBRUARY. A glorious winter's day with a lot of snow and sun, not strong enough to melt the snow.

15 FEBRUARY. Snowfall—sunshine at noon, and snowmelt—mud! Ugh!

16 FEBRUARY. Snowfall—overcast and cold all day.

17 FEBRUARY. Sunshine starting very early; snow gradually melts. There are signs that we will soon depart from here.

18 FEBRUARY. Order comes today to relieve the third infantry division—and so we join up again with the unfortunate tenth corps. The general staff have already moved to Chorlupy:[12] the rest of command will follow tomorrow. Weather not unpleasant, light frost early, sun at noon with snowmelt and mud. I have a terrible cold.

19 FEBRUARY. I travel by car to the new station myself—on the way, I travel to corps command, and report to chief medical officer Dr. Zapatowicz, still in charge of tenth corps. After that I travel to Chorlupy, where I arrive at noon. The place makes a good impression. Command is accommodated in an estate, where the mess hall is also located: nice and spacious, with a glass veranda and an excellent piano. I am accommodated with our lieutenant colonel: this pleases neither of us, especially me because of his many comings and goings; also I do not like sharing my quarters, but today I will have to. Tomorrow I have the prospect of a room to myself.

20 FEBRUARY. Beautiful winter's day. Weather mild, clear air, strong sunshine. Fliers' weather. Soon, we witness a dogfight between our and an enemy flier; it doesn't take long before the Russian is forced to turn back by our antiaircraft guns, and our own pilot to land very near us. His plane has been badly shot up by Russian machine gunfire, and the motor does not function anymore. Major Hoffory, who is traveling with the pilot as observer, has two bullet wounds in the chest and one bullet lodged in his body. He has lost a lot of blood and is taken to our division medical unit. The pilot himself has only been frightened, not wounded. Great agitation in the entire army section, because the major is a personal friend of our army commander, Archduke Joseph

Ferdinand, and has come on a visit just to enjoy a trip in the air. The telephone rings off its hooks, uninterrupted enquiries about his condition. Regimental Physician First Class Dr. Utti is called for a surgical consultation—toward evening the Archduke's personal adjutant arrives, remaining with the wounded man as rapporteur. In the evening, the bullet is extracted. I now have a room to myself: it has been rendered quite livable with whitewash, repair, and some modifications.

21 FEBRUARY. Weather overcast, light frost which lasts all day.

22 FEBRUARY. Increased frost, but still quite tolerable.

23 FEBRUARY. Quite a lot of snow falls during the night, −5°C. At 9:00 a.m. I travel to Kopere[13] with Colonel von Rosenzweig to visit the dentist. He treats my unhappy tooth, which the dentist Dr. Kronfeld unsuccessfully tried to treat in Trieste for eighteen months. He does not fill it because of the threat of periostitis, but thinks that he can save it. Apart from that, I have fresh cavities in the first upper canine and right premolar; I must return in three days' time. Toward evening, Commandant von Sellner returns from sick leave. He looks well and we are all very pleased to see him. Major Hoffory has suddenly died, probably from an embolus.

24 FEBRUARY. Winter continues, but cold is not as bad, only a few degrees below zero—but overcast. Snow air, general mood gloomy, with little to do, as usual with tenth corps. Chief Medical Officer Zapatowicz leaves everyone alone and is happy when he is not bothered. He is a very accommodating gentleman—everything goes smoothly and the number of sick is not raised by even one man. Burial of Major Hoffory at 2:00 p.m.—his body is brought to Palera,[14] before being sent back to Vienna.

25 FEBRUARY. A sudden storm with violent winds starts during the night and lasts all day, making remaining outside impossible. It's very uncomfortable in my room as well, because both windows are exposed to the wind and it therefore cannot be heated.

26 FEBRUARY. Violent wind continues today.

27 FEBRUARY. Wind will not let up—extremely uncomfortable. Durazzo[15] has been taken!

28 FEBRUARY. The storm continues with the same ferocity, but nevertheless I am going to Kopere for my dental appointment.

29 FEBRUARY. Finally, after a series of miserable days, sunshine returns—the wind has also weakened, but cold remains. At 9:00 a.m., Professor Ballner arrives with Regimental Physician First Class Dr. Kulakowski from tenth corps command for an inspection of our hygienic conditions, as representative of the chief of the army medical corps. They first visit all medical units that are in the area and from there travel in two cars to forth brigade command (Major General Prusenowsky) in Pokaszczewo,[16] followed by regimental command and the eightieth infantry command, from there to the north camp,

fourth battalion, and then the position of the eighty-ninth infantry regiment. We must travel to the latter on foot, because the area is already under Russian observation, and they shoot at anyone who shows himself. After a short visit to the eighty-ninth regimental command, we travel to the front through communication trenches in single file one after the other, then through transverse trenches, right, then left, then right again. Finally, after an hour, we arrive in the communication trench and from there to actual fighting trenches. We inspect the shelters; officers' shelters are quite good, clean, and neat, but those for the men are usually extremely poor: they have neither light nor enough air. An unenviable existence—there is urgent need for regular troop relief. Otherwise, tactical installations in the fighting trenches are very impressive and give the overall impression of an unconquerable underground fortress. Foxholes are very interesting—but are they appropriate? Lack of cleanliness in the tangle of trenches is embarrassing. We also inspect the artillery dugouts, from where the Russian positions, the church, and Olyka Castle[17] are clearly visible.

By the time—using the same road—we arrive in Chorlupy again, it's already 7:00 p.m.—The entire command officers' corps are assembled to congratulate our Commander von Sellner on his Military Cross of the Order of Merit Second Class. I join them, while Professor Ballner and Regimental Physician Dr. Kulakowski continue their onward journey. The same order informs us that both Dr. Müller and I have been awarded the Signum Laudis. So, all in all, an interesting and instructive day with a happy conclusion that makes us forget our earlier exertions. Weather very good.

1 MARCH. Weather has completely changed and a storm has been howling all day—overcast with light snow showers. My tooth is starting to act up again, but, in this weather, I cannot make up my mind about a trip to the dentist.

2 MARCH. Bad weather continues, but despite this, I cannot postpone a visit to the dentist anymore and leave at 9:00 a.m. I find the dentist Dr. Kronfeld sick in bed himself: he does not want to touch my tooth, especially in view of the fact that the periostitis is lessening—so I might as well have saved myself the trip. Once I am already here, I pay a visit to Chief Medical Officer Zapatowicz, inform him of the results of our inspection, and by noon am back home. I spend the afternoon reading: a book by Ganghofer: *Trutze von Trutzberg* promises to be interesting. Thawing weather since noon.

3 MARCH. The wind has diminished. Thawing continues, and mud is becoming miserable. The regimental fourth battalion receives an unexpected departure order to encamp in Luck tomorrow: destination unknown, presumably Italy. I have been suffering from headaches since my last inspection. During the past two days, they only started at night, but today they last almost all day—headaches make me feel quite out of sorts, because I have never had them before and have no idea of their cause. According to the latest remit, general staff officers of all high commands are each ordered to the front for fourteen days. In our group, Major Heller is the first one to go: he leaves today for the ninetieth infantry division.

4 MARCH. Temperature has dropped significantly; ground is frozen solid again: overcast, snow air. Our divisional reserve will take the place of half of the eighty-ninth infantry regiment, fourth battalion. For this purpose, they will be stationed in the north camp, where at the same time they will be quarantined because of a louse-borne typhus outbreak. My health is not good anymore: my foot is still swollen, especially in the evening. Yesterday, in fact, both feet were swollen: and added to that the continuing headaches, making rapid walking or mountain climbing very difficult, with dyspnea. But I must put a good face on a bad situation, because my Olga doesn't need to know about all this.

5 MARCH. Overcast, mild weather, thawing weather in the afternoon with mud—light frost toward evening.

6 MARCH. Weather like yesterday, less thawing weather, also with it less mud. Around 10:00 a.m., Chief Medical Officer Zapatowicz arrives at our division medical unit. I accompany him to the . . . battalion of eighty-ninth infantry regiment. Return around 1:00 p.m.

7 MARCH. Weather the same: ground still frozen.

8 MARCH. The same. Moderate wind, becoming stronger by evening.

9 MARCH. Heavy snowfall during the night—wind still bearable. Temperature a little below zero. Morning visit to the dentist to change my filling. By 9:30 a.m. I am already back.

10 MARCH. Snow has disappeared, more been blown away than melted. Another storm at night, which lasts until noon, followed by thawing weather und significant mud by evening.

11 MARCH. Strong winds again, starting during the night, continuing into the day. The ground is frozen solid again. These eternal winds make my room extremely uncomfortable; otherwise the room has become clean and livable, and can be heated when the wind doesn't blow.

12 MARCH. Wind continues during the night, becoming much stronger by noon. The ground is thawing again, moderate mud.

13 MARCH. Weather unchanged. During the afternoon, a German captain gives us a lecture on gas attacks and how to protect against them. They are in common use by both sides on the Western Front, and the

Figure 3.1. Soldiers wearing gas masks in a trench on the Eastern Front. Photograph courtesy of the Leo Baeck Institute.

Russians understand their value as well. Our division currently only possesses five thousand gas masks, but soon they will be made available to everybody.

14 MARCH. Weather the same, sky still overcast. Mud becomes worse and worse. The Russians have become more active lately, with a great deal of artillery fire; we have an average of five wounded daily. Nights are unsettled at the front, but command is not disturbed from their night's rest! The chief of our general staff has returned safely from his valiant fourteen-day stint at the front: his frontline medal is secure! In two days' time, Captain Pistelka will follow him.

15 MARCH. Weather and general situation unchanged.

16 MARCH. Wind has decreased somewhat. Thawing weather and mud have increased together. The sun tries to make a weak appearance toward noon but does not succeed.

17 MARCH. Wind has stopped. Great misery from the mud: the roads are impassable. And now we have a new enemy—Portugal! Germany declared war on Portugal at 9:00 a.m.,[18] after Portugal seized all German merchant ships anchored in its harbor(s), and leased them to the British. We have simultaneously broken relations with Portugal.

18 MARCH. The Russians are still trying to occupy our positions: they attack the eighty-ninth and ninetieth infantry regiments during the night, reach about four hundred paces away, and try to invest our trenches, but our troops bury them again. Weather unchanged.

19 MARCH. Weather and situation unchanged. Horrible mud.

20 MARCH. Overcast, unpleasant weather continues.

21 MARCH. The sun reappears early in the morning—for the first time during this entire month. The telephone rings early, with the news that Archduke Joseph Ferdinand is coming to visit us and will remain here during the afternoon. At 9:00 a.m. the mail brings me the news that, on 16 March, I became one daughter richer. More news than that during one day would have been unbearable!

The Archduke arrives, to personally invest Commandant von Sellner with his new order (Military Service Cross Second Class); a huge honor! He stays with us for a cozy lunch—after that, obligatory photos are taken, and he leaves again at 2:30 p.m. The sun disappears again and the weather becomes more unpleasant; toward evening the wind picks up again and howls like it has for weeks.

22 MARCH. Rain at night, continuing during the day—heavy rain during the night—roads are bottomless, and the entire rearguard is in danger of becoming caught in the mud. The field railway to Chorlupy, which is almost finished, partially sinks into the mud and cannot be used. Luckily, the Russians are faring no better than we are; otherwise things would be very bad for us.

23 MARCH. Overcast, mild weather continues. The mud becomes deeper and deeper.

24 MARCH. Bright sunshine early—everyone breathes easier. Around 9:00 a.m. planes from both sides appear again; they do not get a chance to fight one another, because they are briskly shelled. Weather changes toward noon: overcast, rainy, rain in the evening. No hint of roads drying out.

25 MARCH. Again, early morning sunshine—airplane activity like yesterday: again driven away by shelling. The sun disappears today even earlier than yesterday, and by afternoon it is raining again. The air remains mild—warm.

26 MARCH. Overcast, depressing weather—roads are almost impossible.

27 MARCH. It rains almost all day. A portion of our artillery is relieved by horse-drawn artillery.

28 MARCH. Glorious clear spring day with lots of sun, which lasts all day—ground dries visibly. Toward evening, Dr. Müller returns from vacation.

29 MARCH. More sunshine today; it's so warm that winter clothes have been taken off. The ground is drying significantly. Corps Commandant Martini is visiting our front with chief of the general staff, Major General Kralowetz: they take lunch with us. My Signum Laudis is delivered with the latest dispatch.

30 MARCH. Beautiful early spring weather continues, and becoming warmer, Dr. Scheidl tours our division medical unit today and we invite him for lunch. He is satisfied with what he sees and gives us some practical tips—for example, a very good pasteboard splint for upper arm fractures, etc.

31 MARCH. The lovely spring weather ends. Rain early, sky overcast all day. Luckily roads have dried out so much that today's rain will not make them much worse. A very hot bath at the division medical unit has made me quite lethargic. The Russians have already been giving the ninetieth infantry regiment their special attention; their trenches are only three hundred paces away. To oppose this danger, an attack is ordered tonight. After powerful artillery preparation, Russians are ejected from the trenches and trenches are buried over. This small undertaking costs us eighty dead, sixty wounded, and expenditure of 1,600 rounds of ammunition; the action ends at midnight, and quiet returns.

1 APRIL. Another beautiful sunny early spring day—fliers arrive punctually and are shelled, just as punctually—by both sides. At 9:00 a.m. I travel with the technical adviser Major Hofinger to the north camp to study the question of their water supply. At the same time, I inspect the newly erected baths—splendid, indeed exemplary. By 12:30 p.m. we are back.

2 APRIL. The sun is in a huff and won't come out all day, but weather remains reasonable: dry and warm. As usual, I spend most of the morning at the division medical unit. Today Chief Medical Officer Zapatowicz arrives: we breakfast together and remain together all morning.

3 APRIL. Lovely, sunny weather that starts in the early morning and continues all day.

4 APRIL. Lovely weather continues; the first buds of spring are becoming visible. In the morning, the corps chief medical officer arrives again. He is sent for by chief of the general staff Major General Kralowetz, in whose opinion cleanliness and order in the area of the second infantry regiment, especially in Chorlupy, leaves a lot to be desired. He would be much better off concerning himself with tactical operations and leaving cleanliness to others. As soon as the calamitous condition of the roads disappears and the mud has disappeared, should Chorlupy should look like a garden? What an idiot! If only he had arranged for a road to Chorlupy to be built last fall, instead of building a road for his car and a Swiss chalet which serves as his own personal dining room! He will rue that very bitterly!

5 APRIL. Clear, sunny weather today as well. I inspect the south camp during the morning, and arrange everything according to the wishes of the chief of general staff.

6 APRIL. Glorious early spring weather continues. During the morning, I travel to a private bakery in Zwierow[19] near Kopere, after a case of scarlet fever[20] has appeared among the civilian population. I take Dr. Kulakowski from corps command along with me. The bakery is beautifully equipped; splendid accommodation for my team, and exemplarily neat and clean. I evacuate the adjacent few houses with civilians living in them, a precaution that the corps commandant, on wishes of the civilians, reverses. And I must work properly under these conditions!

7 APRIL. No sun all day today—it remains dry but cold. During the past few days, I have sent my entire winter wardrobe back to Vienna—hopefully, I have not done so too early.

8 APRIL. Weather unpleasant today as well: even colder than yesterday, and a strong wind begins to blow toward evening, which howls all night and cools down the air even more.

9 APRIL. The wind continues, but blows the clouds away; by noon the weather has cleared. I am occupied all morning by a visit from a German senior pharmacist, who has come to visit and examine the quality of our gas masks, made in Germany. Indeed quite a few have been found to be deficient, and discarded.

10 APRIL. The sun appears far too early this morning and disappears just as quickly; pouring rain by 7:30 a.m. Our commandant has just come from the front. How he will grouse! He is returning at 10:00 a.m.

11 APRIL. Real April weather: rain, hail, sunshine and strong wind, all alternating with one another.

12 APRIL. Nice morning, overcast in the afternoon. Wind and rain toward evening.

13 APRIL. Overcast morning, heavy rain by noon, followed by sunshine, and very warm. Vegetation is slowly becoming green, and the bushes already have some green growth; by contrast, in Vienna everything is in full bloom.

14 APRIL. April weather continues. Corps Commandant Martini and his Chief Of Staff Major General Kralowetz dine with us again: they have just returned from our positions.

15 APRIL. Weather unchanged, but roads are drying up relatively rapidly, provided it does not rain every few hours. New code names are distributed today: Lux Kalif instead of Hau Degen for the corps; Lux Duta instead of Hau-Ideal for the division; Army command remains Mars-Vlies.

16 APRIL. Abundant rain early, which lasts all day with a short interruption.

17 APRIL. Weather very unstable, rain at times—mud is bad enough, but by far not as awful as the month before.

18 APRIL. I must depart at 8:00 a.m. to visit the horse-drawn artillery, third and fourth batteries—they only arrived in position two weeks ago, and must leave their positions again tonight. But meanwhile one man has been hospitalized for louse-borne typhus. The road there is still quite bad; the trip takes an hour, followed by an hour on foot, because the terrain is under enemy observation. Their shelters are well built, and they have foxholes at their disposal. After making my examination and taking all precautionary measures, I return via Bakoryn[21] to see whether the first aid station of the ninetieth infantry regiment and their baths are still there. I find the latter fully functional and return at 1:00 p.m. Short period of rain on the way home.

19 APRIL. Weather a bit pleasanter but still unstable, transient rain at noon. The rest does me a lot of good. However, I have significant pain in the small of my back after yesterday's trip, and, in general, don't feel as well as I did during the first year of the war. My heart doesn't feel right, and my foot is still swollen.

20 APRIL. Weather like yesterday. At 9:00 p.m. we attack the Russians with artillery from one part of our position, followed by infantry; still later, artillery begins curtain fire. The Russians return fire at once, and sixteen of our men are wounded, mostly seriously, with a few dead, including Artillery Observer Cadet Brumowski. Unfortunately, we do not know the exact effect of our fire on the Russians.

21 APRIL. The sun is shining and it becomes very warm. The tree buds become ever fuller, and the fields already have a carpet of green. Short downpour in the afternoon, followed by complete clearing.

22 APRIL. Weather nice and warm. The ground is drying rapidly everywhere.

23 APRIL. Easter Sunday! Beautiful weather. Field mass at 8:00 a.m. in the lovely chapel built by the Ulans. Division Chaplain Niezgoda gives an impressive sermon. Then on to Swiçcone[22] with the Ulans, where the table is richly set with all kinds of good food. The entire company joins us at Swiçcone, followed by a festive lunch. There is a sort of fraternity at the front: friend and foe exchange Swiçcone through the barbed wire. Our authorities immediately forbid this in the strictest possible terms, taking prisoner 112 Russians and one cadet, who have come up to our barbed wire barricade. This infuriates the Russians,

who open heavy artillery fire on our positions, to which we respond promptly. Calm arrives after a while.

24 APRIL. Easter Monday! Nice warm weather—quiet at the front. Commandants Prusenowsky and Klein are our luncheon guests.

25 APRIL. Beginning of my medical inspection of the entire divisional area, as has been ordered. I depart early at 5:00 a.m.; the weather when I leave is quite uncertain, strong wind, cloudy. I arrive at regimental command of the fortieth infantry regiment at 5:45 a.m. and, from there, walk to the communications trenches with regimental chief physician Oberstabsarzt I Klasse Dr. Tausz: first we arrive at battalion command, where Major Honsig joins us and takes us into seventh company's trenches. We inspect their positions, shelters and kitchen, and their water hygiene (for tea and coffee), as well as their latrines. The cleanliness in the fighting and transportation trenches is exemplary—like in a parlor. Then we turn back; on the way, I report to third brigade command, Major General Klein, and then with artillery group commander, Colonel Mazza, whom I do not meet personally. I inspect the regimental first aid station, then the second battery of one of the reserve regiments and no. 3/2 Honvéd battery, and return home at 12:30 p.m., tired and weary, with a cold starting. Complete clearing in the afternoon.

26 APRIL. Inspection of the eighty-ninth infantry regiment: I depart early at 5:00 a.m., as before. At this hour, friend and foe—after the uninterrupted shooting and strict observation through the night—are fast asleep. Arrival at regimental command at 5:45 a.m., and then, accompanied by chief surgeon substitute Assistant Physician Dr. Schwab, through the communications trenches to second battalion and the company of First Lieutenant Grünbaum, who takes over with further guidance and clarification. On return, second breakfast at regimental command and photographs taken, followed by a visit to the sick bay, Regimental Physician First Class Dr. Janousek—back home by noon. Weather overcast, quite brisk. Clearing by noon, afterward overcast again: overcast for the remainder of the day. We have a civilian luncheon guest who demonstrates his experiments with a divining rod looking for water. I do not think much of this.

27 APRIL. Inspection of the ninetieth infantry regiment. Departure again at 5:00 a.m. early, first to Pokaszczewo, location of the first aid station. From there, immediately with Chief Surgeon Major Dr. Revesz to the second battalion seventh company, and from there to a battery of the twenty-ninth artillery regiment, and then return to regimental command in the small Hessen-like forest near Pokaszczewo. Back by 10:30 a.m. already. I am miserable and tired, because I get so little sleep at night. I am so anxious not to oversleep that I cannot fall asleep at all, and at 4:00 a.m. it's already time to get up. Added to that the constant trudging around in the positions, and my very bad cold. Weather good, but afternoon overcast—no sign of the sun today at all.

28 april. Inspection of south camp one: no. 1/40 battalion and heavy artillery with Captain Reichel. Depart at 8:30 a.m., return around 11:00 a.m., so quite light and less exhausting—also less dangerous. Weather overcast, afternoon rain—but nature is not as unfriendly anymore. Trees have a clear green covering. My room must still be heated on an overcast day such as this.

29 april. Inspection of north camp, fourth light infantry; and first heavy battery. This camp, which is located in a dense forest, is beautiful and looks like a fairy tale. Medically speaking, it is also splendidly equipped, with drinking water preparation and exemplary bathing and delousing facilities. Troop shelters, partially underground, are splendidly constructed—with pallets, windows, double entrances—electric lighting throughout, just as in the south camp.

Departure 8:30 a.m., back home 12:30 p.m. Weather overcast and cool. The ground is quite bad, because of yesterday's rain. With this, the heaviest and most unpleasant part of my inspections is complete. My cold is somewhat better.

30 april. Sunday: I take the liberty of a rest day but cannot utilize it properly because I undertake the fifth cholera inoculation of members of command. Weather nice—the sun is shining again.

1 may. Beginning of daylight saving time. I felt quite bad early: breakfast doesn't taste good so early at 6:00 a.m. instead of 7:00 a.m.; all the greater is my appetite for lunch at noon. So, difficulties with the changed time are solved.

Figure 3.2. Men lining up for cholera inoculation. Photograph courtesy of the Leo Baeck Institute.

I start inspections of parts of the division situated behind the line, and inspect the bakery in Zwierow for a second time. Depart at 9:00 a.m., return at noon. It is actually a nice trip, in good, sunny, warm weather. There as well I find exemplary order: bread of impeccable quality. Afternoon downpour, followed by a great deal for mud and slight cooling. Oppressive air continues until evening.

2 MAY. Interruption of my inspections—the Russian cadet, whom we took prisoner on Easter Sunday, is returned to the Russians by army command. During the morning, he is handed over to them blindfolded through our position: I have the task of putting a reliable blindfold on him. He arrives at command at noon and swears an oath to our pastor that he will remain silent about everything he has seen and heard while with us. Thereupon, I place a bandage over his eyes and he marches back. He receives a letter for his commandant from Archduke Joseph Ferdinand. Nice weather in the morning, heavy rain again in the afternoon that lasts, with varying intensity, all day and evening.

3 MAY. I continue my inspection—today it's the turn of the entire baggage train. Start at 8:30 a.m., return at 2:30 p.m. The train is scattered all over the place, and inspection takes a lot of time. Weather nice, very warm. Roads on my outward journey still very bad in parts, but significantly better on my return.

4 MAY. I must interrupt my inspection tour today as well: Dr. Müller asks me to take part in the official attestation of his Medical Corps Captain von Cervenka in regard to his requested decoration of Assistant Physician Dr. Hofstätter. Weather nice, sunny and warm.

5 MAY. Inspection of the division ammunition dump. Depart at 9:00 a.m. with Artillery Commandant Colonel von Rosenzweig, return at noon. A pleasant trip, with nice, sunny, warm weather.

6 MAY. Inspection of our own station in Chorlupy. It's very interesting to see what has been made out of this wretched, dirty little farmer's village. Each house has a little garden in front of it, with a birch fence. The roads have been smoothed, spotlessly clean—it looks more like a little town. The division medical unit has also been properly equipped, just as during peacetime. Bathing and delousing facilities are especially exemplary. A large room with a basin and several shower facilities for the men. Cement floor, walls with fiber cement (Eternit) panels—duplicate change rooms for dressing and undressing after disinfection of washing and clothes. Adjacent, an officers' bathing pool with steam rooms, and a fountain in the baths themselves. Large machines for creation of steam, etc. The building is surrounded by a garden.

With this, my inspection tour is completed. During the afternoon, I write my report and hand it in at command, with a copy to the chief medical officer.

Weather remains very nice, even quite warm; a light wind is not unpleasant when it's warm. Nightly attacks occur often now, so also large numbers of daily wounded. Most serious are wounds in the head and abdomen, which are all operated on here in our division medical unit.

During this long war, we have had—also retrospectively—to relearn treatment of the wounded. Before the war, head and belly wounds, even in the medical corps, were still forbidden surgical areas (*noli mi tangere*). But now, the principle is: operate on everything, and as rapidly as possible. We have been provided with qualified surgeons working in our own unit, who operate on everything. This works very well in static warfare. Unfortunately, we do not often get to see the end results, because men have to be evacuated after two or three weeks. Head wounds have proportionally better results than belly wounds, which always seem to come for surgery too late. Peritonitis is almost always present by the time of surgery, and men die after having been operated on.[23]

7 MAY. Finally, a free morning! But not completely, because I have been called as an expert witness at a court hearing. Weather very nice—a storm lasting an hour at noon, but complete clearing thereafter.

8 MAY. Lovely weather, just like yesterday. All the fruit trees are already in full bloom; the other trees are thick with leaves—a beautiful sight. A similar storm at noon, just like yesterday, followed by complete clearing. At the front, despite resting positions, there is fairly lively activity from both sides. Russians try to get nearer and nearer to our positions, in places about two hundred paces from our barbed wire obstacles: presumably, they intend to suddenly storm our

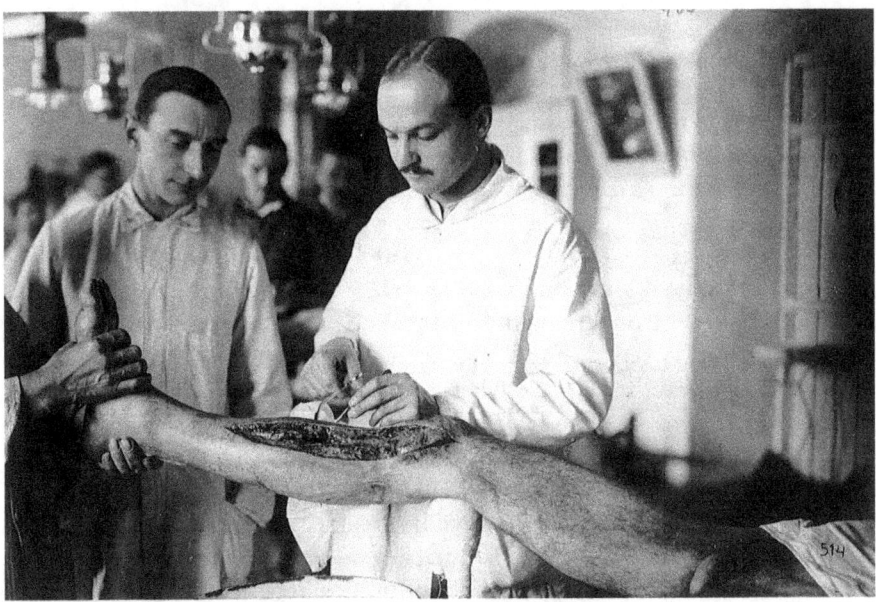

Figure 3.3. An open fracture of the lower leg before plaster of paris application. Photograph courtesy of the Leo Baeck Institute.

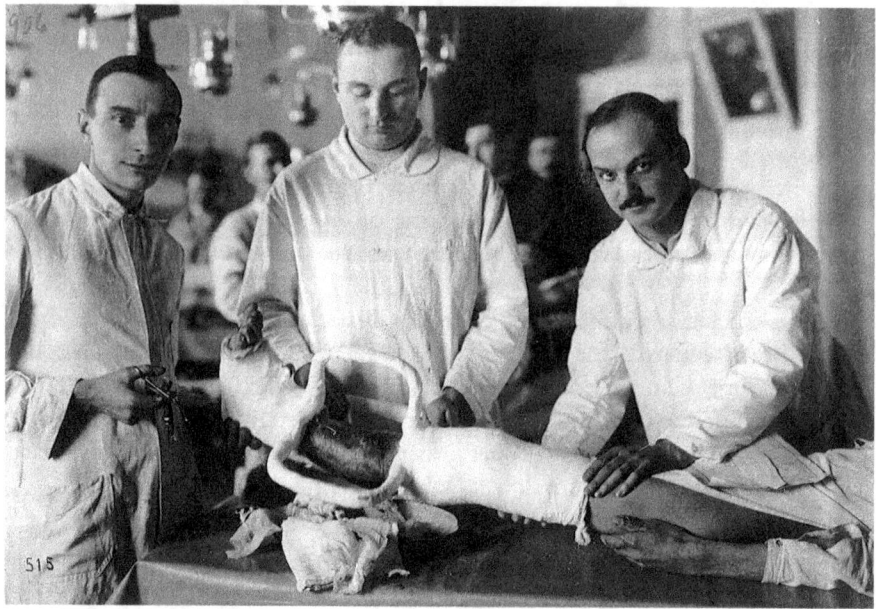

Figure 3.4. Bardach and colleagues look proudly at an aseptically treated lower leg wound that has not become infected. Photograph courtesy of the Leo Baeck Institute.

positions. As a result, we attack their forward positions at night, drive them off, and bulldoze them. But our success unfortunately doesn't last long, and the Russians excavate the buried trenches again. The same thing is again planned for tonight by our ninetieth infantry regiment. During the morning, the corps chief medical officer visits our sick bay.

9 MAY. Yesterday's attack has been postponed until today. No storm today—nice all day, rain only at 9:00 p.m., when an attack would have taken place, so it's postponed from 10:00 to 11:00 p.m. I sit in the mess with the general staff, while the other men seek out their usual fighting positions. Fighting becomes heavy from midnight to 1:00 a.m.; our troops advance very slowly because of slippery terrain and constant illumination of the ramp by Russian floodlights. It's already 3:00 a.m. when news comes from the ninetieth infantry division that our advance has been halted for the night because it's not succeeding. This is naturally conceded by command, and after a lost night, we finally get some rest.

10 MAY. A nice morning, but I am dog-tired because of lack of sleep caused by another frittered-away night. Nothing helps—neither getting up late nor an afternoon nap: such a lost night cannot be quickly replaced.

11 MAY. I feel much fresher after a good night's sleep. At 8:00 a.m. I am already in the division medical unit and stay there until noon; during this time

I do four trepanations of the skull. It's just a pity that, after a few days during which their conditions improve somewhat, they have to be evacuated, so I cannot follow up their progress. The number of sick and wounded here has increased.

12 MAY. The continuing night rain has cooled the weather down significantly, and the first iceman of the *kalte Sophie*[24] has made his presence known.

13 MAY. It remains quite cold today, and I literally freeze during the night. After dinner we say farewell to our beloved quartermaster, Captain Krämer, who must join his regiment (fortieth infantry) tomorrow. Captain Pistelka produces a bottle of champagne: we are joined by Major Heller, Captain Randa, fourth brigade First Lieutenant Baron Hammerstein, Captain Prehalka, and First Lieutenant Zorn; one bottle of champagne follows another, and I do not get to bed until 1:00 a.m. The mood is depressed; Captain Krämer does not rejoice; the occasion is far too sad for him to do so.

14 MAY. Last night, I was so pitiably cold that I make sure my quarters are heated this evening; the more so because of today's brisk, cold weather, despite the sun shining. After dinner Captain Krämer parts from us permanently.

15 MAY. Tonight my room is much cozier, because it's heated, and I sleep significantly better. Also, the weather is a lot warmer today, despite wind, than during the past few days. Cold Sophie still emanates from the warm weather.

General situation unchanged, although many signs point to an imminent Russian attack.[25] Accordingly, there is greater nervousness at our higher command. Toward evening, we bombard Olyka on orders from on high, ostensibly because a Russian command unit is located there. The Russians will take revenge for this, I fear.

16 MAY. Weather overcast but warm—clearing later, very humid. Storm in the afternoon. Just before, visit by the archduke at command. Storm again toward evening, but it doesn't last. Straight after, we receive news of our great victory against Italy: sixty officers and three thousand men taken captive, seven artillery pieces, and eleven machine guns as well.[26] This is apparently the start of our great offensive against the Italians. On that account, the Russians are preparing an offensive against us. Let us cross fingers for the success of our Italian offensive!

17 MAY. A beautiful, clear day. I spend the morning, as usual when I have some free time, at the division medical unit. The corps chief medical officer reappears, and I accompany him to the south camp, about fifteen minutes from the unit. He is very satisfied with what he sees—no wonder, because everything there looks immaculate. Everything in our park is in full bloom, and we will be sorry when we will have to leave our comfortable little nest. We would really prefer to await the peace here if we are not permitted to fight against the wops.

18 MAY. No sign of a Russian attack—our preparations are very thorough. The artillery, which even before this was strong, has been further strength-

ened by the addition of new batteries, and two fresh divisions stand in reserve behind our corps. The twenty-ninth light infantry battalion has already been placed in reserve under our corps. Weather good.

19 MAY. Bathing and delousing facilities that I have already described are only now opened for general use. The weather has cooled down again, so heating is necessary during the evening and night. Noticeably quiet at the front—even if it is the calm before the storm, we are armed and ready!

20 MAY. Weather has cooled down significantly, overcast with rain at times, alternating with sunshine. Today the German Colonel General von Linsingen—commander of the entire northeastern arm group—inspects our position. He arrives at command with his staff early at 9:00 a.m. and is taken to our positions by car. Our commander only returns from there at 4:00 p.m. General Linsingen is generally satisfied with what he sees.

Our Italian offensive is making excellent progress. Until today, we have taken about 13,000 Italian prisoners, including 257 seven officers, 107 artillery pieces (twelve heavy 28 centimeter howitzers), and 68 machine guns. Our troops in the South Tirol already stand on Italian soil—it makes our hearts sing for joy![27]

21 MAY. Weather has become even cooler, so my room is being heated again. We make very active preparations for the expected Russian offensive—large troop and artillery concentrations behind our front. At the front alone, we have eight-four artillery pieces.

22 MAY. Rain during the night, which lasts all morning: correspondingly cold. No sign of Russian offensive, but greater vigilance also means more shooting: therefore, our daily number of wounded has gone up significantly to twenty to twenty-five, mostly serious head and belly wounds. Surgeons at our division medical unit have good results.

23 MAY. Finally, another sunny, warm day, allowing us to move around outside. Mobile army reserve hospital no. 1/10 under the command of Oberstabsarzt I Klasse Dr. Ziepal has been here for the past few days: part of the preparation for the Russian offensive. This precaution is preposterous: first, at the moment it's superfluous, and second, when the battle starts, they will surely be the first to leave.

I am greatly upset by the appearance of Dr. Ziepal. During our military medical scrutiny, he was still a dignified, lively fellow with a carroty moustache. Now he looks like a ruin: his thick moustache and full beard have turned completely white; he is so asthmatic that he can hardly walk ten paces without gasping for breath, and he has to make permanent use of a stick because of his sciatica. It's just awful: he is not even fifty-two years old!

24 MAY. Overcast, cool weather again: it rains at night again. Clearing during the afternoon, cool and overcast again toward evening. During the morning, Dr. Scheidl appears unexpectedly for a conference about accommodation of a group of surgeons when the battle begins. He stays until 4:00 p.m. and dines at the division medical unit, where it is my honor to dine with him. I can now really see how much better the provisions for our kitchen are compared to this one.

25 MAY. Quite warm. Chief Medical Officer Zapatowicz visits the unit during the morning. I tell him that yesterday we dispatched our new memorandum to the Red Cross, concerning change in his previous proposal for the Officer's Badge of Honor for Surgeon Major Dr. Müller and me. If its execution takes as long as its original submission, the war will be finished before the award is given. I also request that the Badge of Honor First Class be put in for our Commandant Sellner, who loves decorations so much. I must naturally make the application.

26 MAY. A very cool, overcast day. We lose our entire fourth brigade—regiments eighty-nine and ninety—they must now serve as reserve for army group Lurmay. As replacement, we receive the eighty-second infantry regiment, a Hungarian regiment, and the twenty-ninth light infantry battalion with five companies. The regiment comprises five battalions. The nineteenth brigade is under the command of Major General von Iwansky.

27 MAY. Quite a cold wind during the morning, clearing in the afternoon. Today agreement comes from the Red Cross that the Badge of Honor Second Class has been approved for Dr. Müller and me—straight after the request to raise the level of the award was submitted two days ago. What a pity! I will try to renew our request; maybe they will make it retrospective.

28 MAY. The relief mentioned above is carried out during the night. There are wounded, but no more than during other nights. The general Russian offensive announced for today has not taken place: in fact, such claims by Russian prisoners have not been corroborated, even in a single case. I spend all morning at the unit hospital, where several larger operations are performed now on a daily basis—for instance, two amputations today alone. Weather today warm and very nice.

29 MAY. The Russians are tormenting us with their new way of waging war. Toward evening they throw mines at the positions that they have built adjacent and right next to our positions—some-

Figure 3.5. A man with bandaged eyes being led out of regimental command. Photograph courtesy of the Leo Baeck Institute.

times no further than thirty paces away. Mines are thrown with great precision, and cause terrible damage. One such mine yesterday killed two officers and eighteen men and wounded many more. This has a very demoralizing effect on our troops. Weather warm, but cool in the evenings.

30 MAY. Still no Russian offensive. Our countermeasures have assumed huge proportions. One would almost think that we are preparing to attack them, and not vice versa. Weather remains good.

31 MAY. During the morning, Chief Medical Officer Zapatowicz appears at the medical unit, and during the afternoon I must travel to him in Kopere, in connection with a very unpleasant matter related to the thirty-seventh division medical unit. At the same time, I hand him my letter of commendation for the Red Cross Medal First Class for Commandant von Sellner: he must now process it further. Dr. Zapatowicz doesn't seem to be a very brainy person. Weather very nice: there is already quite a lot of dust in the streets.

1–3 JUNE. Situation unchanged throughout the three days. Preparations for an eventual Russian offensive are continued. Great excitement, especially on the part of the higher rank superiors. We are kept busy at night, because the Russians have built their positions perilously close to our own. The Russians vacate the advanced trenches, but the very next day they are in them again; such tricks are responsible for a lot of wounded men on our side. Weather remains lovely—during the day quite hot with awful dust.

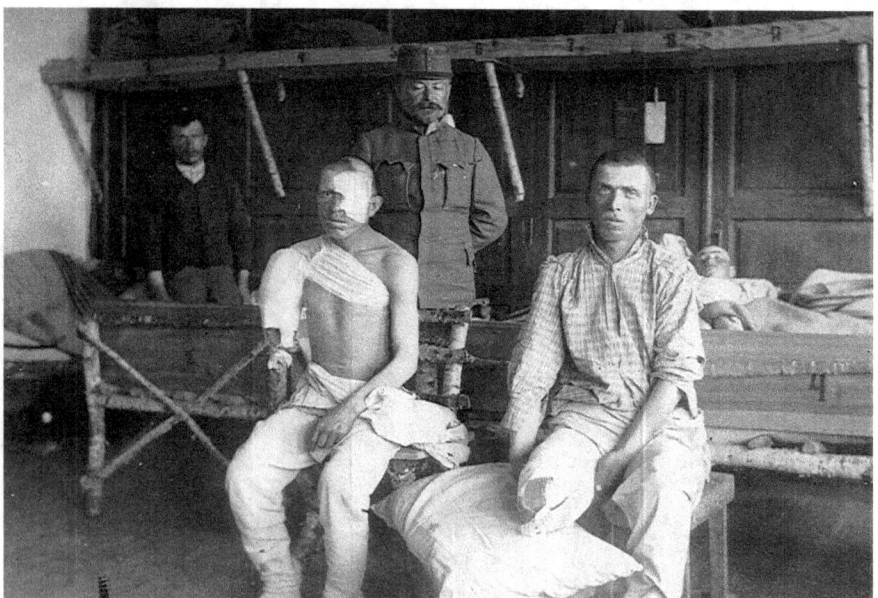

Figure 3.6. A picture of despair. Amputations and eye damage. Photograph courtesy of the Leo Baeck Institute.

4 JUNE. Heavy shooting starts at 4:00 a.m. Its intensity wakes me up and increases more and more: By 4:30 a.m. it's already clear that this represents a violent Russian bombardment and a very serious attack.[28] The bombardment is aimed at us and against the seventieth division, south of us. We make ready to march, and await events. All reserves are brought up, and by 7:00 a.m. immediate command staff are already at the daily vantage point; soon thereafter, thirteenth division command—Vienna *Landwehr* troops—arrive, with Commandant Field Marshal Szcjkaj and Chief Surgeon Major Dr. Oberländer. We have already worked together with this division in front of Olyka: at that time, Prince Hohenlohe was still ordinance officer.

The bombardment lasts, with undiminished intensity, for more than four hours and then diminishes a little, after concentrated demolition fire on our obstacles and positions. A fresh bombardment begins at 5:00 a.m. and then changes to an infantry attack, which is repulsed, as are the next three attacks so that, by evening, we still fully occupy our positions. Losses are relatively light: only a few wounded have been brought into the division medical unit by evening. During the afternoon, Dr. Scheidl arrives with an assistant physician to work with us as surgeons. We are still very confident and in good spirits in the evening when the staff return from their positions.

5 JUNE. Firing from both sides lasts uninterruptedly all night, making sleep impossible. All breakthrough attempts are repelled by our troops. Around 5:00 a.m., Russian firing increases to a violent bombardment that at times reaches such intensity that it makes one's head spin. Individual shots cannot be distinguished from one another anymore: all that we hear is one uninterrupted, steady roar. I go straight to the medical unit, where the surgeons are very busy: I help them as much as I can, and by 10:00 a.m. we are already on the sixth skull trepanation. Suddenly, a shell whooshes over our heads and explodes 180 paces to the right of the unit. This is followed by more shells and shrapnel—everyone in town flees; the horses of the division cavalry run around wildly. The situation becomes critical; we cannot even think of further surgery. Dr. Scheidl, other surgeons, physicians and medical unit staff, and I all retreat to the "west," pursued uninterruptedly by Russian fire; by the time we reach the forest near Romanow, we are quite exhausted, and rest there. The firing gradually quietens down. Dr. Scheidl has sprained his foot during our retreat. After about an hour, we approach the street again, hitch a ride on a wagon, and return to command in Chorlupy. Dr. Scheidl arranges a car from command and whizzes away with his assistant after about an hour and half. His entire project on extended surgical activity immediately behind the front has failed completely, because of enemy shelling.

Terrible news from the front: unbelievable losses—whole battalions, especially of the fortieth and eighty-second infantry regiments, have been trapped during the breakthrough, and trenches are filled with piles of corpses. My heart dies in my throat. We lose many artillery pieces. Our position becomes even more critical, and by 5:00 p.m., the order arrives to evacuate Chorlupy. Command, including the division medical unit, are transferred to the estate in Romanow. Immediate staff only arrives when it becomes dark at 8:30 p.m. We are given our first hot food, which I do not touch: my throat feels strangled. Accommodation with Colonel von Rosenzweig. Our losses of men and material cannot be overlooked anymore. To make things even worse, a violent storm pours down on us that afternoon and again that evening, lasting almost all night.

6 JUNE. A quiet night. The Russians must be completely exhausted as well. Our troops withdraw to the shabby remains of our third position, which are unfortunately very poor. Only time will tell, whether we will be able to make a halt here. This is our worst debacle during the war thus far. We remain here for the moment. Weather overcast, periods of rain.

The third position naturally cannot be held either. We retreat from Romanow at 2:00 p.m. and arrive in Gerazdza, where orders are handed out and we receive a cold snack. I cannot say too many good things about how beautiful, this place—our quarters for a month during winter—looks in summer. A lot of greenery, sandy soil, lovely forests, neat and clean houses. Break camp at 4:00 p.m.: we reach the colony Teremenskaya,[29] home of tenth corps command, where a meeting is held. We only move off late in the evening, arriving in Dworec[30] when it's completely dark; we are quartered there. The road is naturally full of baggage trains: everything is streaming back to Luck in three to four columns; we can hardly get through. Added to that, I have a big scuffle with my horse, which I have not ridden for a few months, and bruise the small of my back quite badly. My stomach is also completely upset: first warm meal at 11:00 p.m.

7 JUNE. I sleep very little during the night: we are living four men in one dirty room, I with the entire artillery brigade. My back is very painful. We hear that the entire forty-fifth infantry division and a German division and cavalry brigade are coming to our aid: will they arrive in time? For the time being, the Russians are attacking Luck in three strong columns. Weather good today, hot, but with storms during the afternoon. The battle for the Luck bridgehead increases in violence form hour to hour. Our fortieth battalion—from which only about four hundred men remain from an original five thousand—are fighting like lions, and have repelled several Russian attacks. They report that there is a 1.5-meter high pile of Russian corpses in front of the barbed wire. All day long, fighting ebbs and flows. Suddenly, around 4:00 p.m., we receive a telephone message that Commandant Martini has been relieved of duty and replaced by Commandant Smejkal as provisional corps commandant. Until Commandant Smejkal arrives, Sellner is in overall charge. Major General Bauer, commandant of the tenth cavalry division, takes command of

our division. Sellner leaves rapidly and gladly for his new position: the situation here is bad and extremely dangerous. Fighting becomes extremely heavy toward evening. The Russians, who have made very little use of artillery during the day thus far, now start heavy artillery fire, which, with the added batteries, soon becomes a violent bombardment. They quickly succeed in breaking into our positions so that we cannot hold the bridgehead anymore. Everyone and everything is streaming backward, and soon the order is given for general retreat across the Styr River. General Bauer, a sharp and unsympathetic man, holds us all in our positions in Dworec until the missiles are almost on top of us. Only then does he allow us to retreat, while he is sped away in his own car. I ride away with two other officers, but roads are so clogged with baggage trains and artillery that we get lost in Luck—I myself only arrive at the division medical unit in Zaborol[31] around 7:30 p.m. The railway station in Luck as well as the bridge over the Styr River are blown up by our sappers. The detonation is huge, and a powerful pillar of fire and smoke rises up into the air. Soon after our arrival in Zaborol, a violent thunderstorm forms on the horizon: in barely thirty minutes, the storm is so violent that streets are under water. In the meantime, I find out that corps command is now located in the church in Zaborol. I take refuge there until the storm has passed. I meet Sellner there as well, resplendent in his new position. Soon thereafter, our chief of the general staff Major Heller arrives, with a portion of our own staff. Corps command soon leaves; we remain lying on a few stalks of straw in the church without having eaten anything all day. We lie down to sleep around midnight, but quiet does not last long: after hardly two hours, we are awoken for handing out of the next day's orders. Only now do we get details of last evening's terrible events. The bridge over the Styr has been blown too soon, and many of our men have drowned: a portion of our few remaining men remained behind on the other side of the bridge.

8 JUNE. A new brigade is created from the remnants of our own, and of the nineteenth infantry brigade, under command of Major General von Iwansky. Morning weather is very good—there is peace and calm for the moment—the Russians appear to need some calm as well. However, it will only remain quiet until they collect themselves and transport their artillery over the Styr, and then it will all start all over again. Our poor remnants will probably be of very little use against them. Will we get out of this horrible situation in one piece, and if so, how? There are no signs of reinforcements yet, and if they come, it will be too late. Nothing can be undertaken amid all this clamorous activity.

Around 5:00 p.m., General Iwansky arrives, completely exhausted; he lies down in a corner of the floor to rest up a bit. Finally, our valiant kitchen assistant Chromy arrives at 7:00 a.m. with breakfast and bad, but hot, tea. It's good to eat and drink something after fasting for an entire day. Command is traveling to Torczyn[32] today: I use the opportunity to travel there by car at 9:00 a.m.

and arrive—after many tribulations and car problems—around 11:00 a.m.: I remain there with our baggage train.

Meanwhile, the battle continues—fighting ebbs and flows. A Russian cavalry brigade is on the march, causing great consternation, so the baggage train immediately sets out for Sierniczki,[33] while I remain in Torczyn, waiting for command to arrive. The deputy of the new corps commandant Smejkal, has already arrived, whereupon our valiant Commander Sellner conveniently reports sick, and leaves: he is the second casualty of this debacle.

Toward evening, I travel to the battle train in Sierniczki, accompanied by Junior Logistics Officer Pelikan; we arrive while the gentlemen have gathered for their normal luncheon, and join them. This is very welcome, because for the past three days we have had almost nothing—certainly nothing decent—to eat. We only return to command, which is now in a hunting lodge near Dabrowa,[34] around 10:30 p.m. By the time we lie down to sleep on a bed of straw, it's already 1:00 a.m.: all in one room, fully clothed as we have been for the past three days—no opportunity to get washing done. We are filthy as pigs!

9 JUNE. I cannot even use the few hours that we have to sleep properly—our room also serves as the general staff's office, so of course the light is on and the telephone rings all night—no question of sleep for me. Within the first hour, an alarming message about a heavy Russian attack arrives: it turns out that—as so often happens in this war—our artillery is bombarding our own troops! But the strike is already over: and so it goes all night. At 4:30 p.m. we rise from our uncomfortable "beds." After not having had the opportunity to bathe for the past three days, this morning I bathe thoroughly, even though I run the risk of being stuck here in the middle of shaving—luckily, I am not interrupted.

Russians are slowly but steadily approaching, and our line slowly gives way just as steadily. At 10:00 a.m., command leaves, first to colony Budki.[35] I travel in the wagon with the general, and my horse is ridden by its stableman. We remain here until 7:30 p.m. A very gloomy day: we constantly receive alarming news about attack by Tatars and other wild soldiers. The fact remains that the Russians are gradually advancing and are already nearing Usice.[36] After an hour's traveling, we arrive at colony Alexandrowka[37] south of Torczyn. Command has only two miserable farm rooms at its disposal. We get our first hot food at 9:00 p.m., in the open air.

10 JUNE. Alarm at 3:00 a.m., and orders to be ready to march. Our troops are naturally not prepared to remain in their shabby positions anymore and retreat as far as the Russians can see. After fortification of our new position, a complete change in disposition arrives: according to this, we must make a strong flanking march past the enemy, in a northeasterly direction. We depart at 7:00 a.m. and are at our destination when another sudden change in orders arrives. Accordingly, we interrupt our march to Chorochorin[38] and instead march to Zubilno,[39] where we arrive at noon. We take up secure positions here,

in case of a Cossack attack, because, other than that, Russian forces here appear to be scanty. They do not advance, and there is very little artillery fire: they seem to have transferred their main forces elsewhere, so the only soldiers in our area are relatively large troops of Cossacks, who, during the night, have attacked our neighboring thirty-seventh division. There is a battle in which even Major General Tabayoly personally participates. The Cossacks are driven off, and a few gentlemen from command wounded. Because of this, we are somewhat more careful and take quarters hardly sixty paces behind our own firing line. Nevertheless, everybody is anxious, and each man carefully guards his own personal weapon. Dinner at 6:00 p.m.: only the second hot meal since the start of the Russian offensive. I quarter with gentlemen from the second artillery brigade in a nice, clean room and again have a thorough wash. By the time we get some rest, it's very late—we still await corps clearance, which only arrives at 9:30 p.m. This is followed by the drafting of our own orders and that of the artillery, so by the time we go to sleep it's already 1:00 a.m. But there is little time for sleep, because by 2:30 a.m., our baggage train departs, and our beds are literally pulled out from underneath us. Army Commandant Archduke Joseph Ferdinand has also become a casualty of our debacle and is replaced by Colonel General Tersztyánszky. High command has finally got hold of the real culprit for this debacle—Corps Chief of the General Staff Kralowetz, who has a great deal on his conscience. Two corps commandants have been relieved because of him—Meixner and Martini—and he becomes commandant of the forty-eighth, seventy-seventh, and forty-fifth infantry brigades. We wish him the best of luck with these, because he won't get very far with the seventy-seventh. Colonel Pusak, commandant of the fortieth infantry regiment, has also been relieved because the breakthrough occurred in his area.

11 JUNE. A defined plan finally takes shape in measures taken by army high command. This morning we continue marching "north." We leave at 4:00 a.m., arriving in Bereck[40] at 7:00 a.m. We should have arrived here yesterday but, for tactical reasons that have become apparent in the meantime, have had to incline back to the west. Now that these problems seem to have been corrected, we can continue our march according to plan. The troops take up a secure position here. The front is to the southwest, about six hundred paces north of the village; we stay in the village itself. The artillery is located behind us—a very unpleasant position, when the enemy artillery begin their work.

According to reports received, enemy cavalry corps are active near us, so a night attack cannot be excluded. Our commander decides to change quarters, and we ride off to Woronczyn[41] at 3:00 p.m., where we take up quarters in the castle together with the thirteenth division. I am quartered in one room with Artillery Colonel Walzl. This is the first night during which I am able to sleep for eight full hours (10:00 p.m. to 6:00 a.m.): this is essential, because I am completely exhausted, more psychologically than physically. The enemy do not seem to be having any fun either, because there appears to be nobody on the other side, yet we must keep retreating. Our definitive new corps commandant, Field Marshal Csanady, has arrived and taken over command.

12 JUNE. Ready to march at 4:00 a.m., on the way to Nowy-Dwor,[42] where corps command is accommodated; the castle is not available to us anymore. We stay in the open for the moment: the weather is very good, and in the afternoon, we march off to Dazwa,[43] because there are no quarters for us in Nowy-Dwor. We finally receive some newspapers at command: we have really longed for these, because our own mail has stopped completely. Happily, we gather from the newspapers, as well as verbal reports from around the front, that our overall situation is not as bad as our own experiences have led us to believe. Both of our flanks are secure, only in the middle have we been driven back, so a significant bulge has formed: the Russians are not yet confident enough to attack us there with infantry, so their cavalry keeps contact without attacking us directly. We are gradually moving to the northwest, to meet up with our reinforcements: two German corps are on the way. Our retreat is very gradual and incremental. A battalion already arrived today and has been immediately incorporated.

Hardly more than 1,600 men remain from the original eleven thousand or so men who started when the Russians broke through at Olyka: so we have lost about ten thousand men. The neighboring division has not fared better: all together, our fourth army has lost about forty thousand men and endless amounts of war material. Our own division alone has lost thirty-six artillery pieces, all our mortars, spotlights, gas masks, two fresh water preparation apparatuses, one steam and three traveling kitchen disinfectors, etc, etc. Artillery ammunition, explosives, and technical material in incalculable numbers, as well as forty-four machine guns.

Arrival at the estate in Dazwa at 4:00 p.m., where I am accommodated in a small room with Colonels Rosenzweig and Walzl. The estate is in derelict condition, under supervision of an old but still blond damsel, who has dolled herself up during the afternoon for our benefit—all in white, apparently to confirm her purity.

13 JUNE. The night passes quietly. Our room is small, but neat and clean. Transient rain toward morning, and then it becomes nice and warm. Quiet throughout the day as well—not a single shot is heard or seen. Our troops recover and regroup—together with the battalions that have been incorporated we again have about four thousand rifles.

Today, for the first time since Chorlupy, a press report arrives: unfortunately, it is not very cheerful: our troops in Bukowina[44] have been forced back significantly and now stand northeast of Czernowitz.[45] Will we be able to repair this damage?

Late in the afternoon the new commandant arrives: Excellency Jemrich von der Bresche, a very unattractive little man. Immediately after his arrival, an insane cloudburst occurs—and it is the thirteenth today! We are very sorry indeed that von Iwansky does not remain our commandant. He is a charming gentleman, keen witted with an excellent sense of humor, sometimes tinged with sarcasm.

14 JUNE. Our division is regrouped, and we march via Swinarin and Czesnowka to Tumin.[46] Departure 7:00 a.m. Weather very unstable, alternating overcast and sunshine/cloudy. Heavy downpour in the afternoon, just while we are marching through the forest: we get a thorough soaking. We remain in Swinarin, home of the corps command of Corps Szurmay, for several hours—we hear that a German division has been incorporated into our left flank. After receiving assignments for the position in question, we ride away. Our commander appears to be a fan of rapid riding: he rides only at the trot, even rapid trot and gallop, and doesn't recognize slow riding. After passing through Tumin, we arrive at Swiczow[47] after seven hours and take up quarters in the school—I am quartered in one room with Colonel Rosenzweig, with a window without windowpanes. Today was exhausting—I haven't felt as tired and wretched as I do this evening, for a long time. Dinner at 9:00 p.m.

15 JUNE. A quiet night, allowing me to feel at least partially rested and refreshed. Heavy rain all night and through 9:00 a.m., also repeatedly during the course of the day, and quite cool. Otherwise, quiet. The Russians are not far but do not advance. German troops—apparently two corps and a cavalry brigade—have already arrived and are making ready. Tomorrow we will begin our general offensive.

16 JUNE. The night is unusually cold, disturbed by handing out of orders after midnight. Fierce cold and overcast: this should be April weather!

The offensive begins; our troops advance at 9:00 a.m. and command arrives at daily vantage point ¤ 225 west of Tumin, where we take up a position in a farmhouse—it's even heated! Some of the men pass the time roasting potatoes.

We advance well but slowly. By 6:30 p.m., we have advanced so far that we are able to leave our daily vantage point and advance farther. We travel at the trot, arriving in Wojnica[48] at 8:30 p.m. On the way, we are soaked by a cloudburst for a second time. Our position is not too dangerous, and command travels to Gubin,[49] but only after long, time-consuming consideration. We take up quarters there in a small school. Mass quarters in a room that otherwise serves as a local dining hall. By the time we arrive, it's already 10:30 p.m.: the baggage train does not get here much earlier than that. We get our first hot food at 11:00 p.m., but it's as bad as it has ever been. Finally, we get some rest at 12:30 p.m. Today could not have been more exhausting if it tried.

17 JUNE. The cold, unfriendly weather continues, although there is sunshine at times. Our division is already waiting at the front: the neighboring division, including the Germans, has not penetrated as far as we have. It's afternoon before the division is ordered forward. The Russians appear to have brought up reinforcements, and complicate our advance. They even go over to the attack, before we even start our own offensive, actually forcing our troops back. But we force them back to their former positions. The Russians attack again toward evening, but again retreat. Because fighting fluctuates, our baggage train is pushed back so that, when things finally calm down by evening, we stand there without batmen, baggage, or traveling kitchen, and must make do with sleeping fully clothed on straw that we ourselves collect, every man for himself. No hot food today. Wretchedly cold, very little sleep. The Germans are doing much better than we are: they reach their given objective and take one thousand prisoners, as well as artillery pieces and two machine guns.

18 JUNE. Unstable, cold weather continues—rain at times. We remain here; advance is very difficult. Our baggage trains have been brought up again, so at least I can sleep decently, despite the fact that we are in mass quarters, ten men at a time. Today's press brings the bad news that Czernowitz has again fallen to the Russians—we are very depressed.

19 JUNE. Our front is relatively quiet: the Russians appear to have retreated from our positions; we are ordered to pursue them. The quiet we have enjoyed all day ceases in the evening. The Germans have advanced very well, so our division is ordered to advance and pursue the enemy. Orders are only handed out toward midnight, and command is ordered to advance at 4:00 a.m. the next day—but then everything is delayed for two hours. Meanwhile, the Russians attack, and our artillery return heavy fire: it doesn't last long, but its intensity brings the Russian attack to a halt. Plenty of wounded on both sides. So, the entire night is spent in movement and restlessness.

21 JUNE. During the night attack, the Russians are driven out of their positions and our division pursues them. We march off at 6:30 a.m.: at first the weather is lovely, but it then become cloudy with rain that, by 5:00 p.m., is pouring down in torrents. We march to Wojmica,[50] where we remain on the telephone for nearly two hours; then farther on ¤ 243 west of colony Dubrowa[51] to a group of barns in a German colony, where we spend the night. Because of the cool weather, I erect my tent inside the barn. We will not attack the enemy this evening. The division medical unit is also brought here.

22 JUNE. I do not sleep well, although I feel comfortable in my tent. In early morning, a violent cannonade emerges, from the German side. But after a short time, things calm down again. At 9:00 a.m. command rides to the daily vantage point at colony Dubrowa right next to the road.

At 10:00 a.m., our own attack and that of the neighboring division begins. It starts with directed artillery fire, which becomes a short but heavy bombardment. Then our infantry advances; the Russians counterattack, and so violent battle ebbs and flows all day. It ends with our not having won much ground, because German troop numbers are not large enough to prevent Russians from repeatedly attacking us. We have about six hundred wounded. All pass through the same road on which we stand. I collect all those able to march, including those who can drag themselves forward with difficulty: we join up with the ambulances that are passing by. I visit the first aid stations of the fourth rifle and eighty-second infantry regiments: I will not do this again, because their organization is miserable, and, each time I suggest something, I get the same stereotypical reply: "Regimental command has ordered it done in this way."

At 8:30 p.m., we return to our night stations. Straight after dinner, a heavy cannonade begins again: the Russians are trying to counterattack our division. No rest for us until the situation is clarified, and by the time the Russians are driven off, it's already 11:00 p.m.

Weather generally good, but at times rain threatens. It remains cool all day.

23 JUNE. I spend a miserable night in the tent, this time because of the howling wind, which does not allow me to fall asleep. It becomes calmer by morning, and the nice, sunny weather lasts all day. Our front is quiet: today our neighboring division are doing the heavy lifting. Only toward evening do the Russians try to attack our section, but are repelled each time. Command does not ride out to the daily vantage point today; in contrast, our division medical unit is fully occupied: the number of wounded in our division alone has risen to more than eight hundred.

24 JUNE. The day starts quietly—an attack is ordered, but troops do not advance as they should, mainly because the neighboring division is in their rear and remains where it is. Also, as has occurred before, we are significantly short of artillery ammunition. Toward evening, the order arrives from corps command to attack the Russian positions. Our troops are repelled and scarcely manage to reoccupy their old positions: this maneuver costs us a lot more than six hundred wounded, and many dead and captured. But corps command is satisfied.

Weather favorable, but significantly cool in the evening; we are quartered in open barns, so it isn't very comfortable. We were not prepared for so long a stay here. A moored observation balloon floats over our area. Toward afternoon, Russians shoot a whole series of shrapnel that whizzes over our heads. It's hard to know whether they meant to hit the troops or the balloon, but in any event, nothing is hit.

25 JUNE. Our front is quiet—today is the turn of the Germans—fierce fighting, but they make no progress. Very busy at the division medical unit: we have had to take care of many wounded during the last few days. Weather lovely—very warm. Command remains stationed here for the moment.

26 JUNE. Quiet at the front continues. Tonight our division is being taken out of the front line, to be used as army reserves, replaced by thirteenth infantry division. Troops remain in their positions, and command also stays put. This is urgent, because our losses are very great: more than 10,000 men in Chorlupy, and again more than 2,500 men during the past few days, so the few replacements we have made during the past few days are completely used up. Weather remains nice and hot—but the dust problem is very bad.

27 JUNE. Our army commander, Colonel General von Tersztyánszky, authorizes (only) the officer's corps of our division to be placed in reserve. All the officers and our immediate staff are to be introduced to him at 3:00 p.m. He appears together with Commander Csanady, accompanied by our corps commanders, introduces himself to the staff officers, and gives a dashing talk to all the officers assembled. The gist of this talk: he is well meaning to those who do their duty but correspondingly "brutal" to those who forget their duty. What a joke!

The weather that has been fine and warm all day so far, becomes overcast and stormy: the storm breaks at 5:00 p.m., heavy rain lasting, with varying intensity, all night.

28 JUNE. Overcast, rainy weather continues—rain at times—very humid. Clearing only after 5:00 p.m. Calm along the entire front: this is the calm before the storm, because we are preparing a large offensive, which should begin in two days' time. General Prusenowsky is a spent force. He has had even less luck with the eleventh division than he had with us. His fall is quite humorous: it occurred at table as follows: Commandant Smejkal had just described recent battles in a very lively, interesting way, developing his opinions of what occurred. Complete silence, interrupted only by a loud snore from General Prusenowsky—that was enough.

29 JUNE. Fine early: warm and humid. At 9:00 a.m. I travel to Wojmica to fetch our corps chief medical officer, because he cannot find us through the mud: he remains with our division medical unit, until afternoon. At 5:00 p.m. weather changes: rainy and cool.

30 JUNE. Weather atrocious—cold, west wind, overcast with rain at times. The immediate staff rides off at 5:30 a.m. to the vantage point of the thirteenth *Landwehr* infantry division—we are given a room without windowpanes—pitiable cold and an awful draft. Each wall has two open window frames; some are boarded up with planks, but still very uncomfortable. I am bleary-eyed after only three hours sleep—it's incredibly boring here, because our division is still being held in reserve.

Our attack does not advance despite repeated artillery preparation and bombardment. The Germans north of us, as well as the Falkenhayn division in the south, do make some progress, though. Around 8:00 p.m., we want to finally march forward but are ordered by corps command to stay where we are until the situation is clarified. By 10:00 p.m. this has still not been done, but in consideration of the late hour, we must again retreat to ¤ 243. What a scandal! What stupidity! Command is literally kicked out because they have become a nuisance. Almost nothing of the battlefield can be seen, either from the daily vantage position or at quarters; there is also the disadvantage of bad telephone communications in every direction. Today's vantage point is hardly one and a half kilometers from our quarters, which doesn't help either. So, in summary, command has been chased away, and it has all been for nothing. Such a day, with nothing to keep me occupied, is enough to drive me crazy.

1 JULY. After return from our so-called daily vantage point yesterday evening at 10:20 p.m., we have our main meal of the day, so it's midnight before we can get some rest. I sleep well until 5:00 a.m., despite rain and cold. Weather overcast early, then clearing. At noon the order comes for our division to attack and relieve the positions of the thirteenth *Landwehr* infantry division. However, by the time proper orders are given it is already 3:45 p.m. We depart for colony Dubrowa, to exactly the same position that we occupied on the 22 June. We ride, as is always the case with Major General von Jemrich, at the trot and the gallop, so it barely takes twenty-five minutes until we arrive at our vantage point.

Advance proceeds very slowly and continues deep into the night. Because there is no space for the entire immediate staff in one house, I ride back to our position with Junior Logistics Officer Pelikan and First Lieutenant Count Varaczyki at 10:30 p.m., so it's already around midnight before we can get dinner and then get some rest.

2 JULY. Despite the night fighting, the position has not completely been taken, so fighting continues into today. The three of us return to command at 9:00 a.m., so the immediate staff is all together again. Weather very nice, warm, and sunny.

The battle lasts, with interruptions, all day, but Russians maintain their previous position at Zaturczy.[52] We have a pile of about three hundred wounded: meals are brought out to us. After dinner, I ride back with the junior logistics officer to our beloved position: by the time we arrive there, it is already 10:30 p.m.

3 JULY. We ride back to command at 9:00 a.m.—there is so little space here that there is nothing for us to do, and we must loaf about idly all day. I would much rather have remained at our night station, where the division medical unit is also located and operates all day. The front is quiet, but only because the Germans are not fighting with us today—they have had enough for the moment, and need to rest and recuperate. If only our superiors understood this too! There is a general feeling of bitterness against our army commandant Colonel General Tersztyánszky, who appears to be a very brutal man: he is eager for his own credit, at the expense of others. Weather very nice until 4:00 p.m., when a storm breaks. Complete clearing after two hours, and, after dinner, I ride back to our night station with Junior Logistics Officer Pelikan: we arrive there at 9:30 p.m.—weather is excellent.

Today is the first real day of summer: very hot and oppressively humid. The same game is played, with the three of us (me, senior logistics officer, and chief medical officer) as during the past few days. We ride off to command at 9:00 a.m. Our army commandant has finally concluded that the position at Zaturczy cannot be taken with the forces he has available, and orders regrouping, which must be carried out that day. Relocation begins during the afternoon. Of course, this does not escape the notice of the Russians, who open up a murderous fire, starting a new attack in all directions. Troop relocation is naturally stopped at once. The artillery fire lasts all afternoon and only quiets down later in the evening: I return to my night location with my medical colleague. This bold idea of troop relocation in the middle of the day has caused us many wounded, dead, and captives.

5 JULY. The heat becomes tropical: it doesn't even cool down in the shade or when we are at rest. We are bathed in sweat all day. I overnight in the same place as before and spend all day at command. As a result, I have absolutely no place to stretch out and rest. It's doubly unpleasant when the weather is so hot: general tiredness and lassitude become unbearable. During evening, exactly when we have to ride back, a storm develops: we have to ride very rapidly to arrive dry at our quarters. The storm does not materialize, but we still arrive back exhausted. The front is quite calm, but heavy rifle fire from both sides.

6 JULY. We finally all transfer to the daily vantage point at colony Dubrowa: very near the front, hardly four kilometers away. But the great inconvenience of riding to and fro, and necessity of spending all day without quarters or a place to rest my weary bones, is gone. I take up quarters in the school next to the Protestant church (prayer house), together with Pelikan and First Lieutenant Martinowicz. I partition my third of the room—which is quite spacious—with my tent canvas, to live more apart from the others. I have become spoiled by living on my own for months in Chorlupy. Weather has cooled down significantly because of a strong wind that begins to blow during the night and lasts all the next day. A storm lasting one hour blows in toward evening.

7 JULY. Cool weather continues into the morning hours. I spend the morning at the division medical unit, ¤ 243. Much warmer in the afternoon. The front is quiet, as though the Russians were who knows how far away. By contrast, our reserves become ever stronger by transfers from the Italian Front—certainly they are only a few battalions—twenty-seventh and seventeenth infantry regiments—but they are reinforcements nevertheless.

Unfortunately, the Russians are advancing in Eastern Galicia: Kolomea[53] fell into their hands again a few days ago. The attack in Italy has had to be stopped to shorten our line there, and we have had to retreat and give back Arsiero and Asiago; The Italians trumpet this as a great victory, of course.

The Germans too have their work cut out for them. The English have started an offensive in the west, and the French are still attacking.[54] Army Hindenburg is being attacked by the Russians at the same time. And so, fierce simultaneous fighting on all fronts, with unbelievable intensity and great bitterness. If only it would all end!

8 JULY. In the morning, solemn decoration of our senior artillery officer: Colonel von Rosenzweig is awarded the Leopold Order by Corps Commandant Csanady in front of the command building in colony Dubrowa. While the order is being pinned on him, cannons on the front shoot salvoes, making an extremely solemn impression. Afterward a modest snack, then the corps commandant departs. Front completely quiet. Weather good: an hour-long storm toward evening. The terrible heat has let up.

9 JULY. The front continues to be quiet. The Russians do not fire even one shot. We arrange an attack on the Russian positions every morning from 3:00 to 4:00 a.m. It doesn't last long, but is enough to interrupt our sleep, especially when the Reichel cannons (10.4-centimeter cannons under the command of Captain Reichel) are shot off, at the same height as and hardly two hundred paces from our house: the entire building shakes, and as if by a miracle the windowpanes are not broken. Weather pleasant: a short-lived evening storm again.

10 JULY. The air has cooled down significantly, and it looks like rain. Nevertheless, I ride to division medical unit in the morning, returning that afternoon, during which time the weather clears up completely. Airplane activity has significantly increased, recently.

11 JULY. Weather very nice and warm. I travel at 8:00 a.m. with Captain Prehal to the quartermaster in Pavloviczy,[55] home of corps command. While he completes his affairs with the quartermaster, I look up dentist Dr. Kronfeld, to finally fill the tooth that he started to treat last winter. So, in the end, the tooth that Dr. Schmidt unsuccessfully tried to treat in Trieste nearly eighteen months ago can finally be saved. We return to command around noon.

In the afternoon, a gypsy from fourth light infantry battalion is sentenced to death by firing squad for repeated desertion, and the sentence is carried out immediately. I have the unpleasant task of acting as witness and confirm his death. A gruesome business. Luckily, the shots hit home and he dies immediately.

12 JULY. Weather overcast and rainy, cooled down a great deal. Lieutenant Colonel Gröschl, an old regimental comrade of mine, has joined the fortieth infantry regiment. We are happy to see each other and have a nice chat about bygone days. Quiet at the front, even with our regular but superfluous firing: the Russians have become used to it and don't react even with a single shot. They must surely think; let the dear Austrians continue wasting their ammunition.

13 JULY. Weather nice and warm, cool toward evening—a violent storm.

14 JULY. I spend the morning at the division medical unit and with the chief medical officer in Pavloviczy. I want to visit Dr. Kronfeld because my tooth

gives me no peace (although by far not as bad as it was in Trieste, no matter how many times Dr. Schmidt wanted to fill it). Unfortunately, Dr. Kronfeld went on leave yesterday, and I return home empty-handed. The pain lessens: I hope that it will disappear.

15 JULY. Weather nice and warm, cloudy again toward evening, as has been the case during the last three days, with the only difference that today it really does rain. Quiet at the front continues.

16 JULY. Weather overcast and cool. During the night there is a heavy Russian attack on the German southern group. We don't know the result of this fighting—the Reichel cannon makes its uncomfortable appearance again toward morning. The Russians are somewhat more active on our front today—apparently they do not appreciate our mortars.

17 JULY. Morning at division medical unit. Weather overcast and humid; just when we sit down in our summerhouse for lunch, it starts to rain quite heavily, and we become very wet. Our general sits where he is: he has his raincoat on. A few more episodes of heavy rain during the afternoon. Lively Russian artillery fire continues today as well. At times, they bombard our location. The heavy Russian attack against the German southern group in Pustomyty[56] continues all morning: its effects are unclear.

18 JULY. A terrible night. The front is very active: continued uninterrupted artillery and infantry fire from both sides; each infantry shot is clearly audible through the warm, misty air and the wind blowing to the east: it is as if they are shooting right in front of us, although we are about four kilometers from the front. Shooting continues until 4:00 a.m., preventing me from even closing my eyes. Because I am so tired, I feel miserable all day and very gloomy, mainly because our latest press reports also sound so depressing. The last two days of fighting have been bad for us. Our troops have retreated to the other side of the Lipa River.[57] The gloomy mood is also influenced by the miserable weather. It rains almost all day, preventing us from leaving our huts. Some clearing only toward evening.

19 JULY. A very calm night, allowing me to sleep well. Overcast early, clearing later—a midday storm, and then more heavy downpours during the afternoon.

20 JULY. Weather very overcast with repeated rain, which cools the air down significantly: it looks like fall already. This bad weather is also very unfortunate for the harvest: it seems to be a generalized, not just localized, weather phenomenon. The front is quiet. For the past two days, my toothache has completely disappeared and I can chew well again.

21 JULY. Rain again all day. It rains through the ceiling into our room in places. Rainwater in the fields and hollows has literally formed into lakes. Rain is driving us to distraction. Quiet at the front.

22 JULY. Rain continues during the night. Morning overcast and rainy—some clearing around 11:00 a.m. Inspection of the fortieth infantry regiment,

located in reserve near us, takes me two hours. More storms at 2:00 p.m., and repeated heavy rain all afternoon. Active artillery and infantry fire during the night from both sides.

23 JULY. Very overcast and cloudy early: I postpone my intended inspection of the twenty-ninth light infantry and send the wagon back to the division medical unit. Meanwhile, it clears up more and more, and the weather is very good by afternoon. According to news from my father, my decoration with the Red Cross Honor Cross Second Class has been published in the Gazeta Lwowska.

24 JULY. Lovely clear, warm weather. I leave with Junior Logistics Officer Pelikan at 8:30 a.m. for my intended inspection, first to twenty-ninth, then on to the fourth light infantry battalion. Impossible to reach the positions themselves; trenches are so full of water in places that one sinks up to the knees and higher in muddy water. I make do with only visiting the first aid stations. By 1:30 p.m. we are back again.

During the afternoon, a German general—an artillery brigadier—and his adjutant come for an inspection. During dinner, he tells us many interesting things about French and English theaters of operation. Unfortunately, we have to give him our own room for the night and must be accommodated in mass quarters in the Protestant church.

25 JULY. Weather nice and warm in the morning; afternoon overcast, but no rain. Increased artillery activity on both sides today.

26 JULY. Nice, warm summer weather. At 9:00 a.m. I ride to the division medical unit, where I also meet the corps chief medical officer; back by noon. Since the return of good weather, airplane activity has significantly increased.

27 JULY. During the course of the afternoon, we receive information from army command that the Russians are soon going to begin another offensive. Great nervousness on the part of our general staff. The brigade's general staff are commandeered, and instructions given to them to take special precautions for the coming night.

28 JULY. Army command is well informed, if a little late. I am suddenly awaked at 3:45 a.m. by heavy enemy artillery fire, and it's soon clear that a true bombardment has begun. We are all immediately up and active. The bombardment is aimed at our southern division, the seventieth. It does not take long for their line to be broken through, and the bombardment is extended somewhat north, to the thirteenth division. This is also soon broken through, and then, early at 7:00 a.m., our own division is attacked, followed by the thirty-seventh Honvéd division, and finally the twentieth Germans. So, a total of five divisions are being attacked during the current offensive. The Russians have complete success against all four Austrian divisions; only the Germans bloodily repulse three attacks, and remain in their positions.

At 11:30 a.m. the fighting calms down along the entire line. In the late afternoon, we counterattack and are able to advance a bit in all locations, into the number two position that we prepared earlier, so that we have lost in total hardly two kilometers of ground, at the cost of many of our men taken captive. Entire companies have disappeared, namely fortieth infantry regiment and fourth light infantry. There are very few wounded; hardly fifteen men are bought in: all the others, unfortunately, remain in Russian hands.[58]

There are certainly quite a few dead during the bombardment, but most of the men are taken prisoner. During the afternoon, 378th German infantry battalion joins us in a counteroffensive: the fighting ends at 7:00 p.m., hardly two hundred paces from our own firing line. Both of our sides together fire plenty of small rifle shots, shrapnel, and shells, and there are many critical moments during the course of the day, but, luckily, we come out unharmed. At 8:00 p.m. we ride back to night quarters at ¤ 243, where we have already been quartered before, hardly three kilometers from the new front. First hot meal of the day at 9:00 p.m.

Weather very good, but oppressively hot at times. Afternoon storms gather but do not occur because the air cools down significantly.

The debacle would not have been as great, and the loss of hardly two kilometers of ground would have meant nothing, if we would have been able to depend in some measure on our troops. Unfortunately, this is not the case!! Our men are completely demoralized, cannot withstand fire anymore, and simply run away after the first cannon shot. That is where the danger lies, the more so because this time the Germans are not able to put as many of their own troops at our disposal as before.

29 JULY. A quiet day. Our troops are in their second positions on the eastern edge of colony Dubrowa; command is in its former quarters in the barns on ¤ 243, where I erect my tent in its former position. I sleep very well, after I have been on the go since 4:00 a.m. the day before. I awake, out of habit, at 4:00 a.m., but then fall asleep straight away again. At 7:00 a.m. I am rousted out of bed by the corps chief medical officer, who wants to speak to me on the telephone.

This rest proves to be the calm before the storm. At 3:00 p.m., the Russians attack our positions again—fighting becomes fierce and unfortunately ends again with their breaking through. As usual, the Russians do not advance, and our troops assemble and counterattack again. Around 8:00 p.m., the old position is again in our hands, and we can breathe freely again. We take dinner in good spirits, and go to bed at 10:00 p.m. Weather very good.

30 JULY. I am awakened at 2:45 a.m. by a violent storm, which pours down onto my tent. After I am convinced that water does not leak in, I calm down again. However, I cannot fall asleep: at 3:30 a.m. a Russian bombardment begins again. We are ordered to be ready to march at once, because—as expected—a breakthrough quickly occurs again. Our baggage train departs at 6:30 a.m., while the fighting carries on. At 7:30 a.m. the Russians fire three shells on our command: two explode fifty paces from us, but we are luckily not hurt, just badly scared. At 8:20 a.m., the division medical unit departs to Pavloviczy—they have hardly left when many wounded stream in from the front—I take the duty over with my medical orderly, collect and look after the wounded.

Toward afternoon, we and the Germans make a combined counterattack that succeeds completely—our troops retake the old positions from yesterday. The division medical unit and baggage train (which arrives at 4:00 p.m.) are ordered back, so we get both lunch and dinner together at 6:00 p.m. Feverish active at the unit: 295 sick and wounded are evacuated, a third of them German. After the morning storm, the most beautiful weather develops, and continues all day. Overcast toward evening, but no rain.

31 JULY. Our front is quiet, but heavy cannon thunder north of us where the Germans are fighting. During the past two days, the Russians have gotten nowhere, thanks to attack by the 378th and 287th German infantry regiments: the Germans fight exceptionally bravely; their regimental commander rides past them just behind the firing line: despite being lightly wounded by a graze on the head, he remains with his regiment. One battalion commander has already fallen and one has been wounded: apart from that, one officer has been wounded and six killed. Our side has not suffered this kind of losses: our gentlemen prefer to be taken prisoner by the Russians—a scandalous situation! During the past several days, more than two hundred wounded Germans have arrived at our division medical unit. Weather overcast early, then clearing, with a strong wind that turns into a storm around noontime.

1 AUGUST. Continued quiet on our front. Continued attack by the twentieth German division north of us that repel all Russian attacks, with heavy losses. Weather fine, warm, and sunny—but no real summer heat.

2 AUGUST. After three days of uninterrupted fighting, the German front also becomes quiet again. Weather nice and warm like yesterday, but we freeze pitiably in our open barns at night because of the strong wind.

3 AUGUST. Field Marshal von Hindenburg has taken command of Army Group Linsingen, including the third army (Böhm-Ermolli)—a well-known, good, solid appointment. German 378th infantry regiment and 217th battalion are transferred to us, and keep our division medical unit busy. Weather overcast early with a few showers, which clear out rapidly.

4 AUGUST. A sudden, violent rainstorm during the night: all of us quartered in barns are woken up—most have to move with their beds because rain comes though defects in the barn roof. I freeze pitiably and sleep very badly. The storm lasts all day, despite periods of sunshine. Our stay in the drafty barn becomes more and more uncomfortable: the men try to repair holes in the roof and erect roofs over our beds. Dr. Müller and the chaplain are invited to dine with us today. A few days ago, I recommended Dr. Müller for the Officer's Cross of the Order of Franz Joseph. Quiet at the front continues. During the night, the

neighboring thirteenth infantry division south of us attacks the Russian position—stupid waste of ammunition, without the slightest success. The Russians don't respond even with one shot. They know our attacks by now and do not react to them.

5 AUGUST. The storm and miserable, damp, cold weather continue—late fall weather. Added to that, our miserable accommodation in the open barn, where we cannot work because nothing is heated: it's enough to drive one to despair. Toward evening, the storm does let up somewhat, but otherwise the weather is unchanged.

6 AUGUST. A very unsettled night at the front—a lot of shooting on both sides. Weather still overcast, damp cold, with a lot of rain. Despite improvements that have been made, it still rains into the barns, and the cold—especially at night—is unbearable.

7 AUGUST. Weather still very unstable. Sunshine alternates with repeated episodes of rain. We are wrapped in coats all day.

8 AUGUST. Early at 4:30 a.m. and ready to march: the Russians are attacking along the entire front. This time no bombardment, only continued precision shooting. It soon becomes clear that the firing has taken the least toll of our own division: it has had more effect on our neighboring divisions to the right and left. The thirteenth (right) is pushed back and retreats. Naturally, the Russians fight in vain against the twentieth (German) division: they try four times during the day and each time are repelled with bloody noses. Toward noon, the thirteenth, together with their reserves, go over to counterattack and win back their old position. When this happens, our order to be ready to march is canceled.

At 7:00 p.m. the Russians again counterattack parts of our thirty-seventh division; again we are ordered to be ready to march. After about two hours, everything peters out and we unpack again. According to prisoner information, the Russians intend to attack at dawn tomorrow—with shock troops,[59] without artillery preparation, and after having built their positions very near to ours today. We will have to take special precautions tomorrow morning at 3:00 a.m. In preparation, I do not close an eye all night: additionally, it's terribly cold inside my tent. At 3:00 a.m. there is a great deal of firing from both sides, but no attack—by 6:00 a.m., things are completely quiet. Weather miserable all day: cold, with innumerable periods of rain.

9 AUGUST. Quiet at the front lasts all day. Even the weather, which was overcast and cold in the morning, suddenly clears nicely around 10:00 a.m. The sun breaks through the clouds and spreads its warmth over everything. Unfortunately, the news came yesterday that our troops have had to vacate the bridgehead at Görz,[60] which we have defended heroically for more than a year. Hopefully this will not have bad consequences: none of us want to grant the wops a victory.

10 AUGUST. A quiet night. Weather good from early on, nice and a lot warmer than yesterday. Complete quiet at the front—not a single shot all day.

11 AUGUST. Nice, warm weather all day—a beautiful evening—full moon. Today our batmen are mustered: my Schweiger has been ruled fit for duty and will have to leave me in November. Quiet at the front continues. However, the press again brings gloomy news: our troops have vacated Stanislau.[61] So, we have now lost Czernowitz, Brody,[62] and Stanislau. If only it would all end!

12 AUGUST. Morning weather nice and very warm. Two transient periods of rain during the afternoon, followed by clearing. Quiet at the front.

13 AUGUST. The eighty-second infantry regiment leaves us, replaced by the fifth battalion of sixty-second and 103th infantry regiment. Weather unstable: sunshine mixed with clouds. I meet with Surgeon Major Dr. Garra.

14 AUGUST. Overcast in the early morning, but rapid clearing and it remains nice and very warm all day. The German Rittmeister von Linsingen, son of the famous General von Linsingen, joins our command today as communications officer between us and group Litzmann, under whom we serve at the moment. A very pleasant, elegant young officer—just a little nervous. He receives a separate tent, built into the barn near my tent. At 10:00 p.m. the 378th Germans attack an advanced Russian trench, take it, and capture a machine gun.

15 AUGUST. Horrible weather. It has been raining from 5:00 a.m.: the rain lasts, with very short interruptions, all day long. Many of us get out of bed early, because rain is dripping onto them: soon all of us are up, to escape rain in our barn. Those who don't have a "flying roof" over their beds now see to it that one is built: by evening the entire barn is divided up into separate cabins.

16 AUGUST. Thick fog since last night: continues into the morning. After that, gradual clearing and, from 2:00 p.m. onward, beautiful, warm, sunny weather. Third infantry brigade command (Major General Klein) with his staff leave us today: there are being transferred to Siebenbürgen.[63] Something is apparently about to happen in Romania. Absolute quiet at the front, until shooting and mortars begin from both sides at night. We are too near the front and so are able to hear each and every shot.

17 AUGUST. Lovely, warm weather continues all day. The Russians have been somewhat active: they apparently intend an attack; a defector tells us that the Russians will attack tomorrow—exactly on Kaisertag. We will see. In any event, preparations for Kaisertag are made; and, at the same time, frontline troops are informed about the possibility of attack.

18 AUGUST. Our Kaiser's birthday! At 9:00 a.m. a field mass in the cemetery chapel—after that, troop decorations are handed out by the commandant, mainly for the telephone section. Festive lunch at 12:30 p.m., to which the German regimental and battalion commanders of 378th infantry are invited. A very fine menu. During the Kaiser's toast, our artillery fires a round at the Russians.

Russians are quiet all day; they only attempt a breakthrough at 7:00 p.m., apparently in expectation that our officers and men would be by this time drunk with too much champagne: They are quickly and bloodily repulsed. By 8:00 p.m., everything is over, and the front is calm again. Weather nice, very hot. A real dog day.

19 AUGUST. During the morning, I inspect both battalion dressing stations of the 278th German infantry. Their dressing stations resemble our first aid stations, but are much better equipped. Each battalion has its own very heavy vehicle for material, and a second ambulance—just as heavy—for the wounded. One should not show our troops such things: if they see them, they will retreat at the first setback.

Today is also a very hot day—I return at noon bathed in sweat. Localized storms toward evening. Today the Russians try again to attack our forward position that the Germans took from them a few days ago. However, they are repelled. At night they try again and this time are successful. During the immediate counterattack, Germans lose five officers and seventy soldiers dead and wounded, and still cannot take the position back.

20 AUGUST. The air has cooled down significantly, but it still stays nice and warm enough all day. In the morning, our Group Commander Litzmann appears—he asks me about the condition of the wounded German officers and, with me as guide, visits them in our division medical unit. He is a stately, friendly old gentleman who expresses himself reassuringly about the general situation.

21 AUGUST. Weather unstable, with rain at times. The air has cooled down significantly. Quiet at the front—nightly shooting has significantly lessened.

22 AUGUST. Overcast in the morning, with repeated periods of rain. Clearing in the afternoon, but the air remains cool and the evening is cold.

23 AUGUST. Weather remains unstable—cloudy and cool. Rain mixed with sunshine. During the afternoon, the German surgeon general of Group Litzmann inspects our division medical unit. He arrives accompanied by two German doctors and Chief Medical Officer Zapatowicz. I report to him punctually and take over the inspection, because our Dr. Müller is in the sick bay. Inspection is rapid and superficial. The German U-boat *Deutschland* with money and goods from America has, despite being pursued, landed safely in Bremen.[64]

24 AUGUST. Weather like yesterday. After dinner I remain at table with Major Heller, Captains von Linsingen, and Junior Logistics Officer Pelikan: we sit comfortably and talk politics until 11:30 p.m.

25 AUGUST. A restless night with a good deal of firing from both sides, especially during the morning hours. Weather good: pleasant and warm—it looks as if summer heat has finally ended. Three days ago, command started to build shelters for our winter quarters about eight hundred paces behind our former vantage point. They will be about one and a half meters under, and about half a meter above, ground.

26 AUGUST. Rain at night, fine during the day, and warm. The night attack announced by the defector does not materialize.

27 AUGUST. A quiet night. Today the defector spoke of another imminent attack—I do not believe him because, according to an airplane report, the Russians have few soldiers and artillery against us. Rain at night—strong wind all day, but sunshine and warm. Toward evening the wind increases and becomes a real storm.

28 AUGUST. A very quiet night; I am able to sleep very well, for a change. During the morning, Chief Medical Officer Zapatowicz visits our division medical unit. Straight after lunch, new cholera vaccinations for command—this time there is no severe vaccine-related reaction: We are all very upset at the news that yesterday Romania declared war against us.[65] Our resentment is indescribable: everyone feels like the whole world has conspired to attack us. Nothing but enemies all around! In the evening, we receive the news that Germany has declared war on Romania, and Italy on Germany. How will Bulgaria react? The circle of our enemies has for all practical purposes closed. Who, at this hour, would dare prophecy at when and how this war will end? Weather nice in the morning, heavy rain in the afternoon, continuing into the night with heavy winds.

29 AUGUST. I sleep miserably. The drumming of rain on my tent roof, wetness inside, and the howling wind outside give me no peace. Additionally, a severe attack of right-sided sciatica. These, all together, are conditions that I have not experienced before. My health is deteriorating sharply, and I will think about these miserable, cold, wet quarters in the barn all my life. Weather overcast and cool, clearing during the afternoon.

30 AUGUST. Despite quiet at the font, my sciatica keeps me from sleeping again. Weather very nice from early morning onward—but my pains are not getting any better. Yesterday afternoon I had, because Dr. Müller was on leave, to travel to the chief medical officer in Pavloviczy by car, which does my sciatica no good at all. We are surprised today at the news that General von Falkenhayn, Chief of the General Staff at German headquarters, has been transferred back and replaced by Hindenburg. What can this mean?

31 AUGUST. A warm day, actually hot—hot at the front as well! The night before is restless—a great deal of shooting—and the Russians start a bombardment at 5:30 a.m. We are immediately made ready to march despite the fact that, as it turns out, the Russian fire is directed at seventieth division south of us. The bombardment lasts four hours, followed by an infantry attack, which is kept in check by our powerful protecting fire. Troops from seventieth division immediately counterattack, and Russians are driven from two of their three positions. The third is taken during the night, so that early on 1 September all positions are again in our hands.

1 SEPTEMBER. Very restless night; heavy artillery, machine gun, and infantry fire lasts all night. By dawn it is finally quiet again, and quiet lasts all day. During the morning, Senior Surgeon General Dr. Hammerschmied gives a talk in our division medical unit about protection against gas: all division physicians attend. I invite him and his physician escort to take lunch with us. During the night comes the news that Turkey has declared war on Romania. Morning overcast, afternoon rain.

2 SEPTEMBER. A quiet night, allowing me to finally get a good night's sleep. Morning weather overcast and rainy at times, clearing in the afternoon.

3 SEPTEMBER. Weather like yesterday, clearing only during the afternoon. Bulgaria declared war on Romania on 1 September, so at least we are relieved of that potential problem: there were rumors that Bulgaria would leave the Central Powers. Unfortunately, Captain von Linsingen is leaving our division today—apparently, he doesn't appreciate his living quarters in the barn, so Papa Linsingen has had him transferred to army command. He is replaced by Dragoon First Lieutenant von Elterlein. My sciatica, which has improved significantly during the past few days, has now completely disappeared.

4 SEPTEMBER. A horrible night: pitiably cold and uninterrupted heavy firing at the front—I barely get two hours sleep. Quiet only returns around 5:00 a.m., but there is great activity among our batmen, so again no sleep. In the morning, a German gas protection officer arrives to train officers and men to protect themselves against gas attack. I am pleased that yesterday evening First Lieutenant Sandig just returned from a course in poison gases in Krems, and that he takes this lecture over from me. The weather is beautiful, but no talk of heat anymore. Fall is arriving with giant steps.

5 SEPTEMBER. Night passes exceptionally quietly, so I manage to get a good night's sleep. Fine weather all day, which fliers make use of continuously: they now appear every day, often in squadrons of five or six. No dogfights so far, despite the fact that fliers from both sides appear at the same time. They make wide detours around one another. In the morning, a talk from the German gas officer about protection from gas attack, for the men nominated for the job of gas protection officers. The talk is not as good by far as the previous one given by General Hammerschmied.

6 SEPTEMBER. Stupid shooting at night again, so I sleep very little, and that badly. The nice, warm weather continues. The officers' public baths at the division medical unit are finally ready for use: I take the liberty of using the facility in the afternoon. I am just finished with my bath when the German consulting surgeon from the Litzmann Army Group, Colonel Dr. Groebl, Professor of Surgery at Breslau[66] University, accompanied by Surgeon Major Dr. Bosmann, Professor of Pathological Anatomy at Breslau University, appear to inspect our division medical unit. Among sick and wounded, which interest him especially, he notices one man shot through his gallbladder. An emphysematous[67] biliary fistula has already formed, for which he can find no explanation. He recommends immediate surgery, which he performs himself. It's a pleasure to see how confidently and elegantly he works.

7 SEPTEMBER. A curious type of fighting has recently evolved in our position. Complete quiet on the front all day except for a few artillery shots here and there. But hardly has it become dark when shooting starts again: infantry, mortars, machine guns, artillery, uninterruptedly all night until daybreak, when everything subsides again. The purpose is to obstruct our work on front positions. But work carries on diligently, except that it costs a few killed and wounded each day, and robs us of sleep, especially because an east wind, which mostly blows here, carries the sound of fighting to us.

Almost every day, we have German officers as guests at table: today, the German Artillery General Hansen and his adjutant, a German captain. He is the commandant of all the artillery in Group Litzmann. Press report: German and Bulgarian troops have stormed the bridgehead at the Turtukal River[68] and taken prisoner four hundred officers (two generals) and twenty thousand men, together with more than one hundred artillery pieces. Great rejoicing: those Romanian swine deserve a nice souvenir of their perfidy.

8 SEPTEMBER. Nightly shooting at the front continues, as does my sleeplessness. The Russians have partially removed their troops from our front, and only three regiments are left. That is apparently the reason for their anxiety, and wild shooting during the night. Some of our battalions use up between four thousand and five thousand shots during one night. Thick morning fog, cool, unpleasant, clearing and warm by afternoon, then quite cool in the evening. During the night, we freeze pitiably in our barn.

9 SEPTEMBER. During the morning, a visit from Chief Medical Officer Zapatowicz at our division medical unit. Weather very nice and warm. The seventieth infantry division has left: probably for Siebenbürgen.

10 SEPTEMBER. Night relatively quiet. The Russians seem to have finally understood that the amount of ammunition used up during the night bears no relation with the losses that they have caused (fifteen to twenty men). Naturally, we are also shooting a lot less now. Weather nice and warm, but an enormous dust cloud has developed. Our fliers have observed the approach of a new Russian guard's corps marching to the southwest from Luck. Press report: Silistra[69] has fallen! Thus, Bulgaria has won back the area lost to Romania in 1913.[70]

11 SEPTEMBER. Night also quieter. During the night, the Russians have directed an unsuccessful gas attack against the German tenth *Landwehr* division south of us. This is the first Russian gas attack in our sector. The subsequent infantry attack is easily repulsed. Weather nice and warm, becoming cloudy toward evening, but no rain.

12 SEPTEMBER. Night completely quiet. Weather nice and warm.

13 SEPTEMBER. Quiet at the front. Weather changeable, mostly overcast with wind and a great deal of dust.

14 SEPTEMBER. During the night, wind increases to storm intensity—some rain early, which has tamped the dust down. But it has become colder, as cold as during late fall. It's all the more unpleasant because we have no proper quarters and are exposed to the elements—we freeze pitiably during the day and at night, if possible even more so. Quiet at the front. There is a rumor that we will soon be leaving this theater of operations. As a result, there is little interest in construction of winter quarters, and the work doesn't budge.

15 SEPTEMBER. We freeze horribly during the night, and the weather has not improved. Windy, overcast, and cold, just like yesterday. Our quartermaster Captain Prehal leaves us today and is returning—after two weeks leave—to his own command, the ninetieth infantry regiment. We have been celebrating his departure since yesterday evening with a large Souper. He sits in the place of honor next to the generals. The official event has had to be significantly shortened because of the beastly cold in the barn and accompanying discomfort. It's to be continued this afternoon. But this did not stop certain gentlemen last night from helping themselves liberally to the champagne. During the afternoon, even more German officers join us at table: they are exchanging company and battalion command with us. Captain Prehal is acclaimed with a large number of champagne toasts, and the fortieth infantry regiment band plays in his honor. Straight afterward he gets into his car: our amateur photographers immortalize the moment, after which we whizzes away while we yell "hurrah" and sound fanfares.

First Lieutenant von Elterlein is leaving command today as well—he is a pleasant, cheerful fellow who has felt very much at home with us. He is taking over a German battalion command.

Relatively quiet at the front, even though the Russians are much more active today than they were during the past few days and are shooting more artillery rounds off.

16 SEPTEMBER. During the night, we freeze again. Around 8:00 a.m., a lively cannonade at the division south of us at Szelwow.[71] A Russian attack is being prepared: we make our own preparations and are soon ready because, after extending in a northerly direction, portions of our division will also come under fire, especially the twenty-ninth light infantry battalion, under Commandant Lieutenant Colonel Gröschl. After a very heavy artillery barrage that ends as a real bombardment, the Russians break into the forward battalion lines; our men withdraw in good time and retreat to positions in the rear. Then a counterattack is made by battalion no. 5/62, a battalion of the fortieth infantry regiment, and a German battalion: after short but heavy fighting, they succeed in throwing the Russians out again. Russians counterattack but are soon brought to a standstill. The same thing happens in other divisions—Russians counterattack, but our positions hold along the entire line, and where the Russians succeed, it's only temporary and they are immediately driven back. During the day, 1,800 Russians are taken captive and four machine guns captured. Russian losses are enormous—but our losses have not been light either; more than five hundred wounded brought in to our division medical unit during the night.

Weather overcast early, followed by clearing, even sunshine in the afternoon. Overcast again toward evening, and very cold. During the afternoon, Professor Dr. Gröbel appears at our unit, to examine his surgery patients: he dines with us at the medical unit.

17 SEPTEMBER. The Russians appear to have had enough—today has been completely quiet at the front. Weather changeable: overcast morning, rain at times during the noonday hours, and transient clearing during the afternoon. Significantly colder during the evening. We huddle in our coats all day and cover ourselves with a cape, because it is too cold in the barn without it. There are no warm corners, where we can at least warm ourselves for a little while. Our kitchen is outside, sheltered from the rain only by a flying roof. Nights are quite unbearable.

Commandant von der Marwitz takes over command of our group from Commandant Litzmann. He visits us at 6:30 p.m. and asks me about yesterday's losses.

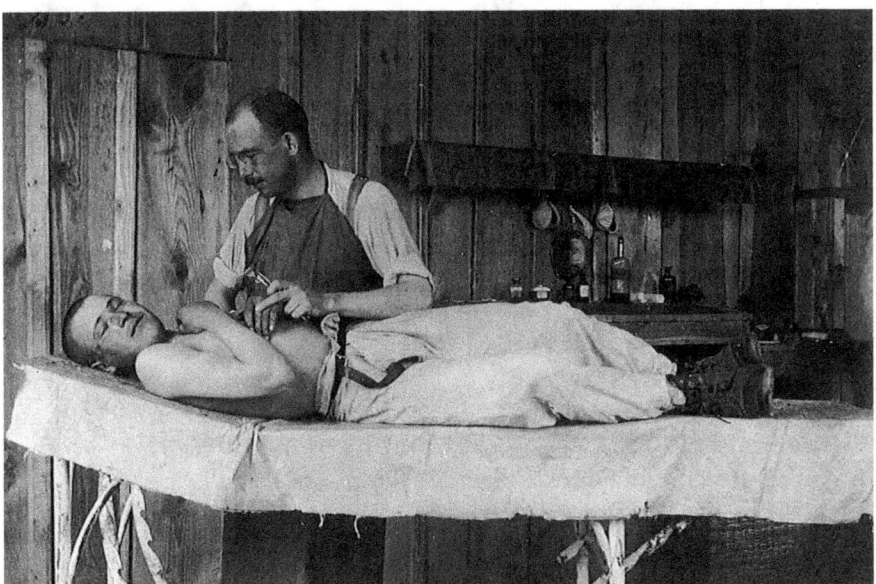

Figure 3.7. Surgeon examining his patient postoperatively. Photograph courtesy of the Leo Baeck Institute.

18 SEPTEMBER. A restless night, stupid shooting of machine guns and artillery from both sides. Cold would have been endurable without this pointless firing. Early overcast, cold weather, a bit of clearing in the afternoon, but increasing cold during the evening. Dr. Müller begins his leave today—naturally at my cost, because I have to wait for my own leave until he returns.

19 SEPTEMBER. Another restless night. Lively firing at the front, and the awful cold in the barns, prevents any of us from sleeping. Around 8:00 a.m., the Russians begin heavy, directed fire against the tenth German *Landwehr* division to the south of us. The firing becomes more and more violent and by 11:00 a.m. has extended to our own division as well. Around 4:00 p.m., the degree of intensity of firing lessens on us but increases on the divisions to the south: the tenth German and our own eleventh. A violent bombardment develops, and lasts, with short pauses in intensity, until darkness falls. An infantry attack does not follow, however. Only around 11:00 p.m. is a forward section of trench transiently captured, but the Russian are immediately driven back.

Weather very nice, even warm around noon in areas where the sun shines. But in the shade it's a lot less warm. I feel especially miserable today, because both my ears are completely blocked from a bad cold, with permanent bilateral whistling.

20 SEPTEMBER. Night is somewhat warmer but, as expected, also restless. The Russians begin a powerful bombardment onto the tenth German and our eleventh division at 2:00 a.m., which continues uninterruptedly until 5:00 a.m. The cannonade is deafening and sounds even scarier at night than during the day.

Eventually, the Russians succeed in breaking through, but an immediate counterattack partially drives them out. Reserves are brought up. From 9:00 a.m., Russian fire is extended to parts of our own division as well, and at 10:00 a.m. we receive notice that the Russians are preparing a gas attack. Command as well as medical unit are ordered to be ready to march off at once. At 11:00 a.m. fighting subsides completely, and there is no infantry attack on our division. It's asserted that the Russians refuse to leave their trenches, even though they are fired upon by their own artillery.

The Germans take their positions back and in the process take 250 prisoners. The Russians are cordoned off in their own trenches, cutting off any possibility of escape, and all who do not give up are killed.

At 6:00 p.m. one of our own flight squadrons, consisting of eleven planes, is soon joined by several Russian planes—a sporadic dogfight ensues, but no one is hurt. Russians drop bombs on our positions and our flank, without doing any damage.

Weather overcast early, nice in the afternoon, then overcast again. But it has become significantly warmer, so living in the barns has become more bearable.

During the night, First Lieutenant Baron von Hammerstein returns from vacation and is greeted warmly.

21 SEPTEMBER. A quiet night—no shooting, and our troops have a chance to rest. I am not feeling well; it always hurts somewhere now. Since yesterday I have severe pain in my right ankle joint—it looks as if another inflammation is developing, as was the case a year ago: the same foot, just another joint. Weather overcast but not cold—rain toward evening, which lasts well into the night and cools the air down significantly.

22 SEPTEMBER. Brisk firing along the entire front during the night; apart from that, rain hammers down on our roofs. Reason enough not to be able to sleep. The overcast, damp and cold weather lasts all day, and our barns become literally unbearable. How we long for a warm room—you cannot imagine! Clearing in the evening, clear, starry sky, but still brisk. Chief Medical Officer Zapatowicz arrives at our medical unit in the morning.

23 SEPTEMBER. The night is horribly cold, and we freeze wretchedly. Brisk infantry and mortar fire on the front—so again no real sleep. Getting up early and washing in this cold barn is almost unbearable. The temperature hardly reaches 4°C. Beautiful weather during the day, warm and sunny.

I start up my round of inspections again, with the fortieth infantry regiment. I leave at 10:00 a.m. and return at noon. The regiment is in reserve not far from us, in colony Dubrowa. Command is lodged in my former quarters, the school. The men are all in covered shelters—how I envy each and every one of them!

24 SEPTEMBER. Another clear, starry, very cold night. I do not take my blouse off to sleep anymore. It's much quieter at the front, yet I sleep very little—because of the damp, cold barn, I have already caught a cold, which gives me no rest. Other men are not much better off health-wise, most are coughing quite badly.

I continue with my inspection during the afternoon, visiting the twenty-ninth light infantry regiment and no. 1/62 infantry battalion. I enter the trenches of the first group but do not like what I see—it's much worse than comparable positions at Olyka. The trench is very narrow; cross trenches are still damaged in many places from previous fighting. Fighting trenches contain foxholes and rabbit holes. The rabbit holes have hardly room for six to eight men, but have the advantage of not being easy to hit and are protected. The large foxholes literally have an outside staircase. Weather very nice—I even sweat on the way back.

25 SEPTEMBER. A lovely, sunny, warm fall day—just beautiful. At 10:00 a.m. I travel to battalion no. 5/103 and visit the trench, accompanied by the local physician. Their communication trench is remarkably wide—German system—and very clean. The position itself is impressively clean and exemplary in every way: where possible even better than in Olyka. This, in contrast with twenty-ninth regiment. Many rabbit holes of the latest type located in the fighting trench. Shelters for the troops, for use as quarters are already being built. They are of impressive size and depth, one for each half company, and absolutely bombproof. However, they are certainly not hygienic: no light, no air circulation possible—this will have to be accomplished artificially in some or other way. Rifle bullets whistle over our heads constantly. By 1:00 p.m., I am already back.

During evening, I transfer my quarters from my barn to our division medical unit. I cannot stand it here anymore—no sleep and I am so cold that I am worried about becoming seriously ill. I take a small room in Dr. Müller's house, which was originally the owner's cowshed but has now been nicely outfitted as an office. The best thing about it is a regular oven that can easily be heated. There is no floor; two windows, one nailed shut with planks for lack of glass panes, the other covered with Billroth bandages.[72] This bandage has the estimable property of letting light in completely, but against this it is opaque, which helps make the room quite cozy. Walls are freshly whitewashed—so in sum, a warm, clean room, which I especially appreciate after so many miserable days and nights in that damned, drafty barn, open on all sides. Simply an Eldorado!

26 SEPTEMBER. Despite this, I do not sleep well the first night: it's the fault of my batman, Schweiger, who has set up my bed without realizing that the ground is soft and irregular. But at least it's warm: that is the main thing.

Today is another warm and sunny day. At 10:00 a.m. I travel to field hospital no. 9/10 in Wojmica to pay a return visit to my old comrade the commandant, Dr. Gara from Karlstadt,[73] and to examine his disinfection oven. It's very practical, requires little material—only bricks and a few pipes—and is based on dry air disinfection. One of these must be built in our medical unit as well. I meet our chief medical officer there. By noon I am back. My cold is better.

27 SEPTEMBER. Weather not so good: overcast and cool, clearing in the afternoon with sunshine. Increasing cold toward evening. At 3:00 p.m. our division stages a heavy rifle and artillery attack on the nearby Russians, to deceive and pin them down, because the Germans are attacking Swiniuchy,[74] south of us, to reoccupy positions occupied by Russians for the past several days. Very heavy artillery fire from our side, which increases to a real bombardment for a few minutes. The entire action lasts for an hour, during which we fire about five thousand rounds: in financial terms—according to the experts—this costs about a quarter of a million crowns. It seems to have paid off, however, because the position is completely retaken, with 41 officers and 2,800 men taken captive, as well as nineteen machine guns and one artillery piece. According to prisoner reports, the Russians planned an earlier attack and made all necessary preparations, including reserves. But we prevented this by attacking first.

28 SEPTEMBER. A cold night, also cold the next morning. Luckily, I notice very little of the cold weather in my nicely heated "room"/cowshed. But the gentlemen in the barn are grousing loudly. It's their own fault: they are all together and have taken no serious steps toward building winter quarters. I obtain a few competent workers from command of the light railway locomotive who, led by their engineer, will build a shelter for me. I make sure that the material is also supplied to my division medical unit. Each man must look after himself—a real scandal! But our chief of staff, Major Heller, with all his noblesse and generosity, is far too extravagantly disposed to worry about little things like shelter, provisions, etc., for his command. He only recognizes the war per se and does not care about anything related to it. This is decidedly unjust, because his duty is much more to care for all aspects of his command and in the first instance to see that the men obtain winter quarters. All that he needs to do is to task one man with this job and make sure that necessary labor and materials are available. But that is a sore point with him—to remove one professional from the troops—that could lose the war! Our commander himself is a poor vassal, who can just whine and complain but never command and who does not trust Major Heller at all. He himself has already developed an ear infection and walks around with bandaged ears, like an old woman, but lacks the courage to order that decent quarters be built for the men.

Weather very nice with a great deal of sun that unfortunately doesn't give much warmth anymore; it's quite cool in the shade.

Today is the second day of the Jewish New Year, and Chaplain Dr. Levi comes to our position by car to hold a service with us. I receive him myself so that he doesn't feel completely abandoned. Participation among the men is very low. Services are held outside. He also cannot understand how we can be accommodated in this wretched way.

29 SEPTEMBER. The weather changes: overcast and cool, with periods of rain toward evening. Our regiment's front is shifting to the north so that, instead of the German 378th infantry regiment on our right flank, now we have the German 348th infantry regiment on our left. Accordingly, command is also moving north to Alexandrowka—exactly now, when I want to see to building my own shelter in the woods!

30 SEPTEMBER. I sleep beautifully, probably because the night is exceptionally quiet at the front. Today we are busy preparing for relocation of command, which should follow at noon. The division medical unit is being moved to Wojmica with an advance section to command.

A great victory in Herrmanstadt[75] is reported. The Romanians have been cut off from their line of retreat at the Red Tower Pass[76] in the Carpathians—about three thousand prisoners and enormous war booty: ten locomotives, three hundred ammunition carriages, seventy automobiles, thirteen cannons, two hundred ammunition wagons, more than two hundred filled baggage wagons, one hospital train, one airplane hangar with two airplanes inside, and large amounts of other miscellaneous war material. This makes us very happy—that miserable rabble deserve everything they get.

1 OCTOBER. At midnight all clocks are put back one hour, to daylight saving time. I am happy to be able to spend an extra hour in bed and to finish the nice book *Das grosse Heimweh* by Rudolf Herzog that I have been reading. But the Russians do not seem to agree with my plan, nor with the fact that we are moving today; at 6:00 a.m., they start a heavy artillery barrage aimed at our sector. So we have no alternative but to get up quickly. Weather very overcast, unfriendly, damp cold, with a strong north wind. The artillery barrage lasts uninterruptedly until 11:00 a.m., and then there is a pause of one and a half hours. This ceaseless hammering on our positions has so far not led to casualties. The men are well protected from this type of firing in their rabbit holes. Meanwhile, the weather has completely cleared; the sun is shining but doesn't warm the weather up much—it remains cool. Leaves on tress are gradually disappearing: many are already red. At 12:30 p.m. the hammering on our positions begins again, lasting late into the night.

2 OCTOBER. A restless night with a great deal of firing. An early frost on fields and roads: it becomes clear and quite warm when the sun breaks through. Hammering on our positions begins punctually at 6:00 a.m., just like yesterday, and by 10:30 a.m. has become a real bombardment that lasts about an hour, followed by a Russian infantry attack against the twenty-ninth light infantry, no. 4/62 battalion, and the German 378th infantry regiment. Only the right flank of battalion no. 5/103 is affected. Fighting ebbs and flows: first the Russians penetrate our trenches, then they are driven away, whereupon they try again, until finally at 1:30 p.m. they are driven off and we are in charge of all our positions again. During the artillery attack, Russians also direct fire to our rear, where they expect our reserves to be. They have placed all lines of approach under fire, and a great deal of shrapnel falls on our position without injuring anyone.

Quiet all afternoon, but our medical unit is very busy—during the course of the afternoon and the night—until 3:00 a.m.—more than three hundred wounded are brought in—among them about sixty Germans and forty-five Russians. After sunset, which unfortunately occurs very early now—around 5:00 p.m.—it becomes horribly cold, and locations in the barn where we eat become quite unbearable. The few men who have fur coats are already huddled in them: the other men freeze. Only a few men have barracks that can be heated—for example, the general and I in Dr. Müller's house, as well as some who have installed themselves in the mess in the forest, which is already complete. We will soon leave this inhospitable place and return at 7:00 p.m. to our well heated barracks. How good that will be!

3 OCTOBER. Night passes relatively quietly. No significant activity during the morning either. We hear from prisoners that the Russians have relieved their frontline troops, of whom only a remnant remain. Straight after lunch, artillery fire begins again: it gets heavier and heavier and soon becomes a real bombardment, followed by an attempt by their infantry to penetrate our positions. Heavy curtain fire pushes them back again, before they get a chance to reach our trenches. These attacks are repeated a few times, each time without success; from 3:30 p.m. they don't try anymore. Our losses today are light, hardly sixty wounded; Russian losses appear to have been much heavier. Weather very bad: overcast, damp cold, strong north wind at times.

4 OCTOBER. Overcast, bad weather continues, a little temporary clearing in the afternoon, heavy fog during the evening. Reasonably quiet on our front—the Russians shoot at us sporadically, but larger actions are reported from our northern and southern German neighboring divisions. Still no Russian successes.

5 OCTOBER. Nice, warm weather in the morning, which suddenly changes toward noon, with heavy west winds. Cold again, with rain at times. The plan to move our command to Alexandrowka seems to have been definitely abandoned. Instead, we are provisionally moving into already completed shelters in the woods. Mass quarters for most of the men in the mess, with exception of the general and Colonel Rosenzweig, whose quarters are ready, and gentlemen from the general staff, quartered for the moment in the telephone exchange. For meals, beds are pushed back against the walls to obtain space for the tables. I suggest remaining in my existing quarters, because on 14 October I want very much to go on leave. Unfortunately, there is no leave because of the Russian offensive. But I still hope for approval by the appointed time. Even quieter on the front than yesterday. Our own firing is also less today.

6 OCTOBER. Weather changeable, cool overcast. Quiet at the front.

7 OCTOBER. Yom Kippur. By invitation from Chaplain Dr. Levi, I travel to Vladimir Volynsky with the general's own car, taking Senior Physician Dr. Deutsch from the second division medical unit with me. The journey takes 1.25 hours; the weather is very unpleasant: overcast, rain at times. I spend the entire day in synagogue in a place of honor next to Chaplain Dr. Levi with exception of the afternoon pause from 2:00 to 4:00 p.m., during which time I visit the local medical supply branch to order supplies. I return to the synagogue and remain there until 5:30 p.m., at which time I return, arriving at command at 7:00 p.m. (The car remains at my disposal all day.) I fast easily and am not plagued by hunger. The sermon is much better than the one for New Year. The service is solemn and very good—an outstanding cantor—but the number of men is a lot smaller, only common soldiers and poor Russian Jews. Around noon the weather improves, and my journey back is much more pleasant than in the other direction.

8 OCTOBER. I am awoken by Russian artillery early at 4:30 a.m.: active fire in the vicinity of the division medical unit. Artillery fire all afternoon, which changes to an actual attack. They try four times, but each time are easily repulsed.

Figure 3.8. Eastern European synagogue: one tiny part of a world destroyed by the Holocaust. Photograph courtesy of the Leo Baeck Institute.

Weather unpleasant all day, rain at times, wind, damp cold. Most leaves on the trees are already yellow.

I spend the morning at the corps chief medical officer in Pavloviczy, related to permission for transfer of my division medical unit to Wojmica. Transfer itself takes place in the afternoon; a section of the northerly adjoining German group has been assigned to Colonel Hueger. Naturally, as has always been the case, wounded assemble in the usual location of the medical unit on the side, from where they are evacuated by wagon. News from the Romanian Front is very good. Herrmanstadt has been in our hands for a while, and Kronstadt (Brasa)[77] has been occupied today.

Today, I start with building of my shelter: military railway commandant Captain Diebel has kindly made skilled craftsmen available to me. The plan has been drawn up by Engineer Lieutenant Tramer, a Viennese. Material taken from tree trunks in the forest are supplied to me by the medical unit; the rest I beg, borrow, or steal from the technical consultants. Every man for himself, instead of command unity. What a scandal!

9 OCTOBER. A stormy wind howls unceasingly all night, only letting up toward morning. Weather remains changeable with repeated rain during the day. Quiet at the front, heavy Russian artillery fire only after 2:00 p.m., but the expected infantry attack doesn't materialize.

Work on my shelter is progressing well—I am already looking forward to its completion. Since the medical unit has left here, I am unpleasantly isolated. At least our mess is very cozy.

10 OCTOBER. Quiet at the front. Weather better, no rain during the day.

11 OCTOBER. Lovely, clear weather, warm, with a fairly strong, warm wind. During the morning I travel to the medical unlit in Wojmica and then to the corps chief medical officer in Pavloviczy to request his support for my leave request. I do the same thing with my general on my return. My request is sent off today. Toward evening the wind picks up and becomes a veritable hurricane around 10:00 p.m. Powerful clouds gather, and a violent storm ensues. I would not mind if my shelter provided me with sufficient shelter from the storm, but it does not. Of my two windows, one is closed with roof board, the other has only one out of six panes made of glass, the rest covered with Billroth bandage. This second window faces west, where the storm originated. The force of the storm against this thin wall of bandages is unbelievable—but, protected by many kinds of counter pressures, it holds. However, water penetrates into all the crevices of the ceiling and walls. I do not sleep a wink all night: at dawn, I see that everything on my table is soaked. The entire morning is occupied taking all my books and equipment out to dry.

12 OCTOBER. Wind howls all morning, letting up toward noon. Afternoon sunshine, but then wind and rain again by evening. The long way from mess to my shelter is very unpleasant. The front is quiet: I am busy all day with building my shelter.

13 OCTOBER. Weather changeable, overcast, cold and damp, but no rain. Quiet at the front continues. My building progresses. There is a real building frenzy all along the entire area. Everyone is building!

14 OCTOBER. Rain early. Weather very unpleasant. A great deal of Russian firing all morning; immediately after lunch, they go over to infantry attack, which is easily repulsed. These attacks are more a demonstration than anything else. More rain toward evening, exactly when I have to walk the long road from mess to shelter.

15 OCTOBER. Lovely clear, warm, sunny weather, continuing all day. The Russians do not allow even such a nice day to pass without an attack. Scattered artillery fire all morning, especially at our barrage balloon south of us: they do not hit it, because it descends in time. Suddenly, at 5:00 p.m., without artillery preparation, they try to advance against our division, but immediate blocking fire from our batteries does not even allow them to reach our barbed wire.

16 OCTOBER. Lovely, warm weather continues today, as does Russian activity. Today, their artillery fire starts very early, at 4:30 a.m.: they fire not only on our trenches, but also on our artillery and reserves in the forest. Firing is so active that it appears to be the prelude to an attack. Because I am so isolated in my new quarters, I get out of bed and walk straight to command. Firing lasts

until 11:00 a.m. but is not followed by an infantry attack. Around 9:00 a.m., I take the opportunity to complete my morning toilet in my quarters, which was interrupted by Russian fire.

According to reports, the Russians have attempted an infantry attack on the twentieth German division next to us this morning. They come on in dense columns but are hurled back by violent artillery fire, with enormous losses.

At 3:00 p.m. there is another sudden Russian artillery attack on our front, followed immediately by an infantry attack. Powerful blocking fire from our artillery, machine guns, and mortars do not allow them to even reach our trenches, and the attack is repulsed. At 5:00 p.m. they try again, with the same result. Very heavy Russian losses, while our own losses are light: five killed, twenty-six wounded.

Russian fire south of us near Pustomity[78] during the evening is much heavier. The air is so clear, with a southwest wind, that each shot can be heard sharply, just as if it would have been in our immediate vicinity despite being twenty kilometers away. The report comes late at night: the Russians are easily repulsed.

17 OCTOBER. Because of yesterday's Russian activity, which lasts into the night, I do not go back to my quarters, but remain at command in mass quarters. In a few days' time, I hope to move into my new lodgings. I need not have bothered: during the night, the front is completely quiet. Weather miserable, damp cold, very overcast, rain at times, a lot of mud.

18 OCTOBER. Heavy artillery fire starting at 4:00 a.m. As it later turns out, this is an artillery attack from the German group north of us on Russian positions. At 9:00 a.m., the Russians begin to fire at parts of our line; it only lasts about an hour. Weather nice and sunny, cloudy in the afternoon: this does not stop me from moving into my brand new quarters which are finally completed. My living room is lovely and friendly—a little too small, 3 × 3 × 3 meters—but very bright. One does not have the feeling of being more than 1.2 meters below ground. Externally, it gives an enviable impression and is built quite stylishly.

19 OCTOBER. A very cold night—it's already −4°C, but I do not notice this at all, because my quarters are beautifully heated. I sleep very well indeed the first night. My mood leaves much to be desired: each letter from my wife—which I am always so happy to receive—lately brings me nothing but disappointments. She says that I am responsible for the fact that I have not been home since Christmas, while she sees so many acquaintances in Vienna during this time. If she only knew how I yearn for leave, she would surely not reproach me in this way. It's an unfortunate coincidence that Russians haven't stopped attacking us since June and that all leave has been blocked. But women often lack insight. Out of pure anger, I have not written home for the past five days, thereby punishing myself more than her: pangs of conscience, inner disquiet, and miserable mood.

Russians have been actively firing artillery and mortars since noon and during our lunch have fired a few heavy shells on command: Luckily they do not hit, because we are all still alive. Thick fog early, and real cold. The sun cannot break through, and all day is overcast and cold.

20 OCTOBER. Firing lasts all night, disturbing my sleep many times. The first snow falls during the night but has disappeared by morning. The sun breaks through and we have nice weather the rest of the day. My quarters are ready today in all their glory and are photographed.

21 OCTOBER. Since noon yesterday, the Russians have been very active firing mortars: firing goes on all night almost without pause, as if their only aim was to interrupt my sleep. Weather overcast early, rain toward noon that lasts until evening and softens our roads. Despite the state of the roads, I travel in the morning to the division medical unit in Wojmica, where I happen to meet our chief medical officer. Return around noon. Permission for my leave still has not arrived, and my impatience rises daily. I cannot make myself do any work, keep myself busy packing and unpacking, but am not sure whether I will really obtain leave. A portion of the small number of our front troops return, so at the moment we only have no. 5/103 battalion at the front. Many consider this preparation for an eventual relocation of the division.

22 OCTOBER. Russian activity at the front continues: mainly mortar fire during the night—extremely unfriendly. Weather cloudy and rainy all day—evening rain—mud becomes ever deeper. Immediately after dinner I hear by telephone that my request for leave has been approved by army command. Limitless joy! I am so excited that I cannot rest. My only thoughts are directed at provisions that I can bring along to my family. In Vienna, according to newspaper reports, shortages have become very severe—people stand for hours in line—sometimes without success—in front of stores to buy something, anything. I would like to spare my family from this, at least during the time I am on leave. So far I have collected a goose and four live chickens: what a bother they will be during my trip! Also: a compartment box full of potatoes, two kilograms of butter, sixty eggs, three loaves of bread, rolls, one kilogram of soap, which is especially scarce, twenty packages of matches.[79]

23 OCTOBER. Morning passes very quickly with packing and all manner of preparations for the trip. Immediately after lunch, I get into the automobile made available to me by command and—with many greetings and wishes for a good vacation by everyone in command, General Jemrich at its head (who is most entertained by my chickens)—I whiz off. My car aide Lieutenant Kuzniar accompanies me to Vladimir Volynsky. The roads are very bad—muddy—and the trip does not go off smoothly. On the way I made a detour at our bakery in Chorostow,[80] where I fetch the flour, eggs, loaves of bread, and rolls. Here I join our baggage train commandant Captain Resch, a very nice man—but he is large and heavy and weighs the car down, so it can proceed only with difficulty: the car breaks down twice on the way, and a one-and-a-half-hour trip to Vladimir Volynsky takes four hours. Near the entrance to the railway station, the car breaks down completely, and we nearly miss the train. We travel farther without difficulty, but have to change trains in Kowel[81] and carry all the heavy packages onto the other train. The chickens go into the baggage car, a great relief for me.

24 OCTOBER. The train is not very full, so I share a first-class coupé with only one other man; I can sleep through the night without having to use the sleeping car. During the day, a dining car is attached to the train, and we are well looked after with provisions. This is very necessary, because throughout the long stretch of railway, there is no food available, despite the many stations like Lublin, Kielce, Ivangorod,[82] etc. In Trzebinja[83] we reach Austrian soil. At 10:45 p.m., according to plan, we arrive in Vienna Nordbahnhof. I cannot find my wife, despite the fact that I gave her my arrival details in good time. A bad woman,[84] I think to myself, and go off myself. I cannot scare up a car at the station, and my goose quacks with impatience, amusing everyone around. For a good tip, the porter finds me a one-horse carriage. Not only do I have great difficulty loading all my baggage, but a woman asks whether I cannot take her with me as well! Luckily she is traveling in a completely different direction; otherwise I would have had to say "no," and she is an officer's wife! The taxi meter moves much more rapidly than the coach, so by the time I finally arrive in front of my home in district VII Kaiserstrasse 62 after a whole hour, it costs exactly eight crowns. The caretaker looks very surprised to see me when he opens the door. Oh my goodness! The lady of the house and her daughter have just returned home from the station: she must think that the Herr Doktor has left her in the lurch! What a scene! It turns out that, immediately in front of the military train with which I arrived, a civilian train—which I was obviously not on—had arrived. When she asked when the next train was due, she was told tomorrow at 7:00 a.m.—they naturally thought that she meant the next civilian train—so she went back home, but the greater was her surprise and joy when she found me there already!

VACATION, 24 OCTOBER TO 14 NOVEMBER. I find my family well, just thinner, especially my Olga. I can see her joy and happiness that I have arrived: she is very animated and will not leave my side—my dear, good wifey, affectionate as a little child.[85] My eldest daughter, Bettina, has become a splendid, lively woman. Her thinner appearance looks very good on her, and she is both modest and lively. She fills me with joy. Ega is a pretty, dear young girl, still doesn't learn much but certainly knows more than she did last year and has made excellent progress in piano playing. She has real talent. Miki is a magnificent young girl, deft and agile, but always modest—she cozies up shamelessly against her Dad and is a real enfant terrible. My youngest daughter, Mary, is dear and sweet:

actually, this is the first time I really see her. This sweet little thing is very good, hardly cries at all, so that one doesn't even know that an eight-month-old baby is there. Time passes too quickly and extremely pleasantly—every day we either receive visitors or pay visits to others; we often go to the theater, which we both enjoy greatly. Performances are all splendid.

Provisions have become very difficult to obtain, and my heart bleeds to see how my two elder daughters have to get up at 7:30 a.m. and stand in line for half a loaf of bread. Our cook and maid do the same thing—that is how daily rations are collected. If one is even quarter of an hour late, there is no bread for the day.

Three meatless days in the week are less difficult to bear and can be compensated by vegetables and flour-based dishes. In any event, the few ounces of meat that one can afford, since everything has become so expensive, so shrivel up in the pot that each person can only take two or three bites, and even this costs at least seven crowns. Less beef is eaten, and fat geese and pork are much more practical, especially because they already contain fat, which therefore need not be purchased. Fat is the most important dietary ingredient at the present time.

A daily newspaper is a thing of the past—Poland's ensuing proclamation of 5 November is completely unexpected and much discussed.[86]

Weather is very good throughout my stay, very mild and even warm, with only two transient periods of rain. And so, the twenty days fly by. Each day shortens my leave and my joy, and before we look around 15 November arrives, and I must travel back.

15 NOVEMBER. I leave the house at 6:00 a.m., accompanied by my dear wife and Bettina, who absolutely refuses to stay at home despite the early hour. My train departs at 7:00 a.m. As soon as we leave Prerau,[87] a complete winter landscape comes into view. It's snowy and cold, and remains so until we arrive in Wolhynia.[88] In places, we suffer from insufficient heating on the train. However, the trip is comfortable, because there are few officers traveling with us. On the way, I find out that my command is located in the same place that I left; I arrive there the next day in time for lunch.

16 NOVEMBER. Hearty welcomes and greetings from all sides. My new underground lodging is still there, and I soon move in there. Winter weather: overcast. Cold, snow.

17 NOVEMBER. Telephone call early; order from tenth corps command that, apart from my regular services, I must take over the duty of our chief medical officer, who is on vacation. Zapatowicz might not even return, because he is favored to be promoted to surgeon general. I travel quickly to corps command, but only get to report to chief of general staff, Lieutenant Colonel Raschky, because the corps commandant himself is at the front. A certain amount of excitement: Colonel General von Linsingen is inspecting our positions today.

The Russians, who have been significantly quiet during the past several days, have become quite active again. Our batteries return fire, and shooting from both sides becomes quite lively.

Weather today overcast again, light snow and cold: the ground has frozen solid.

18 NOVEMBER. Weather unpleasant: snow, cold, temperature below zero, overcast and gloomy, as is the general mood—many men from the mess are also on leave, and the few who are left are nowhere to be seen, because everyone is crouched in his shelter, somehow passing the time there. I do the same thing, which is not too difficult, especially since I am kept busy with extra work by the absent chief medical officer.

Russians are shooting like crazy and appear to be planning an attack. They have gradually built their trenches to within a few hundred paces of our own.

19 NOVEMBER. It has become even colder, −5°C, with strong east wind. Snow again during the afternoon. The division physicians assemble around me again, and we have meetings all day: each one has his own problem—one wants leave, another doesn't wish to cooperate anymore; I must find some words of comfort for each of them. Quiet at the front during the morning, but since noon heavy firing from both sides, mainly artillery.

20 NOVEMBER. At 10:00 a.m., a call comes from corps command that the army physician in chief is arriving in Rogozno[89] at 1:00 a.m. for an inspection: I must be there waiting for him, as representative of the corps chief medical officer. I have very little time, and travel there immediately. I am pleased to expect General Terenkoczy again and quite surprised when, as soon as the train arrives, I see his successor, Surgeon General Dr. Bürkl from the *Landwehr*. Terenkoczy appears to have been removed. Bürkl is inspecting no. 3/9 reserve hospital: we have a good but simple lunch together and then travel together to Wojmica, inspect my own division medical unit as well as no. 9/10 field hospital, and then go on to Pavloviczy to corps command, where we report to Commandant Csanady and introduce him to the others. It's already 4:30 p.m. when he (Bürkl) travels to the thirteenth *Landwehr* infantry division in Kruchyniczy,[90] and I return to my division, arriving around 5:00 p.m.

The new army chief medical officer looks like a nice, friendly fellow: he says that he is a water diviner. Weather better than yesterday—no more wind.

21 NOVEMBER. An overcast, horrible day, thick fog with visibility hardly twenty paces—afternoon thawing weather, mud, strong southeast wind. Accordingly, very little fighting. The boredom is awful, no company at all—our lovely, beautiful mess is totally deserted, except for the two obligatory meals, which are announced by ringing of a bell. Most men leave the mess with their last mouthful still in their mouths. Why? Where is the communal life, which has previously been so well known in our division, where each new man has already heard of our division's reputation and is pleased to join it?! Our com-

mandant is the main cause of this boring attitude. He is a real hypochondriac: every day there is something else wrong with him—his ears are always stuffed with cotton wool, sometimes even with a bandage over them, so at table he can't have even the most rudimentary conversation. No savoir vivre at all! At night he runs to bed at 9:00 p.m.—the mess is either too warm or too cold for him: in any event, he has supposedly caught a cold. It's so true: "The fish rots from the head downward."

22 NOVEMBER. Early sunshine, for the first time since my return from leave. I have almost started to believe that the sun doesn't shine here anymore. Unfortunately, my raised spirits are immediately dashed. As soon as I leave my den, I hear the sad news that came in overnight: our old, so dearly beloved and honored Kaiser Franz Joseph I died yesterday evening at 9:15 p.m.! What effect this earthshaking event will have on the war, and the entire political situation, cannot be foreseen. Good news from the Romanian Front: Crajowa[91] has been taken.

23 NOVEMBER. Weather changeable, sunshine followed by clouds. Snow has disappeared completely, and temperatures are milder. The front is quiet, very little artillery activity, alternating from both sides.

24 NOVEMBER. Nice, warm, sunny weather—other than that, nothing of note. Zapatowicz has taken his ten days' leave; we do not know what he intends to do now.

25 NOVEMBER. Nice, sunny weather continues. At 9:00 a.m. our command takes an oath to the new Kaiser Karl: all the troops and baggage trains in our area are assembled in front of the cemetery chapel on ⌑ 243. The ceremony lasts until 11:00 a.m. On our return we get the news that Field Marshal Mackensen and his men have crossed the Danube in the Dobrudscha[92] area in more than one place. The Romanians are doing miserably—no worse than they deserve.

26 NOVEMBER. Early sunshine with a strong east wind, which causes the sun to soon disappear behind the clouds. Around noon a short period of sunshine. The front is quiet.

27 NOVEMBER. Weather absolutely awful: overcast with rain. Doing anything outside is most uncomfortable. The roads have been greatly softened and the mud has begun again.

28 NOVEMBER. Weather unchanged. Usual desultory firing from both sides at the front.

29 NOVEMBER. Weather the same; also the fighting. Russians are heavily engaged on the Romanian Front but are only concerned about saving their own skins, not about the Romanians, Their left flank is hanging in the air exposed; once Bucharest falls, the way to Odessa is open. Captain von Linsingen and a colonel from the quartermasters section are our guests at lunch: we enjoy each other's company. As previous war comrades, he is very interested in what has happened to us since he left.

30 NOVEMBER. Still no sunshine: overcast and foggy, with mild temperatures. At 9:00 a.m. there is a quiet mass for our dear departed Kaiser. Last night around 10:30 p.m., the Russians attacked the German 378th infantry regiment again with artillery and captured one machine gun. Our fortieth division throw the Russians out of the trenches once more.

Such stupidities occur quite frequently on both sides: in my opinion they make no sense, and the resultant few Russian wounded are completely disproportionate to the large amount of ammunition rounds that are used; we have some losses as well. We should conserve ammunition for the time when we really need it.

Today the Kaiser's funeral is held in Vienna.

1 DECEMBER. Overcast, foggy, cool weather continues. Nothing new at the front: lively mutual firing at one another during the night continues. We are bored, little to keep us occupied, no companionship. The day drags on endlessly. In the morning I travel to Pavloviczy (location of corps command). Zapatowicz has returned from leave, purely for financial reasons, so as to obtain all the war payments due him. He is definitely leaving in a few days and then will obtain half his full salary for the next three months. It sounds petty but has its justification. Several physicians come to say goodbye to him: Müller, Gara, etc.

2 DECEMBER. Early in the morning an official requiem for Kaiser Franz Joseph in the cemetery chapel on ¤ 243. This concludes the official mourning ceremonies. There is a tragic postlude in the form of a railway catastrophe on the Vienna-Budapest route just outside Budapest: the Vienna fast train, overfilled with returning mourning guests, crashes into a local train: about 70 dead, more than 150 wounded. Just awful!

Excellent news from Romania: Bucharest will soon fall soon; it's surely just a question of a few days. Weather like yesterday but less frost, only a few degrees below zero.

3 DECEMBER. A light frost, −1–2°C; cold lasts all day with clouds and wind. Very uncomfortable. Firing on both sides has significantly lessened: nights are much quieter. The Russians seem to have moved a great deal of their artillery to the south. They have begun a strong, but unsuccessful, relief offensive in the "three land corner"[93] of the Carpathians. Romanian troops are useless: the Central Powers' advance continues unabated. Campolungo in Italy has already been taken, and the Army of Mackensen has joined forces with the Army of Falkenhayn at the crossing of the Danube and are now advancing on Bucharest.

4 DECEMBER. Uncomfortable, overcast, windy weather continues; the ground has frozen solid. Nothing new on our front, making the latest press reports on the Romanian front the more interesting.

5 DECEMBER. Weather unchanged. In Eastern Romania, our troops have reached Targovisti,[94] and in the south the Argesu[95] has been crossed. Bucharest was rapidly evacuated by the Romanians several days ago.

6 DECEMBER. We finally see the sun again: it does us good, after so very many cloudy days. But temperature remains below zero, and ground is frozen solid. This beautiful sun doesn't last for long: by noon, it's already completely covered by clouds. At the same time a violent cannonade begins on the front. Only after a great deal of telephoning around do we find out that it's our neighboring division, the thirteenth *Landwehr* infantry regiment, that has commenced a large-scale action to reoccupy the picket guard recently lost to the Russians: the close proximity of the Russians has become "unpleasant." The action is completely successful; the position is taken—and held despite two Russian counterattacks, with forty prisoners taken.

Things have a habit of occurring at the same time; news comes in the evening that both Bucharest and Ploesti[96] have fallen. This is certainly more important than the portion of trench taken by the thirteenth. We don't have all the details, but the Romanians have evacuated the city to at least save men and material.

7 DECEMBER. Yesterday evening a strong east wind began, and continues all day; skies are heavily overcast, and cold continues. Quiet at the front: the Russians appear to be resigned to their losses at the picket guard.

8 DECEMBER. Overcast, cold weather, strong east wind continues. It's just awful—I cannot leave my den.

9 DECEMBER. Weather unchanged: very heavy wind at night. Ground almost frozen solid.

10 DECEMBER. Weather the same; despite this I must travel this morning to the division medical unit for a discussion with our old friend from the Brusilov Offensive Surgeon Dr. Scheidl. He wants written confirmation from Dr. Müller and myself, through fourth army command, that he saw action in the middle of enemy fire in Chorlupy on 5 June during the Russian breakthrough. He naturally doesn't mention the fact that he merely passed through Chorlupy, running away when the first shots were fired; on the contrary, he wants to squeeze a high decoration for bravery out of this affair! After lunch, our commander von Jemrich finally takes four weeks leave.

11 DECEMBER. Oberstabsarzt 1 Klasse Dr. Herzog is appointed the new chief medical officer of tenth corps in the place of Zapatowicz; he will arrive during the next few days.

12 DECEMBER. Thawing weather, rain at night and in the early morning—there is already mud during the day. Extensive repairs of the stove in my shelter: insertion of a new iron plate: the old one has spoiled my comfort in the shelter.

Toward evening, unexpected news comes that the Central Powers have made formal peace proposals to the Entente.[97] We receive this news with mixed emotions. Most are very happy about it. The first serious step toward peace has been taken! The Entente surely cannot say "no" to this with a clear conscience without considering it further: their responsibility to the world would be too great. For us, with the splendid position of our forces that give us such a colossal advantage, the moment has come to magnanimously make the first step. The following days will surely be momentous!

Booty taken in Bucharest is enormous. The fortresses have all been taken intact and fallen into our hands with artillery pieces and a huge quantity of ammunition: also huge stores of grain.[98]

13 DECEMBER. Our new chief medical officer Dr. Herzog has arrived and today is inspecting our division medical unit as well as no. 9/10 field hospital in Wojmica: of course I have to be present for both. He does not make a good impression and will surely make more excessive demands than his predecessor. I return from these inspections at 12:30 p.m. Weather nice and sunny, moderate wind. But there is mud everywhere.

14 DECEMBER. Weather overcast, strong southeast wind, mud. I report to the front at 9:00 a.m. and inspect the no. 5/103 dressing station and then the fortieth infantry regiment, as well as the shelters of the fourth light infantry. They are all situated to the east of the large forest, between the woods and colony Dubrowa. Return at 11:30 a.m.

According to radio broadcast, our peace offer has not been received well: one may already say that it will not be accepted.[99] An English newspaper is so impertinent as to say that discussions could only be possible, if Germany first surrendered its artillery and its entire fleet. That is mean-spirited, in view of our peace offer!

15 DECEMBER. The current data on Romanian war booty include:
    145,000 men, among them 1,600 officers
    150,000 dead, wounded, sick, and scattered
    422 field artillery pieces, among them 25 heavy guns
    364 machine guns
    64,000 square kilometers of land, almost half the entire country
    2,000 kilometers of railway of a total of 3,087 rail routes
    130 locomotives of a total of 700 vehicles
    One quarter of their entire rolling stock
    800 German and Austrian prisoners have been freed.

There are still no figures for captured agricultural products such as grain, oil, petroleum, etc.

The press reports on our peace offer merely to serve to confirm what we have heard on the radio. Noticeably, the Russians have not yet spoken, for or against, but the more so do others—mainly the English. Newspapers exceed each other in the vilest insults to Germany. Word such as thieves, tigers, villains, etc., appear everywhere. Weather mild but overcast and wet.

16 DECEMBER. Early fog that then clears for a few hours. Continued quiet on the front.

17 DECEMBER. At 8:30 a.m. I travel to the front with Chief Medical Officer Herzog, then to the baths at ¤ 243, followed by visit to dressing station

no. 5/103 in the forest, the dressing station of the fortieth infantry regiment and the fourth light infantry camp at the nearby depression to the east, also to reserve position no. 5/103.

Herzog insists on making sure that the men's hair is shaved short, and that stretcher bearers, medical orderlies, and even physicians undergo testing in giving morphine injections. That is ridiculous!

Return at 12:30 p.m., and we have lunch. We both visit my lodgings, where we discuss individual details; then we visit locomotive station no. 6.

I am quite blown away when during discussions he informs me that yesterday he signed my request to award the Order of Franz Joseph to officer Kr. After all, both Chief of General Staff Major Heller and Captain Pistelka had told me that this request had been sent off middle of September. What inefficiency! Weather quite good, even sunshine by noon for a short time, but mud is quite bad.

18 DECEMBER. Early sunshine, cold not so bad, light southeast wind. Suddenly overcast at noon, snow squalls: the snow remains (because of the temperature).

After dinner, I join a lengthy celebration in our mess in honor of Artillery Captain Katzer, who is going on leave tomorrow to get married. He is very jolly: alcohol loosens his tongue, and he tells stories from his time as second and first lieutenant so humorously that we roll with laughter. By the time we part, it's 12:30 a.m.

19 DECEMBER. Complete snow cover, overcast. Temperature a few degrees below zero.

20 DECEMBER. Heavy snowfall overnight, moderate west wind. Snow is very deep in places. I am ordered to report to the corps chief medical officer in Pavloviczy at 9:30 a.m.: I find the chief medical officer of the thirteenth *Landwehr* infantry division there as well. Herzog gives us a long lecture about our professional obligations and then, mercifully, allows us to go. The new broom is still sweeping clean! His main job is to provide busy work, so nobody is bored.

21 DECEMBER. A beautiful, sunny winter's day, less cold, but more snow—the wind is completely still. Inspection with the corps chief medical officer. We leave at 7:30 a.m.: inspection of dressing station at the twenty-ninth light infantry; we go right into the front lines, then the manned first aid stations of no. 4/62 and no. 2/40, then the elaborate position of second field artillery regiment. Return at 12:30 p.m.

22 DECEMBER. Overcast, gloomy weather and quite cold. In the evening in our mess, we hold a wager on the peace offer, which had made many of us so happy and in which many had placed so much faith. The "friends of peace," including our Junior Logistics Officer Pelikan, lose; this costs him two bottles of champagne, to which we—seven men in all—help ourselves, augmented with

four bottles of regular wine: all consumed during amicable conversation. It is 12:30 a.m. by the time we get to bed.

The Entente still has not officially replied—but what they say, and how they say it, in the newspapers, leads us to conclude that we are further away from peace than ever. Their language is not only hostile but scandalous.

All fronts quiet at the moment—maybe the calm before the storm! In Romania, too, progress is now very slow.

Regimental Physician First Class Dr. Fieber from the division medical unit, an excellent surgeon, is being transferred for fourteen days to the twenty-ninth light infantry first aid station: he has been tasked to observe how first aid is given to the wounded immediately behind the front and to suggest improvements. This stupid plan is all Herzog's idea.

Only Herzog, fresh from the hinterland, whose war is only just beginning, could suggest such a thing, after war has already been raging for more than two years. Physicians on the line have developed a way of doing things during this time; we, who have no direct influence on the fighting, may not even try to change any of this. They will, at the decisive moment, do exactly as they have been accustomed to, in ways that they consider best. Quality of care depends exclusively on efficiency of the doctor who is treating the patient. Because we cannot choose our physicians but must take them as they come; the fate of the wounded lies entirely in their hands. Dr. Fieber will not be able to change this in any way.

23 december. Moderate thawing weather, southwest wind—morning rain, afternoon clearing. Piles of deep snow are gradually melting.

24 december. A good deal of snow has already melted: it has become a dirty gray cover. No question of Christmas spirit. The newspapers bring news that President Wilson has asked the warring parties for their peace conditions. We are very upset. After we have made the first peace overtures, the American with the huckster's spirit now wants to appear before the whole world as a peace apostle. And all this time they have had the key to peace in their own hands: if America would have stopped supplying war material to our enemies, the war would have been over long ago. Americans are only interested in making money—human lives are of no importance at all.

At noon we receive only fasting dishes: potato soup with spinach and two fried eggs—that is all. Too little for my "unchristian" spirit. There is certainly a festive meal in the evening, but not to my taste: nothing but different forms of fish: fish soup, jellied fish, baked fish tart. Fish has to be brought in from Lemberg at inflated prices—nine crowns per kilogram. Much more value is placed on drink: we start modestly with decent amounts of beer, followed by a few bottles of table wine—soon it's champagne's turn, and things become quite wild, with General von Rosenzweig—as representative of the vacationing commandant—making a toast to our new Kaiser Karl, followed by one to our families at home. He is an exceedingly refined, elegant, and noble gentleman, but no speaker. Our Major Heller proposes an added toast to get things get going: he is in a jolly mood caused by all the wine, but still in complete possession of his faculties. The general, the logistics officer, and I go to bed at 11:30 p.m.; others remain until 4:00 a.m.: in all, thirty-four bottles of champagne are emptied.

25 DECEMBER. Everyone has a hangover—just like the weather, overcast, damp, strong southwest wind. Only some traces of snow.

26 DECEMBER. Overcast, damp weather continues, with strong west wind. At 9:00 a.m., inspection of our divisional ammunition dump by our corps chief medical officer: I accompany him. From there I go on to our divisional medical unit, where I stay until noon. Sweden has stated that it is prepared to act as peacemaker in the Wilsonian spirit.

27 DECEMBER. Morning overcast, foggy, light east wind, temperature about zero. During the afternoon it starts to snow, and by evening snow has become quite deep.

28 DECEMBER. Complete winter landscape. Snow is very deep—as far as the eye can see—and the forest looks beautiful in its winter clothes. Wind completely still, real snow air, temperature not too bad, around zero.

29 DECEMBER. A beautiful winter's day: a great deal of snow, wind calm, temperature at its coldest −1°C. At 8:00 a.m. I travel to the front with the corps chief medical officer, from there on to the artillery, group north—Assistant Physician Dr. Rodler. From there, on to fortieth first aid station: Dr. Fieber is already there. After long discussions, we travel back. By the time we return, it's 11:30 a.m. Meanwhile, the weather has become overcast, and toward evening snowdrifts are whipped up by a strong southwest wind.

30 DECEMBER. Heavy rain during the night, followed by snowmelt. Most of the roofs of our shelters are not sufficiently watertight. Many gentlemen have to wander around during the night with their beds, looking for a dry place to sleep. My roof still stands, except for a few places: chimney and kitchen. If it does not get any worse, I will be OK.

Great excitement in Budapest today, because Kaiser Karl is bring crowned King of Hungary. The Hungarians are very proud and excited about this and are making tremendous preparations. Hopefully they will have better weather than we do here.

31 DECEMBER. The rain has stopped, and a little frost has fallen—black ice. During the morning I inspect the first aid station of the second howitzer regiment in Alexandrowka, return by noon. Great preparations for New Year's Eve in our mess. Dinner only at 9:00 p.m. Renewed light, granular snowfall toward evening.

Notes

1. Nowosiółki (Poland).
2. Ostrozhets' (Ukraine).
3. Romaniv (Ukraine).
4. Harazdzha (Ukraine).
5. Mount Lovćen; Cetinje (Montenegro).
6. Vorotniv (Ukraine).
7. Lutsk (Ukraine).
8. Franz Ballner (1873–1963), noted bacteriologist and hospital epidemiologist.
9. Viennese for a formal dinner.
10. Botyn (Ukraine).
11. Verkhivka (Ukraine).
12. Khorlupy (Ukraine).
13. Not found.
14. Not found.
15. Durrës (Albania).
16. Pokashchiv (Ukraine).
17. Olyka (Ukraine). Seat of the Radziwills when in the area.
18. In reality the date was 9 March. Austro-Hungary declared war on Portugal a week later.
19. Zviriv (Ukraine).
20. Caused by group A streptococci (contagious).
21. Bakoryn (Ukraine).
22. More accurately święconka. Food blessed at Easter, consumed within the family circle (Polish Easter Custom).
23. Penetrating wounds of the abdomen that compromised intestinal integrity, with leakage of intestinal content into the peritoneum, led to fatal peritonitis in the pre-antibiotic era.
24. Saint Pancratius (see chapter 2, note 51).
25. Bardach's first mention of the imminent Brusilov Offensive.
26. Battle of Asagio (Trentino offensive), 15 May to about 4 June).
27. In the event, this offensive petered out into a draw.
28. Bardach was right in the middle of the Brusilov Offensive and describes all aspects of it in great detail. This offensive, a major Russian attack against the armies of the Central Powers on the Eastern Front, was launched 4 June 1916, and lasted until late September. It took place in an area of present-day Western Ukraine in the general vicinity of the towns of Lemberg, Kowel, and Lutsk. The offensive was named after the commander in charge of the Southwestern Front of the Imperial Russian Army, General Aleksei Alexeevich Brusilov (1853–1926). It broke the back of the Austro-Hungarian Army on the Eastern Front, with about 750,000 killed, wounded, missing and captured. But at the same time, the Brusilov offensive did little to strengthen Russia's strategic position, and contributed to the slow unraveling of her war effort, accelerated radically by the February 1917 revolution. The best work on the Brusilov offensive remains Norman Stone's *The Eastern Front 1914–1917* (New York: Scribner, 1975).
29. Teremno (Ukraine)?
30. Dworec (Poland)?
31. Zaborol' (Ukraine).

32. Torchyn (Ukraine).
33. Sirnychky (Ukraine).
34. Dąbrowa (Ukraine).
35. Budky (Ukraine).
36. Usychi (Ukraine).
37. Not found.
38. Khorokhoryn (Ukraine).
39. Zubyl'ne (Ukraine).
40. Beres'k (Ukraine).
41. Voronchyn (Ukraine).
42. Novyi Dvir (Ukraine).
43. Dozhva (Ukraine).
44. The historical region of Bukowina former part of Moldova and now split between Romania and Ukraine, or the administrative unit Duchy of Bukowina, a constituent land of the Austrian Empire from 1774, and a crown land of Austria-Hungary from 1867 until 1918.
45. Chernivtsi (Ukraine). Capital of Austro-Hungarian Bukowina.
46. Svynaryn, Czesnówka, Tumyn (Ukraine).
47. Sviichiv (Ukraine).
48. Wojnica (Ukraine).
49. Hubyn (Ukraine).
50. Wojmica (Ukraine).
51. Dibrowa (Ukraine).
52. Zaturtsi (Ukraine).
53. Kolomyy(i)a (Ukraine).
54. Battles of the Somme and Verdun, respectively.
55. Pavlovychi (Ukraine).
56. Pustomyty (Ukraine).
57. Zolota Lypa River (Western Ukraine).
58. Whole units were taken prisoner by the Russians.
59. The success of the Russian offensive was helped in large part by Brusilov's innovation of shock troops to attack weak points along the Austrian lines to effect a breakthrough, which the main Russian army could then exploit. Adapted by Ludendorff and Hindenburg during the German 1918 spring offensive.
60. Gorizia (Italy).
61. Ivano-Frankivsk (Ukraine).
62. Brody (Ukraine).
63. Transylvania, part of Austro-Hungary until after the war, when it was incorporated into Romania.
64. One of the very few German vessels that broke the blockade into the United States during World War I.
65. Romania declared war on the Central Powers on 27 August 1916 in an attempt to seize Transylvania—a region with majority Romanian population—the Banat and Bukowina from the Austro-Hungarian Empire.
66. Wrocław (Poland).
67. Gas-filled.
68. Romania.
69. Silistra (Bulgaria).

70. Second Balkan War (June to July 1913).
71. Shel'viv (Ukraine).
72. Billroth Battist, named after surgeon Theodore Billroth (1829–1894), founder of modern abdominal surgery. A yellow, water-resistant type of bandaging material.
73. Karlovac (Croatia).
74. Świniuchy (Ukraine).
75. Sibiu (Romania).
76. Turnu Roşu Pass (Romanian).
77. Braşov (Romania).
78. Pustomyty (Ukraine).
79. From now on shortages—at home and later the front—assume increasing importance.
80. Chorostow (Ukraine).
81. Kowel (Ukraine).
82. All in Poland.
83. Trzebinia (Poland).
84. Bardach uses the word *Frauenzimmer*, which has low connotations.
85. No more talk of *Frauenzimmer*.
86. The Act of 5 November 1916 was a declaration of Emperors Wilhelm II of Germany and Franz Joseph of Austria. This act promised the creation of the Kingdom of Poland out of territory of Congress Poland, envisioned by its authors as a puppet state controlled by the Central Powers. The origin of that document was the dire need to draft new recruits from German-occupied Poland for the war with Russia. Even though the act itself expressed very little in concrete terms, its declaration is regarded as one of main factors in the Polish efforts to regain independence.
87. Přerov, Czech Republic.
88. V(W)olhynia: region in Eastern Europe, now divided between Poland, Ukraine and Belarus.
89. Rohizno (Ukraine).
90. Kruchyniczy (Ukraine).
91. Craiova (Romania).
92. Border area between southeast Romania and northeast Bulgaria.
93. Poland, Ukraine, Slovak Republic.
94. Targoviste (Romania).
95. Arges River (Romania).
96. Ploieşti (Romania).
97. See *New York Times*, 13 December 1916 (2). Germany's peace proposals, which relied heavily on the war's existing status quo and also retention of its colonies, were soundly rejected by the Entente and US President Woodrow Wilson.
98. Necessary to relieve the Central Powers' food shortage caused by the Allied blockade.
99. It included retention by Germany of all its occupied territory in Belgium and northeast France.

CHAPTER 4

1917

*Winter in Ukraine—Inspections—
Blockade—Worsening Shortages*

1 JANUARY. That was a jolly New Year's Eve! We gather in the mess at 8:00 p.m.—General von Rosenzweig, substituting for our vacationing commander, has a small game of whist going, so it's 9:00 p.m. before we sit down for supper: meat pies, Wiener schnitzel with mixed salad, beer, and wine. It becomes very jolly very rapidly: two gypsies from the twenty-ninth light infantry fiddle without interruption. First Lieutenant Schwarz, to whom we are bidding farewell, has some spicy things to say. Before we look around, it's already midnight. Champagne for all: the general proposes a very well-thought-out toast to our Kaiser Karl and Empress Zita, followed by good wishes all round: "Happy New Year" from everyone's lips. Second supper: meatloaf, smoked tongue in aspic, cheese, small baked goods. Things become livelier and livelier: we drink and drink and drink. Rittmeister Baron Hammerstein recites verses that he has composed beautifully: a review of First Lieutenant Schwarz's entire tour of duty at command. If only the refrain were not so vulgar! Much remarkable dancing! It's already 3:30 a.m. by the time we part: some others depart before I do. Despite this, I get up early at the usual time of 7:00 a.m.: my valiant batman, Schweiger, always makes sure that I do, with his clomping about—some men remain together celebrating through 7:00 a.m.: they look like death warmed over! Weather horrible: it rains during the night again: mud, gloomy, foggy and very damp air—also in my shelter.

2 JANUARY. Pouring rain during the night, and by morning it's −4°C. At 7:30 a.m. I travel to the front with Chief Medical Officer Herzog and from there to the first aid station of the fortieth infantry regiment; then with Senior Physician Kantorek to that of no. 3/40 accompanied by the battalion commandant, German Captain Bartosch. On the way back, lively Russian firing on the position, clearly seen through the clear, beautiful snowy weather. Firing becomes critical: when we want to return from the supply depot into the com-

munications trench, an officer whizzes by with the news that Major Strohhofer, commandant of first aid station no. 4/103, has just been wounded. We see a fresh shell hole and large puddle of blood at the entrance to the trench, and rush to the first aid station to which the major has been brought. Herzog enters the trench, quite exposed, to bandage him. It would surely have been better had he left this to regular physicians, who would first have taken the major into the shelter, undressed him, and treated him at their leisure. He is wounded in the thigh and left eye. Although they are only flesh wounds, they are bleeding very heavily—his pulse is very weak. Wounds are washed, emergency bandages placed, and he is evacuated to the medical unit. It's around 11:00 a.m., but, because of the slow journey on bumpy roads, he only arrives at the unit at 3:00 p.m., completely exsanguinated, and dies soon after. The femoral artery had been severed!

Figure 4.1. Medical care in a first aid station. Photograph courtesy of the Leo Baeck Institute.

We are all very depressed about this: he was one of our best staff officers, beloved and honored by his men like few others. Straight after dinner, we are just as depressed to take leave of First Lieutenant Schwarz: a dear comrade and dashing fellow.

3 JANUARY. Snow again during the night: temperature drops below zero. Morning overcast and damp, almost no wind. At 9:00 a.m. I travel to the first aid station of the fortieth infantry regiment, where all doctors have gathered and Dr. Fieber tries his best to tell us about his experiences during his fourteen days at the front, courtesy of our valiant chief medical officer. Trouble is that he has nothing to tell, because, during the entire time, he has sat on his hands at the first aid station of the twenty-ninth light infantry, which had—by chance—very few wounded. It proved impractical to fit treatment of every wounded man around his presence. Our corps chief medical officer doesn't think about the wounding of Major Strohhofer in this context: perhaps if a good surgeon had been at hand soon after, his life could have been saved. Lecture and discussion takes about an hour, after which I go to the dressing station of reserve artillery unit no. 10, then return back: I arrive around noon. The sun tries to peek through during the afternoon, but only succeeds for a very short time.

4 JANUARY. Burial of Major Strohhofer near the medical unit in the Wojmica[1] cemetery. I travel there by car, with several men from command. Corps

Figure 4.2. Burial in the field. Photograph courtesy of the Leo Baeck Institute.

Commandant Csanady, accompanied by several other officers, is also there, with German Group Commandant General Riemer, successor of General von der Marwitz, who has become army commandant on the Western Front. A very uplifting ceremony: many officers and men are present. The funeral cortege is made up from his own battalion, with many wreaths. Chaplain Strzyzowski delivers his usual bad, incomprehensible eulogy—I haven't heard a more miserable speaker for a long time; Corps Commandant Csanady gives a short but pithy and moving eulogy talk at the open grave. By the time we return, it's 11:30 a.m. Weather is very cold: −4°C with a moderate east wind, strengthening during the afternoon, with snow squalls. Toward evening weather suddenly changes: warmer southwest wind with some rain, snowmelt, and thawing weather.

5 JANUARY. Weather very mild, sunshine at times, a great deal of mud, snow completely melted in places. At 9:00 a.m., I travel to the division medical unit to visit the new sick bay of the division ammunition supply depot. Return around noon.

6 JANUARY. Lovely winter's day with sunshine and not too cold, −2.5°C, fairly strong northwest wind. Departure early at 8:00 a.m. with the corps chief medical officer to the fourth light infantry first aid station, then to reserve artillery unit no. 10. Visit with the commandant of nineteenth brigade, Colonel Schmidbacher. Return around 11:00 a.m.

Excellent progress in Romania: Braila[2] is already in our hands, and the enemy has been cleaned out from the whole of Dobrudscha.[3] The Entente has, as is now generally known, turned down our peace proposal. Both we and the neutrals are very disappointed: today, the German Kaiser has given a strict army command informing everyone: he is now determined that peace must be forced upon the Entente by war.

7 JANUARY. A severe winter's day, −7.5°C, with strong east wind, but otherwise clear sky and pure air. At 8:30 a.m. I travel with the corps chief medical officer to the first aid station of the second howitzer regiment in Alexandrowka,[4] also the baggage train of the fourth light infantry, which is also there. We inspect medical equipment and supplies and return at 11:30 a.m. Afternoon: cloudy and overcast, fresh snowfall toward evening. During evening, our shelters glow with electric lights for the first time, making them double as homely. But our beautiful light is extinguished after only half an hour—only a test run, but should be stable from tomorrow on.

8 JANUARY. Morning overcast, damp, cold not so bad, almost no wind. I travel to Pavloviczy[5] at 7:30 a.m., from there together with Dr. Herzog to Chorostow[6] to inspect the bakery and the division troop command. It is noon before we return. Complete clearing by afternoon with sunshine. Focsani[7] has been taken! Ninety-nine officers, fifty-four thousand men, three artillery pieces, twenty machine guns. A very good catch!

9 JANUARY. Nice winter's day with sunshine and not too cold, hardly −4°C with a moderate east wind. At 10:00 a.m., I travel to Captain Grimm's artillery group with Assistant Physician Dr. Rodler; return at 11:00 a.m. Afternoon becomes overcast.

10 JANUARY. Moderate frost and overcast.

11 JANUARY. Beautiful winter's day with moderate cold and moderate east wind. Sunshine. At 9:00 a.m., I travel to the division ammunition depot in Wojmica, whose sick bay has still not been built; after that to division medical unit, return by noon.

At 3:30 p.m. I travel to the corps chief medical officer in Pavloviczy again, as commanded, together with Surgeon Major Dr. Müller. Return around 5:00 p.m. Increasing frost toward evening. For reasons that are unknown to me, we have a small mess celebration this evening: perhaps in honor of the opening of our electric lighting which functions perfectly, starting today. Perhaps because the day after tomorrow our commander returns from leave; as soon as he arrives, we will be back in the doldrums again. Perhaps a preliminary celebration for our Major Heller, who is going on leave for four weeks as soon as the commandant arrives; And, last but not least, perhaps because our riflemen have shot a deer, which tastes wonderful.

Guests include our cavalry commander; also Captain Resch and Major Steinböck from corps command. Our own string quartet, augmented by two men from the fortieth infantry music section, presents a varied program, each piece dedicated to a specific gentleman. Very good red wine and of course no lack of champagne to conclude. It's midnight before I go to bed: some stay celebrating until 5:00 a.m.

12 JANUARY. Nice morning weather, with sunshine, moderate cold, calm winds. Overcast during the afternoon. During the morning, I visit our quartermaster store, established very comfortably in a nearby forest.

13 JANUARY. Thawing weather since yesterday evening, strong east wind. Damp cold, foggy, a great deal of mud. Artillery fire from both sides has increased significantly during the past two days. Airplanes fly over at night, something completely new in this theater of war.

14 JANUARY. Overcast, foggy morning, thawing weather. Sudden clearing in the afternoon, with sunshine. Today there has been a large-scale batmen exchange: my batman, Schweiger, is staying with me.

15 JANUARY. Snow during the night, very overcast and foggy early. Ground is frozen, thawing weather toward evening. During the morning, I inspect baths being built here on the side of the hill—slow progress.

16 JANUARY. Morning overcast, foggy, mud, afternoon rain. Morning inspection of the sick bay in the division ammunition depot in Wojmica, which has still not been finished properly. I visit the division medical unit, return around noon.

17 JANUARY. Ground is frozen solid: west wind. The storm troop corps exercises today on the height: a great deal of rifle practice. The entire command is present at this exercise, myself included. Very interesting: lasts from 9:00 to 11:00 a.m. Afternoon departure of Major Heller for four weeks' vacation. His substitute is Lieutenant Colonel of General Staff Command Stamecka.

18 JANUARY. Moderately frosty weather, with a strong east wind, continues. Overcast, with periods of fog.

19 JANUARY. Heavy snowfall at night, up to ten centimeters deep: snow lasts all morning: −6°C, light east wind. Because of the weather, planned inspection of the division ammunition depot by the corps chief medical officer is canceled. This doesn't help me much, because I have risen early and prepared for the journey anyway.

We are in the middle of a complete reorganization of baggage train and medical units. From 1 February, the division medical unit will be known as the division medical column/convoy. It will have the task of getting rid of heavy conveyances, including ambulances, and only accept locally available[8] vehicles: twenty-four for transporting the wounded and twelve for medical supplies. The number of physicians is reduced from six to five, each division with a permanent field hospital. Our division is assigned field hospital 9/20 that will now receive the number 1009: the first two numbers denote the corps (to which it belongs), and the last two the earlier hospital unit number. Here, as well, heavy vehicles are replaced by local conveyances, twelve for the wounded and sixteen for medical supplies. A great pity about the ambulances: it's true that they are impossible to use in mountain warfare, but, for example, here in Wolhynia,[9] where they can advance easily, they will be greatly missed: a locally available horse and wagon can never replace an ambulance.

20 JANUARY. First really cold winter's day: −16°C at 7:00 a.m. Clear blue, sunny sky. Heavy snow crunches underfoot: just glorious. Light northeast wind. At 9:00 a.m., inspection of baths that are being built at ¤ 243 by the corps chief medical officer: naturally, I must come along.

21 JANUARY. Weather like yesterday, −14°C. At 10:30 a.m., I travel by sled to first aid station no. 462 and the twenty-ninth light infantry. I discuss the latest orders with them and return at 1:00 p.m. A lovely trip.

22 JANUARY. A little less cold, −7.5°C, but sun has disappeared, no more blue sky: cloudy and overcast, with a westerly wind. At 9:30 a.m. I travel with the corps chief medical officer to Captain Grund's artillery group and Assistant Physician Dr. Radler. On the way back, we visit the baths being constructed on ¤ 243 again. Back at 11:00 a.m.

23 JANUARY. Another small decrease in cold: −5°C; overcast, cloudy skies and westerly wind. Afternoon snow squalls. At 9:00 a.m. I travel to division medical unit no. 2, returning around noon. For the past few days, I have been in possession of a telephone box in my room, so I am no longer compelled to run several times a day and night and in all kinds of weather to telephone central. Our new corps chief medical officer finds it necessary to speak to his subordinates regularly, often about minor matters—to document how busy he is. He will keep on with this nonsense until fighting starts up again.

24 JANUARY. Temperature −4°C, light snow starting at noon. The substitute for our Chief of General Staff Lieutenant Colonel Stamecka has slipped while walking in a trench and broken his fourth right rib. After being bandaged, he remains here under my care.

25 JANUARY. Weather like yesterday: overcast, cloudy. At noon, a shy but unsuccessful effort by the sun to penetrate the clouds.

26 JANUARY. Cold, frosty weather continues. At 10:00 a.m. I am with the chief medical officer in Pavloviczy, after that the division medical unit. During the afternoon, Oberstabsarzt 1 Klasse Dr. Rallner arrives—again, we inspect the baths at ¤ 243, then go on to the first aid station of the fortieth infantry division to inspect baths that are being built there as well.

27 JANUARY. Temperature −10°C. In the morning, I visit the quartermaster depot. Afternoon with Engineer Richter at the fortieth infantry regiment regarding construction of baths.

28 JANUARY. Temperature −9°C. Cold weather continues, snow remains deep. At 9:00 a.m., introduction of command to the new corps commandant, General of the Infantry Kritek: our own Commandant Csanady has been transferred, in the same capacity, to sixth corps.

29 JANUARY. Temperature −10°C. Overcast, followed by clearing, sunshine by 9:00 a.m. Travel to the dressing station at the fortieth infantry regiment with the corps chief medical officer, then back to the baths on ¤ 243. Back by 11:00 a.m. Introduction of the corps chief medical officer to our generals.

30 JANUARY. Temperature −11°C. Dr. Herzog has canceled today's planned inspection of the fourth light infantry. I stay where I am: I have enough to do instructing the newly arrived Assistant Physician Dr. Baum and the baths, etc.

31 JANUARY. Freezing: −24°C. The coldest day this year so far, with a biting east wind. Because of the cold and wind, I try to remain indoors, but am summoned to Pavloviczy at 3:00 p.m. by the corps chief medical officer. Snow squalls toward evening.

1 FEBRUARY. Temperature −10°C. Wind has eased up: overcast and very cloudy. Today, field hospital 1009 joins our division and is now called the division medical column instead of division medical unit.

2 FEBRUARY. Temperature −9°C; almost no wind. At 9:00 a.m. I travel to first aid station 103, then to the one at no. 3/40, returning 12:30 p.m. In the afternoon, back to the corps chief medical officer, returning at 5:00 p.m.

3 FEBRUARY. Temperature −10°C, biting east wind and snowdrifts. A horribly severe winter. During the morning, I visit the baths at Ha . . . ofen [illegible], rest of the time at home. Beginning on 1 February, the U-boat war has intensified.

4 FEBRUARY. Temperature −11°C, overcast with a biting east wind: terrible weather, which stops me from going out.

5 FEBRUARY. Temperature −15°C, partly sunny, moderate west wind. At 9:00 a.m. I travel to Alexandrowka to the second howitzer regiment, return 11:00 a.m.

6 FEBRUARY. Temperature −15°C. At 7:00 a.m., thick fog and slight westerly wind. I travel with corps chief medical officer Herzog to the fourth light infantry to inspect their position. Unfortunately, we lose our way and arrive at reserve company command: we obtain a guide who is a stretcher-bearer, but, despite him assuring us he knows the way, we travel for about two hours without arriving at the first aid station. So we cancel the planned inspection and limit ourselves to inspection of the baths on ¤ 243, which, unfortunately, because of the severe cold, are still not finished. From there we return back and arrive at 10:30 a.m. By this time, I am completely numb from the cold. During our wanderings, skies clear up completely: the clear blue sky allows excellent visibility. The Russians use this to open lively artillery fire after 9:00 a.m. on our right flank (twenty-ninth light infantry). It is so active that two gentlemen from command who are outside have to jump into a foxhole, in which they spend a whole hour. In the end, it was good luck that we couldn't find the way to the front today.

7 FEBRUARY. Temperature −19°C: it's getting colder and colder. Early mist. I travel to Wojmica at 9:30 a.m. to inspect the supplies of field hospital 1009 and the medical column itself. Return 1:00 p.m.

8 FEBRUARY. Temperature −10°C, quite a strong northwest wind, which doubles the cold temperatures. At 8:00 a.m., I travel with the corps chief medical officer to the baggage train of no. 5/103 in connection with a case of smallpox[10] and one of dysentery. The smallpox was brought in from the hinterland (Szolnok[11]): the man had returned from vacation the day before. We cannot find any explanation for the case of dysentery: the man has been in the field since November 1916. The entire machine gun section to which the man belongs is examined for carriers of the bacillus.[12] Then we inspect the sick bay in the rear of the twenty-ninth rifles, which is also located with the baggage train, then (again) baths at the fortieth infantry regiment at ¤ 243. Return around 11:00 a.m. In the afternoon, I am summoned again to Pavloviczy by the corps chief medical officer, return 6:00 p.m.

9 FEBRUARY. Temperature −17°C, strong west wind. At 9:00 a.m. I travel to the fourth light infantry, returning 11:30 a.m. All vacations have been blocked from 6 to 28 February, apparently because of transport difficulties: just at the time when my vacation time approaches! We are very upset about Wilson's attitude to the intensified U-boat war. He has broken off relations with Germany: a harbinger of a future war declaration. That false "apostle of peace" has finally shown his true colors! As long as America made a great deal of money exporting food and war material to the Entente, it was comfortable to remain neutral, even in favor of peace—only a theoretical peace, to be sure, with happy, optimistic speeches. But now, when its trade is threatened, America is suddenly on the side of the Entente. How can anyone be more deceitful?

10 FEBRUARY. Temperature −7°C; bitter west wind that makes it feel twice as cold.

11 FEBRUARY. Temperature −1°C, bright sunshine—limited snowmelt during the day. I am ordered to the corps chief medical officer at 4:00 p.m. and return only at 6:00 p.m.

12 FEBRUARY. Temperature −6°C. Endless winter. Sunshine, deep blue sky, absolutely clear air—almost no wind. A beautiful winter's day. I depart at 8:00 a.m. with the corps chief medical officer to Alexandrowka, to the second howitzer regiment, from there (again) to the baths on ¤ 243, which are unfortunately still not finished. Back at 10:30 a.m.

13 FEBRUARY. Temperature −8°C. Hazy, but clearing by 10:00 a.m. with deep blue sky and sunshine. At 8:30 a.m. I travel with Regimental Physician First Class Dr. Meyer to the German no. 3/378 division to inspect their first aid stations, which are to be taken over by our fortieth infantry regiment. They are beautifully equipped—each battalion's dressing station has a delousing fa-

cility with a bath. The sick bay itself is well equipped: really worth a visit. On the way back, the Russians hurl shells at us: we return at 11:30 a.m.

14 FEBRUARY. Temperature −10°C, overcast, heavy clouds, which lift around 9:00 a.m. but then close in again. I travel at 7:00 a.m. with the corps chief medical officer to the first aid station at the fourth light infantry, from there to the position of first company, then back to the aid station, return at 10:30 a.m. Afternoon very cold with a west wind.

15 FEBRUARY. Temperature −6°C, bitterly cold west wind. I inspect the baths on ¤ 243 and then work detachments 1/20 and 1/19. I have a great deal of paperwork to get through during the afternoon.

16 FEBRUARY. Temperature −2°C, with a bitterly cold northwest wind. It feels a lot colder than it did when the temperature was −20°C.

17 FEBRUARY. Lovely winter's day with blue sky and clear air. Wind calm at times. At 9:00 a.m. I travel to the new position of the dressing station at no. 2 field howitzer regiment, from there to the aid station at fortieth infantry division, where I make a special inspection of the baths. Return 11:00 a.m. Afternoon visit to the baths on ¤ 243 with Lieutenant Colonel Stamecka.

18 FEBRUARY. Temperature −7°C, sunshine. Clear blue sky, wind absolutely calm. A fine winter's day. I travel at 7:30 a.m. with Lieutenant Colonel Stamecka to the baths at the fortieth infantry regiment, from there to the fortieth infantry regimental command, then to the twenty-ninth rifle command (Major Wolli), then to howitzer battery no. 3/2 which has been built so well that it is worth a visit. Back at 10:30 a.m. Heavy airplane activity, with a great deal of bombardment. Surgeon General Frisch, chief medical officer in Vienna, inspects the front on Royal Command. First: tenth corps; he also visits medical column no. 2 and field hospital 1009, and is delighted at what he sees. No wonder—in Vienna, they have no clue of what our field installations are like: they are undervalued by many, overvalued by others. There is a perceived need to see everything with one's own eyes: a war decoration, perhaps even with swords, will surely follow!

19 FEBRUARY. Temperature −10°C, overcast skies and strong east wind. Surgeon General Frisch continues his inspection today: promptly at 8:00 a.m., he arrives by car at the baths on ¤ 243, accompanied by the corps chief medical officer. I report to both of them: they inspect several baggage trains and continue on to the first aid station at the fortieth infantry battalion. The general invites me to travel in his car: he wishes to visit the trenches, something that we look on as a piece of bravura. He is especially delighted with the baths at the fortieth infantry division. No wonder: they have been built into a hillside so that, from the outside, almost no trace of them can be detected—only the smoke that rises at times from the chimney, situated at ground level. A real communications trench leads into the baths, which contain a dressing and undressing room, both separated by the baths themselves. Baths are very spacious, with basins with water flowing in and out—plus twelve showers. Adjacent are the officers' baths, with sweat cubicles and douches. A village fountain contributes the water, which is drawn inside. The water is heated in mobile kitchen bowls and a built-in hot air oven takes care of the delousing. Baths are about four kilometers from the trenches.

The Russians do not agree with our plans to visit the trenches: their bombardment is especially strong today. Since 8:00 a.m., the road to colony Debora[13] has been under constant bombardment. Shells exploding about two hundred paces from us make the good Herr Frisch somewhat jittery: "I didn't come here to get shot." He gets into his car with the corps chief medical officer and speeds off in the direction of the thirteenth *Landwehr* division, leaving me with the men from the fortieth regiment, standing in the freezing cold, completely oblivious as to how I would get back to my command. The fortieth takes care of me and sends me back by wagon. On the way, I visit the baths on ¤ 243 that finally are being opened today—another great achievement. The first large divisional soldiers' home is also being opened on ¤ 243: all 180 men who will occupy it today must first be bathed and deloused—a lot of work. Quite a few deficiencies appear, which shows how little interest Engineer Richter really had: he left everything to the workers themselves. But, in general, the facility functions; at least in principle, he has done his duty.

20 FEBRUARY. Temperature −11°C, clear skies and sunshine. In the morning I visit the soldiers' home; other than that I take the liberty of a day of rest.

21 FEBRUARY. Temperature −10°C, overcast, cloudy sky, calm wind. Early departure at 7:00 a.m. with the corps chief medical officer to first aid station 103, then into their lines of fire, and after that the battalion baggage train. On the way back, inspection of the baths on ¤ 243, which are now fully active. Return before noon. At the same time, Major Heller returns from vacation: he has been promoted to lieutenant colonel; Lieutenant Colonel Stamecka leaves us this afternoon. Most sections heave a sigh of relief, because he has made their lives miserable and is now returning to the general staff with all his bad habits intact—in such contrast to Lieutenant Colonel Heller, who is modest and friendly to everyone. I myself cannot complain about Stamecka, perhaps because, from the very first day, he came under my personal medical care.

22 FEBRUARY. Temperature −9°C, very light northwest wind. Overcast early and cloudy, followed by complete clearing. Departure early at 7:00 a.m. with the corps chief medical officer to first aid station no. 4/62. We want to visit their position, but the Russians have just bombarded their communications trench, which has been quiet during the past few days, so the chief medical officer deviates from plan. Instead, we visit the first aid station of the twenty-ninth light infantry, followed by no. [?]/40 and 3/40, return around noon. Engineer Captain Pistelka, assigned to our division staff even before the war, has been transferred to a Honvéd division on the Italian Front. With his departure, we lose yet another old comrade from our division. He was a cheery, dashing fellow: a real, *gemütlicher* Hungarian, who liked to attend every revelry and enjoyed preparing them himself. At such times, enduring friendships are forged, and many aspired to his friendship just to make use of him. It was important to be his friend, because as office director and father of special favors, large and small—so necessary for remuneration requests—he knew how to get around his superiors; once he was securely "in the saddle," he made his power felt to all under him. It was then a question of dealing with his mood, compassion, and coarseness. Other than that, his activity when there was no fighting was minimal. Sergeant Piotrowski, also called "James," was his right-hand man. There were no secrets from him, and, if one wanted information from Captain Pistelka, his typical reply was: "Please refer to James." The good James, very conscious of his indispensability, dealt with officers as though they served under him: this of course made him feel very important.

When it became obvious to James that he would not be awarded both Signa to add to his Service Cross First Class, he ostensibly lost interest in Austrian decorations. But he quietly yearned for the Crown Order, which remained out of his reach, and ostentatiously wore no Austrian orders, only the German Iron Cross. He was obsessively proud of his German decoration and made sure that no one at command other than general staff was awarded it. When the order came not to wear it alone, but always together with Austrian awards, he angrily demanded to at least be awarded the lowest (bronze) Signum Laudis.

We have him to thank for the fact that neither I nor Dr. Müller, commandant of the medical column, have been awarded the Iron Cross, despite having fought shoulder to shoulder with Germans, whose wounded have filled our hospital column, since 1916. He could not obtain this decoration for his boozing buddy Major Rosenbaum—perhaps his only service to the Germans: the same Rosenbaum who once loaned him thirty cooking pots in the Carpathians.

We had a celebration party for Pistelka last evening. The menu was excellent. Music from the fortieth: a few gypsies competed with each other in singing jolly tunes. Even our general sacrificed an hour of his valuable night's rest to his friend and teacher of the Hungarian language: he remained in the mess until 10:00 p.m.—a long time, for him. Colonel Rosenzweig and I stayed an hour longer. The celebrant and a few of his true friends remained there until 5:00 a.m.—long before that time, they were all completely sozzled.

Nice, clear weather today is responsible for much activity in the air. Around 2:00 p.m., there is a dogfight between a German and a Russian pilot. Unfortunately, the German is shot town in the Szelwow[14] area—the officer dead, the machine destroyed. Troops on the front wanted to see the Russian pilot making an emergency landing behind his own lines. Cold comfort!

23 FEBRUARY. Temperature −6°C, biting northwest wind. At 9:30 a.m. I travel to field hospital 1009 and from there to the medical column, returning at noon.

24 february. Temperature −14°C, very cold northwest wind. Weather keeps me in my quarters.

25 february. Temperature −5°C, bitter southwest wind. Thick fog blocks visibility completely. At 3:30 p.m. I travel to the chief medical officer, returning at 5:30 p.m.

26 february. Temperature −1°C: strong west wind and overcast skies. No thawing during the day, light snowfall at night. I spend almost the entire morning at the bathing facility on ¤ 243, to follow the entire business from beginning to end. Everything goes beautifully. Baths are excellent—men enjoy their baths, and it makes them feel very good. Only the delousing disappoints me somewhat. The oven temperature is 120°C, and clothes, etc., remain in it for fifteen minutes, in other words, three minutes longer than the time prescribed. Despite this, when the clothes come out, I find lice still alive in one of the pieces to be washed and cleaned! From now on, clothes coming from the oven will be hung up loosely, not in a pile. I will investigate this matter further.

27 february. Temperature −1°C, southwest wind. Blowing snow and thick fog, which burns off my noon, but snowfall becomes heavier. From today, white bread and rolls are forbidden.

28 february. First temperature above zero (1°C) for many, many weeks. Air is mild, light thawing weather, significant snowfall during the afternoon. The corps chief medical officer is going on two weeks' leave tomorrow—three weeks, travel days included. I must take his place during this entire period and change my accommodation to corps command. I move my quarters at 10:00 a.m., and at 11:00 a.m. report to Commander Kritek: I use the afternoon to install myself in the chief medical officer's office. Comfort at corps command leaves nothing to be desired: food is plentiful and excellent. The only thing is that the commander is a really bad host.

1 march. Snow is still very deep, temperatures relatively mild. Light thawing weather toward noon, black ice in the evening. I make use of the first train at corps command to orient myself both at command and in Pavloviczy. I inspect the dental outpatient clinic and find nice officers' baths and shaving cubicles there. I order a bath for that afternoon, which I enjoy greatly. At 6:30 p.m. all sections meet to report to our commandant. I find this regulation useful: it's very interesting to hear about happenings at different departments, and we must sometimes justify many things that we have done, without prior preparation. The advantage of this is that one is able to raise objections to proposals made by other departments early and thus forestall any argument.

2 march. Weather like yesterday. Light snowfall in the early morning hours, thawing weather in the afternoon, black ice in the evening. At 8:00 a.m. I travel to the field hospital in Berezoviezy,[15] returning 11:30 a.m. The hospital is very good and receptive to the needs of the town as well. Excellent bacteriology laboratory—Commandant Dr. Steindl.

3 MARCH. Temperature −9°C, biting east wind which makes it feel doubly cold. Despite this, I travel at 8:00 a.m. to Rogozno,[16] I inspect the corps ammunition depot (Senior Physician Goldschmidt), and then field hospital 913, still in the building stage. It is meant, at least for the present, for up to eighty beds but does not yet have an operating room; baths are also impractical, though they do have an excellent and efficient delousing facility, which I examine firsthand. A second barrack is being built and a third projected; I meet Commandant Surgeon Major Zulawski. Return around 11:30 a.m.

4 MARCH. Temperature −15°C. Winter continues, but wind is calm, so the cold is bearable. At 3:00 p.m. I travel to my division command to take official leave of Captain Pistelka, and pay a visit to my commander and most of the other staff gentlemen there after I have completed my official duties. Return 5:00 p.m.

5 MARCH. Temperature −11°C, clear sky and icy air. Departure at 8:00 a.m. with Regimental Physician First Class Dr. Just, who has been appointed to serve with the corps chief physician, to the baths in camp no. 5 at the fortieth infantry division, which are finally completed, and will be opened on 8 March. Baths have been built by Acting Sergeant Engineer Kraus, the same man who

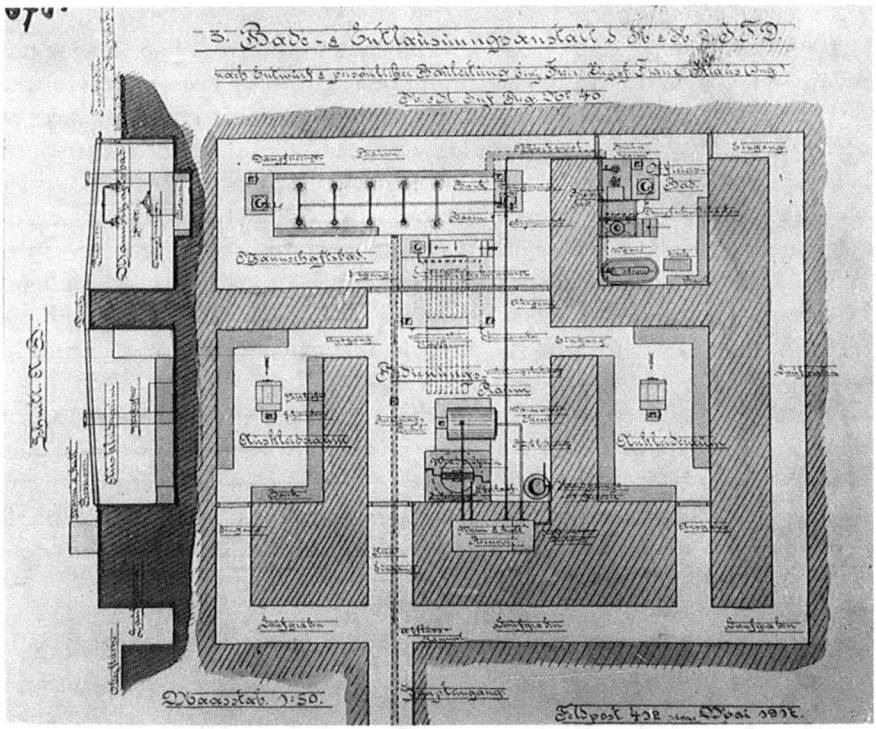

Figure 4.3. Bardach's sketch of bathhouse facilities. Photograph courtesy of the Leo Baeck Institute.

built such beautiful baths in the north camp at Chorlupy.¹⁷ The present baths are also excellent and have the great advantage of being less than three kilometers from the front, so troops can easily make use of them where they are. I have made a sketch of them. They are built into a slope: a communications trench leads into the baths that consist of an undressing room, baths themselves, a delousing room, and a dressing room. The bathing room has a large basin that is not too deep, in which shower water collects and serves as a footbath so that it can then be let out again. Adjacent to it are splendid officers' baths with sweat cubicles and cold and hot water douches. A second communications trench leads from baths into the open. From the outside, nothing can be seen. The ceiling is lighted electrically, and a fountain has been built into the baths. A very artistic creation, wonderful to behold. About four hundred men use the facility daily.

From there, we travel to first aid stations [?]/40 and 3/40, returning just before noon.

Kritek departed yesterday for a three-day visit to General Linsingen. He is ticked off, because our Army Commandant Tersztyánszky has been assigned the third army in exchange with Colonel General von Kirchbach, who is taking over fourth army—which Kritek has rightly aimed for: he is after all only one grade lower (younger).

6 MARCH. Temperature −7.5°C, with light snow flurries. I am staying put today, occupied with tactical work. I find out that I have been put up for the German Iron Cross by my division commander; unfortunately, the chances of getting it, especially now, are very slim, because of a tension that has developed between the German and Austro-Hungarian Armies. Germans find that their physicians do not receive many decorations from us and are waiting for this numerical balance to equalize. The fact that I am part of this problem is the fault of the division general staff, because submission could just as well have been handed in a year ago. After all, we have been working intensively with the Germans for more than a year, and an entire German regiment was assigned to us and treated by our own medical facilities.

7 MARCH. Temperature −4°C. Another significant snowfall. At 8:00 a.m. I travel with Captain of the General Staff Stichy to Rogozno for logistical purposes, return at 10:00 a.m. Car travel saves a great deal of time. The commandant returns at noon, and evening reports start again: each presentation by all departments is subjected to advice and consent so that orders do not clash, acceptable to all.

8 MARCH. Temperature −6°C: a bitter east wind and blowing snow. Underestimating the horrible weather, I travel early at 8:00 a.m. to Kruchyniczy,¹⁸ where I inspect the construction of thirteenth medical column. Beautifully equipped, just like a clinic in Vienna. Surgeons include Regimental Physician Dr. Fieber—assistant to Professor Hochenegg—and Dr. Krasnik, all excellent doctors. I stay there until 10:00 a.m. and then travel with Surgeon Major

Ruzyczka to regimental dressing station, the twenty-fourth *Landwehr* infantry regiment, which is also well equipped, with baths for the entire regiment but a somewhat more primitive mobile delousing facility. Return at 2:00 p.m. The trip back is awful: wind drives the snow in our faces with such force, that it stings like needles.

9 MARCH. Temperature −2.5°C. Wind has almost completely abated—large piles of snow have accumulated again. I stay at home, to finish urgent paperwork.

10 MARCH. Temperature −5°C, winds calm. Complete winter landscape: huge piles of snow everywhere. It doesn't look like March at all. I travel to the dressing station of second artillery and second Honvèd regiment. The artillery of second regiment has been separated from the second division since the battle at Olyka,[19] replaced by reserve cannon unit no. 10. A few days ago, the latter was moved away and our second cannon regiment returned to us. Today's trip was nice, but not easy to complete in one morning: we have to hurry to be back by noon.

11 MARCH. Temperature −4°C. Sunday! I mention this, because—as I have already remarked—only corps command really knows when it's Sunday. During this long war, I never know exactly what day it is. Church service interests me very little. Tables are covered with real tablecloths, not just sheets. Lunch is ample and excellent: everyone is in a Sunday mood. I myself am a little depressed, because of the private notification that my request for the Officer's Cross has been rejected and that now several months more must pass before I can receive some other award, for example, the silver Signum Laudis. Maybe I will have more luck with the German Iron Cross: the request is being sent off today from corps command.

12 MARCH. Temperature −2.5°C. Cold is lessening, but it's snowing. At 10:00 a.m. in Rogozno, I meet Consulting Surgeon Hinterstoisser, primarius [senior consultant] of the Teschen[20] civilian hospital. As representative of the corps chief medical officer, I have the task to meet and bring him here. His task is to inform me of surgical activity in our corps as a whole. He arrives punctually, and we travel to second medical column, where we stay for quite a time because the hospital is very busy and he wants to observe it in action. We have lunch at 1:00 p.m., and then at 2:30 p.m. travel to mobile hospital 1009 in Wojnica, where a suspected case of gas gangrene has just been admitted. Surgery is immediately performed: Dr. Hinterstoisser observes it from start to finish, thereby greatly delaying our trip to Bereżowiezy mobile hospital 0412, and our return even more so. It's pitch dark, 7:30 p.m., by the time we arrive back at corps.

13 MARCH. Temperature −6°C, moderate east wind with sunshine which changes to fog at noon, and the skies darken. We leave for the fortieth infantry division at 7:00 a.m. On the way, we inspect the baths at ¤ 243, then the ones in camp no. 5: the surgeon is especially impressed with the latter; then on to

both first aid stations of the fortieth infantry division. From there, we travel to Kruchyniczy to medical column no. 13 (Dr. Fieber and Senior Physician Krasnik); we find it very busy, and witness an interesting operation: we have lunch there, leave at 2:00 p.m., and are back at command at 4:30 p.m. Dr. Hintestoisser goes back to twenty-fourth corps in Chorow.[21] I find command in great turmoil because of an apparent case of bubonic plague[22] among the Russians: I am tasked with taking the necessary precautions for our own corps at once.

14 MARCH. Warmer: 4°C. Thawing weather. Awful mud awaits us when all the snow melts. I remain busy with the plague issue, and complete the work that has piled up during my two-day absence. Rumors of a revolution in Russia increase.[23]

15 MARCH. 4°C: snowmelt continues. Around noon weather changes, with snowfall that by evening increases to driving snow, with appalling cold. Dr. Hinterstoisser returns from twenty-fourth corps at 8:30 a.m. and is introduced to the commandant, and at 10:00 a.m. we both travel again to medical column no. 2, where we stay till noon, then on to field hospital 913 in Rogozny, where we have lunch; at 2:00 p.m. he leaves by train, and I return to Pavloviczy.

A real revolution has broken out in Petersburg: all the ministers have been arrested, and thirty thousand soldiers are said to have joined the movement. If that is true, we are in for interesting times.

16 MARCH. The cold has started again (−9°C). In the morning, I inspect the dental clinic and look for proper places for isolation of Russian prisoners. Daily orders with various instructions from command regarding the plague issue arrive. All Russian prisoners must be quarantined for seven days: each division has a separate barracks for that purpose. Surgeon Major Dr. Ruzyczka arrives in the morning to discuss this matter with me.

In Russia, things are heating up more and more. The Tsar has abdicated in favor of his brother Michael Alexandrovich, who is only entrusted with the Regency.

17 MARCH. Temperature −4°C. At first: calm winds, but by noon a strong, cold west wind. At 7:00 a.m., I travel via Kruchyniczy—where Surgeon Major Dr. Ruzyczka joins me—to the first aid station at the thirteenth field artillery (Senior Physician Betnig), then to first aid station no. 13 (Regimental Physician First Class Dr. Grotte) and then on to first aid station twenty-fourth *Landwehr* infantry regiment (Senior Physician Mannsfeld), first aid station no. 3/24 *Landwehr* (Ensign Ossana), German first aid station 372nd infantry regiment with bathing facility, first aid station first *Landwehr* Infantry regiment (Regimental Physician First Class Trepper), and first aid station no. 1, twenty-fourth *Landwehr* (Senior Surgeon Nobel); return at 11:30 a.m.

18 MARCH. Temperature −5°C, sunshine, calm winds. Sunday! I remain at home because I have a bad cold. We are still not fully informed about the situation in Russia: whether the revolution has been caused by the peace or the war party. News at the moment is scanty. No matter what, we win, because the people cannot look on unconcerned at what is going on. Afternoon: again clouds and snowfall, after thawing at noon.

19 MARCH. Springlike air (2.5°C), snowmelt, pools of water everywhere. Weather changes repeatedly during the course of the day. I stay at home because of my cold.

20 MARCH. Warmer: 4°C. Overcast, cloudy sky. Snowmelt continues. At 7:30 a.m. I travel to sixty-second first aid station, from there to the twenty-ninth, and fourth light infantry divisions. Roads are terrible: part of the way by wagon, part by sled. For this trip I need twice as much time as usual—it's already 1:00 p.m. by the time I return. Opening of a movie theater at Pavloviczy in the morning. Entry prices very low for men, but more for officers and 1.50 crowns for staff officers. It functions very well and is very entertaining.

21 MARCH. Temperature the same (4°C). Snowmelt, rain at times. Roads are getting worse and worse and will soon be impassable. Around 11:00 a.m., Chief Medical Officer Herzog returns from his vacation. I lunch here, and return to my division in the afternoon. Unfortunately, I have to come here again tomorrow to sign myself out, because the commandant is not here today. The trip to command is absolutely horrible. The roads are awful—potholes everywhere, in every depression water swells into a veritable San River. Horses sink repeatedly to their knees, and the wagon threatens to turn over. I am only too pleased that, after more than thirty minutes travel (usually twenty minutes), I arrive at command.

22 MARCH. Zero degrees. Again, a snow-covered winter landscape: fresh snow falls at night. I will have to get used to the miserly conditions at command again. Even my quarters—a small, low shelter with tiny little windows—make me claustrophobic: there is so little room to move! The room is hardly 3 × 3 × 3 meters, and food has also become progressively worse. I notice this more because of my recent absence. There is no more bread for officers, only usual army bread, which is very bad: it consists mainly of cornmeal, is heavy and crumbly, almost inedible—at least for me—and bread is so important to me! No more milk bread for breakfast, only this lousy corn bread, without butter—horrible![24] At 9:30 a.m. I travel to corps command again, to sign off with the commandant. Travel on the muddy road is extremely difficult, and it's noon by the time I arrive. The commandant is very friendly, thanks me for all the trouble I have taken, and opines that everything is in best order. A few such words from so high a gentleman always make one happy and spurs one on to greater efforts. At lunch we say goodbye to our commandant: he is going on a gas course in Valenciennes (France). What a fine posting—only meant for a high gentleman; such a thing would hardly happen to us.

23 MARCH. Snowy landscape again (−3°C.). Thawing during the afternoon. Conditions in Russia are still unclear—but it's boiling and seething there, perhaps more than we know. Apparently, the Tsar and Tsarina have been taken captive! A fine rabble!

24 MARCH. Temperature −1°C with clear, beautiful, blue sky and strong sunshine, allowing snowmelt to begin in the early morning hours. At 7:30 a.m., I travel to the second division ammunition depot, where I stay for an hour, and go on a sick bay visit with the physician: Senior Surgeon Dr. Sugar, a military physician of the Hungarian school, a complete ignoramus, and dishonest to boot: completely undependable. His medical activity is so bad that I cannot watch it. From there I travel to second medical column: there, surgery is so active, purposeful, and exact that it is a pleasure to see them work. Regimental Physician First Class Bastaczi is an excellent surgeon.

25 MARCH. Sunday: which we hardly notice at command, in strong contrast to the situation at corps. Zero temperature, with a strong east wind, overcast, cloudy sky. Snow is gradually disappearing, but is still very deep everywhere. Unfortunately, I am summoned to the corps chief medical officer at 3:00 p.m. and must obey. His petty attitude has no place here. I only return at 5:30 p.m.; the conference is of no earthly importance: a complete waste of time.

26 MARCH. Warmer (2°C), with rising temperature during the day. Water from melting snow literally forms streams, flowing in the streets. At 7:30 a.m. I travel to field hospital 1009 in Wojmica, where the corps chief medical officer has announced an inspection. He acts as though he is working in a military hospital during peacetime, forgetting completely that the officers and physicians are civilians, who have no idea of what such service is. This delight lasts until 11:30 a.m. Because I have to travel with him at 1:45 p.m. to the division baggage train in Chorostow, I cannot return to my quarters and must remain at table at the field hospital until the train departs at 1:45 p.m. I arrive there at 2:15 p.m., inspect the bakery (Regimental Physician First Class Herrnstadt), and finally return at 6:00 p.m.

27 MARCH. Sunshine (−4°C). It finally looks as though spring is trying to arrive. I spend the morning collecting provisions for my batman, Schweiger, to take to my family in Vienna, during his upcoming trip. At the home front, they have had shortages of everything for a long time: flour, bread and milk are unavailable. Our situation isn't good either. Bread, which is already totally inedible, is now being made with wood flour. I cannot wait to try it. The state treasury has now taken possession of our horses, replaced with old nags, which we now have to ride. In this way, the treasury wants to ensure a supply of horses after the war. I am curious to see how much I will get for my horse. Getting back to Schweiger's trip home: With great difficulty, I have succeeded in buying the following for him from corps command: one ham; two kilograms of sausage; two kilograms of salted, smoked meat; ten kilograms of bacon; thirteen kilograms of flour; two kilograms of powdered milk; three kilograms of peas; five kilograms of beans; one box of potatoes; two loaves of bread from corps command, made of pure rye flour; two of our own loaves (corn bread). In this way, my family will at least have enough to eat for a few days.

28 MARCH. Thawing (4°C), clear, blue sky. We can hardly move one foot out of our shelters: pools of water and mud everywhere. I am happy that I do not have to go out, and can remain here.

29 MARCH. Colder, −1°C, again fresh snowfall. Winter is not finished with us yet this year.

30 MARCH. Snowmelt (0°C). Mud is getting worse and worse. Water is so deep in all the hollows that it resembles the San River. Horses sink up to their bellies in some of these large puddles.

31 MARCH. Warmer, 6°C. Snow has disappeared, replaced by lakes of muddy water that get bigger and bigger. Very nice morning weather, periods of rain in the afternoon, just when I have to go to field hospital 1009 for erection of a new barrack. There is a certain amount of excitement at command: Archduke Leopold Salvator is scheduled here for an inspection. My trip to the field hospital lasts from 2:00 to 4:30 p.m.

1 APRIL. Spring air is blowing (−5°C)! Only a small amount of dirty snow remains in places. Mud gets ever deeper, lakes of muddy water ever larger.

We eagerly and impatiently await daily newspapers with news from Russia. Things appear more serious than newspapers relate. It's certain that the revolution wants to change Russia into a constitutional state: because the Tsar can have no place in this, he has simply been removed. It's just as obvious that there is still a monarchist party, but workers and socialists demand such a wide variety of concessions that the revolutionary party is in an exceptionally difficult position. For the moment, Michael Alexandrovich[25] has not accepted the crown: he will only do this if the nation vote for him to do so. Quite obviously, Russia, in such a condition, is incapable of any meaningful attacks in the field. The Entente is very depressed about this, also by the strategic blow that Germany has dealt the British and the French on the Western Front: immediately before the French offensive, which they have been preparing all winter long, Germans have suddenly pulled back their troops over a distance of one hundred kilometers long and ten kilometers wide (this has also been prepared all winter) to significantly shorten the front.[26] The British and French are now faced with an entirely new task: it will surely take them many weeks to bring up their heavy equipment and artillery, install, and fortify it.

This is a chess move with no historical equivalent and brings Hindenburg even more honor.

Today Archduke Leopold Salvator inspects an artillery placement, as well as a few German airplanes.

3 APRIL. Warmer, 7.5°C: snow almost completely gone. Sunshine and clouds alternating. The ground is starting to dry out. At 3:00 p.m. I travel to the corps chief medical officer, to request four days' leave for the coming festival days.[27] Remarkably, he has nothing against it, so I will leave the afternoon of 5 April and return after four days leave in Vienna. Leave has been granted for everybody again, but our corps command insists on the passing of a full six months since my last leave, and I still need another full month to complete this time period. Will leave be possible then? Everything depends on what happens in Russia: it's already 5:00 p.m. by the time I return from the corps chief medical officer.

3 APRIL. With 10°C, spring is definitely here. Strong west wind, and ground is drying out more and more, but trips to the front are still impossible: it would be a terrible slog for horses. The chief medical officer does not understand this and almost every day fixes a rendezvous for the day after and then cancels it, apparently after the gentlemen in corps command make him see sense. At 9:00 a.m. I travel to the baths on ¤ 243—everything is functioning without a hitch, and delousing is now absolutely reliable, but there are still problems with personnel organization.

At 3:00 p.m. I have a meeting with all the chief physicians in the presence of Dr. Potorau and the head of the bacteriology laboratory, concerning upcoming cholera and typhoid vaccinations. This takes about an hour, after which Senior Physician Holzer (fourth light infantry) photographs us all.

4 APRIL. Cloudy early with a strong east wind that brings clearing with sunshine. I am preparing for my upcoming four days' leave, and time passes quickly. All sorts of service tasks pile up for me today. Afternoon brings the first spring storm, which lasts quite a long time—afterward just rain, then clearing. Sunny, fresh, and warm—accompanied by a plague of flies both sides of the line. Despite command's decision, my leave is approved. I depart at noon to spend at least a few enjoyable days with my family. The trip is very pleasant—by coincidence I meet my old friend and comrade Major Berner from the fourth battalion: he has a lot to tell me, about the year he spent in Schönbrunn Palace, so time passes quickly, and I arrive on schedule in Vienna at 11:00 p.m., where my wife and Tinka are waiting to meet me. The misery in the city is immediately apparent when looking for a conveyance. There are several there, but no one wants to take us unless we gave him a large tip. I don't wish to do this, so we travel slowly by tram as best we can and arrive in the Kaiserstrasse at 12:45 a.m.

7–10 APRIL. Vacation days pass all too quickly. The first and third days are completely rained out, but the other two days are tolerable. The children are very happy to see me: Miki won't leave my side, but Mary (the youngest) wants nothing to do with me—no wonder! She is nearly one year old and this is only the second time that she has seen her dad. She is not used to male company. Conditions in Vienna are very depressing. It is fortunate that, shortly before my arrival, I sent so many provisions with my batman. My wife and children look bad, no wonder! My Olga has the daily grind of finding provisions for seven people. She must be on the street at 7:00 a.m. daily, something to which she is not accustomed. We spend one evening in the Apollo Theater—by 9:00 p.m. all places of entertainment are closed. The show lasts from 6:00 p.m. to 9:00 p.m.

11 APRIL. Train departs at 7:00 a.m. After an uneventful but boring journey, I arrive at command 11:30 a.m. the next morning. The first news I get here is very good. My horse has been purchased by the state treasury commission for the ridiculous price of 2,370 crowns: as long as I stay at command, I can use the money. But happiness is clouded by the fact that the Germans have rejected my Iron Cross application, for the simple reason that they have not been awarding it to noncombatants for the past few months. This is how our high ranked medical superiors now represent our interests! The youngest reserve lieutenant at command already has the Iron Cross, but a senior chief medical officer is not worthy of it! It's a scandal! Our divisional physicians have done such an enormous job for the Germans, who have fought so often and so long in association with us and been treated in our medical units. By contrast, other gentlemen have mostly only dealt with the Germans by telephone!

13 APRIL. Nice, warm weather, already 11°C early. Ground is already hard and dry almost everywhere, so the dreaded period of snowmelt has passed quite quickly, even with the recent temporary closure of the military field railway because of flooding. I travel at 3:30 a.m. to second medical column, where I am summoned by the corps chief medical officer for 8:00 a.m. A very thorough inspection: it is already 11:30 a.m. by the time I return. Soon after, our commandant Major General Jemrich arrives after his trip to France; he talks a lot, but says nothing important.

14 APRIL. Early departure with the corps chief medical officer to first aid station no. 5/103, which has been newly established and looks exceptionally clean and appropriate. Despite this, our valiant Herzog hasn't even *one* word of recognition for Senior Physician Dr. Stein's exemplary achievement, but rather looks for reasons to rebuke and grouse. On the way back, inspection of the baths at camp no. 5: inspection completed at noon.

15 APRIL. Russian Easter Sunday! It rained yesterday afternoon, also during the night, so the new army commandant, Colonel General von Kirchbach, Tersztyánszky's successor, cancels the planned inspection at our division. I am summoned to meet with the corps medical chief at 3:30 p.m., return 5:30 p.m.

16 APRIL. Departure 7:30 a.m. to fortieth infantry ... regimental first aid station—first battalion ... thirteenth company ... return 12:30 a.m. [illegible shorthand].

17 APRIL. I stay at home to deal with urgent office matters. [illegible shorthand].

18 APRIL. Weather favorable, like yesterday. Travel at 8:00 a.m. to the division munitions depot, from there to field hospital 1009, and then finally to second medical column—return around noon.

19 APRIL. Weather overcast, periods of rain; 7:30 a.m. departure with the corps chief medical officer to the fortieth infantry regiment, first battalion, then 3/40—after inspection of the first aid station, we visit the positions of 3/40, then to tenth company. On the way back, inspection of first aid station of second artillery with the twenty-ninth light infantry, return by 12:45 p.m. Russian positions are hardly fifty paces from our own: the Russians walk around quite happily on the ramparts, no shots fired from either side. News from Russia is still confused. The worker and socialist parties seem to be leading the agenda, both striving for peace.

20 APRIL. Unfavorable weather. Early rain, strong southwest wind and significant cooling—I stay at home.

21 APRIL. Our friendly relationship with the Russians has ceased, and they are shooting at us—normal war again. Corps Commandant Kritek visits us in the afternoon, with his personal adjutant Rittmeister Baron Reinlein, representing Chief of the General Staff Lieutenant Colonel Britto, as guest. Our mess is nicely decked out, and food is excellent. Weather nice, dry, warm, sunshine

22 APRIL. Weather overcast, foggy, quite cold. Yesterday I carefully inspected the baths on ¤ 243 and remained there for a few hours. The abbreviated description of the division is now I.D. instead of I.T.D.

23 APRIL. Early 5:00 a.m., the Russians suddenly start an artillery attack, almost a bombardment. All members of command assemble in the officer's mess, awaiting developments. But after hardly thirty minutes, guns suddenly go silent, and calm returns to the field. Fire was aimed mainly at depressions behind our positions and the entrance roads. Positions themselves are more or less intact.

During the morning I inspect the soldiers' home and the workers' section no. 9/1. At noon two Swedish officers appear as guests of our army: one colonel and one captain. They will remain at our command for five days.

24 APRIL. An overcast, foggy day—visibility practically zero. I travel with the corps chief medical officer, who has attached himself to the corps gas officer Captain Petrin, to first aid station of the sixty-second. Inspection also of first aid station twenty-ninth light infantry, and then on to the position of 5/62; on the way back to first aid station fourth light infantry; return at noon. At 3:00 p.m. Swedish officers accompany me on an inspection of ¤ 243, as well as the soldiers' home. Return at 5:00 p.m. Cholera and typhoid inoculations at command.

25 APRIL. Weather still overcast: cool, but not unpleasantly so. At 3:00 p.m. I travel with the Swedish Colonel Sparre and Captain Count Hamilton to Wojmica and give them a thorough tour of the medical column and field hospital. They are delighted at what they see. Back by car, arrival 5:00 p.m.

26 APRIL. Awfully cold at night, a few degrees below zero in the morning, but with a clearer, blue sky and sunshine. Surgeon General Bürkel has arrived

for an inspection. At 3:00 p.m., I wait for him at the baths on ¤ 243, from there I take him to the baths in camp 5, then on to the regimental first aid station fortieth infantry regiment, 4/62, and then back to field hospital 1009. Because we travel everywhere by car, the trip is quick, and we are back at 6:30 p.m.

27 APRIL. Cool today as well but fine and dry, with a strong west wind. Inspection continues today: I travel at 7:30 a.m. to second medical column, where I stay until 11:00 a.m. Surgeon General Bürkel is a water diviner, and his experiments take up a large part of the inspection time. Otherwise, he is very generous, not a carper, so unlike our dear Herzog, whose only task during inspections is to carp and look for problems.

After 7:00 p.m., while we are at dinner, a Russian squadron of six to eight planes appears over our positions and the thirteenth *Landwehr* division. Despite heavy antiaircraft activity, they penetrate ¤ 243 and bomb the thirteenth *Landwehr*. Our pilots report gathering of troops behind the Russian positions, and increased artillery. All these are signs of a coming offensive—just when I want to go on vacation on 10 May! Gypsies play at dinner in honor of our Swedish guests: things become very jolly, and soon champagne appears to toast them. Straight after dinner, Artillery Colonel von Otto is decorated with the Signum Laudis—he is spending time with us as replacement for the vacationing General Rosenzweig.

Figure 4.4. Dress-up pantomime with amateur players. Photograph courtesy of the Leo Baeck Institute.

28 APRIL. Weather changeable, mainly cool, periods of light snowfall, which disappears without a trace. The Swedish officers depart straight after dinner: a moving farewell. We can see that they have enjoyed being with us and would have preferred to stay. The colonel in particular wants quite badly to experience a battle with us. Before they get into the car that will take them to the train station, another quick photograph is taken.

29 APRIL. Weather like yesterday. At 2:30 p.m. I travel by car to the corps chief medical officer: I have been summoned again! The condition of our horses is now very bad. Fodder is extremely scarce—therefore, they must be spared as much as possible. The horses are very tired and saggy; many die each day from exhaustion: we receive cars rather than horses despite the fact that gasoline must also be spared and wheels must run on the rims because of lack of rubber.

30 APRIL. Miserable morning weather. Wind, cool, overcast, clearing only by afternoon. During *Jause*[28] we are entertained by the Burgtheaterensemble in Pavloviczy, home of corps command. I do not participate, because my spirits are low.

1 MAY. First beautiful spring day! Sunshine starts in early morning. Spring vegetation is much delayed because of many cold days and even colder nights. There is hardly a green shimmer to be seen in the fields, and trees are still completely bare. Today the new army commandant, Colonel General von Kirchbach, comes for inspection and takes lunch with us. The corps commandant is also present; each man with his cadre of gentlemen. I am seated beside our general. Two German officers are also our guests, and the mood is very lively.

2 MAY. Beautiful spring weather. At 8:00 a.m. I travel to the division ammunition depot, from there to second medical column, then to field hospital 1009 where, coincidentally, I meet the corps chief medical officer, there with Chief of the General Staff Colonel Raschke, who is having an abscess lanced. He has always insisted on a surgical group for us, as if he had a premonition that he would be the first to use it.

3 MAY. Lovely spring weather continues, even if a north wind makes it quite brisk. At 8:00 a.m., departure with the corps chief medical officer and the corps gas officer Captain Petrin to sixty-second first aid station, where all physicians and gas officers have assembled for a presentation on gas protection. The lecture is long—at the end, we are all photographed, and return at 1:00 p.m. During the afternoon, I work on family food issues: how to acquire more provisions for my upcoming leave. It doesn't look good—even we hardly receive anything anymore.

4 MAY. Weather like yesterday, nice and sunny but the amount of warmth still leaves a lot to be desired. Everything is still cold—hardy a glimmer of green in the meadows. Our poor horses are suffering especially badly. They have received hardly any fodder for many months—hardly one kilogram of mixed fodder per day. The administration keeps making adjustments so that as many

horses as possible can be moved back to the hinterland. This is a double-edged sword, because if we suddenly need to move, half the material must remain behind. Today I receive the sad news from my father that my poor brother-in-law Eduard died on 2 May. Death came as a deliverance for him, because no one should live such a poor and miserable life, and my sister Loreia has long—in effect—been a poor, unhappy widow: her husband was only a burden to her and her family.

In the morning, I inspect the soldiers' home—in the evening I receive approval in the military mail for my vacation. I am very happy about this, but must wait for the return of Dr. Müller, my replacement, before I can leave.

5 MAY. Good weather—it's gradually getting warmer. I am so busy with my thought about vacation that I have no more patience for other matters—today I stay put as well.

6 MAY. Nice weather in the morning, not particularly warm. In my impatience, I get up at 8:30 a.m. and go for a long walk through the forest to the first aid station, second Honvėd regiment, which I reach at 9:20 a.m. I stay there and have a nice chat with Senior Physician Baum, a Bielitzer,[29] who has a lot to tell about the war, until 10:45 a.m., returning, arriving to command shortly before noon. This walk is a little too much for me, and I develop blisters on both soles of my feet. Dr. Müller has just returned from vacation and is waiting for me. The time is right, and now there are no obstacles to my going on leave. Extensive rain in the afternoon, lasting all night.

7 MAY. Beautiful weather, a great deal of sunshine; it's getting considerably warmer, and fields are becoming greener, even if very sparingly. Our poor horses are already trying to get at the small amount of grass: it isn't clever of them—with another week's patience, they will soon have a decent meadow on which to graze. Yesterday's rain did the vegetation a lot of good. Dr. Müller arrives at 10:00 a.m. to take over my position: however, he gives me the unwelcome news that he has taken another one to two days absence in Kowel,[30] because his transfer is pending. Will the grim and grisly Herzog allow me to go on leave before Müller's arrival from Kowel?

8 MAY. I speak with Herzog at 8:00 a.m.—he is not thrilled with my departure but does not hold me back; after lunch at 12:45 p.m., I travel to Rogozno by car, arriving in Lemberg[31]—where I stay at the Hotel Imperial—at 9:30 p.m.

9 MAY. At 5:00 a.m. early, I visit the grave of my dear mother and other dear departed relatives. The cemetery is the only place where there is peace and calm—the only sign of the war is overgrowth and deficient care of the gravestones, which are otherwise so carefully tended. At 8:00 a.m. I visit my father. I hardly recognize the poor man, he has changed so much. He is suffering from the war as well: he is malnourished, and what food there is, is bad. He has come down in the world and become very thin, although, subjectively, he still feels

well. My sister Loreia with her two children is still sitting *shiva*[32] for her dead husband, Edouard. Everyone is very glad to see me; I must, contrary to my original plan, overnight in a hotel and only leave for Vienna on 10 May at 7:00 a.m.

10 MAY. Arrival 10:30 p.m.

VACATION, 10–29 MAY. My wife insists on meeting me at the station despite the late hour. The poor woman looks even worse than she did last time. Daily cares and difficulty obtaining enough food for seven hungry mouths has made her jumpy and very run down. On the contrary, the children look well. Mary my youngest is a lovely little scallywag: she is walking already and is very dear, despite the fact that she wants absolutely nothing to do with me: she is not used to men. Miki is a beautiful young woman: sensible and well educated. One seldom sees so elegant a young lady! Ega also looks well and has made good progress in all aspects. Tinka is a complete young lady but has great problems in school, and I will be pleased when she finally graduates and finishes with it already—she has talent only in certain subjects (e.g., languages), but subjects like mathematics, physics, etc., are closed books to her.

Miki has been coughing very badly for the past three days, and it's clear to me that she is suffering from whooping cough. She played in the garden with a child suffering from pertussis, and the damage was done. The child has been in bed since then, and the coughing bothers her greatly. She was so looking forward to Papa's visit: to the walks and trips that she wanted to take with her Dad, and now all her little plans have been destroyed. The coughing, retching, and vomiting do not let her sleep all night—I cannot sleep either, naturally, because I run to be with her for each attack until she calms down again. I ask Professor Knöpfelmacher to visit her, but he doesn't know how to treat it either, except for a rapid change of location, which is not so simple during wartime. Most summer resorts are hesitant to book, struggling with lack of provisions, even with guests, for whom all sorts of difficulties are made. All bookings must be made by the end of May, with exact details of arrival, departure, and how many days will be spent there. The city will only quasi provide from 1 July to 30 August. Upon recommendation, my wife and I travel to Sauerbrunn, to look at a summer residence rental; but we don't like it there, and return home in the evening empty-handed. Days pass very rapidly with many visits that have to be made. My Olga, who is bothered greatly by lack of provisions and has become very thin, has recovered somewhat during my visit, but my departure falls doubly heavily on her, because she will not have restful nights anymore. Miki's coughing attacks occur mostly at night, and I often have to get up every thirty minutes to an hour. I decide, just before the end of my leave, to ask telegraphically for an extra fourteen days, but will only receive the answer on 29 May. We try again to find a summer residence and finally find one in Radaun, but it's very expensive: seven hundred crowns for July and August. We are appalled to hear, on 29 May, that extension of my leave has not been granted. How typical of the military! I make sure that Olga rents the house in Radaun quickly, and leave the day after.

31 MAY. Arrival at command at 11:00 a.m. Meanwhile, command has been transferred from the forest to Pavloviczy, former location of corps command. I am not welcomed back in a friendly manner because of my vacation extension request. After I explain the situation personally to the general, he is visibly upset that he has done so little to help me. Summer heat is in full swing here—temperatures up to 35°C in the shade. My quarters—in the former barracks (office) of the chief medical officer—are also very hot at a constant 26°C: it's quite unbearable in the afternoon.

1 JUNE. I am kept very busy with my duties but am constantly oppressed with worry about my wife and children at home. I intend to personally request a new leave period from corps command. The heat continues: not a drop of rain, so necessary for seeds to germinate. Only today does the good Herzog have the courage to speak to me by telephone. After I describe my problems at home (again), he asks why I did not request the extension formally, punctually, and in writing. Obviously, he is to blame for the whole affair; Commandant Kaiser, who has recently replaced Corps Commandant Colonel General Kritek, is a charming and gracious man, who certainly would not have said no. I indicate to him my intention to go personally to go corps command with my request: he does not answer me; obviously this makes him very uncomfortable! At 5:00 p.m. a short but heavy thunderstorm, limited to Pavloviczy only.

3 JUNE. Hot summer weather continues. At 8:00 a.m. I depart for the newly expanded reserve position no. 4/62, returning at 10:30 a.m.

4 JUNE. Weather has cooled significantly; we freeze at night. At 8:00 a.m. I depart for division ammunition depot 2, from there to medical column no. 2, then off to field hospital 1009; return at 11:30 a.m.

5 JUNE. Cool, dry, pleasant weather continues. Departure at 8:00 a.m. first to the baths on ¤ 243, then on to sick bay twenty-ninth light infantry, from then on to first aid stations nos. 1 and 3/40—return at noon.

6 JUNE. Very hot early, becoming more humid: around 5:00 p.m. a real thunderstorm breaks out, lasting for an hour. At 7:00 p.m. we meet up with two Dutch officers: Rittmeister Godin de Beaufort and First Lieutenant von Reigersberg-Versluys: they are here to observe our position and facilities.[33] We are not sure what they think of us, so must show everything in the best possible light. All necessary preparations are made: for example, cattle must not graze on sides of the path through which they walk. Meals are ample and well prepared (during their visit), and the gentlemen disport themselves, in very good spirits, until midnight. The founders of the feast partake happily of the wine and champagne until 5:30 a.m.

7 JUNE. The foreign gentlemen observe our positions accompanied by Captain Erben. Lunch today early at 11:00 a.m. because they must depart at 12:30

p.m., again under escort. The men are very pleasant; the first lieutenant especially is inquisitive; they are treated with greatest care. My inspections are held up by their visit: at 3:00 p.m. I travel by car with the logistics officer to the corps chief medical officer in Mikuliczy,[34] twelve kilometers from here. I make a detour at division transport command in Chorostow, and we return at 7:00 p.m. Weather pleasant, not too hot anymore.

8 JUNE. Significant cooling. So much paperwork has accumulated during the past two days that I cannot go anywhere today. It takes all morning before the work is completed.

9 JUNE. We freeze overnight; today my room is even heated. The sun shines nicely early but soon disappears behind the clouds, and it becomes cold again. Violent storm around 6:00 p.m., lasting one and a half hours. Early at 7:30 a.m. I travel to first aid station twenty-ninth light infantry, to inspect the position projected by their corps as a new first aid station. The position is badly chosen and useless, because it comes under the heaviest artillery fire during battle. But that idiot Herzog insists on it. That other idiot (just as bad as Herzog), my Commanding General (Jemrich), doesn't dare make counterproposals. I travel to the fourth light infantry on the way back and inspect the baths in camp no. 5; return at 12:30 p.m.

10 JUNE. Temperature somewhat warmer: at least my room doesn't need to be heated anymore. I am feeling miserable: I had a wretched night with

Figure 4.5. Bernhard Bardach at his desk with accumulated paperwork and reading material. Photograph courtesy of the Leo Baeck Institute.

cold shivers and nausea—during the day, I have a fever and a terribly upset stomach, which reflects the state of my entire disposition. Tales of woe from home: Mary also has whooping cough. Olga does not know what to do anymore: she has had to let the child's maid go because she has been sleeping around, staying out until 1:00 a.m. Olga takes such matters seriously, but they only serve to increase the confusion. I am exiled here, without any prospect of leave.

11 JUNE. After having fasted almost completely for an entire day, I am feeling somewhat better. It's noteworthy that almost half of the entire command is suffering from the same thing, most especially Captain Erben: he has been lying in bed with fever for the past three days. Is this the notorious Wolhynian fever or food poisoning through green salad, which we now eat in large quantities? I stay at home today as well.[35]

12 JUNE. I am feeling much better. I depart at 7:30 a.m., first to first aid station 5/103—and on the way back to first aid station 4/62—that has in the meantime been transferred to the church mill; return at noon. Surgeon Major Gara wastes my entire morning chattering, especially about himself and his personal affairs; he shows little understanding for interests of others, so a proper conversation with him is impossible.

13 JUNE. An early walk to medical column no. 2: it takes only twenty minutes to get there. From there to the field hospital, return by wagon at noon.

14 JUNE. The number of our enemies has increased by one: upon pressure from the Entente, the King of Greece has abdicated in favor of his second son, after the first son didn't suit the Entente.[36] There is no doubt that now Greece will declare war on us. The situation in Russia is totally confused, a great advantage for us. The fact that they are not capable of mounting another offensive lightens our military load and lets us concentrate on uninterrupted fighting on the Isonzo and Tirol fronts. The Italians are wearing themselves out for nothing: they have already had enormous losses during the first ten battles and, apart from Monte Kuk,[37] have achieved nothing. Our corps chief medical officer, Dr. Herzog, has been transferred to Cholm[38] as chief garrison physician: he is being replaced by Oberstabsarzt I Klasse Dr. Alfred Lederer. For Herzog, this is a well-deserved demotion: one would go far to find so mean-spirited a superior. All physicians are happy about his fate, because he has not had a single good word for any of us. By contrast, he has pestered and nagged us at every opportunity. The word "loathsome" describes him very well. I detest him from the bottom of my heart, because he alone is responsible for not prolonging my leave despite my needing it so urgently. When two of one's children suddenly become seriously ill, their mother—all alone—is kept busy full time providing sustenance for seven people, and she needs rapid change of air because of children's' whooping cough—what could be more urgent? God bless and keep him in Cholm—far away from me.

15 JUNE. Weather has been nice for the past few days, warm and windy, but by far not as hot as at the beginning of the month. I depart for inspection at 8:00 a.m. Today it is the artillery's turn: I visit the first aid station of the second field artillery, then the artillery group Major Zaufalek/Assistant Physician Rodler, and at the end first aid station second Honvéd regiment. On the way, I also inspect 5/2 Honvéd battalion, which is especially well installed. Return at noon.

16 JUNE. Today, a big inspection by Field Vicar Bishop Bjelik. He arrives at command at 10:30 a.m., inspects the second medical column and field hospital 1009 in Wojmica, after that the soldiers' home on ¤ 243. He takes lunch with us: all chaplains in our division are invited, also Dr. Müller. After lunch, he travels to the thirteenth rifle division. General Jemrich has not departed yet, and he and I accompany the field vicar on his inspection tour. At 2:00 p.m. he returns to corps command. At night, Russians fire far behind us in the direction Pavloviczy-Wojmica. Our new, long bridge over the swamp sticks in their craw: they have already fired on it four times. This happens at 7:00 p.m., exactly the time when Regimental Physician First Class Bardachzi, the surgeon at second medical column goes out for a walk: he is unlucky enough to be hit in the skull by all four shells and is killed immediately. We are all deeply upset and mourn his loss because he was an exceptionally efficient and hard-working surgeon—the pillar of our medical column. The entire command joins the physicians in mourning this terrible loss. Weather very nice. Rain at night.

Figure 4.6. Memorial service in the field. Photograph courtesy of the Leo Baeck Institute.

17 JUNE. We are far from over mourning for poor Bardachzi—he informs our daily conversations. Today, the ensemble of the Vienna Intimtheater arrives. The entire command turns out for the performance, because net proceeds are for the widows and orphans fund. I do not participate in this entertainment.

18 JUNE. It has become much hotter. Today is a very sad day: our poor Bardachzi is being transported back to his native Bohemia: his brother, another regimental physician first class, has come from Przemysl[39] to take him home. The benediction takes place at 6:00 p.m. Our general takes me to the medical column by car—almost all division doctors are assembled, also many from the neighboring thirteenth rifles division. The chaplain gives an incomprehensible sermon: speaking doesn't seem to be his strong point. His high-flown philosophy is unintelligible, and he doesn't seem to know what he is talking about. In addition, he is a Hungarian with bad German. After him, the chief medical officer speaks, this time movingly and well, making one momentarily forget one's intense dislike. He makes *one* big mistake: when this tragic ceremony ends, he gathers us around him one last time, to say goodbye. This is neither the right place nor the right moment—he has to have seen that the general is waiting for me. He formally asks our pardon for his bad treatment of us. After shaking everyone's hand, he asks the superfluous question whether any of us would like to be transferred to Cholm. General silence! What a scene! It should have been photographed to preserve it for posterity!

19 JUNE. The heat is so unbearable that I am staying at home today. Room temperature 26°C.

20 JUNE. Weather like yesterday: no rain, no cooling down. At 4:00 a.m. the Russians permit themselves an artillery attack on our fortieth that lasts about twenty minutes—it sounds like a bombardment but is not. No losses. Some accidents, caused by clumsy handling of different kinds of ammunition, have recently caused us more losses that those from enemy fire.

21 JUNE. Despite the awful heat, I walk to our medical column at 8:00 a.m., returning by wagon at 11:00 a.m. Serious abdominal surgery: stomach and liver damaged by an infantry bullet. The operation is successful, but the patient dies with the last stitch.

22 JUNE. Heat unbearable: 30°C in the shade; no wind, no likelihood at all of rain. I am jaded and cannot decide whether to depart for the front, especially because I am leaving for field hospital 1009 at 9:00 a.m., where I remain until 11:30 a.m. Finally, the greatly wished-for storm breaks toward evening but brings only a little cooling. We celebrate the decoration of Officer First Lieutenant Kuznierz with champagne (of course)—until midnight.

23 JUNE. Early rainy weather, clearing. But heat just as bad as before. At 8:00 a.m. I travel to first aid station no. 2/40, inspect their redoubts, and return at noon.

24 JUNE. Finally, the rain that everyone is yearning for falls during the night: it starts around 2:00 a.m. and lasts uninterruptedly until noon: then, periods of rain during the afternoon, with clearing toward evening. All the greenery looks freshened up and rejuvenated. Long evening celebration in our mess. Our First Lieutenant Hoffmann, allocated to us as technical adviser, is returning to his command, before being inducted into the air force as a pilot. A small group of us remains until 11:30 p.m.—most remain longer. I have had enough: the champagne doesn't taste good anymore—I was never really excited about these champagne parties, but now they mean nothing to me. The night rain has disturbed the patients in the field hospital because the rain leaks into their barrack.

25 JUNE. Rain again toward morning, followed by clearing. At 8:30 a.m. I walk to medical column, arriving just in time for a serious abdominal operation—I remain there until noon.

26 JUNE. Weather nice again and not too terribly hot. At 8:00 a.m. I travel to first aid station no. 5/103; I go into the position with the physician in chief, returning at noon. The state of this battalion is exemplary: it looks like a well-tended palace garden—clean, neat, and tidy. During my return walk back, Russians fire more shells: I have to choose another way back.

27 JUNE. Weather very nice. Today is another theater day. The Fronttheater of the Vienna Private Stage Company is staging a production for us. Great bustle and excitement in the afternoon. The ensemble of twenty-one people arrives at 10:00 a.m. Quarters and provisions must be prepared for all of them: not so easy with the present scarcity of provisions. Our senior cook, Winiary, is desperate, grumbling unendingly. In the end, difficulties are overcome, especially by the many pretty, young maidens traipsing around our village roads in their small shoes. They take lunch separately from us, because of lack of space and service. The performance takes place at 6:00 p.m.: *The Spanish Fly*, a jolly farce. Everyone laughs, but enjoyment does not last long and everything is finished by 7:30 p.m. The social part of the evening begins after dinner: they dine with us and soon everything becomes very jolly. On my left-hand side, the prompter, Miss Heiger, sits: a nice, serious person; opposite me, the main actor and director, Mr. Lessen, an unmatched, elegant comedian. Next to him, an actress for the masses, with a very large appetite. Things soon become very cozy; the wine does its job, and a Vienna Schrammel quartet plays amusing tunes—Mr. Lessen and Mrs. Felden sing and dance until late. Most of the company is tired from goings-on of last evening and go to sleep at midnight, myself included, although I have had a previous good night's sleep. The rest remain until 3:00 a.m. I hear them passing through the streets singing; then it becomes quiet. They leave Pavloviczy at 9:00 a.m. the next morning, with best possible impressions.

28 JUNE. Slight hangover, so I stay at home today. Weather like yesterday.

29 JUNE. It's already hot and muggy early in the morning, but I still depart at 8:30 a.m., first to the medical column; because there is little to do there, I go on to the field hospital and return at noon. Humidity reaches its climax during the afternoon: finally, around 5:00 p.m., an extremely violent storm breaks out, bringing a little relief. The storm lasts about one and a half hours. Immediately after dinner, the Russians begin a three-hour direct artillery attack on the eleventh division, situated south of us: several thousand salvoes are fired. effect unknown, but no following infantry attack.

30 JUNE. I am suddenly awakened at 4:00 a.m. by heavy firing in my vicinity: I first think that there is shooting in the village, but it's only our antiaircraft guns firing at a squadron of six Russian airplanes. Planes succeed in crossing our lines, and fly farther in the direction of Vladimir-Volynsky,[40] dropping bombs and directing machine gunfire. It takes an entire hour before the last pilot has returned to base, under heaviest possible fire from our antiaircraft batteries. At 8:30 a.m. I travel to second artillery's first aid station, from there I visit the baths in camp no. 5, and on the way back inspect the baths on ¤ 243. Outside is quite unsettled. Austrian pilots are seeking revenge and fly over Russian positions, but are fired on vigorously and lucky to get back safely.

1 JULY. Continuous rain during the second half of the night, lasting until early morning; rain the rest of the morning. Clearing only around noon. The Russians have been active during the past few days: strong forces have assembled near Brzezany,[41] and it looks like a new offensive is likely.[42] Heavy artillery activity on our front and the neighboring position to our right. This is ironic in view of the decision by Russian workers' and soldiers' councils for an immediate peace settlement.

Greece, which now has a new king, has sent us an official billet-doux. One more enemy!

2 JULY. Russian pilots again, only with the difference that they appear very early, at 3:30 a.m. Aerial bombing in places. Losses still unknown. Last time, four men and one horse were wounded in Wojmica. Apparently—irrespective of our heavy antiaircraft firing—they are winding down their activities. The theater company arrives again around noon: two performances are planned for here. Today is *The Rape of the Sabines*, well played and jolly. Just as the performance is about to begin at 6:00 p.m., a violent storm develops, and start has to be delayed thirty minutes because of heavy downpours on the roof of the theater building. After performance and dinner, obligatory get-together in our mess. Music, song, cheerful recitations: time passes quickly and pleasantly, and in no time at all it's 1:00 a.m.

The Russian offensive in Brzezany is in full swing: they are attacking with forty divisions in an area hardly fifty kilometers wide: Against them, we only have ten divisions. Fighting is violent and bitter. Up until today, they have been repelled everywhere: only the village Koniuchy[43] has been lost. Enormous losses: they advance in large, concentrated numbers. Heavy artillery activity on our front.

3 JULY. Weather very unstable—repeated periods of rain. Theater evening again: *Pension Scholler*—a stupid farce, but well played. After the performance, the theater group scatters to the area around Pavloviczy, invited by a few commands. Three ladies and six gentlemen remain behind with us. I leave them to the younger people and go to bed around 11:00 p.m. The remaining revelers stay until 2:30 a.m.

4 JULY. Weather unstable: transient rain toward evening, which does not prevent the announced nature show, at 9:52 p.m., of a total lunar eclipse in a starry sky. It's a full moon: the eclipse begins from the left side of the moon, with significant darkening. This dark strip moves gradually to the other end of the moon: it takes almost an entire hour before the eclipse is total, and the moon appears as a red disc behind the dark streak. A magnificent spectacle! Could this natural phenomenon perhaps be a sign the war will soon end? It is well known that the war started with another natural phenomenon—a total solar eclipse on 21 August 1914. Who dare say?! Russians have hardly begun their new offensive. If they don't have more luck than they have had during the first three days, they will not get very far and will have to retreat.

5 JULY. Russian pilots awaken me early in the morning with their revolting bombs and our antiaircraft firing. This time their bombs drop on the village of Lukaczy,[44] south of the Germans' position. At 10:00 a.m., our new chief medical officer, Dr. Lederer, finally arrives. Hopefully he brings us salvation! Herzog officially hands over all first aid stations and personnel to him. Weather good: very warm again during the afternoon. Evenings cool and fresh.

6 JULY. A horrible day! Hot, humid, exertions all day—newly arrived Chief Medical Officer Lederer inspects the division. He inspects the baths on ⌂ 243, then the sick bay of twenty-ninth light infantry. From there we travel by car; he picks me up at 7:30 p.m. with Dr. Herzog, and we go to the first aid station twenty-ninth light infantry. All the physicians are assembled there for a talk on gas protection given by Surgeon Major Ruzcyzka from third medical column, who has just returned from a gas course in Vienna. From there we travel to first aid stations [?]/40 and 62, and then onward to the baths in camp no. 5. I am back at noon, but, straight after lunch, have to travel to field hospital 1009, where I meet up with the gentlemen again and, from there, travel to second medical column. There I meet Surgeon Major Professor Raubitschek from Czernowitz,[45] who has arrived in his capacity as army hygiene specialist. I have to repeat almost the entire inspection tour from the beginning, and with a wagon, not a car. And again, to the baths at ⌂ 243, then first aid station [?]/40, finally returning at 7:00 p.m. What a day! The new corps physician makes an excellent impression: a kind and worthy gentleman who understands what we have achieved. He has participated in it as a division physician of long standing, in stark contrast to Herzog, who until recently has sat out the war in Budapest. A storm breaks toward evening, cooling the weather off somewhat.

7 JULY. Weather again nice—I allow myself a rest day. News about the Russian offensive is very satisfying: apart from small successes in the beginning, they do not seem to have achieved anything, despite tremendous losses. That is good! A Czech and Slovak brigade is fighting on the Russian side against us:[46] more than eight thousand of them have been taken captive by us—what miserable, faithless baggage they are!

8 JULY. My main task at the moment is copying down the talk given by Dr. Ruzyczka: his talk is well put together, and of even more interest to me, because I have been seconded to attend a ten-day gas course in Vienna starting on 17 July. I am obviously very happy, because I can be with my family again. But my joy is not unalloyed, because lectures are scheduled in both morning and afternoon, 8:00 to 11:00 a.m. and 2:30 to 5:00 p.m. It is highly questionable whether I will be able to reach the rotunda—where lectures are being given—in time by train from Radaun—where my family is located. For the moment, I don't want to spoil my happiness, and hope that everything will turn out all right.

9 JULY. It rains intermittently almost every day. I don't mind, but my family are suffering because they are cooped up in the room and can get no enjoyment form the countryside. Today I am dispatching my batman, Schweiger, with Senior Physician Dr. Baum, who will obtain provisions for my family in Galicia. I am curious as to what he will be able to obtain there. From here, all I could give him were three loaves of bread and a large container of freshly picked strawberries. If they arrive safely, my family will be pleased. I have also sent two kilograms of butter. Food scarcities become worse every day; it looks as if the day is not far, when, even with German money, nothing will be able to be scraped up. Our own provisions have also become very sparse, monotonous, and insufficient. How we used to eat at command sounds like a fairy tale now. Heavy rain for my trip back.

10 JULY. Nice early weather, no more talk of severe heat. Cloudy during afternoon, rain toward evening. In the afternoon, I am ordered to go to the new corps chief medical officer for a discussion. I leave by car at 2:30 p.m. and return at 6:00 p.m., after having made a visit to the baggage train at command at Chorostow. The new chief medical officer requires a detailed report on the division's sanitary and hygienic conditions before I travel to Vienna for the gas course. I have to miss the performance by the Vienna ballet ensemble, which starts at 6:00 p.m. I am not at all sorry: we have had enough expensive entertainment this month. But man cannot escape his destiny: after dinner I attend their song and cabaret performances. Very good—the female singer copies Mella Mars in her heyday excellently, and the piano accompanist is a Bela Laski in another form and name.[47] Very jolly: the female ballet dancer dances delicately and stylishly: real Vienna waltzes. It's midnight by the time I get to bed.

11 JULY. Weather has changed significantly: cold, windy, overcast, cloudy. Temperature in my room today is 17°C. I am busy all day with the preparation of the report for the corps chief medical officer. A huge job, which I am only able to do because of my excellent notes.

12 JULY. Overcast, cool weather, rain at times. I am very busy preparing for my upcoming trip; unfortunately, this afternoon I have to travel to the field hospital Wojmica, which the corps physician in chief is inspecting. He is by far not as strict as his predecessor: more than anything, he is not annoying. From there we travel to the medical column. By the time I return to command, it is 6:00 p.m.

13 JULY. Pouring with rain since early morning. The black bread rolls, which I wanted to collect this morning for my family, have unfortunately fallen into the water. I depart at noon. May God bless my enterprise, and may the bad weather only occur on the notorious "Friday the 13th."

14 JULY. The journey goes off without a hitch, and weather is good. Arrival in Vienna at 3:00 p.m., where Olga is waiting for me at the station. We go directly to Radaun. My children look well, even Miki who has not completely recovered from her whooping cough attack. Mary, my youngest, is developing best of all. She is sixteen months old today but still doesn't want anything to do with me. No wonder: this is only the second time that I am a guest at home, for a short time.

The gas course, which is the real purpose of my trip, begins 17 July in the army gas school nearby the rotunda—in other words, exactly the opposite location from Radaun, where my family are. Luckily, trains start operating at 6:00 a.m., so I can arrive at the school on time at 8:00 a.m. However, I must get up at 5:00 a.m. to catch the first train at 6:00 a.m., arriving at 8:00 a.m. Lectures last from 8:00 to 11:00 a.m. and 2:00 to 4:00 p.m. The intervening time from 11:00 a.m. to 2:00 p.m. is the most unpleasant for me. Too short for me to travel home, and food in the local guesthouse is bad: very expensive and mostly insufficient. I have to carry my bread around in a bag all day: bread has not been provided in any of the inns for quite a while now. I return home at 6:00 p.m., tired and worn out by the heat and long train journey, so I cannot enjoy anything for the rest of the day. Sundays, and the few days after the course ends, are pleasant: I spend them in Vienna or Radaun. The course is extended for two extra days.

2 AUGUST. News from the Russian front is very interesting. As we have heard, the Russians opened an offensive on 1 July in the area of Brzezany and have had some successes. They occupy Halicz on 14 July and Kalusz on 15 July, but with great losses. On 19 July, we mount a sudden and unexpected counteroffensive against Zborow,[48] which quickly turns things in our favor. Whole units of Russians collapse, throw their weapons down, and flee back. We, on the other hand, surge forward, reoccupying Tarnopol.[49]

3 august. The offensive extends to the south: Stanislau, Halicz, Kalusz, Chortkow, Kolomea, Buczacz, Zaleszczyki, Skala, Hussiatyn, and Sniatyn[50] are occupied: with these, the whole of East Galicia—in Russian hands since 1914—is once again in our hands. Yesterday, 2 August, Czernowitz and Kimpolung[51] are also reoccupied. We are well on the way to reoccupy the whole of Bukowina[52]—a phenomenal achievement. That is how our offensive looks: the enemy has melted away like the morning dew.

A few more words about the weather, which was very pleasant in Vienna throughout the entire period. During the past few days, a heat wave has settled over the whole of Central Europe. Heat has become unbearable: it's especially bad during my trip back, so by the time I reach camp, I am tired and wrung out. Another theater group traveled back with me, this time from the Wiener Volksoper. These theater companies have become a terrible pest: they cost us a lot of money, and catering has become so difficult that we are very upset indeed at the delicacies that are offered them. I do not go to the latest performance, nor will I go to any future performances. I have had enough of paying for their catering. Right at the start of the current performance, a severe storm begins and rain lasts all morning of the next day.

4 august. Clearing during the afternoon. I find a few changes at command, which is still located at the same spot in Pavloviczy. Our Chief of General Staff Heller has been seconded to corps command for eight weeks and substituted by General Staff Lieutenant Colonel Britto—I know him well from the beginning of the war, because he has been our guest at tenth corps command several times. A nice, kindly man, even though he is less than knowledgeable and therefore hesitant and nervous (as he has always been). Rittmeister Baron Hammerstein has pushed through his transfer to the Italian front. He is one of the nicest men at command, and in him I lose my best photography supplier.

5 august. Torrential rain during the night: I am lucky that my barracks is still standing and not flooded. Rain causes great damage to the trenches—most are completely underwater. It carries on raining all morning. The theater society has finally departed after having staged two consecutive productions; each time, Lieutenant Colonel Heller came for the performance, and there was a great deal of drinking, lasting through 3:00 a.m.

6 august. Weather has cooled down . . . no rain, but unstable. News from the Bukowina front is very good: Radautz[53] has been taken.

7 august. Inspection of second sanitary train and 1009 field hospital in Wojmica by the chief corps physician at 9:00 a.m.; I arrive there on foot and return at noon; he stays for luncheon. The inspection turns out well. Lederer is not a whiner like Herzog, and has the necessary military experience. Weather good, sprinkles at noon.

8 august. Very warm, nice weather. I remain at home to complete a large amount of correspondence.

9 AUGUST. Continuation of inspection by corps chief medical officer. He arrives in Pavloviczy at 8:00 a.m. and stays there until the entire inspection has been completed. Today is the artillery's turn. We travel to second Honvéd regiment, then Group Zaufalek (Rodler), second artillery, and on the way back we visit the sick bay of twenty-ninth light infantry and no. 4/62 infantry regiment, as well as the provisions officer. By the time we return, it's 1:00 p.m.—very hot. In the afternoon, we visit the dental clinic. Lederer obtains quarters and dines with us. Our general is in a good mood: tomorrow he is going on leave again, and how he likes his leave (perhaps too much)! This might be why he tells me in the afternoon that he wants to put me up for a decoration and requests necessary details. He has taken long enough: I received my last decoration February 1916.

10 AUGUST. We leave by wagon early at 6:30 a.m. directly for 5/103, and from there to fourth light infantry, where we inspect one company's position. Then off to the extreme right flank of our position to fortieth regimental first aid station. It is so oppressively hot and humid that we can go no farther and return straight to Pavloviczy, where we arrive at 12:30 p.m. Everything else is canceled, and chief medical officer Lederer departs back to his corps at 4:00 p.m. It's a pleasure to do inspections with him. He has words of recognition and praise for everything and everybody.

11 AUGUST. It rains during the night, cooling the air down significantly. It remains cool and overcast all morning, clearing and warmer in the afternoon. Our Russian offensive is advancing a little more slowly. In Bukowina, Gurahumora[54] has been occupied: Mackensen is starting to move in Romania and has struck the Russians and Romanians north of Focsani,[55] stopping—for the moment—their further penetration in the Putna Valley.

12 AUGUST. Weather much more bearable: it looks as if the heat wave is over. Resistance by Russians and Romanians appears to have increased. Our progress is now slow, and Russian activity in the air has increased on our front. They are dropping bombs on Wojmica and Rogozno, without success.

13 AUGUST. Command is changing in field hospital 1009. Surgeon Major Gara is being transferred to the hinterland, replaced by Honvéd Regimental Physician First Class Dr. Molnar, who has sat out the war in Budapest so far and shows neither understanding nor desire for this position. Weather good, not too hot. The new army commandant, Weber, is very busy visiting our positions. He has been governor-general in Belgrade for the past year and a half.

14 AUGUST. Once more hot and humid. I travel by train to Vladimir Volynsky at noon, where I order a shirt and trousers at the ready to wear clothing department of the fourth army—the prices there are affordable, even cheap: Both together cost fifty-four crowns, compared to one hundred crowns bought privately. They are still made of wool, already a rarity; everything now is made of cotton. Unfortunately, the first train back leaves at 7:00 p.m., leaving me with a few boring hours in this miserable dump. I arrive in the mess at 8:30 p.m.

15 AUGUST. Hot, humid weather continues, at least with a respite toward evening in the form of a short period of rain. At 8:30 a.m. I travel to the baths at ¤ 243, then to camp no. 5, and then to sixty-second first aid station, and to the advanced first aid station of this battalion north of the fox redoubt. On the war back, I inspect the soldiers' home with our logistics officer: return at noon. Cool, pleasant weather continues.

17 AUGUST. Our first celebration of the birthday of our new Kaiser Karl. Unfortunately, rain starts at dawn and becomes heavy, lasting all day with only a few interruptions. The field mass is canceled, but not the opulent Kaiser dinner. Chicken and new potatoes appear again—delicacies that we have not seen for the past two months. Plenty of champagne, but the mood of the men is subdued. Some of the main drinkers are dead or transferred, others on leave; nevertheless, the celebration goes off wonderfully. The commandant and General Rosenzweig are on leave, probably celebrating with their families. First Lieutenant Zorn has become a captain after hardly six years of service as an officer—there are no more youngsters in this army.

18 AUGUST. Heavily overcast early; clearing around 10:00 a.m., fine the rest of the day. Depart at 8:30 a.m. for the baggage train at fourth light infantry, then to field hospital 1009 and second medical column. Return 11:30 a.m.

19 AUGUST. Weather nice and warm. The Italians have begun the eleventh battle of the Isonzo: hopefully they will have the same luck as they have had up to now. Only now are we informed of the large amount of booty taken in the fighting for Bukowina and Galicia: by contrast, the number of prisoners taken is surprisingly small, only 41,000 men, and 655 officers. By comparison, 257 artillery pieces, 546 machine guns, 191 mortars, 50,000 rifles, 25,000 gas masks, 14 armored cars, 15 trucks, 2 armored trains, 6 loaded railway trains, 26 locomotives, 280 train coaches, several airplanes, and a significant quantity of provisions.

20 AUGUST. Nice warm weather continues, becoming really hot during the course of the day. It's especially noticeable when one must run around sweating, visiting first aid stations and troop positions. At 7:30 a.m. I travel by wagon to first aid station 2/40, then 3/40, 1/40, and finally fortieth regimental first aid station. This trip is exhausting: there are many new first aid stations in the previous vicinity of the thirteenth rifle division.

21 AUGUST. Weather like yesterday; I feel it less because I spend the day at home. In the morning, Dr. Lederer favors me with a visit, because has just gone to the dentist. We chat about all sorts of things until he departs. Lieutenant Colonel Britto is attending the gas course for the next eleven days; Lieutenant Colonel Heller has arrived to substitute for him.

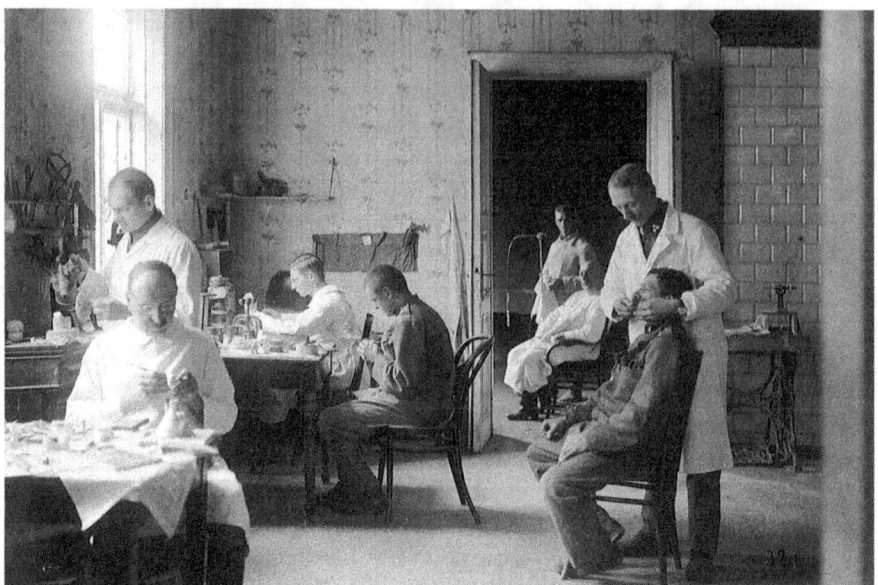

Figure 4.7. A visit to the dentist in the Austro-Hungarian Army. Photograph courtesy of the Leo Baeck Institute.

22 AUGUST. Weather warm, strong wind during afternoon, with a great deal of dust. Overcast by evening, but no rain. I spend the morning at second medical column: I walk there at 8:30 a.m., returning by wagon at noon.

23 AUGUST. Warm weather. Today all baggage trains need to be inspected: I travel with our administrative lieutenant colonel at 9:00 a.m. to the management office, from there to baggage train fortieth infantry regiment, twenty-ninth light infantry, 4/62, 5/103, and fourth light infantry; return at noon. At 3:00 p.m. I travel with Lieutenant Colonel Heller, the logistics officer, and technical adviser Captain Szoljom-Feketc to the bakery and division train in Chorostow, return at 5:00 p.m.

24 AUGUST. Moderate warm weather continues. In the morning I am occupied with office work. During the afternoon, a German officer gives a lecture on the Battle of the Somme, with slides. Many German officers attend. The lecture is interesting—but it's so hot and stifling in the barracks, that it becomes unbearable. After an hour, we come up for air: it's good to breathe fresh air again.

25 AUGUST. The Eleventh Battle of the Isonzo rages for the fourth day, with unheard-of intensity. Apart from small local successes, the Italians have achieved nothing. Our troops are achieving amazing things there. By comparison, the battles in Bukowina, Galicia, and Romania have waned. We get the impression that the existing positions will be held and defended. Weather still nice and warm. Cloudy toward evening.

26 AUGUST. Heavy rain overnight, cloudy in the morning, clearing by noon. We have acquired yet another enemy: now the Chinese have declared war on us!

27 AUGUST. Our Army Commandant Colonel General von Kirchbach has been taken ill several weeks ago—apparently stomach ulcers, maybe even cancer. He is operated on and a gastroenterostomy[56] is done: he is doing better. His replacement, Colonel General Wurm, has been named Commandant of the first army on the Isonzo, and he in turn is substituted by Colonel General Hauer, who up to now has been in command of Cavalry Corps Hauer. He arrives at 9:00 a.m. and introduces himself to everybody. I am present as well and cannot go out and visit the troops, as previously intended.

28 AUGUST. Pouring rain during the night, everything is wet in the morning, but then weather clears. I walk at 8:00 a.m. to field hospital 1009, staying there all morning. Defective barracks have to be repaired and modified, so there is much to advise and to discuss.

29 AUGUST. Very hot again today, but it is even hotter on the Isonzo. Fighting on all other fronts is now overshadowed by that on the Isonzo—even the heavy fighting by the Germans in Flanders.[57] Unfortunately, the Italians have successfully occupied Monte Santo, and our troops have transferred the front back about six to seven kilometers. The Italians are wildly triumphant: they report having captured two 305 mortars. If nothing but this happens, they still will not have won, and Trieste is still beyond their reach. May God let it be so!

30 AUGUST. Today's report is very favorable: the Italians have achieved nothing. After extreme heat yesterday, sudden cooling down today, after a little rain during the night: I almost had to close the windows. I remain in my quarters awaiting inspection by Surgeon Major Wach of fourth army command.

31 AUGUST. Something new: officers are now being sent to the front by order of high command, with the task of listening to requests and complaints from the men, but in reality just another inspection, followed by detailed reports. Today is the field hospitals' turn. At 9:00 a.m. I walk to the medical column, where I meet with Dr. Lederer. At 10:00 a.m., Surgeon Major Dr. Wach arrives in Wojmica by train, met by our Dr. Müller. Inspection of both field hospitals lasts until noon. I travel back; the other two gentlemen remain for lunch and, in the afternoon, travel on to Rogozno. Our newly minted commander returns from vacation with the same train. I greet him at lunch. The two stars and pompous title of "Excellency" haven't changed him a bit: Tepp remains Tepp. Weather, after rain during the night, very pleasant. Some mud, which dries quickly.

1 SEPTEMBER. Doctors Lederer and Wach pick me up by car at 7:00 a.m. We first go to the soldiers' home, then to the baths on ¤ 243, supply depot 2, sick bay of twenty-ninth light infantry, sick bay and first aid station 4/62, and the baths in camp 5. After all these have been inspected, we want to go farther,

but the Russians begin to fire at our area. A Russian plane appears, and it looks as if it is aiming at us, because the pilot flies very low (about four hundred feet) and circles around, despite very heavy antiaircraft fire. One shell after the other explodes, also shrapnel. Hardly one hundred paces from us, a man from the fortieth infantry regiment, who wanted to draw water from a well, is instantly killed by a shot to the head. Both gentlemen, especially Wach, who are not used to this, are overcome with fear, and run into a shelter; Wach, who is in front, stumbles over the step, falls to the ground, and Lederer falls on top of him. I follow them. I am no hero, but have become such a fatalist during the course of this war that when such things happen, I always think, "If a bullet is meant for me, it will hit me no matter what. There is plenty of time for this to happen." We wait for a good half hour: the situation changes every five minutes. We finally make use of such a pause to get to our car, waiting for us in the nearest hollow. Both gentlemen have lost all desire for more inspections, and on suggestion of Lederer, they end abruptly. Because it is still too early, we find the first aid station of second field artillery regiment in the forest and travel directly to Pavloviczy, where we have time to inspect the dental clinic. They allow time for a nice, long, safe visit and around noon travel on to Rogozno, from where Wach departs to his regular station and Lederer travels back to corps command by comfortable car. Lunch today tastes particularly good; after that I have an afternoon nap longer than any time previously in this war: by the time I awake, it's already 4:45 p.m.

2 SEPTEMBER. After a rainy night, weather significantly cooler. I spend the morning in the field hospital, where there is a commission walkthrough of necessary changes by technical adviser Captain Szoljom-Feketc and me. I walk there (as usual), return by wagon.

3 SEPTEMBER. Russians use moonlit nights for flying and aerial bombardment. This time they search out our main traffic hub in Rogozno, where they cause significant damage: one man dead, two wounded, one ammunition depot hit by a bomb, and a portion of the ammunition blown up. Also a German catering store. Weather today very cool: I have already closed the windows. Afternoon transient rain.

4 SEPTEMBER. Germans have taken Riga. A great success, but it does not change our position, especially in view of the fact that we trumpet to the world that we want peace without annexation. It's a pity about each man whom we lose, penetrating deeper into Russia. Our fighting in Galicia and Bukowina is very significant, because we must drive the Russians out of our territories so that we need nothing from them—but further annexation in Russia makes no sense. How much more valuable would it be, if the Germans—with troops at their disposal—would attack the Italians in the Tirol, to relieve us on the Isonzo! But pride and prestige take the lead here. We want to finish up with the wops, as the Germans want to do with the French. Hopefully, we will succeed.

Today it rains all day, with short interruptions. It's quite cold. How good that at least we have a proper roof over our heads—something that we didn't have this time last year.

5 SEPTEMBER. Cool, overcast weather continues.

6 SEPTEMBER. Much warmer today; sunshine, the ground has already dried out. At 5:00 a.m. I visit the field hospital, return at 6:30 p.m. Barracks there are being completely rebuilt, and strict control is necessary.

7 SEPTEMBER. Beautiful, sunny fall day, characteristic cool mornings and evenings. Departure for the front by wagon at 7:30 a.m. Inspection of dressing station twenty-ninth light infantry, 2/40, fourth light infantry. The Russians seem very nervous and are shooting out of fear; we could seek to advance on this front as well, but it makes no sense, because we are really quite weak here! Our entire fourth army consists of the twenty-ninth infantry division, our second infantry division, one German division, and Cavalry Corps Hauer—that is all. Our division consists of eight battalions, commanded by one brigade, one division, and one corps command. No matter how strong the twenty-ninth is, it's understandable that we do not move and are happy that the Russians don't move either, out of mutual fear.

Today's visit relates mainly to troop supplies with medicines and medical material. They have a lot more than their allocation, but complain constantly that they receive too little. Meanwhile, army command is constantly told that supplies must be economized, because they are exhausted.

8 SEPTEMBER. Good weather continues: it has become warmer. The Italians seem to have paused for breath, but, despite attacking it for twelve days already, they still have not taken Monte Gabrieli. By contrast, the Germans are greatly expanding their success in Riga. Their booty is very large: 316 artillery pieces and correspondingly large amounts if other material. The Russians appear to have bolted, leaving everything behind.

9 SEPTEMBER. Weather unchanged, partly cloudy toward evening, no rain. I am very busy with correspondence, plus sending a man from the mess with provisions to Vienna. I have succeeded in collecting six kilograms of bacon, five kilograms of flour, eight kilograms of potatoes and cucumbers—enough so that my family can eat decently for a few days

10 SEPTEMBER. I travel at 8:30 a.m. to the forty-second infantry regiment, which recently has been assigned to us with two battalions. They are demanding so much medical material that I must first see exactly what they already have. Return at noon. I inspect 1/42 and the regimental first aid station: they are being housed in reserve in Kruchyniczy, together with the thirteenth medical column. Weather favorable, really nice.

11 SEPTEMBER. At 9:00 a.m. I go to the medical column. Our own Dr. Müller has been transferred to Cholm. He is very upset indeed that he will have the pleasure of our old friend Dr. Herzog's company again there. I feel sorry for him: he is an anti-Semite in disguise but has always been very decent and upright with me. He is very strict with his subordinates and does not allow any intimacy, which is good for maintenance of discipline but does not endear him to his subordinates. He often does not dine with them in the mess. He has always been erect in bearing, and brave: always at the front of his column, leading them personally, often in dangerous areas. The only thing: he is too much of a Pole and makes no secret of his pro-Polish sentiments. He has apparently no confidence in Austria and has never subscribed to war bonds, despite having a large amount of savings. He believes strongly in Poland's resurrection, and his ideas for new Polish borders are presumptuous—he believes that Danzig must become Polish as well. I avoid political discussions with him in order not to get on each other's nerves. He openly protects Polish officers and physicians in his medical column.

I have put him up for the silver Signum Laudis and handed in a glowing report about him to division command. At 1:00 p.m. I depart for Vladimir Volynsky by train to get the clothes that I have ordered: return by train at 8:00 p.m.

12 SEPTEMBER. The night is noticeably colder: temperature in my room is only 6°C, and I am quite chilled. It does become somewhat warmer during the course of the day and quite hot at noon. During the morning, I have a large amount of office work to complete and a series of conferences during the afternoon.

13 SEPTEMBER. I am granted a raise in pay, retroactive to 1 September. I am very happy about it: if only things were not so expensive at home, I could even manage to save something. But the increased sixty-six crowns a month disappear without a trace with all my expenses. Weather overcast in the morning, short periods of rain in the afternoon, through 8:00 p.m.

14 SEPTEMBER. Weather has cleared, but mud dries slowly. Straight after lunch, Dr. Lederer arrives unexpectedly by car. His visit is really to the dentist: he needs to have a tooth extracted. We travel together to the field hospital and to the column in Wojmica: return at 6:00 p.m.

15 SEPTEMBER. Weather unstable: nice early, then cloudy, strong wind, and cold. Nevertheless, I travel to first aid station fourth light infantry, because several cases of dysentery have occurred there recently. I visit their positions as well. On the way back, I inspect our first aid stations no. 5/62 and twenty-ninth light infantry, returning at 12:30 p.m., just as it is starting to rain. Heavy rain in the afternoon, continuing until evening. It is already quite uncomfortable in my room. I make sure that the room is heated at night; otherwise I would freeze because of lack of warm blankets.

Today the request was sent off by command for an additional financial award in connection with my silver Signum Laudis. It has taken a long time to get this through: the gentlemen don't think of what others are going through, just so long as they get what they want as often as they want it.

16 SEPTEMBER. Weather unstable. Sunshine alternating with clouds—no rain. Temperature somewhat higher. I am busy all day with more and more office duties.

17 SEPTEMBER. During the night, clocks have all been put back one hour: not appropriate for the current conditions, when the whole day is not utilized. At both 5:00 a.m. (old reckoning) and 7:00 p.m., it is pitch dark. According to the new reckoning, one sleeps further into the day, leaving a lot of work for the evening. Weather like yesterday: clearing in late afternoon, temperature pleasant. I take a walk to the field hospital in the morning and bump into Dr. Lederer and then return with him to Pavloviczy where he visits the dentist. Today is Rosh Hashanah: unfortunately, for a while now, our situation with horses, wagons, and cars has not been good enough to allow me—as during previous years—to obtain one of these to travel to Vladimir Volynsky, and train schedules are unsatisfactory.

18 SEPTEMBER. Weather significantly warmer, quite warm during the day. Heating stopped for the moment. At 8:00 a.m. I again walk to Wojmica, after having been interrupted yesterday by Chief Medical Officer Lederer. I visit the medical column and field hospital, returning by wagon at noon. Dysentery cases keep me busy: they are scattered all over the division.

19 SEPTEMBER. Early at 7:30 a.m. I travel to the bakery in Chorostow, after two dysentery cases have appeared there; I also visit second baggage train. What they are doing there is very impressive: they have installed a butcher, a dairy (where butter and curd are manufactured), a vegetable and fruit canning house, and a soda water factory. They manufacture marmalade, pickled cucumbers, and cabbage—they have quite a large concern going: I have heard of nothing comparable in size and scope in the hinterland. Return 11:30 a.m.: weather quite hot.

20 SEPTEMBER. Weather nice today as well, warm, even hot during the day—toward evening very humid and cloudy, as if before a storm: but clouds disappear in the evening and the sky at night is clear. Lieutenant Colonel Heller returns from his seconded position today, and Lieutenant Colonel Britto returns and takes over office directorship. He is probably better suited for deskwork, since his assistant First Lieutenant Patterer does most of the work for him. But he is not suited to be a chief of general staff: he is an idiot in uniform, just like General Jemrich.

21 SEPTEMBER. I travel to Rogozno at 8:00 a.m. to inspect the new hospital in my capacity as corps physician. I am most surprised at what I see—so excellent in its planning and establishment that it could compete with many peacetime hospitals. An exemplary hospital, such as has not been seen in war up to this time. Weather good, but strong wind makes it uncomfortable. Skies darken during the afternoon, but cold weather does not allow it to rain.

22 SEPTEMBER. Weather good; nothing new.

23 SEPTEMBER. Morning begins friendly and peacefully. We have German General von Stocken as luncheon guest: he deputizes for our corps commandant. A very nice lunch with chicken, etc. A band from the fortieth infantry regiment supplies the music. At 4:30 p.m. I receive a report that dysentery bacilli have been found in one of wells used by the fortieth infantry provisions train. I immediately order that the well be buried; to convince myself that this order is carried out, I travel there at once by car. Burying the well is a difficult decision, because it was built at great cost and effort, and was eighteen meters deep. But better to sacrifice it than risk an explosive outbreak of bacillary dysentery. I make sure not to leave until the well has been made unusable. Return at 6:00 p.m. Weather overcast, not as cool, a lot of wind and even more dust.

24 SEPTEMBER. Weather good with some wind, evening quite cool, so my room is heated once again.

25 SEPTEMBER. Early in the morning at 8:00 a.m. I travel to the fortieth infantry provisions train, to convince myself that the well has been completely buried. From there, on to the baths on ¤ 243 and camp no. 5, then to first aid station 5/103 which has been occupied by twenty-ninth light infantry, then to first aid station fourth light infantry. Overcast early with fog, clearing around 10:00 a.m.: I return at 12:30 p.m. in nice, sunny weather.

Unfortunately, bad prospects for Yom Kippur—last year I had a car at my disposal all day and spent the day at the temple in Vladimir Volynsky. Now we are short of rubber and even worse off with horses; the train schedule is no good, so I will have to stay in my quarters.

26 SEPTEMBER. Yom Kippur! I honor the holy day by fasting and absolute rest. Weather very nice, sunny, and warm. I fast easily; unfortunately, I only started last night. We were celebrating the departure of our technical adviser Captain Szoljom-Feketc. I wanted to withdraw from dinner but was kept behind by Lieutenant Colonel Heller. I did not drink any champagne, although I was charged ten crowns for it: it was midnight before I went to bed. At 4:00 p.m. I take a walk to the field hospital, where I remain until 6:00 p.m. After it becomes dark, I travel back and eat alone: a combination of lunch and dinner.

27 SEPTEMBER. Days are still lovely, warm, and sunny, really hot during the afternoon: I take advantage of this weather and, at 8:00 a.m., travel to the front. A good photographer joins me, and I look for the best places to take photos—first, the connection for the locomotive light railway. Then on to camp 5 and its baths, which I also photograph. From there on to first aid station 4/62, where we make a nice photo compilation, including Senior Physician Felter and myself. On the way back, we also photograph the sick bay of the sixty-second, and return at noon.

28 SEPTEMBER. Weather remains good. A restless night, so different from what we have become used to for many weeks. Russians attack our neighbor-

ing division. The cannonade, which occurs around 4:00 a.m., interferes with my sleep, so I go over my depressing thoughts in my mind. I am very worried about my dear Olga. Her current hypersensitivity is getting on my nerves. I remain here. Dr. Müller says goodbye to me—I toss a few well-chosen words at him, which move him so deeply that he embraces me. For a change, I am now reading a great deal. The cats are away, so the mouse can play: the corps physician is on leave, the commandant is at a gas course, and Heller is in Kowel for a meeting, so the only thing left for me to pass the time is reading. Newspapers have become interesting—they report an offensive against the Italians in which Germans have taken part. It costs us prestige, but that doesn't matter as long as the wops finally get what is coming to them. Great transfers are taking place, and all leave is canceled for the next fourteen days. There is talk of our division being transferred "below" (to the Isonzo). The idea does not please me at all. I am already tired of war and pleased to leave its laurels to younger men.

29 SEPTEMBER. Weather change. Cloudy and humid in the morning, heavy rain at times during the afternoon. I travel to field hospital 1009 and return by wagon at noon.

30 SEPTEMBER. The heavens smile again, and the sun shines—but it does not warm us up any more. It's quite cold, and I see to it that my room is heated in the evening.

At 4:00 p.m. I walk with Lieutenant Colonel Heller to the medical column. He absolutely has to peek at the three new nursing sisters who have just arrived and are said to be very pretty. At the same time, he inspects the entire unit: what is he trying to achieve? Has he been ordered to do this, or is it just the matter of the three nurses? From there we go to the field hospital, which he also inspects from top to bottom. I do not see the point of initiating the three nurses at the medical column. As long as static war continues, good—but if we move, they will be a burden on the unit. They need transport for their baggage, and today we do not even have enough transport for ourselves, so a lot would have to be left behind. Then they will need quarters; the unit often works and sleeps outside in the open. If a small house would become available, they surely would not get it. The situation is completely different for the field hospital, twelve kilometers or less behind the column. The nurses can have a permanent base in which to work there, but they will have to be immediately evacuated if we have to move. Over and above this, they do not make a good impression or reflect the seriousness necessary for their profession. Two of them are young girls who would be more suitable as cashiers, and the third older one is too buxom. But I don't want to jump the gun—let us see. Return 5:30 p.m.

1 OCTOBER. The weather has suddenly changed again: it rains in torrents almost all day. The weather corresponds with how I feel. My innate pugnacity, and my wife's hypersensitivity, does not help matters.

2 OCTOBER. Weather remains cloudy all day; nevertheless, I visit the medical column and then the field hospital with Senior Physician Wechsler in the late afternoon, return at 6:30 p.m.

3 OCTOBER. Weather lovely and clear again, sunny and warm. Ground has dried out completely. Unfortunately, I cannot go to the front today no matter how much I would like to, because I am occupied with providing my batman, Schweiger, with provisions for my family: 6.5 kilograms of flour, 3.25 kilograms of bacon, 1 rucksack of potatoes, 2 kilograms of nuts, 3 loaves of bread, 100 eggs, 9 kilograms of chicken fat, 1 kilogram of sausage, some tea, biscuits, 5 lemons, and a pair of shoes for Ega. This should be of some help to them; in Vienna, conditions and provisions are too sad to contemplate. Apart from this, I have to travel to the medical column and field hospital again with the technical consultant to inform him about the work that must be performed there. Return around noon.

4 OCTOBER. Weather nice, sunny and warm especially during the afternoon. In the morning at 7:30 a.m., I travel with Surgeon Major Dr. Konopki—the new commandant of the medical column—to the front; after that to the provisions store at fortieth infantry regiment to see whether new wells have been dug in correct places. From there, we visit the soldiers' home, the fortieth infantry regiment convalescent home, then the fortieth infantry regiment first aid station, [?] first aid station which is being newly built and finally the position of [?]40, which doesn't impress me at all. Back at noon. The staff physician is delighted at everything: all is new to him, because so far he has spent the war in the rear.

5 OCTOBER. Weather still good, but I stay at home again to deal with office work.

6 OCTOBER. Rain at night, overcast all day, heavy clouds and uninterrupted rain all afternoon, which softens the ground.

7 OCTOBER. Very overcast, rain hanging in the air. Despite this, I travel to the field hospital 1009 by wagon to send some provisions home with someone who is traveling back to Vienna. One must use every possible opportunity. This time I cannot send much: three loaves of bread, five kilograms of flour, two kilograms of beans, and five kilograms of apples.

8 OCTOBER. Weather somewhat better, only quite cold because of a strong north wind. At 8:30 a.m. I travel to field hospital 913 in Rogozno, again accompanied with Dr. Konopki, to inspect their building progress, which is not good: work has stopped because they have no nails. Return at noon. During the afternoon, we receive the news that our Kaiser will visit fourth army in Vladimir Volynsky tomorrow at 9:45 a.m., so there is naturally great excitement. Our commander has just returned from a gas course; his main current concern is how to obtain (and boast with) with the Crown Order First Class. Maybe after having spent the entire afternoon working on this, this idiot might even learn something from what he sees here!

9 OCTOBER. Sun appears early: maybe this is Kaiser weather? Unfortunately, it gets cloudy very early and, from 9:00 a.m., rains heavily. The deputation to welcome His Majesty consists this time of one officer and one soldier per corps; from command, only the commandant and his chief of general staff, Lieutenant Colonel Heller. Some clearing toward afternoon, which doesn't last long. Starting at 4:00 p.m., it pours with rain. Von Kirchbach has taken over army command from Hauer, after having returned from sick leave. He has had problems with his stomach for a long time and had to undergo surgery. I could not find out whether it was a stomach ulcer or carcinoma. Surgery was very extensive—a gastroenterostomy. He has recovered so well that he is able to take over command again—just in time to welcome the Kaiser.

10 OCTOBER. Strong southwest wind cleans clouds from the sky. The sun shines again in all its glory but cannot warm anymore like it did earlier. I take out my small fur collar, which makes me feel very comfortable.

11 OCTOBER. Significant rainfall overnight—I did not hear it, but the many puddles and the mud testify to the rain. Soon it's clear again, sunshine and blue sky. At 7:30 a.m. I travel with Dr. Konopka to the front. First to fourth light infantry baggage train, where I present the armorer with twenty-five cigarettes as payment for a beautiful frame for my wife's photograph, which now decorates my writing desk. From there, we travel on to the baths on ¤ 243, camp 5, after that to the first aid station twenty-ninth light infantry, which now includes the position of 5/103. We visit their position, and return. The visit

Figure 4.8. Kaiser Karl praying with the troops. Photograph courtesy of the Leo Baeck Institute.

lasts until noon. It becomes very hot during the afternoon, and we sweat during our visit to the positions.

12 OCTOBER. Weather quite good, sharp, cold northwest wind that dies down by noon. Around 9:00 a.m. I go to the field hospital and observe the surgeons at work, then on to the medical column. Travel back by wagon around noon. Fall is in full swing, leaves are turning, and what is left of the greenery is limp and fading.

13 OCTOBER. Nice, sunny morning—all roads dry again. At 8:30 a.m. I travel to the first aid unit, the second field artillery regiment; inspect 4/10 sapper company and then first aid station third artillery regiment; return at noon. The mail brings me the Honor Cross Second Class from the Red Cross. A nice decoration: I will consider whether to put in for the Officers Cross. Rain toward evening, then clear skies.

14 OCTOBER. Pleasant summerlike weather: everything shines again. It's Sunday, and I stay home.

15 OCTOBER. Warm, sunny weather continues. Lederer is back from vacation, and we have already spoken by telephone.

16 OCTOBER. I leave for the medical column at 7:30 a.m.: Dr. Lederer is also there for the inspection: we arrive at more or less the same time. From there, on to the field hospital; it's already noon by the time I return alone, while he goes back to the corps.

At 4:00 p.m. another artistic delight. This time four gentlemen and four ladies, led by a German captain—a Berlin ensemble who produce and present plays. The enjoyment lasts until 6:30 p.m.: actually, it really is quite jolly. A Viennese lady is naturally part—and certainly the best—of the troupe. After the performance, there is a communal supper, which in such cases always lasts long into the night. I remain until 11:30 p.m.; the bulk of the staff leaves an hour earlier. Enough, already.

17 OCTOBER. I meet Dr. Lederer at 8:00 a.m., and we set off together for our inspection tour. First the soldiers home, from there to the storm battalion, then to baggage train 4/62, twenty-ninth light infantry (sick bay), then the baths at ¤ 243, provisions depot 2, baggage train fortieth infantry regiment. Return at 12:30 p.m. Lederer remains here overnight. Beautiful morning weather, heavy fog early, then complete clearing. Overcast in the afternoon. Senior Physician Felter leaves tomorrow for the gas course in Vienna; I give him ten kilograms of flour, two kilograms of sausage, and three loaves of bread for my family, and send the shoes back to my Olga.

18 OCTOBER. Rain begins during the night, lasting all morning. Because of bad weather, the corps physician interrupts his inspections and travels back at 8:00 a.m. Before leaving, he participates in the official decoration of General von Rosenzweig with the Iron Crown Order Second Class. Clearing in the afternoon, rain again toward evening.

19 OCTOBER. There is already a significant amount of mud. Overcast in the morning, clearing during the day, starry, clear night.

20 OCTOBER. Rain begins early and pours down in torrents all day. Some clearing in the afternoon, but overcast again toward evening. Traveling on such a day is out of the question, and I fill the hours with paperwork.

21 OCTOBER. Dark, gloomy, damp cold weather with fog—a real fall day, just like November. Leaves are falling off the trees in large numbers: they will soon be completely bare.

Vacation leave is once again permitted, but for how long? My darling wife is completely to blame for the fact that I do not wish to take advantage of this. Her hypersensitivity and sour, sarcastic manner have made me very angry. Because of this instead of going home, I keep busy with application for the Charles Cross. I have only been in frontline service in the fourth battalion since 15 October 1915, for a total of seventy-four days, and eighty-four days of frontline duty (reckoned from the day of leaving for combat) are required; I lack twenty-seven days.[58] To make up this time, I want to serve as regimental physician first class in the fortieth infantry regiment, while Senior Physician Kantorek goes on leave. This decision is facilitated by the fact that my wife is making me so miserable, that it is easier for me to take such a risk. Ten months or so ago, I might perhaps have thought more about this: my wife had not yet shown her true colors.

22 OCTOBER. After everyone in charge has agreed with my plan, I leave for the regiment tomorrow: today I am busy full time with preparations for the trip. Weather like yesterday: cloudy, overcast, dark, fog, damp cold.

23 OCTOBER. Beautiful fall day, a great deal of sun, deep blue sky. After completing all necessary formalities, I depart for the fortieth infantry regiment at 10:00 a.m.: arrive one hour later: the regiment is located eight kilometers from division command. Good horses and very good roads facilitate my rapid arrival. Conditions here are different, and I will have to get used to them. Regimental Commander Lieutenant Colonel Raktelj is very pleasant and friendly to me; his adjutant Captain Fuchs has just gone on leave, and the other ten gentlemen in command are only first and second lieutenants of the reserve. In other words, we have little in common, which makes for difficult table conversation. Rations are also worse than at division command: this, according to the young waiter who brings the food—the amount is for example "three potatoes per officer" and no more cooked dessert. For dinner, only two potatoes each; half a roll daily, and we must bring our own bread for meals. The same thing with coffee: each man gets tinned coffee that must last for ten days, and half a liter of milk daily. We must supply more of this ourselves, because breakfast and *Jause* are not included. We get daily cigarette rations and about one liter of petroleum per week. This is perhaps necessary for so large a corps of soldiers. I take over the dugout from the vacationing Dr. Kantorek, including the ubiquitous mice, cats, and dogs. A wonderful, safe shelter, right up to the thin ceiling, which isn't even good enough to withstand a light shrapnel attack. I will have to get myself a better one soon: I must obtain the necessary windowpanes.

24 OCTOBER. Yesterday's beautiful day was an exception—today again the same miserable, overcast, foggy fall weather, and I must make the long trip to the medical units in Wojmica: about twenty-four kilometers both directions. I leave at 8:30 a.m. and arrive at 10:00 a.m. Soon after that, Surgeon General Bürkel arrives for an inspection, accompanied by the corps physician. He arrives because of an anonymous denunciation about immoral activities of the three Red Cross nurses who were assigned to the unit three weeks ago. There you have it! They are too pretty to be decent and will be removed. I take lunch at the field hospital and arrive back to the regiment during quite a heavy rainstorm.

25 OCTOBER. Weather is somewhat better, but the sun cannot penetrate. No rain all day. Quite a lot of mud, but the sandy ground dries up quite quickly. I visit the first regimental battalion that is waiting in reserve on a daily basis: they have no physician, only an officer orderly.

Yesterday, the twelfth battle of the Isonzo began:[59] it differs from the previous eleven in that we are taking the offensive. Unfortunately, we are doing this together with the Germans, who will surely take all the credit. But it makes no difference as long as the wops get the thrashing they deserve. And they will: from the first day, we are successful, with ten thousand prisoners including division and brigade commanders and a vast amount of war material. We have penetrated their positions. The offensive starts off in Tolmein;[60] the artillery is fighting in the Tirol, which is where the advance is taking place.

26 OCTOBER. Things are going beautifully on the Isonzo: thirty thousand prisoners and more than three hundred artillery pieces. The entire Italian first position has been taken. Weather still unstable, but no rain and not unpleasant. Early in the morning, I visit the fourth regimental battalion, which is at present in position. I inspect their first aid station and their medical supplies, and then, with Assistant Physician Lang, go to sixteenth company, which is the battalion reserve, housed in foxholes in the middle of the forest. Back around 11:30 a.m.

27 OCTOBER. Beautiful fall day, glorious blue sky, strong sunshine. This morning I visit the second battalion (Assistant Physician Seitz). His new first aid station is still being built, but when it is finished, it will be very nice and secure from firing. Back at 11:00 a.m., in time for the press report that seventy thousand Italians have already been taken captive, with seven hundred artillery pieces. More soon.

28 OCTOBER. Things are going better in Italy than anyone expected. The number of prisoners has risen to eighty thousand, with six hundred artillery pieces. Amazing! Görz[61] has been retaken. Morning weather very nice. Like yesterday, afternoon cloudy and overcast, moderate wind. Today I travel to first aid station 5/103, because of the report of several cases of diarrhea in a unit that has come from Vladimir Volynsky. Then on to first aid station 3/40, back around noon. I have a lot of paperwork to do during the afternoon—so the day passes quickly. It seems like forever for me to have to remain here until 20 November. I have no one to talk to: the men are all so young, and the good Raktelj is an old grumbling bore who can only criticize.

29 OCTOBER. Weather nice, warm and sunny, wind early on that calms down quickly. Usual early inspection of first battalion, then the splendid regimental convalescent home. I inspect the entire area, and return around 11:00 a.m. Things are going excellently in Italy. Our troops have already taken Monfalcone and Cormons; the Germans have taken Cividale and stand in front of Udine. The number of prisoners taken has increased to one hundred thousand and the number of artillery pieces to more than seven hundred. The amount of other war material cannot even be calculated. The Italian second army has been routed. Trieste can breathe again—this is surely the last battle of the Isonzo.

30 OCTOBER. Overcast early, clearing later. Moonlit nights are beautiful. Very inviting to go for a walk, if it wasn't so dangerous here. Rifle bullets whistle all over in the evening. News from Italy becomes better and better: Udine has been taken, so fighting is already taking place on Italian soil. The number of prisoners now exceeds one hundred thousand, and the number of artillery pieces is now nine hundred. A huge number.

31 OCTOBER. Good weather, with sunshine and deep blue sky; just a fairly brisk north wind. At 8:00 a.m. I travel to the first aid stations of fourth and then twenty-ninth light infantry, return at 11:00 a.m. In Italy, the front is moving south to Caporetto; more than 120,000 prisoners have been taken.

1 NOVEMBER. Weather overcast, clearing around noon. Temperatures generally mild. In the morning, I travel to first aid station 2/40. Construction of the new first aid station is proceeding slowly. Return around 11:00 a.m. A colossal victory has been reported from Italy. Our forces have succeeded in defeating the Italians, who have been blocked from streaming home by the high waters of the Tagliamento River. We have cut off their path of retreat and taken 60,000 prisoners and 600 artillery pieces, for a total of 180,000 prisoners and 1,500 artillery pieces so far. These are tremendous successes, such as have not occurred in the war so far, and are all the more praiseworthy because we are quite exhausted in the fourth year of the war.

2 NOVEMBER. All sorts of troop augmentations, consolidations, and transfers are taking place. Weather still mild. Overcast morning, clearing during the afternoon.

3 NOVEMBER. Weather like yesterday, but nevertheless I travel with Medical Corps Lieutenant Skoczek, my adjutant, to first aid station 3/40 (Assistant Physician Vissich) to inspect the first aid station whose building has been deployed to the forward redoubt; I bathe in the officer's facilities there and return at 11:30 a.m. In Italy, our troops are in Tagliamento; the entire left side of the river has been cleared of Italians. The number of prisoners taken is now more than 200,000 and of artillery pieces more than 1,800.

4 NOVEMBER. Heavy fog, but mild. I travel by foot with my adjutant to first aid station 2/40 (Assistant Physician Seitz): we go together to the position of fifth company, because of a case of dysentery, return 11:30 a.m.

In honor of the Kaiser's name day, the quartermaster surprises us at dinner with two bottles of champagne; the gramophone provides music, and with the music, a cheery mood develops in all present. This is significantly raised when suddenly at 10:00 p.m. the telephone rings: one officer per battalion must appear as billeting officer tomorrow at 10:00 a.m. Additionally, one officer must appear early at 6:30 a.m., for receipt of important tasks. So, naturally, the regiment is marching off to Italy! On to Udine! Great rejoicing! Two more bottles of champagne, wine, and one bottle of liquor are trotted out. With music and cheering, the evening passes in a very jolly way. Around midnight, a *drugi obiad* [Polish second dinner] is served; everyone chips in with his own provisions—sausage and fine baked goods, and there is tea, a drink that is not usual at regimental command. By the time we part, it is 1:15 a.m.

5 NOVEMBER. An overcast, foggy day, which becomes very rainy: plenty of mud. Officers returning from the brigade bring us disappointing news: the regiment is remaining where it is; only two battalions are being transferred! Tonight we go to sleep earlier than last night: by 8:30 p.m., the mess is empty.

6 NOVEMBER. Rain, mud, nothing but mud and rain—I cannot even go out of my hut, and the time passes twice as slowly.

7 NOVEMBER. No more rain; the ground is beginning to dry out again. The sandy, loamy soil allows it to dry fairly rapidly. I cannot decide whether to make a long inspection tour and in the end just visit the soldiers and convalescent homes: even this takes me one and a half hours on foot. The Italians seem to be avoiding battle more and more to save what is left of their army—there is no real resistance against us in Tagliamento, and they are in headlong retreat—also on the Tirol front. Our own territory is now completely cleansed of wops, and our troops are near Venice. The Italian desire to "liberate" Trieste has been replaced by worry about retaining Venice!

8 NOVEMBER. Overcast early, but complete clearing by 10:00 a.m. and beautiful sunshine with corresponding warmth. Because of the good weather, I travel at 8:30 a.m. with Adjutant Lieutenant Skoczek, who is leaving tomorrow for Constantinople, where he will be responsible (together with Senior Physician Holzer) for a field hospital at Kaldini camp, to which a battalion of the fortieth infantry regiment is coming; baths of the second division of the fortieth; first aid station 4/62; fourth light infantry (Holzer); 3/40. Back around noon.

9 NOVEMBER. Weather pleasant and sunny: ground has already dried out completely. After Lieutenant Skoczek's departure, I go with my new adjutant

Medical Corps Lieutenant Teitelbaum to first aid stations 4/40 and 2/40, return around 11:00 a.m. Continued excellent news from Italy: the Italians have already retreated behind Livenza. About 350,000 prisoners and 2,300 artillery pieces.

10 NOVEMBER. Very foggy early, then warm. Fog changes to rain that lasts for most of the day. Wild activity in Russia: Kerensky's government has fallen: he himself has fled, and most of his ministers have been arrested. The Russians want peace at any price. We obviously want peace as well, but it still seems far away. Serves England right!

11 NOVEMBER. Early sunshine and pleasant weather: I prepare for a longer excursion. But soon heavy clouds roll in and it starts to rain. I travel at 7:45 a.m. to Wojmica (about twelve kilometers), inspect medical column no. 2, then on to field hospital 1009; on the way back, I visit my command in Pavloviczy which looks as it has disintegrated. Commandant Jemrich is on vacation for a change. His rich aunt is in the process of dying again, and he must absolutely see her before she passes away. Up until now, she has caused him to take several short vacations, and no one knows how much she is leaving him. But she appears to want to part from this world even less than from her money.

Lieutenant Colonel Heller has been seconded to the gas course in Sedan, which no doubt pleases him well. Life in France must surely be better than that in Pavloviczy. It is 12:45 p.m. by the time we get back to the regiment.

In Italy, our troops are already on the Piave; Venice and Verona are trembling. The wops have gotten what they deserve.

Tremendous upheaval in Russia continues. The new authorities—there is still no new government—have apparently requested a three-month cease-fire. Is this true? For the moment, Russian artillery is even more active than before.

12 NOVEMBER. I am busy all morning with office work. Apart from this, weather is not very inviting, so I stay at home. It's overcast and humid; rain hangs heavy in the air. In the evening we get the news of our Kaiser's accident in Italy—he nearly drowned, but thank God all turned out well—that's all we Austrians still need!

13 NOVEMBER. Pouring rain all day. Appalling mud—no one can move anywhere

14 NOVEMBER. Weather like yesterday. Rain and mud, nothing but rain and mud. Under such conditions, time passes very slowly, and I cannot wait for this isolation to end. Good news from the Italian front continues: our troops are already in Feltre—everything is going according to plan. Confusion in Russia continues.

15 NOVEMBER. Some clearing; rain has stopped. Sun has not penetrated through though. At 9:00 a.m. there is a thanksgiving service for the saving of the life of our Kaiser, in which I participate.

16 NOVEMBER. Weather like yesterday; no rain, but nice days are becoming less and less common. The trees are almost completely bare—fall is in full swing.

Around noon, Senior Physician Kantorek returns to the regiment from vacation. My stay here cannot last much longer: command here is beginning to get on my nerves. I will definitely remain here through tomorrow though.

17 NOVEMBER. Weather no better than the past few days, but I still go out, inspect the baths at 2/40, which has now been taken over by the Germans and been renovated. Like all their other baths at the front, it is constructed according to their own system: a small, narrow yet functional room, oven sufficient for eight to ten uniforms. There is no room for more than these eight to ten men to bathe together, yet, properly used up to about 150 men can use these baths on a daily basis. From there I walk with Dr. Kantorek to the newly built first aid station 2/40, which is finally ready and very nice. There are still working on the foxhole. Back around noon.

I spend the entire afternoon with regimental work. The regimental medical staff have been badly neglected: nobody thought about recognizing their importance. This is a special gift from Regimental Captain Fuchs, who has always been doctor-unfriendly. But now that he has been on leave during my entire time here, I try to make amends. Lieutenant Colonel Raktelj, a very upright gentleman, approves all of my suggestions: I put thirty-two men up for the Bronze Medal for Bravery, promote and put several up for Iron and Silver Service Crosses. I must complete this work today.

There is a festive meal at dinner, not only in my honor but primarily to honor Communications Officer Lieutenant Westphal, who is also leaving the regiment tomorrow: Westphal established communication between the 377th German infantry regiment and our fortieth infantry regiment. Not that this was difficult or demanding, but he still managed to endear himself to the regiment, so much so that all subalterns call him "du." That says a great deal about a German officer.

An excellent supper, chicken and stewed fruit: also—as a special treat—onion bread that is one of my favorites. There is plenty of wine and schnapps, as well as music. The bandleader comes out with his zither, which he plays well. Lieutenant Koprzywa takes turns with him playing his guitar and singing (both very well). A jolly atmosphere quickly develops; the German officer starts the proceedings off with a rambling speech about the regiment, and the Lieutenant Colonel responds. Many other speeches follow, and high spirits become even higher. Of course I am honored as well, especially by the Lieutenant Colonel.

Speeches become ever-more abundant and maudlin. Long before midnight, the German lieutenant passes out, followed by several others, who disappear without a trace. My adjutant Lieutenant Teitelbaum feels morally obliged to give an especially flattering speech about me, which pleases me no end: he is one of the few men who is still sober and whose words don't come out of a bottle. Apart from the three chaplains, only we three physicians remain sober the whole time. At 8:00 a.m. the next morning, our number has almost melted away and the party is finally adjourned.

18 NOVEMBER. Obligatory photography at 8:30 a.m., before the Germans depart (myself as well). The lieutenant colonel does not appear because he has forgotten about it and already gone. The other gentlemen are still in bed with terrible hangovers and have to be dragged out. Eventually, photos are taken at 9:00 a.m., and I depart immediately thereafter. Weather miserable, wet, a strong, biting wind—short periods of snow, which melts almost immediately. Finally, after a detour at the fortieth baggage train, I arrive at command at 11:00 a.m. and am greeted noisily by some of the gentlemen. I spend the entire afternoon reinstalling myself—everything is topsy-turvy here, and I cannot even have my afternoon snooze, which I really need today because I hardly slept three hours last night. Hopefully I will sleep better tonight, because lately I have not been sleeping well at all: I wake up at 3:00 a.m. and then cannot go back to sleep. Additionally, there is a lack of petroleum oil at the regiment, so I must toss and turn in bed for hours, without even being able to read a letter: awful, and it makes one really tired.

19 NOVEMBER. Weather somewhat better; the sun even tries to break out during the afternoon but doesn't succeed. Conrad von Hötzendorf's Italian Army is active south of Asiago—going is very heavy in this mountainous region, and they must slog from place to place. The front on the Piave remains static. In Russia, no noticeable resolution of the chaos.

20 NOVEMBER. Weather: horrible. Rain, wind, overcast gloomy sky, appalling mud. And yet I must go out today. First to the baths on ¤ 243, then to baggage train 5/103. But at the last minute, I must cancel the trip and send the wagon back: it is just raining too hard.

21 NOVEMBER. It pours with rain all night. The ground has softened horribly, and going out is impossible. At 9:00 a.m., we have a mass for the first anniversary of the death of Kaiser Franz Joseph. I must unfortunately stay at home today as well: it's raining too hard, with little interruption, all day.

22 NOVEMBER. It's snowing hard: roofs and ground are snow-covered. The last leaves of fall have fallen, and winter has arrived.

23 NOVEMBER. Snow has disappeared. Temperature during the night around zero. The weather looks good, and I make ready at 8:30 a.m. to walk to the units in Wojmica. Ground is very soft in places; I sink into the mud several times and arrive at the field hospital in a sad and muddy state. I remain in the operating theater until 10:30 a.m. In the meantime, a strong southeast wind develops, and I request a wagon to the medical column. I return from this expedition around noon.

24 NOVEMBER. Wind howls violently with periods of rain the whole of yesterday and last night. It's so bad today that we cannot leave our quarters.

The new Russian government, which still is not stable, is now in the hands of workers, soldiers, and farmers with Lenin at their head.[62] Lenin wants peace at any price, at the very least a three-month cease-fire.

Renewed fraternization at the front: Russians walk unarmed around their positions freely during the day and converse with our people, after they have first ensured that we will not shoot at them. There is no more firing: our propaganda is hard at work. We hear that the Russian government has given the Entente an ultimatum with a maximal period of two days to fix their immediate war demands, or else they will make a separate peace. The days to come should be very interesting indeed.

25 NOVEMBER. Wind howls unabated, and we are forced to stay in place. Colds are the order of the day. My poor batman, Schweiger, has had it, and coughs pitiably; his cheesy-pale face is quite frightening—like someone suffering from nephritis. He is off to hospital today.

26 NOVEMBER. Wind continues to rattle and shake windows throughout the night, and from 3:00 a.m. I cannot sleep anymore. By morning it dies down and appears to have swept the sky clean, because, finally, the sun appears early. I cannot stay inside anymore and leave at 8:30 a.m. for the twenty-ninth light infantry battalion in Kruchyniczy, which is stationed there as army reserves. Weather is still unpleasant, wind blows sharply in the ears, although there is no frost. But mud and puddles of water are deep and ubiquitous.

Return around 11:00 a.m., by which time the sun has disappeared again and the gray, overcast sky of the past few days has returned in full force.

In the evening, we hear that, for a change, Jemrich is taking another eight days' leave—the rich aunt doesn't even give him rest even after death, but why should he mind? I take the opportunity to present my request for three weeks leave to him. I am not disappointed, because he says to me: "Of course, go. You have not been home for a long while." I want to file a request for today as well, but this must be discussed beforehand with Dr. Lederer.

27 NOVEMBER. Weather not bad, dry everywhere. Sky still mostly cloudy, even though sun breaks through at times. At 9:00 a.m. I am off to the baths on ¤ 243, which has been prepared well and functionally for the winter. This is the only facility that functions perfectly, without problems: troops use it more and more. Senior Physician Wechsler, its supervisor, takes great care of it. I inspect the new well in the fortieth infantry regiment battle train, return 11:00 a.m.

28 NOVEMBER. A violent storm breaks during the night: it tugs so violently at the windows and doors that at times I am worried that my barrack might be blown over. The whole day, there are alternating periods of rain, although sun shines early. This unstable weather lasts all day. My medical orderly, Demkowicz, has finally returned from his expedition home and his visit to my family in Vienna. This time, unfortunately, I was not able to give him a lot in the way of provisions: seven kilograms of bacon at sixteen crowns, half a kilogram of butter at twelve crowns, three kilograms of flour at sixty-four heller, six liters of six-rowed barley, three liters of millet, and three liters of beans: all together for fifty crowns. These are horrendous prices, but one must be happy to obtain any provisions at all. As a small compensation, I send them, for free, twenty kilograms of potatoes, some vegetables, one kilogram of sausage, a few eggs, and bread.

29 NOVEMBER. Weather the same. Strong southwest wind, which often rises to gale force. Hardly does the wind calm down when it starts raining again. Going out of doors is impossible, and time passes twice as slowly. I am writing up my request for three weeks' leave, after having first conferred with all personnel involved with its approval.

30 NOVEMBER. Weather same as yesterday. Wind only dies down toward noon. Intermittent periods of rain, which last all day. It remains overcast the whole time, skies are deathly gray.

Things are quite peculiar on our front. The new powers that be in Russia—one cannot yet talk of a government because it still has not been formed—yell for peace, or at least an armistice. In an attempt to counteract this, the secret agreement between Russia and the Entente of September 1914 is published, to the effect that no one is allowed to make a separate peace. The Entente wish to divide our Austro-Hungarian Empire up. Alsace Lorraine must return to France, and the German states on the West Bank of the Rhine must act as buffers, separated from Germany and made independent.

This is how the Great Protectors look at the smaller countries! A few northerly situated, special German divisions are said to have, on their own initiative, agreed to an armistice. It is hard to say whether this is true: what is a fact is that today a Russian staff officer, with a first lieutenant as peace envoy, appeared in front of the lines of section 5/103, and that Major Mrekewa with an interpreter went to meet the same two men in front of our own lines, both to negotiate a cease-fire. Negotiations are not yet complete. However, since I have returned from the fortieth infantry regiment, there is almost no more shooting. A few artillery salvoes here and there, answered by our own guns. A direct hit yesterday caused five wounded, by coincidence in the same 5/103 section. How careful one must be!

1 DECEMBER. Weather mild and calm. Only mud keeps me indoors.

2 DECEMBER. A historic day of the first magnitude! An armistice between the Central Powers and Russia has been drawn up! News came this evening during dinner, through an official telegram from Army Group Linsingen. General Linsingen has concluded an armistice in the name of his entire army group, and there is no doubt that this will—either simultaneously or very soon—be extended along the entire front. Another armistice has been concluded in

Kowel, in the presence of a Russian government representative. Conditions are purely military in nature. The armistice begins at 10:00 p.m.: troops must remain in their existing positions, and no commerce between the lines is permitted, only at specific points on the front. During the first three days, no soldier may be removed from the front; after that it's permitted. The same applies to improvement of their positions, but not with a view to new fortifications and establishment of new barbed wire obstacles. Fliers are allowed to fly over enemy positions, but no firing or bombing is permitted. This applies for the next forty-eight hours: during this time no attacks or hostility are permitted.

Joy over the news is mixed. Is it apathy caused by this endless war, or does the upcoming peace hold in it a sort of disappointment? Who can say? I freely admit that I, personally, fear material loss: this peace can lead to a future drop in the stock market, in which I am invested. Other than that, I am in a bad mood today because corps command has only approved fourteen days' leave instead of the three weeks that I requested. It's clear to everyone that today is a day of enormous historical significance. Lenin is the hero, who has dared—independently, and against the will of the Entente—to accomplish this great task. It is certain that peace with Russia will soon come. What is the Entente going to do now? That is a complete mystery at the moment.

I spend the morning at field hospital 1009, return around noon. The weather is good: clear, sunny, ground already dry in places, mild temperatures.

3 DECEMBER. I get an early call from Lederer that according to military gazette no. 226 of 28 November 1917 I have been awarded the Signum Laudis with swords. I am obviously very pleased about this, even though I could and should have received this a year ago.

Otherwise, I am very pleased about the cessation of hostilities. A discussion between our commander and the Russian representative between the lines has been set for 2:00 p.m. General von Rosenzweig, substituting for our vacationing Commander Jemrich, arrives punctually but must wait a whole hour for his Russian counterpart. The Russian commander does not appear in person, only a lowly staff captain (major) and an ordinary soldier as representatives of their commandant. Asked why the commander has not come himself, the soldier responds: "It makes no difference: we speak in his name." It becomes clear that the Russians only know about a three-day cessation of hostilities and have come only to ask for an extension. Our general clarifies that cessation of hostilities is for an unspecified time, with a forty-eight hour termination period. This satisfies them; we share cognac, cigarettes, and cigars, and part company. Weather good, increasing wind in the afternoon and cold, some snow.

4 DECEMBER. Temperature −5°C, complete snowy landscape, first real winters day. Nice blue sky, wind quite calm—snow around noon—just when I am leaving for vacation on 6 December and have potatoes to take along! Today's military gazette has finally fulfilled what we have wanted for a long time:

(1) Rank above auditors in judge advocate's office: It's about time! A pity that it needed this murderous war to be approved, to differentiate between those who do and those who don't serve at the front.

(2) Rank at performances and parades. This problem has also needed to be solved for a long time. Assembly by rank, and, among rank, according to succession. That is the way it should be! Because of lack of clarity in this paragraph of the regulations, physicians have had to put up with many humiliations.

(3) Service armband exactly like other officers of soldier's rank.

(4) Military Service Badge exactly the same as other officers of soldier's rank.

They still have not approved a change in how junior noncommissioned officers are treated. There are still no clear differences between first and second class and full combatants.

5 DECEMBER. Vacation draws closer. This morning I am busy packing, down to the last small details; −7°C early, so winter continues. It seems that I will have to forgo my potatoes completely. Toward evening it gets even colder: at 6:00 p.m. it is already −15°C. Happiness about my leave has become a bit clouded. The armistice, better said truce, that has just been concluded has been canceled, and hostilities begin again at 10:00 p.m. How, when, why? Don't ask, no one knows. It is all beyond our comprehension.

6 DECEMBER. Temperature −5°C, light snowfall. Still too cold for my potatoes. I am not here anymore in spirit. I quickly pack the last of my things. I have collected a great deal: 16.5 kilograms of flour, 5 kilograms of fish, 1.8 kilograms of peas, 5 kilograms of barley, 3 kilograms of bacon, 60 eggs, three-quarters of a sausage, 1 goose, 2 tongues, 4 loaves of bread, 1 bottle of wine, 1 jar of cucumbers, 1 tin of tomatoes, 1 of marmalade, 4 tins of sardines, 200 grams of tea, 1 crate of potatoes (despite the weather!), 1 kilogram of butter. Added to that, a brass Russian samovar and plenty of other miscellaneous things.

Yesterday evening, before the end of the armistice, there was a meeting between the lines of our intelligence officer and a deputation of Russian soldiers. They are very sorry that, because of a misunderstanding, they have only signed off on a three-day armistice—but ask that we do not shoot at them anymore, and keep to the present conditions: we agree. After the discussion is complete, we empty another bottle of cognac and depart. This interruption in the truce appears to have only occurred on our front: the armistice holds everywhere else.

Punctually at noon, I am on the train; an hour later, I am still on the train. In Chorostow, according to plan, I receive my crate of potatoes and one kilogram of butter from corps command. After a long layover in Vladimir Volynsky, we depart for Lemberg, where we arrive at 9:45 p.m. To my sorrow, we do not meet my father there, although I have informed him of our proposed meeting by telegraph. As it turns out, despite it having been sent a day earlier, it only arrives at 9:00 p.m. the next day, when he is already in bed. At 11:30 p.m. I travel on to Vienna, unfortunately in an unheated coach with six people in the coupé. And so we arrive in Vienna on 7 December at 5:00 p.m., two hours late. My Olga is waiting for me. Because of the many packages, I have to take a one-horse carriage, which costs fifteen crowns. The potatoes are not on it: I arrange for them to be delivered the next day by carrier, which costs another 4.80 crowns. Despite the cold, they are in very good condition; I do not regret the expenditure.

I find all of my children well. Tinka has become quite slender, but she looks good like that and, thank God, she is still in an almost jaunty mood. She is a splendid person, my pride and my greatest joy. I have no idea why she rankled me so much as a child. She looks so much like my unforgettable Henia of blessed memory, whose picture I always have with me.[63]

Ega is, by contrast, calmer, and serious for her age—she is thirteen and has thawed out somewhat during my absence, much livelier than before. These two young girls hang on to me and won't let go. Miki is a delightful young scamp, bright and lively, but doesn't look too well and is somewhat pale. However, she is healthy, strong, with a good appetite. The youngest, Mary—eighteen months old—is very cute and looks well. She is talking a great deal already, but doesn't understand strangers. She is strong-willed and very well developed. All the children make me happy: only my Olga looks very, very bad. She has great difficulty with the hired help, who are now worse than useless. Only demands—no feelings of duty. Apart from that she is most irritated that I am constantly in the field, while so many of her acquaintances have been at home with their families for a long time. Not everyone can—or wishes to—fake illness.

The first three days I have quite a bad cold, after the trip in the unheated coupé, especially in view of the fact that I already had the sniffles when I left. It does not improve, and I must spend a few days in bed, but then I improve and am fine for the rest of my vacation. Time passes only too quickly, and very pleasantly. Of course, many visits and receptions; four times in the theater. We see *The Rose of Stamboul*, a delightful operetta; *Procurist Pold*, an excellent comedy of a Jewish nature; *The Beautiful Saskia*; and operettas, beautifully outfitted and played: the music is not popular yet. And finally *Der Blaufuchs*, a comedy, with Konstantin as guest player, and a Berlin lady who makes a great sensation with her dated and unnatural movements.

It's soon 30 December, and I must depart. I travel again via Lemberg to see my father. He is supposed to be at the station on 31 December at 7:00 a.m., but prefers to wait for me at home, because I have two and a half hours between trains. However, my train is again delayed, this time for about two hours. My father does not reckon with this delay, so I must travel off again without having seen him. Around 9:00 p.m. on New Years Eve, I arrive unexpectedly in the middle of our celebrations. Despite being exhausted—the train was overfilled and I couldn't sleep a wink the previous night—I have to remain seated as long as the commander is present: it is 1:00 a.m. before I finally can go to bed.

Notes

1. Voynitsa (Ukraine).
2. Brăila (Romania).
3. Dobruja or Dobrudja is a historical region in Eastern Europe situated between the lower Danube River and the Black Sea, and includes the Danube Delta, the Romanian coast, and the northernmost part of the Bulgarian coast.
4. Aleksandrovka (Ukraine).
5. Pavlovychi (Ukraine).
6. Khvorostiv (Ukraine)? Too far to be likely.
7. Focşani (Romania).
8. The word *landesüblich* used in this context really means horse-drawn wagons. It may be assumed that the motorized medical columns used up to now were rendered increasingly useless because of the blockade, and that the word "column" instead of "unit" did not change its basic function.
9. W(V)olhynia is a historic region in Central and Eastern Europe straddling Poland, Ukraine, and Belarus.
10. A breakdown in the smallpox vaccination system must have occurred.
11. Szolnok (Hungary).
12. Bacillary dysentery is a fecal-oral infection caused by bacteria of the genus *Shigella*.
13. Di(u)browa (Ukraine).
14. Shel'viv (Ukraine).
15. Berezovychi (Ukraine).
16. Rogoźno (Poland).
17. Khorlupy (Ukraine).
18. Krukhynychi (Ukraine).
19. Olyka (Ukraine).
20. Cieszyn (Poland) and Český Těšín (Czech Republic). Town lies on the border of both countries.
21. Khoriv (Ukraine).
22. A communicable bacterial disease transmitted by bite of the rat flea, or directly by droplet infection (the "black death" of the Middle Ages).
23. Bardach's first mention of the First Russian Revolution (8–15 March N.S.), which deposed the Tsar who was replaced by a provisional government headed by Kerensky.
24. Lack of provisions (military and especially civilian)—first noted mid-1916—will gradually assume catastrophic proportions.
25. Brother of Nicolas II.
26. Operation *Alberich* was a planned withdrawal to new positions on the shorter, more easily defended Hindenburg Line, which took place between 9 February and 20 March 1917 and eliminated the two salients that had been formed in 1916, between Arras and Saint-Quentin and from Saint-Quentin to Noyon, during the Battle of the Somme. Bardach does not mention the scorched earth policy of the Germans along the withdrawal route, nor the French suffering caused by it.
27. Passover began the eve of 6 April 1917.
28. Afternoon Viennese coffee, cakes, and perhaps something more solid.
29. Bielsko Biała (Poland).
30. Kowel (Ukraine).

31. Lviv (Ukraine).
32. The first seven days of mourning following a first-degree relative's death.
33. Holland remained neutral during World War I.
34. Mykulychi (Ukraine).
35. Wolhynian (trench) fever, a louse-borne fever caused by *Bartonella quintana*. About one-fifth of the Austro-Hungarian Army in World War I were infected with trench fever. Green salad prepared in contaminated soil or water would have transmitted fecal-oral pathogens such as *Salmonella* (including typhoid fever), *Shigella* (bacterial dysentery), cholera, and amebic dysentery.
36. In June 1917, King Constantine abdicated, and his second son, Alexander, assumed the throne as king. Prime Minister Venizelos assumed control of the entire country, and Greece officially declared war against the Central Powers on 2 July 1917.
37. Monte Cucco (Italy).
38. Chełm (Poland).
39. Przemyśl (Poland).
40. Volodymyr-Volynskyi (Ukraine).
41. Berezhany (Ukraine).
42. The Kerensky Offensive (1–19 July 1917) was the last Russian offensive of the war, but collapsed by 16 July.
43. Konyukhy (Ukraine).
44. Lokachy (Ukraine).
45. Chernivtsi (Ukraine). Capital of Bukowina (see note 52).
46. The Czech Legion.
47. Viennese cabaret couple.
48. Zboriv (Ukraine).
49. Ternopil (Ukraine).
50. Ivano-Frankivsk, Halych, Kalush, Chortkiv, Kolomyya, Buchach, Zalishchyky, Skala (Podilska), Husyatyn, Snyatyn (Ukraine).
51. Câmpulung Moldovenesc (Romania).
52. Historical region of Bukowina, former part of Moldova and now split between Romania and Ukraine, or the administrative unit Duchy of Bukowina, a constituent land of the Austrian Empire from 1774, and crown land of Austria-Hungary from 1867 until 1918.
53. Rădăuți (Romania).
54. Gura Humorului (Romania).
55. Focșani (Romania).
56. Surgical creation of a connection between the stomach and jejunum.
57. The Battle of Passchendaele (Third Battle of Ypres) was a major campaign fought by the Allies against the German Empire on the Western Front, from July to November 1917, for control of the ridges south and east of the Belgian city of Ypres in West Flanders. It aimed to break through and capture German U-boat pens on the English Channel. Nothing of the kind happened, and terrible slaughter ensued under atrocious rain and mud. The offensive was a failure. See Robin Prior and Trevor Wilson, *Passchendaele: The Untold Story*, 3rd ed. (New Haven, CT: Yale University Press, 2016).
58. This does not make obvious sense but is exactly what is written.
59. The Battle of Caporetto (also known as the Twelfth Battle of the Isonzo) took place from 24 October to 19 November 1917 near the town of Kobarid (now in northwestern Slovenia, then part of the Austrian Littoral). The battle was named after the Ital-

ian name of the town (also known as Karfreit in German). Austro-Hungarian forces, reinforced by German units, were able to break into the Italian front line and rout the Italian forces opposing them. The battle was a demonstration of the effectiveness of the use of storm troopers and infiltration tactics. Use of poison gas by the Germans also played a key role in the collapse of the Italian Second Army, and the retreat of Italian forces one hundred kilometers to the west.

60. Tolmin (Slovenia).
61. Gorizia (Italy).
62. The second (Bolshevik) Russian Revolution occurred on 7 November (N.S.).
63. Bardach's deceased first wife.

CHAPTER 5

1918
Treaty of Brest Litovsk—Crippling Shortages— Piave—War's End

1 JANUARY. Unpleasant weather in Vienna the whole time I was there. The sun only appeared twice or three times for hardly one hour around noon: otherwise overcast, foggy, cold. Two days before I left, it snowed more heavily than we have seen for the last sixteen years. It was doubly as unpleasant, because there is nobody available to clear away the snow. There is also a lot of snow on the way back—it only disappears when we are in East Galicia. Here in Pavloviczy[1] there is also little snow, but much more stormy wind.

Great changes while I have been away. As is well known, there is an armistice on the front, with active discourse between peace envoys from both sides. They are currently busy arranging exchange of goods between the two sides—that is not so easy. Russians are very mistrustful. Our front is now very long: it extends from the Turia[2] to Szelwów,[3] and on this long stretch, we only have five battalions. Germans are withdrawing many troops; we will do the same. Everything speaks for doing this. Our division is gradually being diminished to normal strength. Two battalions have been withdrawn from the fortieth infantry regiment and formed into a new regiment, the 110st. We are awaiting one battalion each for the fortieth and 130th; 4/62 has already received one battalion, carrying the name 128th infantry battalion; 5/103 has got off unscathed. The Russians have already left a part of the front. One of our patrols has marched four kilometers in their direction, without having seen a single Russian. It's my job to organize medical facilities for these troops—a great deal of work. The weather is so bad that I cannot go out.

2 JANUARY. During my vacation in Vienna, my family informed me that, on 8 December [1917], my batman, Schweiger, died of acute nephritis in the hospital into which he was admitted 25 November. I cannot describe how this moves me. He was with me for about two and a half years and did his job perfectly—a good, intelligent, dutiful lad. He never really was healthy, despite

being strongly built and clever. But noticeably pale, bloated face was always suspicious. May he rest in peace! My new batman, a Ruthenian,[4] has come with me during my Vienna vacation, but as soon as we reach the station I release him so that he can go home and enjoy his own vacation (*Rawasurka*), on condition that on the 26 December he must return directly to Pavloviczy. I am astonished to find that he still has not returned when I myself get back on 31 December. Today I am going to telephone his regional gendarmerie.

3 JANUARY. The storm that started last night with blowing snow rages all night, continuing through today. Walking in roads is unbearable. My new batman finally arrives at 11:00 a.m. During his vacation, in a fit of drunkenness, he apparently beat a civilian half to death (as he said, he smacked him up a bit)—not surprising to me, given his size and strength. He was arrested and taken to Vladimir Volynsky,[5] then brought here under guard. I'm just pleased that he is back and that I do not need to depend on someone else.

4 JANUARY. A critical day of first importance. Today, negotiations in Brest Litovsk[6] were supposed to have resumed, after a week's interruption to give the Entente time to reflect whether they should participate in general peace talks. Yesterday, the Russian representative sent a telegram to the Central Powers representative informing him that the Russian government has decided to continue peace negotiations in a neutral nation. Our representative rejected this completely; we are anxious to know what will happen.

5 JANUARY. Temperature −10 °C, very strong wind. But I must go to Kruchyniczy[7] to meet with the bacteriologist there about establishment of a disinfection station. The trip takes about one and a half hours.

6 JANUARY. Thawing weather. Wind strong, light rain at times, black ice; snow does not disappear. The Russian delegation has not yet arrived in Brest Litovsk, but the Ukrainian representative has come, and we are negotiating separately.

7 JANUARY. Zero degrees. Thawing weather and snowmelt. Last night, our large bathing facility in camp 5 burned down completely. I cannot describe how upset I am about this. They were our finest and most functional baths, right behind the front, the pride of our division: I have immortalized them in many photographs.

8 JANUARY. Warmer, +5 °C, snow gone, black ice in places, also mud. At 8:00 a.m., I go out to inspect the burned down baths and salvage what we can from pieces of iron and bricks that remain. From there, I travel with the chief physician of the 128th to the new 2/128 battalion, which has replaced the 5/103. I inspect the position, returning at noon.

9 JANUARY. Heavy snowfall during the night, continuing all day. Temperature −2 °C.

10 JANUARY. Colder, −6 °C. Snow carries on during the night but stops in the early morning. Skies clear.

11 JANUARY. Toward morning a violent wind develops, blowing and drifting snow, so bad that one cannot keep one's eyes open in the road. Roads are impassable in places, and freezing cold. I have no idea how cold it is: there is no thermometer outside.

12 JANUARY. Temperature −2 °C. The storm has abated. Piles of snow in places, otherwise not too bad. I go out at 8:30 a.m., first to the burned-down baths at camp 5. The bath complex is a heap of rubble, all wooden parts have disappeared; only iron parts such as pipes, basins, bars, and bricks remain—maybe they can be reused. From there I travel to baths nos. 1 and 2 on the way to the brigade and at the same time inspect first aid station 3/40, now called 1/110. Great aggravation everywhere, none of the baths are in use—water has been heated for bath no. 2, but not the delousing oven. There is a shortage of wood, and no one bathes. No. 1 has been completely devastated, a picture of misery, no one guards it, many windowpanes are missing. The oven, which just needed some repair, is half gone, bricks stolen. This type of vandalism is so common during war! At the first aid station, wood is chopped away under the eyes of physicians. The sick there are crawling with lice, despite their having a functioning bath (no. 2) only two hundred paces away. This is all the fault of the indolence of our nonmilitary physicians. After have properly yelled, berated, screamed, and cursed at everyone in sight, I return home.

13 JANUARY. Zero degrees, thawing weather. But snow is now so thick that it does not really have any effect. Peace negotiations in Brest Litovsk have started again, after the unpleasant intermezzo has been concluded in our favor. Trotsky has appeared as the head of his delegation and has had to give in to our representatives continuing the negotiations. Ukraine has sent a separate delegation to represent them at the negotiations.

14 JANUARY. Temperature −2 °C, dry, harsh air. Frosty weather increases in the afternoon: at 5:00 p.m. the thermometer shows −12 °C. I have the opportunity today to send more provisions to my family via a noncommissioned officer: 10 kilograms of flour, 5 kilograms of kasha, 2 kilograms of millet, 4.2 kilograms of bacon, 25 eggs, 1 goose, 4 loaves of bread, some sugar, and butter.

15 JANUARY. At 7:00 a.m., −12 °C. Beautiful winter landscape, deep snow crunches underfoot, blue sky, sunshine, harsh air. At 8:30 a.m. I travel to the new first aid station for the fortieth infantry regiment near Szelwów—lovely sled journey of about one and a half hours, return around noon. The sky darkens during my return journey—in the afternoon, temperature rises significantly, but toward evening another violent snowstorm with blowing snow. After dinner, I have to wade through the snow from the mess to my quarters.

16 JANUARY. In the morning, temperature is warmer (+5 °C), but weather is still stormy. Snow has almost disappeared from trees and roofs, but roads are becoming ever blacker, dirtier, and muddier. Puddles of water, some quite large and deep, are everywhere.

17 JANUARY. Temperature −1 °C. Ground completely dry, some black ice, very little snow, moderate wind. At 8:30 a.m. I take a stroll to the medical column and field hospital. I spend the morning there, return at noon. In the evening, we have a theater performance for a change: this time consisting of military performers, cabaret singers, and dancers in civilian life. The performance takes place in the mess after dinner and is quite cozy. Ends at 10:00 p.m.

18 JANUARY. Beautiful morning, deep blue sky, clear sunshine, not very cold—unfortunately, my batman has destroyed my thermometer.

I would have been pleased to go out had I not been ordered to the mess at 11:45 a.m., as logistics officer. As it turns out, the silver Signum Laudis decoration is to be conferred on little me as well as the ... [illegible]. By noon, weather becomes cloudy, with significant snowfall in afternoon and evening. Yesterday's theater society appears again in our mess with lantern slides and presentations. Very amusing.

19 JANUARY. Rain, horrible mud, overcast. Snow melts again: significant rise in temperature.

20 JANUARY. Lovely springlike weather: blue sky, afternoon temperature 12 °C. I have a new thermometer. The mud keeps getting deeper and deeper.

21 JANUARY. Nice, warm weather continues: I cannot stay in my room anymore. At 8:00 a.m. I depart for the 128th, where a case of smallpox has occurred.[8] Because of awful roads and the miserable state of our horses, I change them at the 128th, and continue on, with a trip to first aid station Mulde. Back by 12:45 p.m. Today I receive confirmation that my family has received the provisions. I was very concerned, because on 15 January there was a bad railway accident near Rzeszow,[9] and I was worried that all my supplies had been destroyed. The number of train accidents has increased lately.

22 JANUARY. Fine weather continues—it could not be nicer even in Trieste this time of year. Mail is very irregular—there is a general strike throughout lower Austria: even newspapers have joined in, so hardly a single newspaper has appeared in Vienna today. Workers want to force peace, and use the opportunity to do this when the flour ration in Vienna is reduced again.

I travel again to Kruchyniczy today—a new disinfection apparatus has been built there. Back at 10:30 a.m.

Negotiations in Brest have halted again for eight days, after Trotsky apparently has to return to Petersburg for consultations. Negotiations seem to have reached a dead end. Russians want immediate evacuation of all occupied areas so that a national referendum can be held there. Germans obviously cannot agree to this, because, with current confused conditions in Russia, they cannot be sure what tomorrow may bring. The current regime might collapse overnight, and a new one may restart war, forcing us to occupy conquered territory all over again. They are of course correct—no matter how much they desire peace, they cannot agree to this in the current circumstances. Today I receive confirmation that I have been awarded the Charles Cross.

23 JANUARY. Beautiful springlike weather continues. The only problem is the mud. Dr. Lederer and Chief of General Staff Lieutenant Colonel Britto both appear here at 8:00 a.m. for a large-scale exercise. Actually, Britto only came to visit the dentist and, scandalously, for a made-up inspection to justify his trip. We travel to Kruchyniczy, where we inspect the new steam disinfector that is still in construction stage. Then a chat in my quarters until the gentlemen return from their exercise; they leave around noon.

24 JANUARY. The nice days in Wolhynia[10] appear to be at an end. Mud continues, nothing freezes, but the skies are full of fog, awfully gray, damp cold. At 8:30 a.m., I leave with General von Rosenzweig, who is substituting for the commander, to units that he has not yet seen. First to the field hospital, where an appendectomy is being performed that the general wants to see. The commandant of this group is Senior Physician Zahradrieck, a proficient surgeon and an excellent military physician, who is also organizing the renovation of barracks into operating theaters in an excellent way. I have put this splendid man up for the highest decorations a long time ago, but nothing I do makes this happen. I am sure that politics are being played here. From there we travel on to the medical column, returning at 11:15 a.m. The general is very satisfied at what he has seen.

25 JANUARY. Overcast, damp weather a lot of mud, roads scarcely passable.

26 JANUARY. Weather the same: we cannot go anywhere.

27 JANUARY. Weather the same, but mud is starting to dry out. Ground has already absorbed all the moisture it can.

28–29 JANUARY. Weather unchanged: cloudy, foggy but mild. We are losing the twenty-ninth light infantry battalion, which is currently being decamped, departing in an unknown direction. We are all sorry to see them go: they have been one of our best.

30 JANUARY. Weather unchanged, but I cannot stand staying indoors anymore, and depart at 8:30 a.m.: first to our previous position in the forest on ¤ 243, where I order a copper tub, in which to bathe off this muck—it's in full use, and available for me whenever I come unannounced: everything is functioning perfectly. Then on to the baggage train at the twenty-ninth battalion, but there are no physicians there for me to meet. I do not travel farther because of bad roads and even worse condition of our horses. Every trip is torture: the horses are in a very bad state because of lack of fodder.

31 JANUARY. Weather becomes colder at night, but no question of frost. I send my batman to Vienna to supplement provisions that by now have been used up by my family: five kilograms of bacon, ten kilograms of rendered fat in a crate, four kilograms of flour, four kilograms of barley from my sister-in-law Frau Seidmann, 131 eggs (I pay twenty-six crowns for 140). The five kilograms of bacon is also terribly expensive: twenty crowns per kilogram! Normal prices

for the other items, fifteen crowns. Also three loaves of bread, two kilograms of fine sausage, three-quarters of a kilograms of pressed sausage, six leberwursts. So they now have plenty of sausage. Then another goose, because the previous one tasted so good, and one bottle of rum, which I always obtain from the fortieth. Also one hundred cigarettes for bartering, some constituents to install electric lamps in the kitchen.

I attend another ridiculous (and totally superfluous) concert today, with four women and a man. The gang consists of Professor Schramm (piano), Miss Fried (violin), Mrs. Haas (Cello), one female singer, and one female dancer. Of course, they are our guests at dinner—very cozy, although all the women are surpassingly ugly: but they are very amusing, and Miss Fried plays the violin excellently. After the notables leave, there is some dancing. I stay for a bit, but return to my quarters at 7:00 p.m.

1 FEBRUARY. Overcast, foggy but quiet, fairly mild weather. A little frost only at night and in the morning.

2 FEBRUARY. Weather unchanged, nothing of importance except that the Italians have attempted a small attack. They have a little success, taking some of our supplies and, according to them, 100 officers, 2,500 men, 6 artillery pieces, and diverse material. With our counterattack, we take 15 officers and 650 men prisoner. So their success is not great, certainly not decisive!

3 FEBRUARY. Weather and situation unchanged.

4 FEBRUARY. Ditto. I walk to the medical column at 8:30 a.m., spending all morning there: return by wagon at noon.

5 FEBRUARY. During the night, hoarfrost covers all trees, bushes, and grass. A beautiful picture: as if each tree has put on a white cover. But all telegraph wires are covered in ice.

Otherwise nothing special—I am reading a lot, *Lord Nelson's Last Love* by Schuhmacher, an excellent book from the end of the eighteenth century from the time of Maria Theresa and King Ferdinand of Naples and Sicily. I find details of which I had no idea before.

6 FEBRUARY. Weather remains unpleasant and uncomfortable. Food shortages, which have now spread from the hinterland to the front, have assumed dimensions that threaten to become catastrophic—even most essential foodstuffs are not replenished. Each man receives only 250 grams of bread per day: that's a piece that is not even enough for *one* farmer's meal, never mind the whole day. Lunch consists mainly of tinned food, maybe with a couple of potatoes or cabbage. Morning and evening coffee—that's all! Signs of undernourishment with all their consequences are appearing. An average of ten to twenty men per company are visibly emaciated and weakened, making them incapable of fighting.

Things aren't much better at command. We get the same bread in rationed slices, with a small piece of roll for each meal, half as big and heavy as we got during peacetime: it contains three to four bites. No vegetables, other than potatoes and cabbage. The only difference is that we still get fresh meat daily, instead of in cans. But I fear that tinned goods are in our future as well.

There are strikes in the hinterland: they have started with us and spread to Germany. Things are stricter in Germany, though. Ringleaders have been locked up, war enterprises have all been militarized, and workers discharged from private enterprises. The Entente know exactly what is going on: no wonder they are rattling their sabers even more loudly and will not hear of peace.

7 FEBRUARY. A beautiful winter morning, with blue sky and sunshine. I arrange for a wagon to come and pick me up to 8:00 a.m. for a trip to 2/100 in the Caldini woods, about an hour away. From there we go on in a group on foot to inspect new baths near the convalescent home of the fortieth infantry regiment: return 11:30 a.m.

Weather has changed and become overcast, but temperature has risen and thawing is occurring; in a few hours, all the trees will be free of their white frost cover. Light snowfall during the night.

8 FEBRUARY. Thawing weather with mud continues. At 9:30 a.m. I travel with Junior Logistics Officer Pelikan to the supply depot to take possession of a batch of sauerkraut; return 11:30 a.m.

9 FEBRUARY. The most important occurrence today is the news that today at 2:00 p.m. a peace treaty with the Republic of Ukraine has been signed in Brest Litovsk.[11] So a start has been made. May it continue! This is a modest beginning—but who is to say what will develop from it? In any event, Ukraine is a very rich country, an agricultural state of first magnitude with rich sources of foodstuffs, which we desperately need to feed our half-starved soldiers and civilians. We are short of everything!

The second piece of news is less important: our corps commandant Weber has been transferred to Vienna Military Command for an undetermined period to keep order in Vienna and surroundings. Valiant Commander Jemrich, hardly back from vacation, has taken over our corps command and been transferred to Mikuliczy[12] (site of corps command). We will not miss him: Weber is a boring host, who has disturbed all fellow feeling in the mess. Weather overcast with mud. Rain in the evening.

10 FEBRUARY. Nice, clear morning with blue sky and sunshine: but mud is awful! One cannot move outdoors!

Our spirited commerce at the front about which I have already written continues in great style. We buy horses, gas masks, provisions, etc. In ten days, we have already obtained nine hundred masks at ten crowns apiece. When we think about the fact that we can manufacture ten of our own from the components of *one* Russian gas mask, this comprises a significant number. Our soldiers returning from the front increase daily: We progress without difficulty through Russian territory; our front is not held up anywhere, with only the mopping up of the last enemy remnants necessary. More than three thousand men have been freed up from our division alone for frontline service.

11 FEBRUARY. Peace has been concluded with Russia, in its own particular way! Trotsky, president of the delegation, has declared that he regards the state of war between Russia and the Central Powers as over and will order immediate demobilization, but without a formal peace treaty. Diplomatic relations have been resumed, and negotiations can now continue. On the entire Eastern Front, only Romania remains as our enemy, and they will eventually also have to make peace, because they are completely isolated and are, in fact, at war with Russia. Weather today is appalling, strong winds, rain, endless mud.

12 FEBRUARY. Weather not much better than yesterday. We are still under influence of the peace agreement, and all sorts of orders are being issued, especially concerning our division. The question in every mouth is: Will we remain here, and for how long? The wording of the peace agreements has been issued: among other things, they call for "immediate start of evacuation of the occupied areas, as soon as peace has been ratified." Opinions are mixed—*I declare myself for ending the war here and now. I am sick—sick to death—of this war.* Most others are of the same opinion, but lack the courage to say so openly.

13 FEBRUARY. Newspapers, which only arrived today, are filled with enthusiasm over the peace agreement with Russia. The bitter taste of lack of a formal peace treaty remains, but we try to get over it. The stock market has reacted very favorably, which pleases me because I am invested in the state railway and Anglobank, whose value has dropped significantly. We are all excited, awaiting further developments, especially from overseas newspapers, which have not arrived yet.

Our prisoners in Russia appear not to be waiting for formal evacuation but are streaming back en masse. The daily number passing through our front has risen to one hundred—they are already causing us embarrassment, because we are not prepared for so many at once.

14 FEBRUARY. Temperature a bit lower. The ground is starting to freeze. Recent great political events are now being thoroughly exploited by the newspapers. At the moment, Poles are making the biggest fuss, because a portion of the region around Cholm[13] has been cut off; they are now acting against our interests and refusing to pass a budget. Apart from them, other local opposition is feared, and we have sent several battalions to the hinterland already to assist in calming things down.

Our surgical group has been transferred to eleventh army in Italy. As much as we are sorry to see them go—because they have performed so excellently—it must be conceded that they have no more reason for being here since conclusion of the armistice. So we let them go in peace.

15 FEBRUARY. Colder: −4 °C at 8:00 a.m., fairly strong wind, which makes it feel doubly cold.

16 FEBRUARY. Frosty weather continues. Nevertheless, I go to the field hospital on foot at 9:00 a.m. to bid an official farewell to the surgeons. I assemble all unit officers and nurses in the officers' mess and say goodbye to the surgical group in the division's name. Tomorrow I will send a commendation in our divisional dispatch. From there I go with Regimental Physician First Class Schwelger to the medical column and return by foot around noon.

We must consider carefully before we travel by horse, because there is such a shortage of fodder that it pains us to use them. Apart from that, roads are very bad: Road tracks in the mud made during the past few days have now frozen solid. So travel by sled is the only possible way, and I prefer walking.

17 FEBRUARY. Beautiful, clear winter day, moderate frost, wind calm.

18 FEBRUARY. For a change, today is another theater day. Comedy ensemble from Lemberg:[14] six men and four women. They will eat us to death. Of course I am not going to attend: it is not worth the price of six crowns. But I cannot escape the evening in the mess. It begins, as usual, with a plentiful dinner: actors and actresses become jollier and jollier, and start performing. A cabaret actor beautifully declaims two couplets, which he accompanies himself on the piano. He could be mistaken for our Captain Schulhof—also in his behavior. He presents the couplet "Servus du" wonderfully. A female singer presents the car song made famous by Mella Mars[15] beautifully, except that the refrain is not as good. Another actress develops stomach cramps, so bad that she needs my attention. Finally, obligatory dancing: I take the opportunity to disappear at 11:45 p.m. Winter weather continues.

Figure 5.1. A theater group: not all the soldiers appear to be appreciative. Photograph courtesy of the Leo Baeck Institute.

19 FEBRUARY. Our joy about the concluded peace is short-lived. The Germans are not satisfied with Trotsky's peace formula. Bolsheviks increase their mischief in Estonia and Finland, so Finland finally has to request German aid. Germany does not wait to be asked further, simply takes the opportunity to pocket these provinces! They do not feel bound by Trotsky's formula and are rather of the opinion that the armistice on 10 February has already been announced. After seven days have passed, they set out again: not sure where, probably to Estonia and Finland, with another division sent to Luck.[16] It appears we will not be cooperating with the Germans in the Baltic; we will wait in case Ukraine is directly threatened by the Bolsheviks. So, war between Germany and Russia has been renewed. These earthshaking events don't stop me for asking for leave: Dr. Lederer will go to a gas course on 2 March, and on leave thereafter, so I am stuck here until the middle of April. I take the opportunity of requesting leave now: It's approved, and I travel off tomorrow, back the end of the month.

20 FEBRUARY. Morning passes rapidly with my preparations for the trip. The main issue now is to collect as many provisions as I can. I succeed in obtaining the following:

5 kg bacon @ 14.50 = 72.50
ca. 5 kg ham @ 11.50 = 65.50
1 kg smoked meat @ 8.00 = 8.00
1 kg sausage @ 12.50 = 12.50
0.5 kg butter @ 20.00 = 10.00
2 kg green beans @ 2.00 = 4.00
25 eggs @ 30 heller= 7.50
4 loaves of bread @ 1.20 = 4.80
1 lb. tea @ 26:00 = 26.00
2.5 kg sugar @ 1.36 = 3.40
TOTAL: 214.25 [crowns]
70 kg potatoes: free

With this small pile, which has cost so much, I set off for Vienna: the journey goes relatively smoothly, after I have become so used to overfilled, unheated carriages. I arrive with a short delay of about an hour, at 4:30 p.m. on 21 February.

I am met at the station by my dear Olga. The poor woman still looks terrible: emaciated—almost down to skin and bone—and depressed. At home, the children await me impatiently; poor little Miki is, especially, pale from excitement. My wife's birthday is today: her siblings have sent her lots of flowers; even her aunt old Frau Krieger has arrived to congratulate her personally. After she hears that I am coming, she feels duty-bound to wait for me. She is a dear, sweet old woman—but visits from others are not wanted exactly now: she should know that.

My few days of leave do not bring anything new and very little enjoyment. Anxiety about provisions become greater and greater, inflation is awful, and meat unavailable for days at a time. No vegetables, and bread is miserable. We live mainly from food brought in from the outside, which I anxiously see disappearing. My Olga is not well at all, has cold shivers at night, temperature early in the morning 38 °C, so she must stay in bed all day and preserve her strength.

Her strength is gradually dissipating because the stress of my years-long absence. She does not feel capable of carrying the full burden of supporting the family, worrying about all the domestic issues at the same time. I find myself compelled to request a visit with our fourteenth section and request Surgeon General Frisch to permit me work in Vienna until the end of the war. This is not easy for me to do, and I do not like to make such requests, because I know that when one has no influence, there is seldom a willing ear—I have none. He opines right at the start that Vienna is out of the question, so I will have to be satisfied with another German garrison, for which he will take me under priority consideration.

The smallest of my children surprises me—Mary, who is twenty-three months old, is making splendid progress: she develops more each day and already speaks very clearly. She is pretty and loving and has almost made friends with me—but she keeps calling me *Onki*.[17] Miki is making great strides, although it has hardly been six weeks, she is already reading well, writes very neatly, and her arithmetic is excellent. She is a lovely little thing.

The two older sisters are already of an age when, in such a short time, one sees few marks of progress. Tinka is a devil of a girl, and Ega is also lovely. And so, all too soon, it is the afternoon of 27 February, and I must part from them. Olga and Tinka take me back to the train, arriving at 2:20 p.m. They tell me that this train has been canceled for today, and I can only take the evening train at 8:20 p.m. So, back home again and in a few hours, this time alone, back to the station.

During my trip, I am appalled to hear that, by order of command, all those on leave must remain where they are for a further fourteen days to take pressure off the railway traffic. Too late for me: I cannot go home again, and must simply go back to my unit. In Lemberg, where I arrive at 2:00 p.m. on 28 February, I have to wait until the next day at 8:50 a.m. for the connecting train. I don't mind this at all, and spend time with my father and sister: this makes me very happy—then I travel on.

1 MARCH. I arrive at command at 8:30 p.m. and am welcomed back warmly. They are highly amused that I have returned so soon: I was only expected on 14 March. So I have to put up not only with the inconvenience but also with their teasing. I try to escape this unpleasant situation as best I can, asserting that I knew of the order but still returned to allow Chief Medical Officer Lederer to attend the gas course. This does not help, because a replacement for him is already available and he could have attended the gas course anyway. Once I am there, I take over his position, but remain at division command.

Many recent political changes. Russians, terrified by tremendous German military advances, have put feelers out again, and declared themselves ready to sign a peace treaty according to German conditions. Today, negotiations in Brest have resumed. German conditions are very harsh, much harsher than before, and the treaty must be signed within three days of the meeting. Even these negotiations do not stop the German advance: they proceed and take enormous war booty and provisions. Finally, our own army has agreed to participate actively. Ukrainians have asked us to advance, with the troops of our second army—Böhm-Ermolli. We advance in the direction of the Dniester and Odessa, while the Germans have entered Kiev[18] on one side and Reval[19] on the other.

2 MARCH. Beautiful early spring weather, milder than it's been for several weeks. I'm busy taking over service (from Lederer).

3 MARCH. Lovely early spring weather with sunny blue sky continues. A coat is almost not necessary anymore. But this change in the weather has given me a cold. Peace with Russia was definitely signed today at 5:00 p.m.[20] Peace negotiations with Romania continue and should be completed soon.

4 MARCH. Weather overcast, quite cold, strong east wind. Around 2:00 p.m. I receive the alarm: "Fire at the medical column!" I go there at once—the fire is very bad, visible from far away; I am reassured when I can confirm that at least the sick barracks are intact. The officer's mess, with quarters in it for three physicians, as well as officer's kitchen, have burned down completely: similarly, the house with the commandant's quarters and officers' sickroom. In other words, the two nicest and most important buildings in the complex!

5 MARCH. Weather like yesterday, otherwise nothing special. This is my worst cold in a long time. Yesterday I handed in my request for a transfer. A difficult decision! What I would have given to—as undertaken—participate in war to its conclusion! But my wife's needs overcome my own. I confess that my selfishness has also played a role, because I live better here, relatively speaking, than in the hinterland. Provisions like we get here are impossible there—also from a service point of view, things here are going famously for me, better than in my entire military career so far. Grounds enough for me to want to hang on to my position. But my wife appears to see through me and refuses to keep on shouldering all domestic burdens and obstacles of obtaining provisions in the hinterland. She also sees that I am doing disproportionately better than she—reason enough for her to want me to come home. As much as my wife loves me—that much is obvious—I cannot assume that it is only her love that forces her to want me home so badly. Neither of us have anything with which to reproach each other, so I give in.

6 MARCH. For a change, a complete winter landscape. Snow as far as the eye can see, but not too deep. In the evening, news about peace with Romania arrives, at first only a preliminary peace treaty.

7 MARCH. Sunny, clear weather, with a small amount of frost, which allows me to travel to the medical column to inspect remnants of the fire. It is a great pity about the destroyed building: so much surface space is lost after new accommodations and mess are erected from salvageable rooms. I return at noon on foot. The condition of our horses is now so bad that wagons cannot even be obtained for travel anymore. Each day, more horses die of exhaustion, and those that are still alive are in a pitiable state. No wonder—hard fodder has not been available for months—Instead, a mixture of useless ingredients, with a terrible shortage of hay. We have very little meat to eat. Many horses have been butchered: men have been eating this for weeks. Lively trade at our customers' depot in Zaturczy:[21] mainly horses are purchased, some to be butchered at once for meat.

8 MARCH. Nice, sunny weather, deep blue sky. Light frost in the morning, which soon ends: mud becomes steadily worse. Snow has disappeared everywhere.

9 MARCH. Nice weather continues. I sit in my room like someone who is banned, and cannot go out to the men because I do not have any transportation. There is almost no office work, and little to do in the corps. I spend the day reading.

If only letters from home were not so dreary! Letters of pure misery, mainly lack of food: even here, everything is so scare that I am desperate. Today I bought five kilograms of beans that cost me twenty-five crowns—a horrendous price.

10 MARCH. Lovely, clear warm spring weather.

11 MARCH. Weather like yesterday. Our Kaiser and Kaiserin have a new son: the fifth child in this happy marriage.

12 MARCH. Nice, warm spring weather only holds until noon, then it clouds up. My wife's misery about obtaining food has never been as acute as now. Conditions in Vienna must be just awful, even with rationing. Bread is now unavailable without contacts and, even with them, of very bad quality. Meat has not been mentioned for a long time: all meat supplies are exhausted. Even here, it is now extremely difficult to obtain food. My friend Felter in Lublin is bartering twelve kilograms of flour today for fifteen packages of tobacco. If money for it were available, it would cost eight to ten crowns per kilogram! On 14 March, I am sending a man to Vienna: maybe by then I will be able to get hold of something for them. Rain in the evening.

13 MARCH. Cloudy, gloomy weather. Our troops have entered Odessa.

14 MARCH. New snow falls during the night—not so cold—but a damp cold wind is blowing. I am busy all morning dispatching my batman to Vienna with 14 kilograms of flour, 4.5 kilograms of ham, 2.2 kilograms of sausage, 5.5 kilograms of beans, 5 kilograms of peas, 1 kilogram of barley, 4 loaves of bread, 1 small box of sauerkraut. Also two pair of shoes for my wife: one new, one repaired.

15 MARCH. Overcast, cold morning, clearing by noon with sunshine. Our fourth army command is leaving its troops, en route to Odessa on its own. The quartermaster section remains, and the troops here are now those of second army command (Böhm-Ermolli), based in Lemberg. From now on, we are called "Section Wolhynia." No one is thrilled about corps command transferred to the stinking town of Vladimir Volynsky. They have established themselves so splendidly in Zaturczy and, with summer coming, would have much preferred a stay in the country.

16 MARCH. A beautiful early spring day, sunshine and lovely sunny sky—quite warm. The air is literally narcotic. If only it were not for the mud, we could go out into the fresh air and open spaces. But with the mud, and without transportation facilities, we must hunker inside, in such glorious weather. What a waste!

17 MARCH. Weather like yesterday. I travel with the father-in-law of Captain of Gendarmerie Bezala by car to Zaturczy to our control and purchasing position. We leave at 7:30 a.m. and arrive there after only an hour, returning at 11:00 a.m. A lovely journey and very interesting visit. I see a Russian posi-

Figure 5.2. Bathing facilities carefully marked for rank-and-file soldiers only. Photograph courtesy of the Leo Baeck Institute.

tion, earlier no-man's-land, full of rotted, decomposing corpses and pieces of equipment. Only bones remain. A terrible sight! The customer station is very interesting. Very little is brought here and what is, is very expensive. Mainly legumes, then soap, tea, glycerin, brass casings of ammunition, bandaging material, degreased antiseptic gauze, bread, hotcakes.

18 MARCH. Nice weather continues, already quite warm during the day, so I do not need a coat anymore. Only mud, and pitiable condition of the horses tie me to my room. The poor horses need to be spared at all costs.

19 MARCH. Weather the same; ground is starting to dry out. In the morning, I walk to field hospital 1009 to inspect the newly built baths and delousing unit. It is splendid, exceeding all expectation. Efficient, practical, and very comfortable. The builder is a sergeant—apparently "Engineer" Kraus. I return on foot as well: all together I walk four kilometers—enough already!

20 MARCH. During the afternoon, I travel by train to Vladimir Volynsky corps command, which was transferred there yesterday. I go there to offer my resignation as corps physician representative. Representation at such a distance proves impossible. I have received no tasks of importance, nothing to complete. Senior Physician Baum signs everything with "A.B."; I am not oriented on anything: throughout the entire period, all I have to do is a commendation request and a leave request to approve. There has already been a revolt, after the request was submitted on 3 March: I only received it for approval on 14 March, and

Figure 5.3. Delousing facility. Photograph courtesy of the Leo Baeck Institute.

corps command held me responsible for the delay. If command makes me responsible for such nonsense, how much more so with more important issues! And I can do nothing about it. My verbal deposition is understood by all; before I return from the trip this evening, the telegram has already arrived that I must immediate report to corps command. I won't be able to leave for there before 22 March.

21 MARCH. Nice morning, overcast in the afternoon. During the morning, I quickly inspect the baths on ¤ 243, then the baggage trains and sixty-second battalion, and order a picture frame at the fourth light infantry rifle detachment.

22 MARCH. Morning preparations for transfer to Vladimir Volynsky, leave for there at noon. I take up accommodations prepared for Chief Medical Officer Lederer: a nice, furnished room, just a little far from the office, where I will hold office hours. The office itself is near corps command, which is being housed in rooms of fourth army command. The mess is splendid and food first class, disproportionately better than a year ago, when I was also a substitute here. In France, the German Offensive has begun in full force; our artillery are participating.[22] Weather overcast, no rain yet.

23 MARCH. In the morning, I travel to Oberstabsarzt I Klasse Dr. Latzel in the Kowel[23] garrison, which is more than thirty minutes by foot from the town. I am very tired and must return without having seen him.

24 MARCH. Weather unpleasant, but temperature still mild. Very little to do, just a little office work. Unfortunately, troops are so far away that I cannot even consider a visit. Senior Physician Dr. Baum, who has been posted here, has organized his office work in a complicated way, which keeps him constantly busy. Every stupid detail must be marked multiple times in different books, so all he does all day is to exhibit, remark, and copy. Otherwise, it is very pleasant here. Provisions are not only splendid but plentiful, with a great deal of variation. Disproportionately better than under Kritek—Kanik, who is substituting for Weber as corps commandant, is a nice fellow, says little, and only leaves the mess after the last morsel has been consumed. He shows little interest in the medical service, hardly even listens to my report, and does not ask a single question.

25 MARCH. Unpleasant morning weather, then afternoon rain that changes rapidly to large, watery snowflakes that melt almost immediately. Only toward evening, with lower temperatures, does the snow start to accumulate, and by morning the whole town is snow-covered. Constant snow until noon. Temperature drops toward evening, so around 9:00 p.m. it is so cold that the snow crunches underfoot, like midwinter.

The Germans, who began their offensive against the British on 22 March between Cambrai and La Fère, are having surprising success, which increases with every passing day. On 26 March, they have already crossed over the enemy's third line of defense, the Somme, and are west of their earlier position during the famous summer Battle of the Somme in 1916. About 45,000 prisoners, 960 artillery pieces, thousands of machine guns, and an untold quantity of provisions and clothing captured; the advance continues.

27 MARCH. Still a completely winter landscape; temperature remains low today as well. Corps command now has to transfer again to Lemberg and must arrive there by 31 March. Staff Gentlemen are not thrilled about this: they would have preferred to stay here and continue playing Pasha: they don't like service in the big city anymore. It would suit me fine if they took me with them: I would like to stay there for a few days until Lederer returns.

Peace with Romania has been concluded and the most important parts already signed. Economic details are still under negotiation. When these are completed, the treaty will be signed again.

Because of a case of typhus at the division in Chmielow,[24] I go there for an inspection: travel by train at 7:14 a.m. to Podgajce[25] on the route Vladimir-Wojmica.[26] Here I await Regimental Physician First Class Herrenstadt and travel there by wagon. Inspection ends at 10:00 a.m., and we travel on by wagon to Chorostow, to division transportation command, where I take lunch, returning to Vladimir Volynsky by train at 1:20 p.m.

On the way, a serious accident could have injured or even killed me. The wagon on the way back from Chmielow was a poor sand wagon, which I had to ascend backward. Hardly was I inside it and horses harnessed, when I lost my balance and fell backward out of the wagon, with one foot still hanging inside, pulled along by the horses. Luckily, Dr. Herrenstadt and a first lieutenant helped me up. Otherwise, I would have fallen with the back of my head on the frozen ground and been dragged forward by the horses. Certain death!

29 MARCH. I travel to Lemberg with corps command; second division command is transferred to Vladimir Volynsky. I travel by train to division command early at 7:00 a.m., pack my things, make preparations for the transfer and, after lunch (Lenten food: it's Good Friday), Return by train. So I have some diversion. I make large food purchases at command, prepare a *Typenzug*—as this kind of expedition is now called—and send it on to my family in Vienna.

I'm sending them on account today fifty eggs; one fresh, good liver; and a blood sausage, which I have procured from the medical column through Sergeant Heinisch, a decent, friendly, reliable type.

It is still a wintry landscape, night temperatures still very low and sun during the day is too weak to melt the snow.

30 MARCH. Departure with the immediate staff of corps command with a separate fast train at 10:00 a.m., under lovely weather, to Lemberg. Noon rest in Sokal,[27] where a mess is prepared for us. Arrival in Lemberg at 4:00 p.m.: I travel in a very elegant car—meant for but refused by corps command—with Lieutenant Colonel Breuer, to the Hotel Europe. Our office staff are quartered in the fourth technical gymnasium. I go at once to my father; neither he nor my sister Loreia are at home, only her son Max who is studying for his state examinations. Soon thereafter, they both arrive and are astonished but overjoyed at my arrival.

31 MARCH. I have nothing work-related to do! Troops are far away, telephonic communication impossible, so conversations out of the question—communication only by telegram, and even these mostly arrived garbled. So I take care of my private interests and spend the afternoon at the Kimmelman family. Weather very nice, just somewhat cool.

1 APRIL. Changes in command are gradually become clear. Second general command—stationed in Lemberg—has been built up out of the fourth quartermaster section and tenth corps command. With this change, quite a few personnel have become superfluous and transferred to army high command. This is the case for Dr. Lederer, whose loss affects me greatly. Oberstabsarzt I Klasse Kauder remains with general command. I remain here for the moment, because the corps chief medical officer is only arriving on 3 April.

2 APRIL. Weather very nice—warmer every day. I am having a good time here, only everything is terribly expensive. We dine in the officers' mess, where we obtain a meal allowance until our own kitchen arrives. But the little that one wants extra, for example, breakfast, is exceptionally expensive. A cup of coffee with bread costs 2.20 crowns. But one pays it gladly, just for the chance of spending a few days here. I visit the Jewish theater in the evening, which I enjoy very much—excellent ensembles, performing very good pieces.

3–5 APRIL. Nothing special for my diary. Nothing to do militarily, I live in chaos of more transfers. Second army transfer is going very slowly; apparently, they cannot part from the nice quarters here, and we are currently working as stopgaps. It is very warm.

6 APRIL. I finally send my batman to Vienna with a *Typenzug*, containing: ten kilograms of bacon, four and a quarter kilograms of rolled ham, three kilograms of very good, homemade sausage from the medical column, one kilogram of (purchased) sausage, two kilograms of pressed sausage, fourteen kilograms of flour, five and a half kilograms of kasha, eight kilograms of millet, five and a half kilograms of fine barley, four kilograms of coarse barley, three kilograms of shelled peas, two hundred eggs at thirty-five heller each (it has never been so expensive as now!), one loaf of bread, three aspirin rolls, and three packets of toilet paper. Food comes, in part, from my sister-in-law Frau Seidmann. Hopefully my batman will deliver everything punctually and properly, so as not to case me any distress. I have so little confidence in him! Weather is nice and warm, even if today there are a few showers. I have already put my coat away and switched off the heating in my room.

7 APRIL. The German Offensive in France has been halted, apparently to bring up provisions, reserves, and equipment for a powerful drive on Amiens. This position is far too important for the Germans to stay put and not advance.

Thus far, they have taken 90,000 prisoners, 1,300 artillery pieces, and huge numbers of machine guns and other military equipment.

I spend days here as if on vacation—there is nothing to do. Telephone communication with the troops is impossible, and even written correspondence is very slow. It is good for a few days, but what will happen to my successor, and how he will manage, is his problem. Weather nice and warm, although it rains several times today.

8 TO 11 APRIL. I live in dolce far niente. Agenda for the corps physician has already been transferred to fourth general command—Senior Physician Baum is extremely busy, but I have nothing more to do. I await—with the approval of general command, Oberstabsarzt I Klasse Dr. Kandor—the return of Dr. Lederer so that I will be able to return to my good old second division. I spend most of the day with my father, in business dealings, or corresponding faithfully with my dear Olga. Weather is very pleasant. Trees and bushes already have green sprouts. Farmers have begun crying for rain: now and then, God allows a sprinkle.

12 APRIL. Chief Medical Officer Lederer has arrived and is extremely upset over the new arrangements. It is a very eerie feeling when one suddenly becomes literally jobless, as if the chair has been pulled out from under one. But there is nothing else for him to do but to accept the unavoidable and await orders from army high command. Maybe he will obtain a congenial position. I spend most of the day with him.

13 APRIL. I report to general command, but only wish to depart tomorrow. In the morning, I unexpectedly meet my old friend Dr. Mosler from Czostkow.[28] We are very pleased to see each other and spend almost two hours exchanging memories. We spend the evening in the Café Residenz, together with Drs. Lederer and Baum. The evening would have been very enjoyable in this small circle, but other less congenial guests arrive: Dr. Mosler's brother, the physicist Dr. Mosler from Buczacz,[29] with his wife, to whom I have an extreme aversion; an additional family; and finally Dr. Mosler's daughter Hela, a contemporary of Tinka—and her aunt, Dr. Mosler's third sister—we remain together until 11:00 p.m.

14 APRIL. Depart at 8:45 a.m. for Vladimir Volynsky, where I arrive at 2:30 p.m. Everyone greets me: Unfortunately, Lieutenant Colonel Steller has gone: six weeks ago he was commandeered to the Italian Front—at his request. My quarters are two rooms and a smaller room in a villa with a nice garden. Apart from the kitchen, the rest of the villa is occupied by an officer who is a newcomer. The furniture is passable, with a very good bed. The smaller room is adapted as an office for my medical orderly. Telephone connections and electric light.

Troops are still being shifted around and everything is so confused that it takes a while to orient myself again properly.

Since 10 April, our cigarette ration has been canceled. Instead, we receive 2.50 crowns a day and can buy as many cigarettes as this subsidy allows. If the subsidy is too small, we can always smoke the money ... But it goes to show: even I were to buy the cheapest cigarettes, we can now buy only 80 percent of the earlier brand, and even less of the more expensive brand, like Memphis. It makes little difference to me, because I have practically given up smoking and mainly use cigarettes to barter against provisions, and in place of money to pay the shoemaker, tailor, etc. But heavy smokers are very upset.

15–18 APRIL. Nothing special to report. Troops are still being transferred around. They will soon all be under division command. The nineteenth infantry division is now joined with the staff and the fourth battalion in Vladimir Volynsky, with the second in Zarecza[30], and the [?] in Ustilug.[31] Fourth light infantry moved to Rawa Ruska,[32] twenty-ninth light infantry to Sokal,[33] and 110th infantry division later to Cholm. Two *Landsturm* battalions go on ahead to dismantle the position, leaving a small formation on ¤ 243. We will have to wait, with all this transferring, to see what happens with field hospitals. Weather good, somewhat cool at times but no rain: we could really use rain at the moment.

19 APRIL. Surgeon General Cavick has arrived today to inspect the returning prisoners' camp, which causes us much concern. Inspection follows inspection: we did not expect their sudden influx and were not prepared for them. Shelters are gradually being built: they will be housed or held in quarantine in camps for fourteen days: this is essential, because they are bringing in all manner of infectious diseases, especially louse-borne typhus. There have been several typhus cases in the division lately. So far, they are isolated; hopefully no epidemic will occur. We are on summer time since 15 April: this was originally proposed for 1 April, but the Germans prefer 15 April, and we must follow suit. Everyone is used to it; life carries on as usual.

20–22 APRIL. Nothing special to report. Our branch of general command has been transferred from Kowel to Vladimir-Volynsky, with Surgeon Major Dr. Wach as chief medical officer. I visit him today: while I am there, a telegraph arrives ordering him to general command in Lemberg; Dr. Lederer will be assigned in his place. I am pleased: whether he will be is another question. It is a demotion for a corps physician when he is suddenly sent to a branch section that is nothing but a transit position, without any decisions to be made, with Major Poppi as commandant. Weather has cooled, rain at times but very little of it. Everything is becoming lovely and green, and fruit trees are starting to blossom. It is cool at night, and I have had to start heating my room again.

23 APRIL. Today I am ceremoniously awarded the Military Service Badge Third Class by our commandant for twenty-five years of active service.

24–26 APRIL. Nothing of importance—but yes, something did happen! Today's military gazette contained an order specially meant for children of married men in service: each child is granted a special subsidy, dependent on the father's rank and responsibility: The higher the rank, the lower the subsidy, which is really quite right. I receive twenty-five crowns per child per month. Because I happily have four children, starting on 1 April, I receive an extra one hundred crowns subsidy. Not too bad, even if I can do little with it. During 1917 alone, I spent the unheard of sum of twenty thousand crowns, almost exclusively for household expenses: we don't participate in anything, live modestly, and have made no particular acquisitions. Weather remains nice, summerlike and warm during the day. Fruit trees are in full bloom, and vegetation has become green early, which is important for the horses: the poor animals are so emaciated, and are dying like flies.

Today I approach our commander with a request for the fourteen days' leave due me—according to latest regulations that permit leave after four months of field service. Approval must now be given by both the division commander and the corps commandant. I receive prompt approval and hope to be able to leave on 1 May. My family is very excited indeed about this—of course I am too, no less than they.

27–28 APRIL. Nothing of importance, except for the fact that our troops are being used significantly in the hinterland, for subsidiary work: two battalions of the 110th infantry division have suddenly been ordered to Lemberg—strikes are feared during 1 to 3 May. Political conditions are miserable—each nation follows its own interests and wants to get as much as possible out of this war. This applies mostly to the Czechs, who have almost all fallen short in this war. They initially crossed over to the other side in droves, and many now fight against us on the front, turning their weapons against their own kith, kin, and fatherland. They are also the ones who treated our prisoners—those with German nationality—most barbarically. That speaks volumes—nothing else need be said. Weather still dry, not a drop of rain, so badly needed for cultivation of the fields.

29 APRIL–1 MAY. Spent in preparations for my leave, which starts on 2 May, so I depart on 1 May at 2:30 p.m. I bring as much as I can with me, managing to collect the following:

- 22 kg flour @ 6.00: translates to five bags flour/package of Memphis cigarettes = 132.00
- 2 kg candy @ 5–6 = 11.00
- 2 bars of soap @ 6 = 12.00
- 3 loaves of bread = 3.60
- 2 packets of biscuits = 7.60
- 150 eggs = 36.00
- 10 kg green beans = 55.00
- 1 goose = 30.00
- 2 kg sugar = 3.00

1 ham = 3.30
3 rolls toilet paper @ 42 heller = 1.26
70 kg potatoes: free
TOTAL 294.46 crowns

2–22 MAY. I arrive in Vienna on 2 May at 4:00 p.m.: as usual, my wife is waiting for me at the station. The poor woman still looks miserable, perhaps even worse than before. But the more so do my children surprise me with how fresh and healthy they look.

This time I have to deal with an entire series of household problems. Poor Olga is in no condition to see to everything: she encounters nothing but difficulties and must often leave without having obtained what she needs. For example, when she asked for half a liter of milk for the baby, she was rejected, despite a medical certificate, and told that the child can only obtain a quarter of a liter of milk for the entire day. Awful! My first duty is to the latter: I go directly to senior city physician Dr. Böhm, who now occupies the post of Oberstabsarzt I Klasse, and he immediately approves the requested half of a liter of milk per day. Further, he provides twenty tins of Nestlé for the little one, despite the fact that this can only be obtained after deposit of a milk ration card good for one can, that must last fourteen days. I also see to the state of everyone's shoes and obtain a small supply of leather. There are many other greater and smaller chores that require my attention, and there is no time for leisure, also no spirit to enjoy it. Additionally, my Olga has recently developed an awful boil on her left thigh, which requires lancing. For this purpose, I take her to a reserve hospital in Schmelz, where she is operated on under ether by Primarius Dr. Moskovitz. She is left with a large, deep wound that will take weeks to granulate and heal. Dr. Schwarzwald will take care of her postoperative treatment. My youngest daughter, Mary, now two years and two months old, is very dear. She is making developmental progress that is more noticeable every day. She does not call me *Onki* anymore but Papi: when she errs, I correct her at once. The food situation in Vienna is awful. At least there are now reasonable supplies of fresh, green vegetables that are not too expensive. Asparagus 4.60 per kilogram, spinach 1.30, etc.; we live mainly from the food that I have brought with me. Lack of meat is striking. One doesn't even get the prescribed few ounces per person per week regularly anymore and must depend on fowl, which is horrendously expensive (twenty-two crowns per kilogram).

My Miki is making wonderful progress in her studies. She is a splendid girl, strong, obedient, and loving. I can't even speak about my two eldest: they hang on to me with love that moves me more than I can say.

19 MAY. Unfortunately, I must think of going back again. My family are preparing themselves as well and are all very sad. My Olga is inconsolable and cannot understand why my request to be transferred to the hinterland, after nearly four years in the field, has been rejected.

22 MAY. Olga, Ega, and Mikerl accompany me to the station. I leave at 2:30 p.m. A very humid day, and the train is so jam-packed that I have to spend the entire afternoon and all night in a sitting position. My father awaits me in Lemberg early: after spending about an hour with him, I travel farther and arrive in Vladimir Volynsky at 2:30 p.m. of 23 May.

24 MAY. Little has changed here: our artillery has been withdrawn to the southwest theater. Command goes with them, as well as General von Rosenzweig. I am especially sorry to see him go: he arrived at division at the same time I did; maybe that is why we got on so well together. We also often shared quarters together on marches. He is an exceptionally calm, kindly, charming man with a noble attitude; that cannot be said about many in our command.

I inspect all hospitals in the Kowel garrison accompanied by the commandant: there are four hospitals there, including one for internal medicine one for surgery under command of staff surgeon Marconi, whom I know well from Trieste, one hospital for epidemic infectious diseases and one for eyes, ears, etc. It is interesting to see what can be made out of ordinary garrisons: very comfortable, well equipped, everything necessary for good hospital hygiene. The head is Chief Garrison Physician Dr. Latzel.

25–31 MAY. Provisions problems are getting worse and worse, even for the army in the field. Men get almost no bread and little of everything else. As a result, complaints are brewing among troops and cases of indiscipline—let us speak honestly, mutiny—are increasing, when the men refuse to follow orders. We are entering dangerous times: these two months between now and the new fall harvest will be most difficult of all.

Weather generally good. After more than six weeks drought, it finally rains: rain lasts for three days and does the agriculture good. Nice days follow, but morning and evening temperatures remain cool, and young shoots freeze at night.

Because there are no prospects for our division to leave in the foreseeable future, I have decided to move my family here. My wife, the two smaller children (Miki and Mary), together with the cook who will function here as a nanny. My two older daughters, Tinka and Ega, will be invited to my sister-in-law Frau Seidmann in the country: they are glad to go there. My wife is very happy, and I am busy with preparations. In this way, they avoid the enormous problems of obtaining food in Vienna, at least until the new harvest.

Unfortunately, they are coming at a time when, even here, we have problems obtaining sufficient food—but our food is still good and sufficient. I will of course obtain food from the mess for my family, against paying double board—ten crowns per person daily. In such a way, we can show that they are being fed from private supplies that we buy ourselves, and not from government-run sources. This bending of the regulations does not come cheap.

1–2 JUNE. The weather has completely changed: cold and windy, with storms and rain. It is so uncomfortable in our quarters that they must be heated again, and I must install a double window. My best-laid plans to bring the family here have encountered difficulties. First, branch command, in the person of Lieutenant Colonel Poppi, has turned down the travel request for our housemaid. All requests and proposals, also by my old patron Dr. Lederer, are unsuccessful. Also, news arrives that my sister-in-law Frau Seidmann is gravely ill with uremia. So we all stay where we are!

Because of all these problems, I write to my wife to cancel the plans to come to Wolhynia, instead to take up the original plan for a summer residence in Hanna, or else find another summer nest in Austria.

3 JUNE. I rethink the matter overnight and write to Olga that perhaps it might still be possible to come here with all four children, without the servant. The two older daughters could take turns looking after Mary; mess provisions for three people would come to a total of 909 crowns. I suggest this to my wife and put in a travel application for the two older daughters to obtain cheaper military train fares for them.

At 8:00 a.m., I travel with the commandant to inspect returning prisoners in the Kowel and Ulan barracks. Very interesting. At the moment, there are five thousand men there. One sees how much work and organization is necessary, to bring order to and feed this mass of different peoples—no wonder it did not work at first, thousands suddenly streaming back, without authorities expecting or being ready for them all. How could we reckon with the fact that Russia would suddenly open its doors and let all their prisoners out, saying, "You are now all free and can go where you want"?[34]

The tour takes two hours. A Hungarian—a true Magyar—shows us how he saved his regimental banner from being taken by the enemy. He has carried it around with him for three years and hidden it under sometimes difficult conditions so that he can finally bring it home.

4–5 JUNE. I have travel approval for all four children. Cool weather continues, rain with hail at times. Temperature 7.5 °C. I have had to heat my room for the last three days. Today I send my batman to Vienna with:

    11.5 kg bacon @ 20 = 230
    5 kg beans @ 4 = 20
    7.5 kg kasha @ 4 = 30
    5 kg rice @ 17 = 85
    2.5 kg coarse rice @ 80 h = 7
    4 kg sausage
    1 kg butter = 15
    2 kg semolina @ 1.60 = 3.20
    2 kg curd @ 2.50 = 5
    310 eggs @ 20 h = 62
    200 cigarettes @ 8 = 16
    TOTAL: 443.20 [crowns]

6–10 JUNE. Nothing of importance

11 JUNE. After so many cold days and colder nights, even with frost, finally warm summer weather has arrived: the question is for how long. Crop damage by frost has been reported from many regions of Hungary.

12 JUNE. Nice warm weather continues. I travel by car with Lieutenant Colonel Schulz at 7:00 a.m. to the storm battalion in Falemiczy,[35] where I remain until 11:00 a.m. Unfortunately, troops are now so scattered and dislocated that I can rarely visit them. It would be better if I could do this more often, because younger doctors need strict control, at least initially.

13–30 JUNE. Our Italian offensive begins on 15 June simultaneously on the Piave and in the mountains.[36] Surprisingly successful—thirty thousand troops captured in the first attack. Our troops reach the west bank of the river, penetrating into the enemy's third defense line. Unfortunately, we are not in a position to exploit this breakthrough, and Italian resistance becomes ever stronger, especially in Montello. Weather is also extremely unfavorable, with rain and storms. The level of the Piave keeps rising, crossings are swept away, and availability of additional provisions and ammunition becomes increasingly problematic. The Italians take advantage of this and attack our bridgehead on the west bank with greater and greater force, while we cannot send any reinforcements to the divisions that are already there. Heavy fighting lasts until 21 June, when the order to retreat is given, and we must give up all the territory that we have gained. We retreat to our original positions with heavy losses. We do take 50,000 prisoners, but the Italians take 12,000 of our men, and our killed, missing and wounded comprise 70,000 men. The Italians have lost (prisoners included) about 150,000 men. Our offensive ends on a very sad note!

In the meantime, I prepare to welcome my family, who are coming here for the summer to relax as best they can, because conditions in Vienna are now appalling. The bread ration has been cut in half to quarter of a loaf per person per week, no more; 1.2 kilograms of meat every ten days. My replenishments from here become ever-more difficult, so life there is unbearable; we decide that the family must all come here.

Diary by Olga, Bardach's wife

After all preparations for the trip have been made (new permits, passports, etc.) and after my dear acquaintances have painted terrifying pictures of the dangers to which my children and I will be exposed in enemy territory, I leave Vienna with my four children. My brother Richard accompanies me to the station. Because of his connections to the railway personnel, we are able to get into the train two hours before departure through a back door of a train waiting to leave. Thus, we can comfortably arrange our five seats without pushing and shoving. Traveling at the moment is a real torment. When doors are finally opened for all, there is endless pushing, shoving, and cursing: I am happy that my children have been spared this misery! We travel second class, but by 1918 coaches are in such terrible condition that leather covers are torn and dirty, papers lie everywhere, a dreary picture of filth and neglect. At the moment this does not concern us, and the children are all in a carefree, happy mood, because they can spend the whole vacation with their father. I would otherwise also be very happy, but (in an adult's life there is always a "but") I have many worries, and perhaps after these four dreadful years I don't have the strength to enjoy anything anymore. I am concerned that all our travel documents and passports are in order, and breathe easier when the inspector does not query anything. On this trip, papers must be shown continuously: the carriage door is flung open, and inspectors keep coming, even at night. After twenty-one hours' train journey, at 8:00 a.m. on 18 June, we arrive in Lemberg, washed out, tired, and dusty. My father-in-law is waiting for us at the station: he is enormously happy to see the children, who want more than anything else to sleep in a clean bed where they can stretch out properly. I leave our baggage at the station (we have three coupé suitcases) and just take a hand case with the necessities for the day in Lemberg. We get onto a very dirty tram and travel to my father-in-law's house, which he shares with his eldest daughter, my sister-in-law. We are greeted in the friendliest possible way: my sister-in-law Loreia is a very intelligent woman and always very nice to us. My father-in-law is one of the most mentally alert people I know and belongs to the class of Jew for whom I have nothing but greatest respect and appreciation. He is a patriarchal, dignified, honest, selfless man—the kind of person who is becoming very rare in all nations of the world, despite study, science, and cultural progress. We are given a hot breakfast and then stretch out comfortably and catch up on our sleep. I do not sleep for long but sneak into the kitchen to have a nice chat with my sister-in-law, helping her with lunch preparation. My father-in-law is in the photography store, where he substitutes for his absent grandson, who owns it. I do not have much happy news for my sister-in-law, but—after I have turned my back on the miserable, worry-filled life in Vienna and am now looking forward to better things—happiness gains the upper hand and I feel very welcome in the house of my husband's family.

Bernhard again

My family leave Vienna the morning of 17 June, arriving in Lemberg at my father's early the next morning. They rest up there. On the same day, I travel to Lemberg, to pick them up, arriving next day. They feel at home here, like everything, and are much enthused with the food in our mess. So much, so excellently prepared—they have not eaten like this for ages. It's a pure coincidence that provisions are so plentiful and good here: Jews and farmers from the entire area bring us food, just like the time we changed army command. Our cook, Winiary, is pleased to take everything—against payment of course, just as I pay for my family. They are looking visibly better; the children already looked good when they arrived, but my Olga looked awful: even she is now looking better.

Unfortunately, this happiness doesn't last long. On 28 June, the order comes to move the entire division command to Lemberg. Olga is inconsolable. I could take them all with me to Lemberg, but where would they live? Even if I could find somewhere, where could we find a garden, so necessary for the children at this stage of their young lives? There is nothing for them in the city during high summer. For the moment, we all remain together here and enjoy the clean air and better food. If only we would remain in Lemberg. But that is not at all sure—we could easily be ordered to Italy or somewhere else in the hinterland where we are still fighting. Workers are restless, and soldiers' mutinies the order of the day. Masses of returning prisoners bring Bolshevik tendencies with which they infect our brave soldiers. These mutinies extend right up to the front. We have recently had an unpleasant case in our unit. Shackling and "binding" have had to be reintroduced, because they are necessary to keep soldiers in line. It happened that a company commander ordered this punishment; other soldiers objected and demanded him to be unbound. When the commander refused, a spokesman said to his comrades, "Bring the rifles." They didn't get their way, were overpowered, and sixty-two men were immediately put under martial law. Three men were sentenced to be shot, and the rest received long prison sentences. Executions were carried out immediately.

In sixth infantry regiment in Neusatz,[37] things were even worse: many soldiers who had just returned home demanded leave; because it wasn't granted to them that very month, they boxed the colonel's ears and threatened him with shooting. Unfortunately, the colonel begged them for mercy on his knees, which inflamed them even more. They did the same with fifteen other officers and could only be subdued by a large military contingent. They won't escape their just desserts, but it's another sign of the deep inner corrosion.

Weather changeable, mostly bad, a lot of wind, overcast skies, storms, a lot of rain. Sun shines now and then but not with the strength and warmth that it should this time of year. Vegetation in this part of Wolhynia has correspondingly not developed as usual.

1–16 JULY. The Lemberg plan has fallen away, replaced by incomparably worse news: what I said, and feared most, has occurred—Italy! The order has come: "The division must depart for the southwestern theater of operations as quickly as possible." A few say they are pleased about this because they want to be seen as heroes, but I am convinced that, in their hearts, they feel just like I do. No wonder! After four years of uninterrupted war service, a man feels so tired of war that he has no more strength for fresh fighting. Especially, for me, whose family is so important! The poor creatures have just arrived here to rest a bit, and now they have to go back to Vienna, where there is practically nothing left to eat!

During the next several days, things calm down somewhat, and we have definitely decided that my wife and family must remain here (for the moment). I will make sure about housing, and they will draw rations from the branch of army command. They can remain here through end of August.

The division is busy getting ready to march out on 10 July. The medical column and field hospital have already left, and command will follow on 17 July. The commandant himself gave me the idea to leave my family here. He returned from vacation on 5 July, oriented himself, and after only two days sent Captain Müller for his family, who arrived on 10 July.

Weather has become quite hot the past several days; we sweat a lot and are tired. How will it be in Italy? I think about this, and shudder.

The old faithfuls of our division are getting fewer and fewer. Our Junior Logistics Officer Pelikan left us on 1 July: he has been transferred to a division on the Italian front, not realizing that we would follow him so quickly. His successor has not yet arrived, and he is being substituted at the moment by Junior logistics officer Klech—not for long, because he also suddenly left on 7 July and has not returned. Because his revolver could not be found, we suspected that he committed suicide: this proved to be the case. His body was found in a little wood on 13 July. The cause appears to have been the death of his cousin from tuberculosis about three weeks ago. It really wasn't his cousin as he gave out, but his dear bride. We buried him on 14 July.

I am having great difficulty looking for a place for my family to live, mainly because I would prefer them to be near the mess. Finally, on 16 July we find accommodation in 21 Ustilugstrasse with an orthodox Jewish family, Adjacent to the mess no. 1 of the branch of fourth general command, where they will perhaps eat better than in mess no. 2.

17 JULY. Preparation of our command to march off. We arrive at the railway station at 7:30 a.m. even though we only depart at 10:45 a.m. My children arrive at the station at 9:00 a.m. to say goodbye and are pleased—as I am—that the train hasn't left yet. They stay with me until the train departs. The journey is very slow: the train stops in Rawa Ruska for about three hours, apparently because of a machine defect, and we only arrive in Lemberg next day.

18 JULY. At 5:30 a.m., departure for Stryj[38] at 6:45 a.m., arrival at noon. Arrival in Lawoczne[39] at 8:15 p.m.

19 JULY. Arrivals: Szatoralja lejhely, 8:15 a.m.; Miskolez, 1:20 p.m.; Hatvan 10:00 p.m.,[40]

20 JULY. Arrival in Budapest at 8:00 a.m. and in Kelenfeld[41] at 9:45 a.m. Arrivals at: Hercegholom, noon; Komarom, 3:30 p.m.; Gyor, 6:00 p.m.; Papa, 10:30 p.m.[42]

21 JULY. Arrivals: Szombathely, 4:00 a.m., Kormend, 6:00 a.m.; Szentgothard, 11:00 a.m. (rain); Fehring, noon; Graz, 10:00 p.m.[43]

22 JULY. Arrivals: Marburg, 3:30 a.m.; Pragerhof, 5:45 a.m.; Steinbrück, noon; Laibach, 7:00 p.m. (overcast).[44]

23 JULY. Arrivals: Opcina, 6:00 a.m.; Nabresina, 7:00 a.m.; Monfalcone, 9:45 a.m.[45]

Hardly have we arrived when one of our heavy artillery pieces fires off a salvo. Apparently greeting defensive fire! Ferocious foretaste! It seems that these explosions represent mine blasts from our side. Monfalcone itself is completely destroyed. Terrible devastation: not a single building is undamaged, no stone unturned. Arrival in Cevignano 4:30 p.m.; arrival in Portogruaro 8:30 p.m.

Italian Front

24 JULY. We arrived in Portogruaro last night at 8:30 p.m., decamping at once: by the time we get to our quarters with our baggage, it is 1:00 a.m. I organize my own quarters today. I am given three rooms in a palazzo: very comfortable, but my quarters are on the second floor, and climbing stairs has become difficult. Heat and flies are going to be serious problems. We will stay here three weeks before taking our positions. We now belong to the twenty-third corps of the Isonzo Army under command of Commander Ciecsic, who is at the moment on vacation. Commander Boroević is in charge of group command. I will look up Oberstabsarzt 1 Klasse Heiss, and Surgeon General Thoman during the next few days.

The area itself is large and typically Italian: Narrow, dirty little alleys crisscrossed by canals that reach right up to the houses and remind one of Venice. We are about thirty kilometers from the front; from time to time, we hear dull sounds of shooting, but the area itself is spared, at least for the moment. The air is full of pilots dropping bombs.

The medical column and field hospital are both in our area. The first is not established yet; the second is badly accommodated.

25 JULY. I am busy setting up my home and office. The heat is unbearable: 28 °C in the shade.

26 JULY. At 7:30 a.m. I travel by car to corps commands in San Sebastiano with Lieutenant Colonel Schütz, Captain Erben, and First Lieutenant Zorn. A pleasant trip. The road is splendid, as if made for an automobile, only very dusty. The corps physician gives me all necessary information; I also visit the Chief of the General Staff Colonel Richtermoc—an old regimental comrade, he recognizes me at once and is very friendly. While we are still there, a violent storm breaks, changing over to heavy rain, which accompanies us all the way back. We arrive home at noon.

27 JULY. Heavy rain today, clearing later; the air has cooled down significantly. Here too I meet an old acquaintance, District Commandant Colonel Andrealta, from the Trieste garrison hospital. I use this connection to arrange good quarters for our medical column—in nice rooms that tenth medical corps had refused us before. He immediately put these rooms at my disposal; the medical column is again comfortably accommodated.

28 JULY. Temperature has cooled down significantly—only 22 °C in my room. The twenty-first light infantry battalion has been added to the division.

29 JULY. Nothing special today either. Temperature still acceptable.

30 JULY. At 8:00 a.m. I travel to the twenty-first light infantry battalion in Malcantone, which has been without any physician, medical orderly, or ensign for several weeks after a very long march from Tonale. They have a strikingly large number of sick. Yesterday, I send a physician and medical ensign there; today I inspect the entire battalion, returning around noon. Things are not too bad now, but they do lack medical treatment. Today warmer, but still bearable.

31 JULY. Professor Cori gives an interesting lecture on malaria—command's main health problem, because we are in a malarial zone. Conditions are going to deteriorate even further, as soon as we arrive at our positions on the Piave. Higher temperatures again: 25 °C in the shade.

1–5 AUGUST. In general, nothing new. Officers and men are acclimatizing very slowly, with many cases of fever, as well as dysentery—up until now seventeen cases, mainly with the dislocated fortieth infantry. We believe the fault to lie in the Lemene River flowing through the area. All town canals flow into this river and toilets are washed into it. Not only do people bathe in the river, but they also do their washing—probably including eating utensils—in it. Corrective actions have been taken.

On 3 August, I inspect the second and third battalions of the fortieth infantry regiment, which is now in Portovecchio. I travel there with the bacteriologist Regimental Physician First Class Kaunitz.

4 AUGUST. I inspect battalion 1/40, now located here.

Things are not going well for the Germans on the Marne. They have had to retreat to the Soissons-Rheims line, thereby giving up three-quarters of the territory gained during the past offensive. Their fate on the Marne is the same as ours on the Piave.

6 AUGUST. At 4:00 p.m., inspection of the fourth light infantry battalion in La Sega, where some cases of dysentery have occurred, in bacteriologist Dr. Kaunitz's regiment. On the way back, we inspect the horses in second replacement section, also because of dysentery.

7–8 AUGUST. Nothing special. Weather has cooled down significantly, after a violent storm during the nights of 6–7 August. It rains today as well, until noon. Twelfth corps command has arrived, but no troops have yet been transferred into it.

9 AUGUST. At 2:00 a.m. we greet the Italians for the first time since we arrived here. The detonation wakes me up—I count four violent explosions and immediately think of aerial bombs. but am not hit, so I try to go back to sleep. In the morning, I find out that they have hit the railway station, but only the station to treat the sick (and wounded, killing two men—one sergeant and one infantryman—and wounding five).

During the morning, I inspect the bakery, also because a case of dysentery, and on the way back, also the place where the bomb attack took place. A terrible sight, but I am amazed that so little damage really occurred. A bomb also fell on the street, damaging the water mains, but damage is repaired during the morning.

The bakery is of Italian construction, beautifully and hygienically built, with a douche for the men and hot and cold running water, below each trough an outlet tap. This bakery was apparently built especially for the Isonzo Front.

During the morning, Kaiser Karl arrives at army command in St. Vito.[46] A deputation of all the highest-ranking commanders is sent.

Today's military gazette no. 133 from 31 August 1918 finally brings word of the swords for my Signum Laudis—it has taken long enough. Now my array of decorations is complete. At the same time, these are also awarded to Captain Zorn and First Lieutenants Sandig and Filar: Filar has long been dead from a florid laryngeal infection. He was a good comrade—a refined Pole, something that cannot be said of all his countrymen. Morning weather very nice, afternoon overcast and very humid.

10 AUGUST. Our commander returns after ten days' leave. After Lieutenant Colonel Heller speaks to him about the shame and humiliation inflicted on me, we have a discussion, in which he quasi-apologizes, in his typical stupid way. Forget it! My decision remains as it was! Now, away from the division.

11 AUGUST. At 4:00 a.m. I travel by train to St. Vito, the seat of army command: the trip takes an hour. Soon after 8:00 a.m., I report to the office of the chief medical officer, where I must wait until 9:00 a.m. for Surgeon General Dr. Thoman. During the ensuing time, I orient myself with the rear echelon and confirm its unfortunate small size. Because it intersects with the border, its position is undesirable, belonging to the coastal area: Trieste, Fiume, and Abbazia-Volosca.[47] The chief is extremely friendly, in a way that I do not expect from my medical superiors. He remains friendly even after I tell him how I feel and after he expressly asks me where I really want to go. Naturally, my response is Trieste. This does not bother him. Just the contrary: he is impressed that I know the town so well, tells me that I should apply for the posting, and hopes that the application will be successful. I return from the trip very satisfied. Weather nice, but increasing heat.

12 AUGUST. My main task today is composition of my request and handing it over to command. It will only be sent tomorrow morning.

13 AUGUST. Nothing significant. Our commandant has endorsed my application.

14 AUGUST. Surgeon General Thoman arrives here early in the morning, on his way to visit a malarial area. When we meet, his first question is whether I have handed in my application yet, because he wants to see to it as soon as possible. Around 10:00 a.m., I travel with the station bacteriologist to the 110th infantry battalion, arrive back at 12:30 p.m. Dysentery cases occupy much of my time. I have never before experienced so bad an epidemic—already sixty-six confirmed cases in fourteen days. Morning inspection of the telephone section, where three dysentery cases have occurred. Precautions taken. Weather remains fair and hot.

15 AUGUST. Morning inspection of the telephone section, in which three cases of dysentery have already occurred. Precautions are taken. Good weather continues—very warm.

16 AUGUST. Morning conference with Senior Physician Kantorek from the fortieth infantry regiment, who has returned from leave.

17 AUGUST. The Emperor's birthday! At 10:00 a.m. a high mass in the local cathedral. Festive luncheon; our commander proposes a very tired-sounding toast, whose content is simply that our Emperor should live a long life so that he can experience peace as well!

After the opulent luncheon, there is dinner with salted meat, kraut, and dumplings. Can you imagine? I of course did not touch it, rather brought it for my batman, so he also knows that today is the Emperor's birthday.

18 AUGUST. Morning conference with Regimental Physician First Class Janceck from the ninety-fifth infantry regiment, who joined our regiment yesterday. Who knows whether he will be named my successor if my application is successful? The regiment is accommodated in Portogruaro.

19–20 AUGUST. Nothing special. Very warm. Slight cooling off by evening. A severe plague of mosquitos toward evening, which is very worrying, because we do not know whether they include infected Anopheles.[48] The number of malaria cases increases continuously, although they are far fewer than those in the malarial zone south of Portogruaro. From this zone, an average of up to two hundred men with malaria per day leave the area from our corps alone, which consists of five divisions.

During the evening the new corps commandant of twenty-second corps—Kletterer—with his staff, are invited to us for supper.

21 AUGUST. Afternoon very hot—even worse for me because I have to be outside a great deal. During the morning I visit Dr. Kaunitz in the bacteriology laboratory. He works in a palazzo that is worth a visit. At 4:00 p.m. we both travel by train to the twenty-first and fourth light cavalry regiments, because there are still dysentery cases in both regiments. It's 6:00 p.m. by the time we return: I really feel how oppressively hot it has been today.

22 AUGUST. Heat still oppressive, room temperature already 26 °C. Morning inspection of medical column, afternoon conference with Surgeon Major Konopka and a newly arrived physician. Salary request for the former drafted. With this, I begin to prepare for my transfer, although there is no trace of its approval.

23–25 AUGUST. A great deal of work for us at the moment. The dysentery outbreak is getting continually worse: we already have 120 cases. Malaria cases are also increasing sharply, although we are not in the malaria zone. Anopheles mosquitos do not keep to lines drawn on a map. Heat gets worse and worse, and our rations are becoming concomitantly smaller. Even officers are now allowed only two hundred grams of meat per day: no more, even from our own funds.

Aerial visits from the Italians over Portogruaro are increasing, especially at night because of full moon. For the moment, they have not been so rude as to burden us with bombs, the more so do our antiaircraft batteries shoot at them. In any event, our sleep is disturbed. I can hardly expect approval of my request under these circumstances.

Days pass quickly with conferences, writing—including one or two private letters. No time to read, I can only glance though the newspaper.

26–27 AUGUST. A great deal of work, including paperwork—mainly caused by the epidemics of dysentery and malaria. The first does not lessen at all, and the second increases all the time. Our commandant is suffering from intestinal catarrh: we hope of course that this will not become dysentery. Interestingly, he now only allows me to treat him. Apparently, he wants to compensate for his broken promise to me, when his daughter became ill.

On 26 August, I travel to Cordovado with Senior Physician Friedecker; after I hear that provisions—especially rice and grappa—might be obtainable there for private purposes, I deny myself the grappa—let the men have it. But I do want some of the rice. Commandant Colonel Vogelhuber, a grim old man, is in a bad mood and only allows me one kilogram of of rice, which I laughingly reject, whereupon he approves the obligatory two kilograms that he gives almost everybody, for eight crowns. With this, I leave.

On 27 August, Captain Pistelka passes through on his way on vacation; he belongs to the same corps and is our neighbor: an old and dear companion of second division. I do not spend much time with him, except during dinner. From 26 to 27 August, severe storms during the night cool air significantly.

28 AUGUST. At 9:00 a.m. I travel off by car, accompanied by Professor Cori, the local malaria researcher, and Colonel Heller, who comes with us just out of curiosity. We are going to the twenty-first light artillery, who have had thirteen malaria cases recently. It is interesting to see how he searches out the mosquito breeding places in puddles. He takes all necessary sanitary precautions, the section (machine gun company) are all given quinine, and they obtain material to build nets for doors and windows, so hopefully this outbreak will soon be controlled.

29 AUGUST. Morning conference with Dr. Kaunitz. Weather good, significant cooling down.

30–31 AUGUST. Nothing significant. The dysentery epidemic seems to have lessened, but by contrast, the number of malaria cases has significantly increased. Until today, 150 cases of dysentery have occurred, which have not been bacteriologically proven but have been properly clinically diagnosed, so must be called dysentery. Patients are severely ill and have to be evacuated. Including today, we have seen sixty-one cases of malaria—a large number, given the fact that we are not in a malarial zone.

1 SEPTEMBER. An interesting meeting this morning with Captain (now Colonel) Pollak—an old and dear regimental comrade from the seventy-ninth infantry division. He was captain, and I, the youngest regimental physician—now we are both old and gray, he naturally more than I. Otherwise, he has not changed at all: a sly fox, as always. We revel in each other's company, because we are very close friends. He is a senior officer in our neighboring division. Interestingly, we spoke about him just yesterday at table, because our commandant also knows him well.

2 SEPTEMBER. Weather has cooled down significantly, with rain at times today. Our division will shortly be transferred to the front, to relieve the fifty-seventh division on their southern flank on the Piave. A very unpleasant area, the epicenter of the malarial zone. We leave the domain of twenty-third corps and will now be part of the twenty-second, commandant Kletterer, chief of staff Lieutenant Colonel Rausch. Oberstabsarzt I Klasse Hoffmann who has already been transferred and is to be replaced by Oberstabsarzt I Klasse Feyertag, who has not yet arrived.

3 SEPTEMBER. Extensive preparations for transferring the division. Initially *one* brigade (fortieth and 110th infantry regiments) will be placed in position; the other brigade remains here. There is a great deal to do regarding malaria prophylaxis.

4 SEPTEMBER. Large expedition of my medical orderly, Demkowicz, via Vienna to Vladimir Volynsky to bring my family back to Vienna on 10 September. He takes with him twenty-four kilograms of flour at three crowns; six meters of farmer's fabric at fifty crowns; ten meters of calico for washing at eighty-five crowns; four loaves of bread.

He leaves everything with our neighbors in Vienna and travels to Vladimir Volynsky with empty coffers. Hopefully he will bring everything safely to Vienna: then at least a part of the flour is secure. I buy eighty kilograms of flour at three crowns from the ninety-fifth, who have just returned from Ukraine and bought a great deal of provisions, including flour, with them. I am trying to mail this to Vienna in ten-kilogram packages. I am very anxious about this expedition.

5 SEPTEMBER. At 7:30 a.m. I travel by car with Surgeon Major Konopka, Captain Müller to our new position in Rotta; from there to the future position of our sanitary train medical column in Boccafossa. On the way back, I meet up with the new corps physician of the twenty-second, Oberarzt I Klasse Dr. Hoffmann, in Torre di Mosto. The outstanding work in this column made it a very interesting trip. Yesterday there were more than seven hundred malaria cases; every day two hundred more cases come in, and three hundred are evacuated out. Return around 2:15 p.m.

Preparations for departure—making sure that I have enough safeguards against malaria—take up a lot of my time: enough quinine, mosquito netting to protect hands and for sleeping. The following data show the quantities necessary for everything: although only one brigade is going into the malarial zone, for about 8,000 men, we still need 250,000 quinine pastilles for twenty days!

6 SEPTEMBER. The fortieth infantry regiment is already in their positions.

7 SEPTEMBER. The 110th infantry regiment marches into the position on the ninety-fifth infantry regiment, which is transferred to Sumaga.[49]

8 SEPTEMBER. The sanitary train marches to Boccafossa. Weather generally nice, still very warm, rain only at times with storms, which cause violent downpours, the likes of which we never see at home.

9 SEPTEMBER. Much packing and preparations for transfer of command, whose first squad is already departing for Rotta. We follow early tomorrow morning.

10 SEPTEMBER. Transfer of command to Rotta, replacing the fifty-seventh division. After packing my things onto a field hospital wagon and sending them off posthaste with my batman, I travel by car with Lieutenant Colonel Heller and Captain Schufler at 8:00 a.m. At 9:00 a.m. we arrive at corps command in Torre di Mosso. Here finally I can breakfast, courtesy of Dr. Hoffmann: Nice buttered bread with excellent coffee. From there it is five minutes to Rotta. Another miserable place to stay, in complete contrast to Portogruaro. However, I am well accommodated in the command building. The room is empty, so it is good that I brought a few things with me from Portogruaro: an excellent bed, two chairs, a washbasin, a table, etc. I commandeer a few extra things and install myself comfortably. The same picture of war here: barrage balloons in the air, squadrons of fliers, etc. Our commandant returns during the night from Vienna—it looks as if his daughter is not doing well at all: he is depressed, and it looks bad—probably tuberculosis.

My family start their journey home today—hopefully their trip from Vladimir Volynsky will be smooth and problem-free.

11 SEPTEMBER. The twenty-ninth light artillery are again in our purview and are staying in Portovecchio for the moment. Weather cool and overcast, clearing only during the afternoon. Big alarm toward evening. The Italians

seem to have destroyed one of our pickets. It's being kept secret at the moment, just whispered about.

12 SEPTEMBER. Early at 9:00 a.m., inspection of second medical column in Boccafossa. There is a very high incidence of malaria there; doctors do not know what to do anymore: the daily number of sick stands at about seven hundred. In addition, Assistant Physician Dr. Lamberg became ill in March and had to be evacuated to hospital in Stino;[50] Oberstabsarzt I Klasse Friedecker is attending a gas course, returning on 17 September. Meanwhile, his absence is very much felt. I return at 12:30 p.m.

At noon, the new Chief Medical Officer Feiertag arrives: the third since we have been here. He has been in the War Ministry for years, but has been hospital commandant in Graz for the last few months, and this is his first time at the front. So, in sum, ignorant and inexperienced as a newborn babe, although friendly and forthcoming. He wants to look at the second medical column, so I have to take him there. For the moment he just wants to orient himself, not change anything. By the time we return, it's 7:00 p.m.

News about the capture of our picket is confirmed. A disgrace both for the fortieth regiment and for division command. On a bright, clear day, a small Italian patrol crosses the river, despite it being about three hundred meters wide: they attack our watch post, whose soldiers must have been asleep; otherwise this would have been impossible. They awaken our men by boxing their ears, and take one lieutenant and eleven men captive in their boat, after which they cross over themselves.

13 SEPTEMBER. I am very depressed by news from Olga. They are still sitting in Vladimir Volynsky, waiting in vain for their liquidation money: it will take time for them to find money from another source. My medical orderly, Demkowicz, whom I sent to help them with resettlement on 4 September, is still not there on 9 September. Additionally, he takes so many provisions with him, to lay aside in Vienna, that he should have written to me what happened. I have not heard a word from him; my impatience grows by the day.

14 SEPTEMBER. The matter of my children's inheritance, after the death of their Uncle Bernhard Kimmelman, is in progress. Today I received the first statement about it from their notary requesting that I send him my written power of attorney. I must go to Portogruaro to our judge advocate's office to get this done. Departure from here at 4:00 p.m.: the issue is easily seen to, I return by train at 9:00 p.m. Unfortunately, the train is delayed one and a half hours, so I arrive in Stino at 11:30 p.m. instead of 10:00 p.m. and have to travel six kilometers by wagon, so I only get to bed around midnight.

15 SEPTEMBER. Italian activity in the air becomes greater; there is talk of an approaching Italian offensive. They drop bombs in various places, and dogfights are taking place. Even Rotta is hit now and then by pieces of flying metal, no damage so far. From tomorrow at 2:00 a.m. wintertime begins. All clocks one hour back. Weather remains good.

16 SEPTEMBER. Yom Kippur! I fast easily until dinner. No opportunity for praying. On the contrary, today I must travel with Lieutenant Colonel Schütz, first to the medical column in Boccafossa and from there to smaller formations like the electric company; I visit a splendid electric pump, which emits thirty thousand volts. The electricity central is in the Venetian Alps, drawing from the many pumps whose job it is to hinder floods in the Piave area. On the other hand, these pumps allow us, in an emergency, to flood the area, providing an insuperable obstacle for the enemy. We carry on by car farther to the south. We would have had to cross only one ford to reach the sea. Unfortunately, the ford is too weak to support weight of a car, so we have to turn back and take another way, returning around noon. A lovely trip in beautiful summer weather.

17 SEPTEMBER. I remain at home today to see to paperwork: there is more than enough of that! I request fourteen days' leave, which is approved. However, at the last minute, Captain Müller, the office director, creates difficulties: the request must go up to corps, exactly according to the rules.

18 SEPTEMBER. I travel to corps at 10:00 a.m., requesting the aide to see to my request as rapidly as he can: he promises to do so. I visit the corps physician, still very friendly. Corps command is near, scarcely ten minutes by wagon, in Torre di Mosto. Return at noon.

19 SEPTEMBER. I must visit corps again—this time to request butter from the logistics officer for my vacation: he promises to send me one kilogram tomorrow, and does so.

20 SEPTEMBER. Great deal of packing, no time to rest. The hour of departure approaches—I confirm a car for noon to travel to the railway station in Motta di Livenza, which is thirty kilometers away. Just before my departure, an intermezzo occurs: Our valiant commandant will not give his car up, so I have to postpone my trip a day, because I cannot get to the train in time by wagon today: it leaves at 1:40 p.m.! Later, however, he deigns to appear in my room and magnanimously allows me, by way of exception, to use the car. I finally begin my trip, heavily laden with provisions: forty kilograms of flour, the balance of the one hundred kilograms that I already bought; fifteen kilograms of rice; five kilograms of beans; five kilograms of lentils; five kilograms of barley; one kilogram of butter; one jar of cucumbers, one of marmalade (cornelian cherry); one bottle of raspberry juice; four loaves of bread; eighty decagrams of soap; seven meters of cloth for coats; twenty-two meters of Oxford; six meters of other cloth; three spools of twine; one pair of leather soles.

21 SEPTEMBER–9 OCTOBER. Arrive in Vienna Südbahnhof only one and a half hours late, so around noon. This time Tinka and Miki are waiting for me. At home we have a small hospital. First the cook gets the Spanish flu,[51] then Ega and Tinka do not feel well and next day are both in bed with fever, where they remain for eight days. Flu is raging here: there is hardly a house that is spared; most houses have more than one sick in bed.

My family are, as always, exceptionally happy about my arrival. My Olga is quite beside herself with joy. Mary, the youngest, has made great developmental progress. She is a dear, sweet girl, especially when healthy. But when she is sick, she can become impossible. I see this during the days that pass, when she also gets sick with the flu. Thank God, the course of the flu is mild with all my children.

I try to do what is necessary for my family, but everything has become more difficult. Prices are ridiculously high—and there is nothing to buy for an ordinary person who is not a war profiteer. There is a great trade in clothes and furniture: one can see it when selling things. Prices that are being paid are unbelievable, for used and new items. I use the opportunity to get rid of some old things and am amazed at the prices they fetch. For an old black military greatcoat that I have not worn for nine years (superfluous in Trieste, even more so during the war): six hundred crowns. For my civilian winter jacket, which I have had for fourteen years, five hundred crowns. For my civilian topcoat, which is old, unfashionable, and worn, but is silk-lined: three hundred crowns. I want to sell my two civilian suits as well, but make the sad discovery that the waistcoat of one and trousers of the other have been stolen. The remaining waistcoat is moth-eaten. Yet, I receive three hundred crowns for one jacket and the one waistcoat. For one pair of shoes, bought in 1914 as military gear and already resoled once, 150 crowns. For one rubber washbasin, which cost nine crowns and I hardly ever use, sixty crowns; for one raincoat that I do not wear, sixty crowns. Now I understand why a new suit costs two thousand crowns and why prices of other clothes and commodities are so high.

Shattering political events are developing during my time here. At the end of September, the Bulgarian Front is unexpectedly broken through; Bulgarians lay down their arms and request an armistice, which they are given, but with hard conditions: Immediate loss of all their occupied areas, handing over of weapons, allowing the Entente passage through their region. They agree to everything, and so the fall of Bulgaria is, for us, a fait accompli. King Ferdinand will abdicate in a few days in favor of his son. This is a hard blow for us: we must retreat from Albania, clearing the way for the Serbs to return. Apart from this, things are going very badly for the Germans on the Western Front—they are retreating, although slowly and gradually. Germans have underestimated American manpower and technical equipment, especially tanks,[52] against which they are powerless. Such a tank attack begins with small tank wagons advancing on a broad front, creating thick smoke. They are few in number and cannot be properly attacked. Even if some are destroyed by our fire, the wall of smoke is still there: protected by the smoke, real tanks now advance, destroy the barbed wire obstacles, penetrate through our positions into our frontline artillery, which they pin down. Behind them come the so-called tank autobuses with storm troops, who then occupy the front line and hold it until the mass of infantry arrive, The Germans counterattack, but in most cases the front line cannot be taken anymore, and they have to withdraw. Germans have no countermeasures for a battle against machines.[53]

Internal developments constitute a third critical issue. With us, everything is turning on its head. Czechs, Poles, South Slavs all want independence from Austria. They peek at the Entente, who of course offer them full support and hope for their success. Germans appear tired of war and don't want to know anything more about fighting. Added to that, terrible shortages of everything: for example, we cannot obtain schoolbooks for children anymore, and, understandably, the Germans ask President Wilson for cessation of hostilities on 5 October, and declare the Central Powers to be prepared to accept his fourteen points. Great anxiousness about his answer, which is given on the 9 October and is gloomy: Wilson sets as a condition evacuation of all areas occupied by us and Germany.

Weather has been nice through the end of September: warm and pleasant. On 1 October, it changes, suddenly becoming very cold and overcast, with periods of rain. This weather continues. Our home is very uncomfortable: we cannot heat it, simply because we don't have any coal. Stoves have not been maintained, and it is difficult to get someone to do this. I have tried unsuccessfully to find someone since I arrived home. Meanwhile, I have caught a bad cold and have to stay in bed for two days. I call a physician from regional command: Chief Medical Officer Pabst from the *Landwehr* arrives and requests my leave to be lengthened by five days so that I return on 15 October instead of 10 October.

10–15 OCTOBER. Germany gives Wilson its answer on 11 October. It agrees to all of his terms and asks for a commission to advise on evacuation of occupied territory.

My cold is getting better, and I am going out again. Although Chief Medical Officer Papst had given me leave until 16 October, I will leave on 14 October. I must still see that the stove is fixed, but have also bought a substitute stove for 105 crowns, which would surely have cost 15 crowns before the war. I cannot get any coal yet and must wait patiently until my brother-in-law Richard obtains some.

I depart the evening of 14 October. Most trains have been canceled because of—as they say—traffic problems, so I must take the night train, although it is not convenient for me because I now have to travel to Motta; Stino would have been much nearer command. The train is packed; we sit in groups of six right through the trip, and finally arrive in Motta at 5:00 p.m. on 15 October. From there I finally arrive at command at 7:30 p.m.

16–19 OCTOBER. Today Wilson's answer arrives: he bombastically rejects any dialogue, from which it can be concluded that he demands safeguards to ensure permanent superiority of the Entente—he appears also to demand the German Kaiser's abdication. He has given us no answer to our first note.

The weather here is awful, it rains without a stop—roads impossible, even a wagon cannot pass through them. The Livenza River has risen a great deal—several canals at the font have already flooded; if it continues like this, we might all drown.

Things in our hinterland have been turned inside out. Czechs, Poles, South Slavs demand separation from the monarchy. Our Emperor is forced to proclaim Austria as a federal state—consisting of German-Austrians, Czechs, South Slavs, and Ukraine—on 16 October. Poles are released from the federation: they can join the Congress Poles and then decide their fate together. This does not satisfy the nations either; they want their fate to be decided by the Peace Congress.

20 OCTOBER. My medical orderly goes on leave today; I take the opportunity to give him a few things for my family: four live chickens, five kilograms of bacon, five kilograms of kasha, five kilograms of millet, twenty kilograms of potatoes, three and a half kilograms of fresh meat, a quarter of a kilogram of butter, four loaves of bread, aspirin, several rolls of cotton wool.

The sun comes out today, after so many gloomy days, and everyone breathes easier. Italian pilots are busy again. Chief Medical Officer Feiertag appears during the afternoon, and we both travel to the medical column. Surgeon Major Konopka has been transferred to field hospital no. 405, replaced by Surgeon Major Janceck from the ninety-fifth infantry regiment. So there is a change for everyone except me: I am apparently fated to finish the war as division physician. I fear that my request for Trieste will not be successful. Surgeon General Thoman seems ticked off that I went on leave, and this is his revenge. I want to ask staff physician Fiedler about the fate of my request, but the Surgeon General himself answers the telephone because he has given Fiedler leave. He says I must be patient, because I have not done anything useful for him yet: first we were in Rucorvo, and straight after that, I took a few weeks' leave. Just as I thought: really mean!

21 OCTOBER. The sun appears today as well, but only around noon—At least the ground is drying out and one can go outside again. The anxiously awaited response from Wilson to our monarchy finally comes, and mocks our hopes. Many thought that Wilson might deal compassionately with us, to alienate us from Germany—they were all wrong. His reply is meaner than anything he has said before: he believes that he is not dealing with Austria but rather with Czechoslovakia!

Hungary responds to the initiated disintegration of Austria into a federation with separation from Austria and foundation of a personal union. Our people seem to have lost their heads completely: at a time when the Entente countries are becoming closer together, we are tearing ourselves asunder. Terrible things are going to come out of this, and I wish everything possible that is bad on these gangsters. Everyone is convinced that our peoples would rather live in peace next to one another in cozy Austria, but the gangsters, these traitors to the Fatherland, want it otherwise!

21 OCTOBER. Germany answers Wilson's note by stopping increased U-boat attacks. They justify the alleged destruction in France during their retreat of February 1917 and have transferred the decision of war and peace to the Reichstag. Lovely warm, sunny weather, which dries the ground out well.

23 OCTOBER. Nice, warm weather continues today; it is our mood that is gloomy. By coincidence, I get my hands on a Graz newspaper that I have not yet seen: I at once read about the death of my best friend, Colonel Pistotnik. He was sixty-three—I did not think that he was that old; he always looked so smart and sprightly!

24 OCTOBER. Rain and overcast weather again, but not as bad as previously.

25 OCTOBER. Weather still mild, overcast in the morning but sunshine in the afternoon. Wilson has answered Germany, and prospects for peace look dimmer and dimmer. He is literally demanding Germany's destruction. For example, he states that he will not negotiate with the current government, who are responsible for the war. Of course he means the German Kaiser. He wants to present terms for cessation of hostilities to the Entente, who will formulate conditions. In any event, there must be a guarantee that, even if peace negotiations are broken off, Germany will never again be in a position to defend itself. In other words: capitulation!

26 OCTOBER. Overcast in the morning with fog. Newspapers are forbidden at the front and sent away at once. That is a very hard precaution, but its purpose is not to allow subversion into the army. Because what is being said in our parliament and written in the newspaper makes one want to tear one's hair out. For example, representatives of each nation are demanding that their soldiers be called back from the front. Hungarians and Poles want their soldiers back: they do not even think about how dangerous this is. If this really happens, conditions will become like in Russia, with Bolshevism. Wonderful times await us!

27 OCTOBER. During the night of 26 October around midnight, the Italians suddenly begin a violent bombardment, which lasts uninterruptedly through 9:00 a.m.—mainly north of us; firing is less on our positions. Then they start attacking, during the course of the day penetrating an area twelve kilometers long, and about five kilometers wide.

28 OCTOBER. Fighting continues—fairly quiet on our front, only heavy artillery fire.

29 OCTOBER. News from the front is not good: a few Hungarian regiments, the twenty-sixth division and sixty-third infantry regiment, have mutinied, refusing to advance. So Italians have been able to break through our front, quite far north of our position, south of Montello. When we get the news, we immediately start moving back our heavy baggage trains, as well as the heavy part of the medical column—about thirty vehicles—so that only one section with physicians remains.

30 OCTOBER. Italians broaden their breakthrough. An entire Czechoslovak division has unilaterally left the front and marched to Görz.[54] The situation for our division has become critical because, the more the Italians advance in the north, the greater our danger of being completely cut off. The order to retreat arrives during the morning hours, but it will be about noon before we can leave beautiful Rotta.

The ride to Olmo goes well, although our commandant gallops wildly, as if the Italians are already on our heels. In Olmo we have quite a long rest, and new assignments are distributed. Our dear Heller wallows in these orders so long that entire hours pass without agreement. It's already dark before we ride on. Very soon, we meet up with the baggage trains, which block the roads completely, so we can only advance gradually. The roads themselves, along the Lemeni River, are miserable, narrow, with appalling potholes; mud from the recent rain is so bad that horses can hardly drag their feet forward, let alone people. So we are left with nothing else but to dismount, leading the horses through by hand. At least our commander makes one of the men go in front of him with a lantern, which those of us right behind him can see and follow. Otherwise, night is so pitch black that we cannot see one pace in front of us. I am in particularly bad shape: the horse's hooves have trodden on my feet several times, once so badly that that I fell into the thick mud and landed under the horse. But the old nag was valiant enough not to move until I had extracted myself. We march like this for almost two hours, until most of us are completely exhausted; our valiant commander asks us to remount.

The baggage trains make absolutely no progress: most are forced to unload most of their baggage or throw it into the river, so they can progress with wagons only half-full. Entire artillery pieces—especially heavy ones—are cleared out of the road in this way because they are impossible to take farther, and the road must be cleared for the remaining baggage train. Entire conveyances must be cleared from the blocked streets in this way.

After much trouble and exertion, we finally are in Concordia at 1:00 a.m. We are all quartered together. The mess is in the same room as the kitchen.

31 OCTOBER. We crowd around the Italian stove to warm ourselves. The civilians do the same; we are happy to allow this, because there are some really beautiful women among them. We stay here today; this suits us fine, after last night's exertions. If only my quarters were a bit better.

1 NOVEMBER. We march on from Concordia to Latisana. This time I travel in a car, much more comfortable than even the best horse. We are quartered in an elegant-looking castle where I obtain a room with a comfortable bed. Inside, the castle is battered. Italian pilots fly low over us all day, following our marching columns, strafing them with machine guns, causing many wounded and killing ten horses. Other pilots throw bombs: they destroy a bridge over the Tagliamento just before our troops should have crossed over. So the men have to be redirected across the still undamaged railway bridge, and the baggage train across the bridge in Latisanotta. Because of this, they have to march an extra four kilometers. Obviously, all of this doesn't leave us with a comfortable feeling: each man is afraid for his life.

2 NOVEMBER. We continue our march, arriving in Manzana—a real Italian dump—but despite this, I find a halfway decent place to stay, in the same house as our commander, with an old Italian lady whom I impress with my Latin. She even makes a mattress and clean linen available to me. Italians are much quieter today: one hardly hears any shooting. But pilots in Latisana increase their scary bombing all the more.

3 NOVEMBER. A historic day of the first magnitude. The peace that everyone has yearned for so long has arrived: cessation of hostilities between us and the Italians and our other opponents was signed last night. News only arrived to us this morning at 9:00 a.m. By the time we receive the news, which spreads like a wildfire through our troops, we have already marched from Manzana to Cervignano. Opinions about it are divided. Almost everywhere, there is happiness that this terrible war, with its endless losses in life and property, is finally over. On the other hand, we active officers are filled with heartache over its unhappy ending, the more so because it might not have had to come to this. We were victorious on all fronts, against a world of enemies. The fighting front stands stable and undamaged—but the front at home! There is the problem! The hinterland has failed completely. It has struck us in the back like a dagger that so many nations are using exactly this moment to achieve their egotistical aims, making collapse inevitable. They have been working against us for weeks and months. People who are currently on leave are kept back by all possible means from returning to their units—thereby, discipline is badly affected, also demoralizing troops at the front. Hungarians are yelling at their troops to return home, Czechs are leaving the front unilaterally in droves and marching to Graz, ostensibly to restore order there.

Every hour brings gloomier news. A command comes from our Emperor that individual nations will form their own armies, and all members of the army who are in the hinterland must immediately report to the relevant command of whichever army they choose until they return to their demobilization stations.

Despite the fact that I was born and bred in Lemberg, I refuse to choose the Polish Army and will not belong to such a dissolute, corrupt, indolent nation. The Germans are not kindly disposed to the Jews, but at least they are cultivated, assiduous, and more honest, so I will join them.[55] How much it must have pained the Emperor to set his hand to such a document! It releases us from our oath to the Empire and allows us to swear loyalty to whatever nationality we wish.

We have just been informed of the armistice conditions for our fleet—they are terrible! We seem to have intuited and wanted to prevent it, in that our Emperor wanted to make a gift of it to the Yugoslavs, whose nation has just been recognized. Nothing helps, and Italians order us to give up our fleet in a very commanding tone—the time has been given at which all our ships must be positioned in the harbor in Venice. Commerce vessels are directed to different harbors, where they must lie at anchor. We also have to hand over the plans of our mines; the Yugoslavs want their piece of the pie, do not permit our troops to march under arms to Krain,[56] and demand that all troops disarm.

Our supplies of food, which we wanted to send in large quantities to Trieste and Laibach, have been confiscated; apparently the Yugoslavs intend to collect as much food and war material as possible so as to be able to outfit and feed their new army. Obviously, we cannot agree to such terms. Commandant Ciecsic has been sent to the Yugoslav National Council for negotiations, but there is the distinct possibility that they will force their way through militarily.

According to a newspaper report from 1 November, Count Tisza has been assassinated.[57] Thus, all our best men have been cleared out of the way by the Entente, to clear the field for agitators.

4 NOVEMBER. We leave Cevignano at 7:00 a.m., traveling rapidly by car to Pieris. In Cevignano, most of command is housed and fed in the small castle of an Austrian irredentist.[58] I am quartered away from the castle, next to Lieutenant Colonel Schütz and two ladies who are friendly enough to make bedding available to us.

Pieris is a small town, but our quarters are good. Our troops are caught up in the enormous confusion of the armistice and the upcoming peace. They can hardly be controlled anymore—everyone wants to go home, and, because we so often arrive in abandoned provisions centers where rum and alcohol are readily available, men get drunk and vandalize everything. Today, soon after our arrival in Pieris, a man, drunk as a skunk, grabbed a rifle and shot it off all around. Everyone panicked and feared for their lives—he rampaged through the street, attacked everybody, shot into the houses, and none of the soldiers dared to attack and disarm him. Eventually, Captains Schaufler and Langauer and First Lieutenant Trichtel plucked up enough courage to pursue the man, who had already fled into a ground floor room. He attacked them, and when Captain Schaufler tore the rifle away from him, he attacked the Captain with a rifle butt. A bullet from Captain Langauer's revolver struck him down, with a second unnecessary bullet from First Lieutenant Trichtel. So he lay on the ground, dying from chest and belly wounds—he died later that evening.

Rumors swirl around all day that the Italians, despite the armistice, are going to advance and attack our forces. We do not believe them, but a hatless, tattered man arrives during dinner at 7:00 p.m., announcing himself as Colonel Hummel of the general staff; he tells everyone that he was taken captive by the Italians toward noon in Cervignano. He escaped from them, changed clothes, and walked here. It turns out that we were informed of the beginning of the armistice a full twenty-four hours earlier than when it really began. That is the reason for the great confusion, with all its attendant unpleasantnesses. The de facto armistice only begins at 4:00 p.m. today. Despite this, the rumor spreads that Italians will not honor the armistice. Because divisions situated behind us are already marching by, our commander orders that we immediately march off. I am rousted out of bed at 11:15 p.m., after I scarcely went to sleep at 9:30 p.m. We drive off by car to Monfalcone, where we arrive at 1:00 a.m. and enter the post office. The twenty-second corps command, who are already there, give us something to eat and drink; they march off an hour later, but we wait until dawn and enjoy ourselves with the female workers, as much as is possible, under the circumstances.

Lieutenant Colonel Heller lies on the bed in the telephone room, snoring loudly. Some men remain sitting in the car and sleep, while I chat with the postmistress. We leave, but must stop for long periods of time because the road is blocked by baggage trains. Finally, we get room to move and whizz along to Krajna,[59] where we arrive at 11:30 p.m. Our baggage train only arrives at 8:00 p.m., so during the past twenty-four hours, we have neither sleep nor food. Additionally, I observe sadly that my batman has not arrived with the baggage train and my belongings are nowhere to be seen in the vehicle. The carter and his lads say they have not seen him since the last station. So I am really in a pickle: all my things are there! I do not even have the essentials—toiletries, bedclothes, nothing: only the clothes I have on my back, and that is not much. I am quite desperate and cannot believe that he made off with all of my belongings. I would rather believe that, early in the morning two days ago when I left my quarters, the baggage train was not there, and my things landed on another one. Understandably, I spend a sleepless night: no headrest or cover, and nights are quite cold here. I cannot wash early next morning and just have to travel onward.

6 NOVEMBER. I forget my leggings, which I have worn since the beginning of the war, at last night's station. We march to Divaca,[60] where we arrive by car at 1:00 p.m. Quarters in a villa with Lieutenant Colonel Schütz. Conditions here are awful. Bolshevism is in full bloom, baggage trains are plundered, and soldiers sell what is on the trains: horses, cattle, every kind of war supply. Most men pack everything up, go to the station and storm trains. Continuous firing in the streets: one literally takes one's life in one's hands going into the street. Women also take active part in the plundering. The National Guard is too weak against these gangs; they have asked the Italians for help and, toward 6:00 p.m., an Italian company with three officers and machine guns actually arrives in the town, occupying the railway station and other important points in the town. Quiet soon returns, and we invite the three men to dine with us. It's sad enough that, despite an entire division being near and in the town, together with division command, we need enemy troops to keep order.

The officers are very pleasant: young and reserved, excellent table manners. They too do not seem to have had much to eat today.

Soon after our arrival, to my great joy, my batman suddenly turns up with my things—it was as I thought: he did not meet the baggage train, so he took another and arrived here—it turns out that he is, after all, a decent type. Soon after arrival, I telegraph my Olga. She will be somewhat calmed when she receives the telegram, because she has heard nothing from me for the past two weeks.

7 NOVEMBER. We travel farther to St. Peter in Krain, where we arrive at 9:15 a.m. Troops and baggage train naturally arrive a few hours later. We are supposed to pack up and leave here, but the national guard do not supply us with rolling stock, out of fear that Italians might take it for themselves, because they have done so up to now, so we must travel on as we are.

Our demarcation line has been fixed as Unter-Loisch—Triglan—Schneeberger, Nanus, etc.[61] Italians could arrive here at any moment, so we march off in the afternoon to Koce,[62] where I take quarters with Lieutenant Colonel Schütz. He is a pleasant enough room companion, but there is only one bed per room in these quarters, which he takes for himself, so there is only an improvised bed left for me. The baggage train arrives in the late evening, around 10:00 p.m.—our housekeeper gives us a very nice meal: fresh potatoes with fresh butter, very good schnapps, etc.

8 NOVEMBER. We leave at 8:00 a.m., arrival in Unter-Loitsch at 11:30 a.m. Unfortunately, I leave my bayonet and bayonet belt behind—a great pity. Quartered again with Lieutenant Schütz, again with only one bed. This is too much for me, and I look for a room for myself: I find a splendid room with an excellent bed and finally have a very good night's sleep. I empty out my superfluous baggage, send my mattress back to Vienna, together with some books. All service books and paperwork (files, etc.) are burned by my batman in the company of a senior Polish Colonel whom I do not know. We dine in a restaurant: very expensive, bad food.

Czechs have occupied the Brenner Pass in the Tirol, to hold the Italians up. We have lodged a formal complaint so that we can at least end the war in our own country. But Italians have arrived and taken everything over, not even letting trucks through. Requisitioning will doubtless start shortly. Yugoslavs will soon see what it means to invite the Pied Piper in to restore order: he will have to be paid! Serves them right. Rain tonight, after a long stretch of pleasant weather.

10 NOVEMBER. Despite the fact that the train only leaves at 6:00 p.m., we arrive at the station at 2:30 p.m. We receive three [?] class carriages, and leave at 6:30 p.m.

11 NOVEMBER. Arrival in Vienna at 4:00 p.m. The trip passes rapidly. Only the two small children are at home: everyone else is out. Gradually everyone gathers together, Olga last of all. She is pleasantly surprised to see me. We need such surprises in our lives. So the war has ended for me, and I close my diary!!

12 NOVEMBER. Rest day!

13 NOVEMBER. Inquiry at regional command as to where I should go. I apply in writing to the German-Austrian Army but have to report personally in Graz, where my appropriate command is located,

15 NOVEMBER. Departure for Graz at 9:00 p.m.

16 NOVEMBER. Departure back to Vienna at 11:00 p.m.

17 NOVEMBER. Arrival in Vienna at 11:00 a.m. The trip is miserable, and superfluous because they have enough doctors there. I must come again on 1 December. I will consider carefully whether I should.

20 DECEMBER. Report to Garrison Hospital Hof, where I am interviewed. I receive my honoraria from here from now on.

22 DECEMBER. Begin my cure for rheumatism, which is quite bad, in Dianabad.

1 JANUARY 1919. Enter Clinic Finger for training as a specialist in skin and venereal diseases.

Notes

1. Pavlovychi (Ukraine).
2. Romanian river north-east of Braşov.
3. Shel'viv (Ukraine).
4. "Rus/Rusyn" peoples, living in Poland, Russia, Belarus, and Ukraine.
5. Volodymyr-Volynskyi (Ukraine).
6. Brest (Belarus).
7. Krukhynychi (Ukraine).
8. Breakdown in vaccination.
9. Rzeszów (Poland).
10. Historic region in Central and Eastern Europe straddling Poland, Ukraine, and Belarus
11. After the collapse of the Russian monarchy, Ukrainian political leaders declared complete independence of Ukraine from Russia in January 1918. Bolshevik forces were sent to regain Ukrainian territory, but after the peace treaty between the Ukraine and the Central Powers was signed on 9 February 1918, Russians were forced out by German troops. Ukraine was to be a vast source of provisions and raw materials for the blockaded Central Powers. After the 11 November Armistice, Ukraine became the site of a civil war, ultimately won by the Bolsheviks.
12. Mikuliczy (Belarus).

13. Chelm (Poland).
14. Lviv (Ukraine).
15. Cabaret actress.
16. Lutsk (Ukraine).
17. Short for *Onkel* (uncle).
18. Kyiv (Ukraine).
19. Tallinn (Estonia).
20. The Treaty of Brest-Litovsk, signed on 3 March 1918 between the new Bolshevik government of Soviet Russia and the Central Powers (Germany, Austria-Hungary, Bulgaria, and the Ottoman Empire), ended Russia's participation in the war. According to the treaty, Soviet Russia defaulted on all of Imperial Russia's commitments to the Entente. Bolshevik Russia ceded the Baltic States to Germany. Russia also ceded its province of Kars Oblast in the South Caucasus to the Ottoman Empire and recognized the independence of Ukraine. Furthermore, Russia agreed to pay six billion German gold marks in reparations. Congress Poland was not mentioned in the treaty, as Germans refused to recognize the existence of any Polish representatives, which in turn led to Polish protests.
21. Zaturtsi (Ukraine).
22. The German Spring (Michael) Offensive was a series of German attacks along the Western Front, beginning on 21 March 1918, which marked the deepest advances by either side since 1914. However, Germans were unable to move supplies and reinforcements fast enough to maintain their advance. Fast-moving storm troopers leading the attack could not carry enough food and ammunition to sustain themselves for long, and all German offensives petered out, in part through lack of supplies. By late April, the danger of a German breakthrough had passed. Instead of seizing victory, the German army began a six-month retreat, finally recognizing in August that it could not win the war.
23. Kowel (Ukraine).
24. Chmielów (Poland).
25. Pidhaitsi (Ukraine).
26. Voynitsa (Ukraine).
27. Sokal (Ukraine).
28. Czostków (Poland).
29. Buchach (Ukraine).
30. Not found.
31. Ustiluh (Ukraine).
32. Rava-Ruska (Ukraine).
33. Sokal (Ukraine).
34. This is not exactly what happened; some Austro-Hungarian Russian prisoners only got home in 1921.
35. Hungary (until 1918). Unclear afterward.
36. The Second Battle of the Piave River, fought 15–23 June 1918. After some initial successes, the Austro-Hungarians, lacking supplies and facing attacks by armored units, were ordered to retreat by Emperor Karl, who had taken personal command, on 20 June. By 23 June, the Italians recaptured all territory on the southern bank of the Piave, and the battle was over. So was effective Austro-Hungarian military resistance to the Allies on all fronts.
37. Novi Sad (Serbia).

38. Stryi (Ukraine).
39. Lavochne (Ukraine).
40. Sátoraljaújhely, Miskoic, Hatvan (Hungary).
41. Kelenföld (Budapest train station).
42. Herceghalom, Komárom, Győr, Pápa (Hungary).
43. Szombathely, Körmend, Szentgotthárd (Hungary); Fehring, Graz (Austria).
44. Maribor, Pragersko, Zidani Most, Ljubljana (Slovenia).
45. Opicina, Aurisina, Monfalcone (Italy). Unless otherwise specified, all other towns are in Italy.
46. San Vito di Cadore (Italy).
47. Opatija-Volosko (Croatia).
48. Two species of one genus (*Anopheles gambiae* and *Anopheles* funestus) carry the malaria parasite.
49. Sumirago (Italy)?
50. San Stino di Livenza (Italy).
51. The 1918 influenza pandemic (January 1918 to December 1920) was an unusually deadly influenza pandemic, the first of the two pandemics involving H1N1 influenza virus. It infected five hundred million people across the world and resulted in the deaths of an estimated fifty million to one hundred million people (3 to 5 percent of the world's population).
52. Error: The United States did not field any American-built tanks during World War I.
53. This would change radically in World War II.
54. Gorizia (Italy).
55. The irony of this statement requires no emphasis.
56. Kranjska (Slovenia)
57. Count István Tisza de Borosjenő et Szeged (1861–1918), a Hungarian politician, prime minister, political scientist, and member of the Hungarian Academy of Sciences. The prominent event in his life was Austria-Hungary's entry into World War I, when he was prime minister for the second time. He was later assassinated during the Chrysanthemum Revolution on 31 October 1918—the same day that Hungary terminated its political union with Austria.
58. Irredentism (from Italian *irredento* for "unredeemed") is any political or popular movement intended to reclaim and reoccupy a "lost" or "unredeemed" area; territorial claims are justified based on real or imagined national, historic, or ethnic justification.
59. Krajna Vas (Slovenia).
60. Divača (Slovenia).
61. Logatec Dolenji, Mt. Tryglav, Mt. Snežnik, Nanos Mountains (Slovenia).
62. Koče (Slovenia).

APPENDIX 1

Medical and Nonmedical Ranks in the Austro-Hungarian Army (Simplified)*

The Austro-Hungarian Army was divided into three sections:
(1) The Common Imperial and Royal (*kaiserlich und königlich* or k.u.k.) Army, which was provided by both sides of the Empire. Because the ranks in the other two sections differed somewhat, only ranks in the k.u.k. army are given
(2) The Imperial Hungarian Honvèd (*königlich-ungarischen* or k.u.);
(3) In the Austrian half of the Empire, the Imperial-Royal (or k.k) *Landwehr* (standing army)

    Mannschafte: According to service arm: rifleman, dragoon, ulan, hussar, artilleryman, pioneer, train soldier, etc.
    Chargen: Private first class
    Unteroffiziere: Corporal, platoon commander, sergeant, staff sergeant, cadet warrant officer, warrant officer, ensign
    Offiziere
        Second Lieutenant (Assistant Physician: *Assistenzarzt*)
        First Lieutenant (Senior Physician: *Oberarzt*)
        Rittmeister: rank of a commissioned cavalry officer in the armies of Germany and Austria-Hungary, typically in charge of a squadron or company, the equivalent of a Hauptmann
        Captain/Hauptmann: *Regimentstarzt erste und zweite Klasse*
        Major (surgeon-major): *Stabsarzt*
        Lieutenant Colonel: *Oberstabsarzt zweite Klasse* (no exact English medical equivalent)
        Colonel: *Oberstabsarzt erste Klasse* (no exact English medical equivalent)

---

*Simplified from Erwin A. Schmidl, *Habsburgs jüdische Soldaten 1788–1918* (Vienna: Böhlau Verlag, 2014), 205–207; Manfried Rauchensteiner, *The First World War and the end of the Habsburg Monarchy, 1914–1918* (Vienna: Böhlau Verlag, 2014), 51.

Generals
    Major General: *Generalstabsarzt* (Surgeon General)
    Feldmarschallleutnant: *Generaloberarzt* (Senior Surgeon General)
    Feldzeugmeister: General of Artillery, etc.
    Colonel General
    Field Marshal

Ranks with No Exact English Equivalent

Intendant. I have translated this as logistics officer (senior and junior). Denotes administrative activity. Because the experts whom I consulted differ as to corresponding formal army rank, I have not attempted to use captain, major, or lieutenant colonel.

Divisionär. A function of activity (for example, brigade commandant) without formal rank. For the sake of simplicity, commander or commandant are used throughout the text.

APPENDIX 2

Medical Corps in the Austro-Hungarian Army (Simplified)

Responsibilities

Surgeon General: overall organization of a division and often corps
Regimentsarzt: structure of a regiment or brigade

Structure

The wounded (including the enemy) first arrived at first aid stations. Further surgical treatment then took place at dressing stations. Those fit to be moved were then transported either by ambulance or horse-drawn wagon to field hospitals and sick bays.

Starting in fall 1914, there were also sixty-five medical automobile columns (*Autokolonne*), each of which consisted of ten motorized ambulances for transportation of four to six sick or wounded each. Starting in 1917, coincidental with the taking out of service of motorized ambulances, Bardach starts to call "units" "convoys/columns," although the functionality of the two concepts seems identical.

In addition, there were also fixed and mobile fixed medical units (*Anstalten*) at the front and in the rear. Civilian hospitals were also used for treatment of the sick and wounded.

Bibliography

Bardach, Bernard. *War Diaries: Bernhard Bardach Collection*. New York: Archives of the Leo Baeck Institute [1918], AR 6632.

Ernst, Petra. "Der erste Weltkrieg in deutschsprachig-jüdischer Literatur und Publizistik." In Österreich, *Krieg: Erinnerung. Geschichtswissenschaft*, ed. Siegfied Mattl, Gerhard Botz, Stefan Karner, and Helmut Konrad, 68–72. Vienna: Böhlau Verlag, 2009.

Grössing, Tanja, *Der Bleistift zitterte und das Herz zitterte, als dieses Manuskript entstand: Untersuchungen der Kriegstagebücher von Egon Erwin Kisch und Bernhard Bardach*. MA thesis, University of Graz, 2015.

"Miki G. Denhof Née Bardach, Editor and Designer." In *Biographia, Lexicon österreichischer Frauen*, volume 1 A-H, Vienna, 2016.

Mokotoff, Gary, and Sallyann Amdur Sack. *Where Once We Walked: A Guide to the Jewish Communities Destroyed in the Holocaust*. Teaneck, NJ: Avotaynu, 1991.

Prior, Robin, and Trevor Wilson. *Passchendaele: The Untold Story*. 3rd ed. New Haven, CT: Yale University Press, 2016.

Rauchesteiner, Manfried. *The First World War and the End of the Habsburg Monarchy, 1914–1918*. Vienna: Böhlau Verlag, 2014.

Rozenblit, Marsha L. *Reconstructing a National Identity: The Jews of Habsburg Austria during World War 1*. New York: Oxford University Press, 2004.

Sands, Philippe. *East-West Street: On the Origins of "Genocide" and "Crimes against Humanity."* New York: Knopf, 2016.

Schmidl, Erwin A. *Habsburgs jüdische Soldaten 1788–1918*. Vienna: Böhlau Verlag, 2014.

Schuster, Frank M. *Zwischen allen Fronten.Osteuropäische Juden während des ersten Weltkrieges (1914–1919)*. Cologne: Böhlau Verlag, 2004.

Stone, Norman. *The Eastern Front 1914–1917*. New York: Scribner, 1975.

Winter, Jay. *Remembering War: The Great War between Memory and History in the Twentieth History*. New Haven, CT: Yale University Press, 2006.

———. *War beyond Words. Language of Remembrance from the Great War to the Present*. Cambridge: Cambridge University Press, 2017.

Index

Note: Page references marked with an *f* are figures

academic career of Bardach, 2
aerial bombing, 207
Alexandrovich, Michael, 190, 193
Alexandrovitsch, Captain, 18
Alexandrovitz, Captain, 24
Alexandru, Pharmacist, 95
ambulances, 135, 146, 179
amputations, 126*f*
Andrealta, District Commandant Colonel, 269
Anschluss, xii
anti-Semitism, 3, 6, xvi, xx
armistice: cancellation of (5 December, 1917), 235; conditions of (3 November, 1918), 283
Army Brudermann, 25
Army Group Linsingen, 143, 233
Army Hindenburg, 139
Aschkenasy, Mrs., 18
Austria: Brusilov Offensive (1916), 8; citizenship in, 10; incorporation of the German Reich, 11
Austro-Hungarian Army, xi; Brusilov Offensive (1916), x, xi, xiii; infantry (*see* infantry); medical corps in, 291; ranks, 289–90
Austro-Hungarian Empire, 233

bacillary dysentery, 220
bacillus, 182
bacteriology laboratories, 186, 271
Baczi, First Lieutenant, 48

baggage trains, 128, 129, 133, 134, 142, 143, 161, 162, 179, 209, 214, 224, 231, 284
bakery inspections, 270
Ballner, Professor, 109
Bardach, Bernhard, 8, 9, 202*f*; academic career of, 2; awareness of home front shortages, xii; biographical sketch of, 1–16; birth of, 2, xvi; children of, 3; citizenship in Austria, 11; citizenship in the United States, 13; civilian life (overview of), 10–11; collection of photographs, xix; compensation, 12–14; as dental specialist, 3; education of, 2; family of, xix; first day of fighting (24 August, 1914), 21; funeral for brother-in-law (Edouard), 199, 200; humiliation, 11–12; Italian Front, 268–86; marriage to Henia, 3; marriage to Olga, 4; military decorations, 4, 6, 7; move to New York, 12; Oberstabsarzt I Klasse (colonel), 10; oil painting of, xvii*f*; painting, xi*f*; pension, 11–12; as physician in the war, x; practice of Jewish faith in army, 6; promotion to Oberstabsarzt II Klasse, 7; purchase of horse, 18; service evaluation (1912), 3; transfer from Eastern Front (April, 1918), 9; volunteer for military service, 2; war years (overview of), 4–10; work in medical facilities, xvii–xviii; writing to home, 160
Bardach, Bettina ("Tinka" [daughter]), 8, 163, 236, 250, 262
Bardach, Ega (daughter), 8, 262

Bardach, Henia (first wife), 3
Bardach, Mary (daughter), 8, 162, 194, 210, 262
Bardach, Miki (daughter), 8, 10, 11, 13, 200, 236, 249, 250, 261, 262
Bardach, Olga (second wife), 4, 11, 102, 162, 163, 200, 201, 203, 210, 236, 249, 250, 261, 263, 266; death of, 13; diary of, 264–65; letters from, 47; letters to, 82; vacation (29 June, 1915), 78; writing to, 40
Bardachzi, Regimental Physician First Class, 204
Barlogi (Poland), 82
Bartosch, German Captain, 175
Basrig, Colonel, 30
Bastaczi, Regimental Physician First Class, 192
baths, 101, 115, 120, 124, 180, 186, 187f, 188, 189, 220, 230, 241, 242, 253f
batmen, bad luck with, 71
battalion no. 5/103, 153, 156
Battle of Turobin (28 August, 1914), 22
battles: Battle of the Somme (1916), 214, 256; in Bukowina, 214; first day of fighting (24 August, 1914), 21; in Galicia, 214; of the Isonzo, 213, 214; at Nisko (23 October, 1914), 34; Przemyśl (Poland [26 May, 1915]), 73, 74; in Romania, 214; Zaturczy (Ukraine), 137
battle trains, 130
Bauer, General, 129
Baum: Assistant Physician Dr., 181, 199, 258; Senior Physician Dr., 209, 254, 255
beggar in Grubieszow (Poland), 84f
Beigel, Commandant Surgeon Major Dr., 35
Belgium, entrance into World War I (31 July 1914), 17
Bellegarde, Count, 64
Belzyce (Poland), 81
Bereck (Ukraine), 131
Berezoviezy (Ukraine), 186
Berger, Surgeon Major Dr., 33, 34
Berner, Captain, 89
Beykowski, Surgeon Major, 60

Biblo (Ukraine), 72
Bielsko-Biała (Poland), 4
Bilgoraj (Poland), 26, 27
Billroth bandages, 154, 159
binding, 266
biographical sketch (of Bardach), 1–16
Bircza (Poland), 70
Bisenius, Colonel, 21
Bjelik, Field Vicar Bishop, 204
bodies in the battlefield, 44f, 45
Bogoluby (Ukraine), 92
Bohemia, 205
von Böhm Ermoli, Eduard, 90, 143, 251, 253, 261
Bolshevism, 284
borders, Poland, 218
Boro (Poland), 48, 54, 56
Boroević von Bojna, Svetozar, 71, 73, 268
Bosmann, Surgeon Major Dr., 148
Branewka (Poland), regiment in (25 August, 1914), 21
bread rations, 264
Brenner Pass, 285
Brest Litovsk, Belarus, 87; negotiations in, 241, 243; signing of treaty in, 246
Breuer: Lieutenant Colonel, 256; Surgeon Major Dr., 76
Britto, Chief of the General Staff Lieutenant Colonel, 196, 211, 213, 244
Brody (Ukraine), 145
von Brudermann, Rudolf, 25
Brumowski, Artillery Observer Cadet, 117
Brusilov Offensive (1916), 8, 16, 107–74, x, xi, xiii, xvi
Brzoza-Krolewska (Poland), 76
Bucharest (fall of [Romania]), 165, 166, 168
Buczacz (Ukraine), 258
Budiaczewo (Ukraine), 87
Bukowina, battles in, 214
Bulgaria, 147, 277
Bulgarian Front, 277
burials, 176, 177f
Bürkel, Surgeon General, 164, 196, 197, 226
Buruchewo (Ukraine), 88
Bykow-Siedliska (Poland), 75

cabaret singers, 243
cannons, 142, 189; howitzer, 71, 124; Reichel, 140
card games, 94f
Cavalry Corps Hauer, 215, 217
Cavick, Surgeon General, 259
Central Powers, 148, 233, 241, 247, 278, xii, xiii
Cetinje, Montenegro, 108
Charas, Colonel Dr., 60
Charles Cross, 225, 244
The Charterhouse of Parma (Fabrizio), xiii
Chmielow (Poland), 256
cholera, 39, 40, 42, 85, 100, 119f
Ch(H)orlupy (Ukraine), 110, 114, 116, 127, 128, 136, 188
Chortkiv (Ukraine), 3
churches, 45f
cigarettes, 259, 260
Cistelka, Captain, 80
citizenship: in Austria, 10; in the United States, 13
Clinic Finger, 10, 286
code names, 117
coffee, 25
colonialism, 4
communication trenches, 112, 188
concerts, 245
confidential communications, 67
Cori, Professor, 269
Cossacks, 88, 91, 131
Cracow (Poland), 40, 45, 46, 78
Crajowa (Romania), 165
cross trenches, 153
Crown Order First Class, 74, 222
Csanady, Commander, 132, 136, 177
Czarna (Poland), 31
Czeben (Poland), 87
Czysta Debina (Poland), 24

dancers, 243
Dankl, Captain, 27
Danneberg, Oberstabsarzt I Klasse Dr., 101, 107
Das grosse Heimweh (Herzog), 156
Dazwa (Ukraine), 132
death, bodies in the battlefield, 44f, 45
de Beaufort, Rittmeister Godin, 200

Deischel, Captain, 41
delousing facilities, 120, 124, 182, 183, 186, 254f
demarcation lines, 285
Demkowicz, medical orderly, 232
Demmer, Regimental Physician First Class Dr., 96
Denhof, Miki, 1
dentists, visit to, 214f
von der Bresche, Excellency Jemrich, 133
von der Lilie, Chief Medical Officer Count Vetter, 81
von der Marwitz, Commandant, 151
d'Este, Franz Ferdinand (murder of), 17
Deutsch, Dr., 6
Deutschland (German U-boat), 146
Diappa, Captain, 19
diaries: Bardach, Olga (second wife), 264–65; civilian life (overview of), 10–11; war years (overview of), 4–10
diarrhea, 226
Diebel, Captain, 158
disinfection facilities, 101
district VII Kaiserstrasse 62, 162
divisions, 30. *See also* infantry; regiments
Dolchstosslegende (stab in the back myth), 9
douches, 188
dress-up pantomime, 197f
drugi obiad (Polish second dinner), 228
Dubiecko (Poland), 75
Dubno (Ukraine), 89
dysentery, 42, 220, 269, 270, 271

ear infections, 155
Eastern European Jews, 5, 10, 38f, xviii
Eastern European synagogue, 158f
Eastern Front, xix; daily life on, xii, xiii; gas masks, 113f; transfer from (April, 1918), 9
Easter Sunday (1916), 117
education (Bardach's), 2
eighty-ninth infantry regiment, 23, 109, 112, 113, 118
eighty-second infantry regiment, 145
electricity, 90, 119
von Elterlein, First Lieutenant, 150
England, entrance into World War I (31 July 1914), 17

Entente, 167, 170, 177, 182, 203, 233, 246, 279, 280
Erben, Captain, 201, 203, 268
Ernst, Petra, 1
erysipelas, 99
eye damage, 126f

Fabrizio, Stendhal, xiii
Falemiczy (Hungary), 264
von Falkenhayn, Erich, 147, xi
Falkenhayn division, 136
false alarms, 58
fasting dishes, 170
Feiertag, Chief Medical Officer, 275, 279
Felter, Senior Physician, 220, 252
Ferdinand, Joseph (Archduke), 110, 111, 114, 120, 131, 277, xi
Feyertag, Oberstabsarzt I Klasse, 273
Fieber, Dr., 170, 171, 188, 190
field hospitals, 207; 9/20, 179; 913, 187; 1009, 181, 193, 195, 212, 221, 254
Fighting trenches, 112, 153
Filar, First Lieutenant, 270
first aid stations, 118, 135, 171, 176f, 190, 196, 205; 1, 201; 1/40, 213; 2/40, 213, 227, 229, 230; 3/40, 188, 201, 213, 227, 242; 4/40, 229; 4/62, 170, 215, 228; 5/103, 226; 278th German infantry, 146; inspections, 217, 218; Mulde, 243; no. 5/62, 218
first *Landwehr* infantry regiment, 87, 190
First Lieutenant Patterer, 219
flu, Spanish, 276, 277
flying roof, 145
food poisoning, 203
forbidden surgical areas, 121
fortieth infantry regiment, 109, 140, 150, 180, 220, 224, 225, 231, 233, 242, 273
Fortress Ivangorod (Russia-Estonian border), 81
forty-fifth infantry, 68, 128
fourth brigade (Prusenowsky), 91
fourth cavalry division, 68
fourth infantry brigade, 42, 223
fourth light infantry, 119, 182, 194, 214, 269
foxholes, 112, 153, 226
Frampol (Poland), 26

France, 26, 139; entrance into World War I (31 July 1914), 17; German Offensive in (7 April, 1918), 257
Franz Joseph, Kaiser (death of), 165, 166, 231
fraternization with Russians, 232
Friedecker, Oberstabsarzt I Klasse, 272, 275
Friederich, Army Commandant Archduke, 66
Frisch, Surgeon General, 183, 184, 249
frostbite, 56
Fuchs, Regimental Captain, 230

Galicia, 30; battles in, 214; map of Brusilov Offensive (1916), 16
Gara, Dr., 154
Garra, Surgeon Major Dr., 145
gas attacks (Western Front), 113
gas masks, 113f
Gerazdza (Ukraine), 107
German 378th infantry regiment, 155, 156, 166
German army, capture of Russians, 40
German-Austrian army, 10
German Iron Cross, 185, 189, 195
German tenth *Landwehr* division, 149
German U-boat *Deutschland*, 146
Germany, 147, xii; 278th German infantry, 146; 378th German infantry battalion, 142, 143, 145; agreement to Wilson's terms (1918), 278; break off of communication (Woodrow Wilson), 182; declaration of war on Portugal, 114; entrance into World War I (31 July 1914), 17; murder of Franz Ferdinand d'Este and his wife Duchess Sophie Hohenburg, 17; offensive against Great Britain (25 March, 1918), 25; talk of surrender, 168
Giedlarowa (Poland), 76
Ginzel, Major, 43
glass syringe (*Rekordspritze*), 67
Glogowiecz (Poland), departure from (20 August, 1914), 19
von Glossner, Captain, 31
Golden Medal of Bravery, 77
Goldschmidt, Senior Physician, 187

Goluchowski, Lieutenant Count, 37
Gorenice (Poland), 39
Gorlice (Poland), 34, 68
Gorlice-Tarnów Offensive (1916), xvi
Görz (Italy), 144, 226, 281
Gorzyce (Poland), 34
Great Britain, 25, 139. *See also* England, entrance into World War I
Great War. *See* World War I
Grebow (Poland), 33
Greece, declaration of war (14 June, 1917), 203
Grinchowski, Private First Class, 35
Grocholice (Poland), 36
Groebl, Colonel Dr., 148
Groër, Major, 82, 99, 100
Gröschl, Lieutenant Colonel, 139, 150, 151
Grössing, Tanja, 1, 4
Group Litzmann, 149
Grubieszow (Poland), 84f
Grund, Captain, 180
gypsies, 185, 197

Habsburg Army, 2, 6
Habsburg Empire, 5
Habsburg Monarchy, 10
Habura, Slovak Republic, 51
Hammerschmied, Senior Surgeon General Dr., 148
Hammerstein, First Lieutenant Baron, 123, 175
Hansen, General, 149
Hauer, Colonel General, 215
Hauerstein, Baron, 60
Heiss, Oberstabsarzt 1 Klasse, 268
Heller, Major, 55, 77, 93, 113, 123, 129, 155, 169, 178, 179, 184; Lieutenant Colonel, 211, 284
Herrenstadt, Dr., 256
Herrmanstadt (Romania), 155, 158
Herrnstadt, Regimental Physician First Class, 192
Herzog, Oberstabsarzt 1 Klasse Dr., 156, 167, 168, 170, 175, 176, 181, 191, 195, 199, 200, 202, 208, 209
High Holiday services, xiii, xvi
Hindenburg, 59

von Hindenburg, Paul, 143
Hinterstoisser, Consulting Surgeon, 189, 190
Hoffmann, Dr., 274
Hoffmann, First Lieutenant, 206
Hoffory, Major, 110, 111
Hofinger, Major, 115
Hohenburg, Sophie (murder of), 17
Hohenlohe, Prince, 127
Holzer, Senior Physician, 194
home front shortages, xii
honoraria, 286
Honor Cross Second Class, 224
Honvéd regiment, 212
horses, 56, 128, 191, 192, 195, 198; exchange of, 32; purchase of, 18
Hotel Europe, 256
Hotel Poller, 46
howitzer cannons, 71, 124
Hueger, Colonel, 158
Huta Turobinska (Poland), 25

illnesses, 247; bacillary dysentery, 220; cholera, 39, 40, 42, 85, 100; colds, 38, 154; diarrhea, 226; dysentery, 42, 269, 270, 271; erysipelas, 99; food poisoning, 203; infections, 122f; inflammation of foot, 153; intestinal catarrh, 272; louse-borne typhus, 117; malaria, 272, 273, 274; peritonitis, 121; sciatica, 148; Spanish flu, 276, 277; swelling in foot, 99, 100; Wolhynian fever, 203
infantry: 378th German infantry, 155, 156, 166; 110th German infantry, 259, 273; 278th German infantry, 146; 377th German infantry, 230; 378th German infantry, 142, 143, 145; eighty-ninth infantry, 109, 113, 118; eighty-second infantry, 145; first *Landwehr* Infantry, 87, 190; fortieth infantry, 109, 150, 180, 224, 225, 231, 233, 242, 273; forty-fifth infantry, 68, 128; fourth infantry, 42; fourth light infantry, 119, 182, 194, 214, 269; nineteenth infantry, 177; ninetieth infantry, 115; ninety-fifth infantry, 271; ninety-ninth infantry, 89; seventieth infantry, 149; third infantry, 110; thirteenth *Landwehr*

infantry, 136, 137, 164, 167, 169, 184, 197; thirty-seventh *Landwehr* infantry, 33; twenty-first *Landwehr* infantry, 68; twenty-fourth infantry, 22, 189, 190; twenty-ninth light infantry, 125, 153, 156, 200, 212, 214, 215, 223
infections, 122*f*
inflammation of foot, 153
injuries: amputations, 126*f*; eye damage, 126*f*; infections, 122*f*; leg fractures, 121*f*. *See also* illnesses
inoculations, cholera, 39, 100, 119*f*
inspections, 108, 109, 183, 221; bakeries, 270; baths, 230; eighty-ninth infantry regiment, 118; first aid stations, 205, 217, 218; fortieth infantry regiment, 140; fourth light infantry, 119; hospitals (Kowel garrisons), 262; medical columns, 275; telephone sections, 271; trenches, 118. *See also* Ukraine
intestinal catarrh, 272
Iron Crown Order Second Class, 224
Isonzo, battles of the, 213, 214
Italian Front, 9, 138, 226, 228, 258, 267, 268–86
Italians, xviii
Italy, 147, 227, 229; battles of the Isonzo, 213, 214; control of financial affairs, 12; declaration of war, 73; offensive against (16 May, 2016), 123; resistance, 264; retreats, 266; transfer to (14 February, 1918), 247; transfer to (April, 1918), 9
Iwansky, General, 129
von Iwansky, Major General, 125
Izbugya-Belá (Hungary), 64
Izdebno (Poland), 23, 24

Janceck, Regimental Physician First Class, 271
Janousek, Regimental Physician First Class Dr., 118
von Jarocky, German Brigadier General, 73
Jasliska (Poland), 47
Jelen, Captain, 55, 58, 59, 83, 90, 93
Jemrich, Commander, 246
von Jemrich, Major General, 137, 195, 204, 219

Jesenski, First Lieutenant Baron, 57, 58
Jewish refugees, 28*f*
Joseph, Archduke Karl Franz, 108
Jozefow (Poland), 35
The Jubilee Memorial Medal of the Armed Forces, 4
Judaism, practice of Jewish faith in army (Bardach), 6
Jun, Dr., 73
Just, Regimental Physician First Class Dr., 187

Kaiserfeld, Captain, 42
Kaiser Weather, 108
Kalab, Officer, 55
kalte Sophie (13–15 May), 70
Kamienczyce (Poland), 38
Kandor, Oberstabsarzt I Klasse Dr., 258
Kantorek, Senior Physician, 175, 225, 230
Karl, Kaiser, 171, 175, 213, 223*f*, 229, 270
Karlstadt (Croatia): arrival in, 18; start of journey to, 17
Kaschau (Hungary), 66
Kaspazek, Regimental Physician First Class, 97
Katowice (Poland), 5
Katzer, Artillery Captain, 169
Kauder, Oberstabsarzt I Klasse, 257
Kaunitz, Regimental Physician First Class, 269, 273
Kazmierow (Poland), 79
Kiev (Ukraine), 251
Kimpolung (Romania), 211
King Ferdinand of Naples, 245
King of Hungary, 171. *See also* Karl, Kaiser
von Kirchbach, Army Commandant Colonel General, 198, 215, 188, 195, 223
Kisch, Egon Ernst, 4
Kiwerczy (Ukraine), 88
Klasse, colonel Oberstabsarzt I, 10
Klein, Colonel, 24, 31, 32, 37, 54, 101, 118; confidential communications, 67; Major General, 145; return of, 70; rib fracture, 67
Knights Cross Award, 6, 7
Kobelnigg, Captain, 30, 61, 62

Kolbe, Commandant Surgeon Major, 48
Kolomea (Ukraine), 138
Konopka, Surgeon Major Dr., 222, 223, 274, 279
Konrad, Helmut, xii
Konstantinowka (Ukraine), 90
Koprzywa, Lieutenant, 230
Kötschet, Lieutenant Colonel, 41
Kovel (Ukraine), 7, 86, 101, 162
Kowno (Lithuania), 85
Koziolek (Poland), 31
Kralicek, Commandant, 94
Kralowetz, Major General, 115, 116, 117, 131
Krämer, Captain, 36, 37, 45, 62, 102, 123; as pianist, 100; travel with, 66
Krasnik, Dr., 188
Krasnostaw (Poland), 83
Kraus, Acting Sergeant Engineer, 187
Krautwald, Corps Commandant, 58, 64
Krieger, Frau, 249
Krinninger, Lieutenant Colonel, 29
Kritek, Commander, 186, 196, 201
Kronfeld, Dr., 139, 140
Kronstadt (Brasa), 158
Kruchyniczy (Ukraine), 241
Krynica (Poland), 66, 67
Krzeczkowa (Poland), 71
Kuchinka, Lieutenant Colonel, 108
Kujawi (Poland), 37
Kulakowski, Regimental Physician First Class Dr., 111, 116
Kutchinska, Lieutenant Colonel, 88
Kuzniar, Lieutenant, 161
Kuznierz, Officer First Lieutenant, 205

Laborcza River (Slovak Republic), 58
Laborczradvány (Hungary), 63, 64
Landsturm, 26
Lang, Assistant Physician, 226
Langauer, Captain, 283
von Langer, Major General, 52, 54
Latzel, Oberstabsarzt I Klasse Dr., 255
leave, permissions, 161, 199, 200, 260
Lederer, Dr., 203, 208, 212, 213, 216, 219, 234, 244, 249, 255
leg fractures, 121*f*
Lemberg (Austria), 2, 10, 25

Lenin, Vladimir, 234
Leo Baeck Institute, 1, 7, 10, 11, 14, xiii
Leopold Order, 97, 139
Levi, Chaplain Dr., 6, 155, 157
lieutenant colonel (Oberstabsarzt II Klasse), 7
von Linsingen, Alexander, 92, 124, 145, 148, 163, 165
Lipošćak, Anton, 33, 36, 43, 54; command in Bukowina, 79; confidential communications, 67; return of, 64, 65
Litzmann, Group Commander, 146, 151
Litzmann Army Group, 148
Lord Nelson's Last Love (Schuhmacher), 245
louse-borne typhus, 117
Lower Szebeny (Hungary), 57
Luck (Ukraine), 95, 101, 112, 129, 249
Luger, Dr., 25, 97
Lugow (Poland), 82

Mackensen, Field Marshal, 165, 166, 212
von Mackensen, August, 76, 82, 83
mail, 243
malaria, 272, 273, 274
Malin (Ukraine), 93
map of Brusilov Offensive (1916), 16
Maria Theresa, 245
Martini, Corps Commandant, 74, 115, 117
von Martini, Captain, 19, 77, 78
Martinowicz, First Lieutenant, 138
mass quarters, 157
medical column inspections, 275
medical corps in the Austro-Hungarian Army, 291
medical school (Bardach), 2
medical units: tending to the wounded (2 October, 1916), 156; Wojimica (Ukraine), 159; wounded soldiers (*see* wounded soldiers)
Meixner, Corps Commandant, 52
Meixner, Feldzeugmeister, 39
memorial services, 204*f*
Meyer, Regimental Physician First Class Dr., 182
Mező-Laborcz (Slovak Republic), 46, 48
Mikuliczy (Ukraine), 202

Military Cross of the Order of Merit Second Class, 112
military decorations, 4; Charles Cross, 225, 244; Crown Order First Class, 74, 222; German Iron Cross, 185, 195; Golden Medal of Bravery, 77; Honor Cross Second Class, 224; Iron Crown Order Second Class, 224; Leopold Order, 97, 139; Military Cross of the Order of Merit Second Class, 112; Military Service Badge Third Class, 259; Military Service Cross Second Class, 114; Officer's Cross of the Order of Franz Joseph, 143, 224; Order of Franz Joseph, 62, 169; Red Cross Badge of Honor Cross Second Class, 141; Red Cross Badge of Honor First Class, 125; Red Cross Badge of Honor Second Class, 125; Red Cross Medal First Class, 126; Red Cross Medal of Honor, 80; Red Cross Officer's Badge of Honor, 125; Service Cross First Class, 185; Signum Laudis, 100, 112, 115, 185, 189, 218, 234
Military Jubilee Cross, 4
military performers, 243
Military Service Badge Third Class, 259
Military Service Cross Second Class, 114
Ministry of Finance, 13
Molnar, Honvéd Regimental Physician First Class Dr., 212
Moscicska (Ukraine), 73
Moscovits, Captain of the Reserve, 65
Moskovitz, Dr., 261
Mosler, Dr., 258
mosquitoes, 272
Motta di Livenza (Italy), 276
mountain warfare, 180
Mrekewa, Major, 233
Müller, Surgeon Major Dr., 56, 87, 95, 97, 98, 100, 109, 112, 115, 120, 143, 147, 152, 154, 178, 221

Nagymihály (Hungary), 46
National Guard, 284
National Socialism, 14
National Socialist Germany, 12
Nazis, xii

negotiations: in Brest Litovsk, Belarus, 241, 243; peace, 283
Neusatz (Serbia), 266
newspapers, 132, 247, 280, 283
Niezgoda, Division Chaplain, 94, 117
nineteenth brigade, 177
ninetieth infantry regiment, 115
ninety-fifth infantry regiment, 271
ninety-ninth infantry battalion, 89
Nisch, Serbia, 98
Nisko (Poland), battles at (23 October, 1914), 34
no. 4/62 infantry regiment, 212
no. 9/10 field hospital, 164
Novosiolki (Ukraine), 96, 107
Nowica (Poland), 67
Nowo Georgyevsk fortress (Poland), 86
Nowy-Dwor (Ukraine), 132

Oberländer, Chief Surgeon Major Dr., 127
Oberstabsarzt II Klasse (lieutenant colonel), 7
Oberstabsarzt I Klasse (colonel), 10
Oderberg (Czech Republic), 102
Officer's Cross of the Order of Franz Joseph, 143, 224
Olyka (Ukraine), 88
Olyka Castle (Ukraine), 112
110th infantry regiment, 259, 273
110th *Landsturm* brigade, 33
Opatow (Poland), 36
Order of Franz Joseph, 62, 169
Örmező (Hungary), 66
Ostrozec (Poland), 96, 97, 107

Pabst, Chief Medical Officer, 278
Packeny, Major General, 26
Palikije (Poland), 81
Pavloviczy (Ukraine), 178, 181, 182, 186, 190, 201, 206
peace, 282, 283
Peace Congress, 279
peace formulas, 249
Pelikan, Junior Logistics Officer, 130, 137, 138, 141, 169, 246, 267
pension (Bardach), 11–12
Pension Scholler, 208

peritonitis, 121
Petna (Poland), 68
Petrin, Captain, 196, 198
petroleum oil, lack of, 231
Pfaff, First Lieutenant Auditor, 69
Phlebs, Surgeon Major, 65
photography, 231
Piane (Ukraine), 93
Pick, Oberstabsarzt I Klasse Dr., 82
Pilzno (Poland), 29
Piotrowski, Sergeant, 185
Pistelka, Captain, 93, 96, 114, 169, 184, 187
Pistotnik, Colonel, 280
Ploieşti (Romania), 167
Pockel, Captain, 55
Podgajce (Ukraine), 256
Podgrodzie (Poland), 29
Pokaszczewo (Ukraine), 111
Poland: borders, 218; proclamation of 5 November (1916), 163
Poletylo, Count, 83
Polish Army, rejection of entrance into, 9
Polish second dinner (*drugi obiad*), 228
Pollak, Colonel, 273
Poppi, Lieutenant Colonel, 263
Poreby Kedzielski (Poland), 31
Por River (Poland), 25
Portugal, declaration of war by Germany (17 March, 1916), 114
Posada Olchowska (Poland), 70
postoperative examinations, 151*f*
Potowski, Count, 81
Prachowny, Captain, 72, 75
Prehal, Captain, 139, 150
Přerov (Czech Republic), 163
press reports, 132, 134
Prihalto, Commandant, 86
prisoners, 53*f*, 120, 155, 209, 258
proclamation of 5 November (1916), 163
prostitutes, 41*f*
provisions, 192, 235, 244, 245, 246, 249, 260, 261, 263; difficulty to obtain, 163; for family, 222; lack of, 191; trains, 220
Prusenowsky, Major General, 88, 107, 108, 118, 136
Prussians, 26
Przeginia (Poland), 40

Przemyśl (Poland), 62, 64; battle for (26 May, 1915), 73, 74; departure from, 75
Przepiorow (Poland), 37
Przeuszyn (Poland), 36
Przeworsk (Poland), 78
Przylek (Poland), 31
Pustomyty (Ukraine), 140, 160

quarters, 157
quinine, 272

rabbit holes, 156
Radautz (Romania), 211
Raday, Oberstabsarzt I Klasse Dr., 93, 99, 101
Radczy, Chief Medical Officer Dr., 76
Radler, Assistant Physician, 180
Radochonce (Ukraine), 72, 74
Raktelj, Commander Lieutenant Colonel, 225, 230
Rallner, Oberstabsarzt 1 Klasse Dr., 180
Randa, Captain, 123
ranks: approval for, 235; Austro-Hungarian Army, 289–90
The Rape of the Sabines, 207
Raschky, Colonel, 163, 198
rations, 22, 25. *See also* provisions
Ratniewo (Ukraine), 93
Raubitschek, Surgeon Major Professor, 208
Red Cross, 61, 62, 63, 67, 125; Badge of Honor Cross Second Class, 141; Badge of Honor First Class, 125; Badge of Honor Second Class, 125; Honor Cross Second Class, 224; Medal First Class, 126; Medal of Honor, 80; Officer's Badge of Honor, 125; refreshment train, 60
Redel, Captain, 23
refugees, 28*f*, xii
regiments: 110th infantry regiment, 259, 273; 377th German infantry regiment, 230; battalions formed out of, 24; eighty-ninth infantry, 23, 109, 112, 113; first *Landwehr* infantry, 87; first *Landwehr* Infantry, 190; fortieth infantry, 180; fortieth infantry regiment, 220; German 378th infantry,

156, 166; German 378th infantry regiment, 155; Honvéd, 212; ninety-fifth infantry regiment, 271; no. 4/62 infantry regiment, 212; retreats, 24, 26, 28; second Honvéd, 204; swearing in (12 August, 1914), 19; thirteenth *Landwehr* infantry, 167; twenty-fourth *Landwehr* infantry, 189, 190. *See also* infantry

Reichel, Captain, 119
Reichel cannon, 140
von Reigersberg-Versluys, First Lieutenant, 200
Reinlein, Rittmeister Baron, 196
Reitzes, Dr. M., 72*f*
Rekordspritze (glass syringe), 67
relocation, 161
Resch, Captain, 161, 178
resistance, Italy, 264
rest days, 27, 31
retreats, 24, 26, 28, 29, 127, 132; Boro (Poland), 56; Italy, 266; Russian 2nd army, 68; Russian army, 88; Staszow (Poland), 36
Rhine River (Germany), 233
Richter, Engineer, 180
Richtermoc, Chief of the General Staff Colonel, 268
Rodler, Assistant Physician Dr., 171, 178
Rogozno (Ukraine), 164, 216, 219
Rohrbach, Lieutenant, 99
Romania, 145, 147, 148, 170, 177; battles in, 214; peace with, 256
Romanians, xviii
Rosenbaum, Major, 185
Rosenberg, Senior Logistics Officer, 54, 56, 60, 61, 83, 93, 96, 99
von Rosenzweig, Colonel, 45, 46, 47, 54, 56, 77, 111, 120, 128, 175, 244; General, 234, 262
Rosh Hashanah, 29, 219, xvi
Rowno (Ukraine), 89
Rozenblit, Marsha, xix
Rubeš, Dr., 25, 31
Ruda (Poland), 31
Rudawka Rymanowska (Poland), 69
Rudnik (Poland), 78
Rudniki (Poland), 27, 28

Russia: abdication of Tsar (1917), 190; arrival in (20 August, 1914), 20; Battle of Turobin (28 August, 1914), 22; entrance into World War I (31 July 1914), 17; fraternization with Russians, 232; launch of Brusilov Offensive (1916), x, xi; map of Brusilov Offensive (1916), 16; murder of Franz Ferdinand d'Este and his wife Duchess Sophie Hohenburg, 17; political changes, 251; rumors of revolution in, 190; travel to border (13 August, 1914), 19; wounded soldiers, 166

Russian 2nd army, 23, 68
Russian army, xi, xviii; Bilgoraj (Poland), 27; bodies in the battlefield, 44*f*, 45; prisoners of war, 53*f*; retreats, 88
Ruthenians, 92
Ruzcyzka, Surgeon Major, 188, 189, 208, 209
Rymanow (Poland), 46, 47
Rzedzin (Poland), 30
Rzuchow (Poland), 77

Saint Basiloarda, monastery of, 57, 59
Saint Hubertus Hunt, 98
Sandig, First Lieutenant, 148, 193, 270
Sandomierz (Poland), 34
San River (Poland), 33, 34, 70, 76, 191
Scheidl, Colonel Dr., 97, 109, 124, 127, 167
Schejwl, General Staff Captain, 43, 48, 97
Schipek, Major Dr., 60
Schlesinger, First Lieutenant Count, 48, 58, 61
von Schlichting, Lieutenant Colonel, 73, 75
Schmidbacher, Colonel, 177
Schmidt. Dr., 139, 140
Schneider, Captain Auditor, 75, 96
Schufler, Captain, 274
Schulhof, Captain, 248
Schütz, Lieutenant Colonel, 268, 276, 284, 285
Schwab, Assistant Physician, 118
Schwartz, Captain, 40, 41
Schwartz, First Lieutenant, 175, 176
Schwarz, Assistant Physician, 85

Schwarz, Captain, 23
Schwarzwald, Dr., 261
Schwelger, Regimental Physician First Class, 248
sciatica, 148
second Honvéd regiment, 204
Seidmann, Frau (sister-in-law), 244, 257, 262
Seitz, Assistant Physician, 226, 228
von Sellner, Commandant, 85, 101, 112, 114, 126, 129, 130
Serbia: entrance into World War I (31 July 1914), 17; murder of Franz Ferdinand d'Este and his wife Duchess Sophie Hohenburg, 17
Service Cross First Class, 185
seventieth infantry division, 149
shackling, 266
sick bay, 122
Siebenbürgen (Transylvania), 145
Siedliska Wielkic (Poland), 23, 83
Siemuszowa (Poland), 70
Sienna-Olechow (Poland), 35
Sierniczki (Ukraine), 130
Signum Laudis, 100, 112, 115, 185, 189, 218, 234
Skala (Poland), 39
Skoczek, Medical Corps Lieutenant, 227
sleep, 23, 27
sleeping equipment (23 August, 1914), 20
Sluszczyn (Poland), 35
Smejkal, Commandant, 128
Sobieska Wola (Poland), 22
Spanish flu, 276, 277, xix
The Spanish Fly, 206
von Spanochi, Lieutenant Colonel, 97
stab in the back myth (*Dolchstosslegende*), 9
Stach, Dr., 32, 33, 61
Stamecka, Lieutenant Colonel, 179, 183, 184
Stanislau (Ukraine), 145
Staniszewskie (Poland), 28
Stany (Poland), 33
Staszow (Poland), 37
Steinbock, First Lieutenant, 34
Steinböck, Major, 178
Steindl, Commandant Dr., 186

Steiner, First Lieutenant Quartermaster, 18, 24, 74
Steller, Lieutenant Colonel, 258
Stetter, Chief of General Staff, 75
Stichy, Captain of the General Staff, 188
von Stocken, General, 220
Strohhofer, Major, 176
Struze Wielkie (Poland), 70
Stryj (Ukraine), 267
St. Vito (Italy), 270
Styr River (Ukraine), 129
Sugar, Senior Surgeon Dr., 192
Suk, First Lieutenant, 21
Surgeon Major Professor Raubitschek, 208
surgeries, 205, 206
Sweden, 196, 197, 198
Swiçcone (Polish Easter meal), 117
Swiczow (Ukraine), 133
Swiniuchy (Ukraine), 154
Swojkow (Poland), 37
Szcjkaj, Commandant Field Marshal, 127
Szelwow (Ukraine), 150, 240, 242
Szoljom-Feketc, Captain, 216
Szwejkowski, Lieutenant, 43

Tabayoly, General, 131
Tanew River (Poland), 77
Tarlow (Poland), 35
Tarnogrod (Poland), 27
Tarnopol (Ukraine), 210
Tarnow (Poland), 30
tarok game, 94f
Tausz, Oberstabsarzt I Klasse Dr., 118
tea, 25
Teitelbaum, Medical Corps Lieutenant, 229
telephone section inspections, 271
tenth German *Landwehr* division, 152
Teremenskaya (Ukraine?), 128
Terenkoczy, Chairman Surgeon General, 77, 95, 97, 109, 164
Tersztyánszky von Nádas, Karl, 131, 136, 137, 188
theater performances, 206, 207, 208, 211, 236, 248f, 257
third infantry division, 110
13–15 May (*kalte Sophie*), 70

thirteenth *Landwehr* infantry regiment, 136, 137, 164, 167, 169, 184, 197
thirtieth infantry regiment, 3
thirty-seventh Honvéd division, 141
thirty-seventh *Landwehr* infantry division, 33
Thoman, Surgeon General, 268, 271
378th German infantry, 142, 143, 145
377th German infantry, 230
Tisza, First Lieutenant Count, 48, 64, 283
toilettes, 21*f*
Tokary (Poland), 25, 26
trains, 57, 90, 92, 161, 162, 179, 209, 210, 214, 216, 235, 256, 284; baggage, 128, 129, 133, 134, 142, 143 (*see also* baggage trains); battle, 130; fortieth infantry division, 220, 224, 231; fourth infantry brigade, 223; Red Cross refreshment, 60
Tramer, Engineer Lieutenant, 158
transfers, 81
transports, wounded soldiers, 35
von Trautmannsdorf, Count, 48, 53, 65, 69, 96
travel documents, 265
Treaty of Brest Litovsk (1918), 240–88
trenches, 115, 153; communication, 188; cross, 153; fighting, 112, 153; inspections, 118; vacated by Russians, 126; visits to, 184
Trieste (Italy), 17, 227, 228, 279
Trzebinia (Poland), 162
Trzesowka (Poland), 31
Tumin (Ukraine), 133
Turia River (Romanian river north-east of Brașov), 240
Turkey, 148
Turtukal River (Romania), 149
Tuschner, Lieutenant Colonel, 18, 19, 24, 25, 26, 29, 41
twenty-first *Landwehr* infantry division, 68
twenty-fourth infantry division, 22
twenty-fourth *Landwehr* infantry regiment, 189, 190
twenty-ninth light infantry, 125, 153, 156, 200, 212, 214, 215, 223
278th German infantry, 146

Tylawa (Poland), 68
Typenzug, 257

U-boat wars, 182, 280
Ukraine (winter in [1917]), 175–236
United States, 13, xii. *See also* Wilson, Woodrow
University of Graz, 1
University of Vienna, 2
Usice (Ukraine), 130
Ustilug (Ukraine), 85
Utti, Regimental Physician First Class Dr., 111

vacations, 194; requests (29 June, 1915), 78; in Vienna (2 January, 2018), 240
vaccines, cholera, 85
Valenciennes (France), 191
Varaczyki, First Lieutenant Count, 137
Vetter, Chief Medical Officer Dr., 85
Vienna ballet, 209
Vienna *Landwehr* troops, 127
Vienna Military Command, 246
Vienna Nordbahnhof, 162
Vienna Private Stage Company, 206
Vienna Volunteer Rescue Association, 60
Vistula River (Poland), 31
Vladimir Volynsky (Ukraine), 91, 157, 207, 212, 218, 227, 235, 254, 255, 256, 275
Vyšna Radvaň (Slovak Republic), 58

Wach, Surgeon Major Dr., 215, 259
Walzl, Artillery Colonel, 131
war booty, 155, 168
war's end (1918), 240–88
washing, opportunities for, 27. *See also* baths
Wechsler, Senior Physician, 222, 232
Weichsel River (Poland), 34, 35
Werndorf, Dr., 96
Western Front, 113, 177, 193, 277
Westphal, Communications Officer Lieutenant, 230
Wiener, Captain, 88
Wiener Volksoper, 211
Wierzchowiska (Poland), 80
Wilczkowice (Poland), 45

Wilson, Woodrow, 182, 278, xii, xix
Windischgratz, Duke Otto, 64
Winter Jay, 5, x-xiii, xix
Wislok River (Poland), 69
Wojimica (Ukraine), 134, 159, 161, 192, 207, 210
Wolhynia, 180
Wolhynian fever, 203
Worczyn (Ukraine), 86
World War I, 1, 14, xx
Worotniewo (Ukraine), 98, 101, 108
wounded soldiers, 23, 55, 60, 81, 100, 115, 123, 131, 135, 143, 156, 160, 179, 205, 207; Artillery Observer Cadet Brumowski, 117; average number of, 114; because of thrown mines, 125, 126; Captain Deischel (22 November, 1914), 41; Captain Kobelnigg (21 March, 2015), 62; Captain Schwartz (17 November, 1914), 40; Captain Wratschil (22 November, 1914), 41; and civilians, 87; Colonel Klein (4 September, 1917), 24; frostbite, 56; loss of officers, 146; number treated (2580), 42; Oberstabsarzt 1 Klasse Dr. Herzog, 176; reality of war, 5; restless nights, 22; retreats, 83; Russia, 166; shot through gallbladder, 149; surgery, 121; tending to (2 October, 1916), 156; tending to (24 August, 1914), 21; transports, 35; Zaturczy (Ukraine [2 July, 1916]), 137
Wratschil, Captain, 41
Wscislak, Colonel, 45
Wurm, Colonel General, 215
Wysocice (Poland), 44, 45

Yom Kippur, 6, 9, 91, xvi; 1914, 30; 1917, 220; 1918, 276
Yugoslav National Council, 283

Zabratowka (Poland), 75
Zagrody Nakliekic (Poland), 77
Zaklykow (Poland), 79
Zaleszany (Poland), 33
Zapatowicz, Chief Medical Officer, 33, 60, 110, 112, 113, 115, 125, 146, 147, 149, 153, 163, 166
Zaturczy (Ukraine), 137, 252, 253
Zborow (Ukraine), 210
Zdziary (Poland), 29
Zielonka (Poland), 28
Ziepal, Dr., 124
Zita, Empress, 175
Zorn, Lieutenant, 55, 213, 268, 270
Zulawski, Commandant Surgeon Major, 187
Zwierow (Ukraine), 116, 120